153

SCOTT'S NOVELS
THE PLOTTING OF
HISTORIC SURVIVAL

SCOTT'S NOVELS
THE PLOTTING OF
HISTORIC SURVIVAL

FRANCIS R. HART
THE UNIVERSITY OF VIRGINIA

THE UNIVERSITY PRESS OF VIRGINIA

CHARLOTTESVILLE

Those who read me know my conviction that the world, the temporal world, rests on a few very simple ideas; so simple that they must be as old as the hills. It rests notably, among others, on the idea of Fidelity.

— *Joseph Conrad, Preface to* A Personal Record

So far as I move on the level of possible existence, I recognize the deeply historical nature of my situation. . . . The awareness the self has of its historicity, Jaspers says, is originally a personal one. I become aware here of myself communicating with another personal reality; as for myself, I am linked in time to a succession of situations and data each of which is unique in time. . . . It is hard to resist the thought that Jaspers has discovered on his own initiative the distinction Peguy illumined with such extraordinary force, notably in Clio. *Didn't Peguy adhere to such formulations as: "What has bounds, and is determinate when viewed from without, is inwardly the manifestation of authentic being. The person who loves only humanity does not love; he only loves who loves a specific human being. The person who is logically consistent and keeps his commitments is still not a faithful being, but only the person who shoulders his act and his past love as his own burden and admits that they are binding on him."*

— *Gabriel Marcel,* Creative Fidelity

— *History, Stephen said, is a nightmare from which I am trying to awake.*
From the playfield the boys raised a shout. A whirring whistle: goal. What if the nightmare gave you a back kick?

— *James Joyce,* Ulysses

PREFACE

THIS is a critical interpretation and comparative assessment
of all of Scott's novels. It attempts to analyze their fictional
rhetoric and thematic currency without significant prejudice, but its very undertaking and completion imply a
genuine and growing respect and affection for Scott's fiction
which I hope is never concealed. In the absence of a
definitive edition of all the novels, this study is forced to rely
on the Dryburgh edition, which purports, albeit ambiguously, to embody Scott's final revisions. Until the early,
uncollected editions are systematically studied, the critic will
remain unsure how to use them and feel obliged to turn
elsewhere.

In undertaking an interpretive survey of all the Waverley
Novels I have been anxious to allow myself as much analytic latitude as possible and to avoid the restrictive imposi-
tion of a single controlling thesis or narrowly argumentative
pattern. To some readers this will prove an inconvenience;
to them the result may seem a succession of independent
essays – and this I would find preferable to an artificial and
dogmatic unity. But it is not, as I hope will become clear to
those willing to take the inquiry as an honestly inductive
one. It may be unnecessary to point out that my subtitle

identifies what I take to be the underlying thematic problem and pattern of the novels or that the epigraphs signal the importance to that pattern of the idea of fidelity dramatized in conjunction with the sense of history as nightmare. The four-part arrangement represents, I hope, a meaningful classification of the materials Scott used to explore that problem and to play significant variations on that pattern. To those missing a thesis in my introduction, it is only necessary to hint that the book's total argument is recapitulated in its final seven paragraphs.

Many pertinent questions are only touched upon in this essay; I wish space allowed otherwise. The relation of Scott as poet, antiquarian, and man, to the Author of Waverley, occasionally noted, must be explored elsewhere, but only after the Author of Waverley has been critically defined. The fascinating problem of narrative styles has for the most part been postponed, although the effects of stylistic differentiation and the related theme of language as a cultural problem have been traced in individual works. Since space, preparatory concern for the artificial English of the Scot, and criteria for other than the superficially negative judgments already traditional are lacking, I have saved the general problem of Scott's style for separate analysis.

My method of classification, while allowing for the assessment of diverse topical impulses, necessarily submerges the question of chronological development, although it is noted occasionally and is implicitly present throughout. An answer is also implied: references to the early and to the later novelist should be made and understood cautiously; the Author of Waverley was already a mature talent when born in 1814, still mature when Scott struggled through *Anne of Geierstein* (1829), and erratic in development in between. The early "Tales of My Landlord" – *Old Mortality, The*

Heart of Midlothian, The Bride of Lammermoor – are superior; much later, *The Abbot, Quentin Durward, The Fair Maid of Perth,* by virtue of their protagonists, their ordeals, their versions of an authentic historical pessimism, are also unexcelled. The spectacle of development shows neither dramatic fruition nor dramatic degeneration.

Finally, the impress of milieu and public on the Author of Waverley, his impact on European fiction, his place in a Scottish literary tradition, all three little noted here, have been the subject of enlightening recent speculation by David Craig, Donald Davie, Alexander Welsh, and Kurt Wittig. All of these matters are essential to full assessment. My essay can therefore well afford to resist ambitious or dogmatic generalization.

For permission to quote from copyright materials I am grateful to the following: George Braziller, Inc., for *Beyond the Tragic Vision* by Morse Peckham; Chatto and Windus, Ltd., for *Scottish Literature and the Scottish People* by David Craig; The Clarendon Press for *The Oxford History of English Literature, English Literature 1815–1832* by Ian Jack; Columbia University Press for *Sir Walter Scott, Bart.,* by Sir Herbert Grierson; Criterion Books, Inc., for *Love and Death in the American Novel* by Leslie Fiedler; Duke University Press for *The Political Reason of Edmund Burke* by Francis P. Canavan, S.J.; the editor of *ELH: A Journal of English Literary History* for "Waverley and the Unified Design" by S. Stewart Gordon; Farrar, Straus, and Giroux, Inc., for *Creative Fidelity* by Gabriel Marcel, translated by Robert Rosthal; Harcourt, Brace and World, Inc., for *Aspects of the Novel* by E. M. Forster; Harper and Row, Inc., for *Realism in Our Time* by Georg Lukacs, translated by J. and N. Mander; Holt, Rinehart and Winston, Inc., for

The English Novel by Dorothy Van Ghent; Macmillan and Company, Ltd., for *Collected Essays* by W. P. Ker; The Merlin Press, Ltd., for *The Historical Novel* by Georg Lukacs, translated by H. and S. Mitchell; Oliver and Boyd, Ltd., for *Literary Essays* by David Daiches and *The Journal of Sir Walter Scott* edited by J. G. Tait; Oxford University Press, London, for *The Hero in Eclipse* by Mario Praz, translated by A. Davidson; A. D. Peters and Company for *The Living Novel* by V. S. Pritchett; Princeton University Press for *Mimesis* by E. Auerbach and *Anatomy of Criticism* by Northrop Frye; The Regents of the University of California for *Nineteenth Century Fiction*: "The Bride of Lammermoor, A Novel of Tory Pessimism" by R. C. Gordon; "Providence, Fate, and the Historical Imagination in Scott's *The Heart of Midlothian*" by P. F. Fisher; and "The Fair Maid, Manzoni's *Betrothed*, and the Grounds of Waverley Criticism" by Francis R. Hart © 1963 by The Regents of the University of California; The Regents of the University of Wisconsin for *Romantic Narrative Art* by Karl Kroeber; Routledge and Kegan Paul, Ltd., for *The Heyday of Sir Walter Scott* by Donald Davie; The Tweedsmuir Trustees and Cassell and Company, Ltd., for *Sir Walter Scott* by John Buchan; University of Pennsylvania Press for *Theme and Symbol in Tennyson's Poetry to 1850* by Clyde de L. Ryals; University Press, University of Minnesota, for the essay "Scott's *Redgauntlet*" by David Daiches in *From Jane Austen to Joseph Conrad*; Yale University Press for *The Hero of the Waverley Novels* by Alexander Welsh.

Begun in 1961, this book has already benefited from recent signs of a Waverley revival. It was completed and revised too late, however, to profit from the various major efforts of Edgar Johnson, Thomas Crawford, Christina Keith, and Coleman Parsons (and no doubt others unknown to me). It might never have been completed at all without the kind encouragement of James C. Corson, Albert B. Friedman, and Edgar Johnson, and the provocative suggestions of Roy Harvey Pearce and Marshall Waingrow, though they have been spared seeing the result until it faces them in print. Others less fortunate have seen it often and have done what they could to rescue it from the author's oversights and extravagances. Such efforts include the acute, constructive, but regrettably anonymous strictures of the readers for the University Press of Virginia, the painstaking paperwork of Adele Hall and Betty Jean Blincoe, the editorial and clerical marvels of my wife Lorena and her mother Ruth Laing. Finally, of the many students who have helped shape my reading of the novels, one is, in the course of the book, singled out for special posthumous gratitude. In memory of Robert MacConnell, therefore, and to my indispensable and indefatigable wife this book is dedicated.

FRANCIS R. HART

Charlottesville, Virginia
January 1965

CONTENTS

CONTENTS

SCOTT'S NOVELS
THE PLOTTING OF
HISTORIC SURVIVAL

INTRODUCTION

AFTER reading *Waverley*," said Goethe to Eckermann in 1828, "you will understand why Walter Scott still designates himself the author of that work; for there he showed what he could do and he has never written anything to surpass, or even equal, that first published novel."[1] The eidolon Author of Waverley appeared in 1814; his sesquicentennial brings signs of renewed critical interest. But Goethe and the Romantic century would be surprised at how long it has taken. Nineteenth-century readers knew all we do about the imperfections of the Author of Waverley; we merely rehearse their strictures and omit or overlook their admiration: Hazlitt's complaints about political and social blinders; Balzac's objection to the lack of that French delicacy, *passion;* the charges of Carlyle, Bagehot, and other Sages of a want of religious depth and earnestness.[2] The list of those who, voicing their reservations, remained fervent admirers comprises a nineteenth-century Hall of Fame. Flaubert and George Eliot found him unrivaled in the British tradition. Balzac, Pushkin, and Manzoni would see

1

the truth in Bradford Booth's suggestion that the Author of Waverley's appearance was perhaps the "most important event in the history of fiction."[3]

Yet, while there is exaggeration, there is basic truth in such assurances as those of Compton Mackenzie and V. S. Pritchett that Scott is now the Great Unread. There is wishful thinking, but also some fact, in David Craig's condescending, "The Scott vogue is now a famous curiosity of the past."[4] If the vogue is dead, so are obstacles to fresh appraisal. A new look at the novels is facilitated by their present neglect. We can envision a future free of high school editions of Ivanhoe and The Talisman. We can see an end to sarcastic allusions to the tinseled exoticism of Abbotsford's mercenary antiquary. True, we cannot yet find freedom from academic prejudice. One weary junior professor pleads, "Scott's something I figured long ago I could afford to ignore." His militantly Liberal senior, bent still on exorcizing the Waverley demon of drab Gothicism from his own nineteenth-century culture, "wouldn't allow a Waverley Novel in my classroom." Many stereotypes and cultural anxieties stand between the Author of Waverley and the academic non-reader. But the resultant innocence is conducive to fresh assessment.

The innocence cannot, of course, remove all obstacles. As Donald Davie wisely observes, there are neither means nor reason for readers of "James or Conrad or Ford" to disown their expectancies.[5] But at least there is evidence – notably in the theoretic essays of Wayne Booth and Albert Cook – that the rhetoric of fiction has been recovered from the orthodoxy of narrow realisms. At least we may weigh the artifices of earlier novels without prejudgment and read them as works of fiction. And this means confronting honestly the charges of such severe analysts as David Craig and Dorothy Van Ghent: the novels lack significant coherence; their "life" is false because Scott was blinded to the possibilities of his matter by slipshod methods, conventional forms, and stereotyped moral attitudes.[6] It means challenging the dogmas that the Tory in a revolutionary age was bound to the one-eyed fiction of propriety, and that the regionalist lost his inspiration when he deserted Life and turned to Books as a resource. It means recognizing the Author of Waverley's various subject matters, each of which produced its masterworks: *Waverley, Old Mortality, The Heart of Midlothian* – but also *The Abbot, Quentin Durward, The Fair Maid of Perth,* and *The Bride of Lammermoor.*

Such a reassessment has already begun. What is new about the present effort? First, it attends to all of the novels. Second, it seeks to avoid certain distractions or distortions which qualify the success of recent discussions.

There remains, first, the hardy tendency to submerge or prejudice practical criticism in arid debate over whether Scott is Romantic or anti-Romantic.[7] Scott was of the late Enlightenment – spiritually at home with his Edinburgh teachers, his friends Mackenzie and Crabbe, the late Augustan Tory satirists, even Francis Jeffrey. His editorial efforts were in behalf of Dryden and Swift; his sympathy for Johnson was so deep that during his final muddled months he confused himself with that *ultimus anglicorum.*[8] For some Victorian admirers his work was a bulwark of enduring English manliness against the alien or effeminate strains of Byronic or Keatsian Romanticism.[9] But these facts, puzzling in one who, with the "anti-Romantic" Byron, created European Romanticism, cannot be sorted with such facile categories. If Scott differed sharply from "the typical Romantic writer," who is *he?* Patrick Cruttwell's "basic trends of true romanticism" were variously distasteful to Wordsworth, Coleridge, Keats, Hazlitt, and Byron. Donald Davie makes the sound suggestion that Scott is Romantic insofar as he adopts the premises of the anti-Jacobin organicism of Wordsworth's tirade on the Convention of Cintra.[10] Such premises become, in the novels, a new social vision. The proposition, derived from Leslie Stephen,[11] that the Author of Waverley is fictionalized Burke has much truth; the term "anti-Jacobin" will prove suggestive for what follows. But one should take precautions. One should weigh Georg Lukacs's demonstration of how profoundly the Author of Waverley differed from those whom Lukacs lumps together (Burke, Joseph de Maistre, and other Legitimists) as antirevolutionary pseudohistoricists.[12] *Waverley* is not Disraeli's *Sybil*. Scott was no more and no less *Romantic* anti-Jacobin than Edward Gibbon. But he lived his adult life after 1789. The failure of the French Revolution, Morse Peckham writes, was "what he expected and hoped for, yet it made him realize that eighteenth-century conceptions of society were inadequate." It is going too far to say that Scott "experienced the negative isolation and alienation of Werther and Harold, and thus he, too, lost control of the present."[13] But he was of the counter-enlightenment. It is as misleading to call him anti-Romantic as it is to call him Romantic. It is more useful to classify him with Byron and Thackeray, perhaps with Browning and Austen, as an ironist for whom Romantic values are an essential part of a serious ironic vision.

A second distraction – more insidious because more useful and inviting to the critic – is the habit of confusing Scott the writer of fiction with Scott the cultural force. Literary appraisal is lost in the celebration of the discoverer of historicity and his new conception of man in traditional

society or in undue emphasis of his dramatization of historic
event in its felt impact on private life. Varieties of this
distracting praise come from such different interpreters as
Lukacs, Pritchett, Daiches, Kettle, and Peckham. Some
were anticipated by Scott's contemporaries; Lockhart himself warned against the confusion of Scott the novelist with
Scott the genius of a new historiography.[14] Yet the question
of the nature and extent of Scott's historism must be central
in any formal or thematic analysis of the novels. What, then,
is the danger? It is in what Kenneth Burke calls "essentializing." The habit is everywhere evident, but the following is
one good illustration: "the best of Scott is not to be sought in
his conventional pictures of Gothic manor-houses and
effects of storm-ridden Nature or unbridled passions – pictures in which he inclines towards the oleographic; but, as is
well known, in his descriptions of Scottish habits and
customs, such as those that occupy the whole of the first part
of *The Pirate*,"[15] and so on. Every attempt to segregate the
"best of Scott" from the "conventional" risks comparable
absurdities.

At its most plausible the habit appears in the tradition
stretching from Coleridge to Lukacs and David Daiches of
finding the subject of the Waverley Novels in an ambiguous
vision of human history. The tradition has recently been
called Coleridgean, but Coleridge, Lukacs, and Daiches
differ significantly. Coleridge defines the Waverley "idea" as
an "omnipresent conflict of social humanity," the conflict
between a "religious adherence" to the past and permanent
on the one hand and the "mighty instincts of *progression*
and *free agency*" on the other. Lukacs sees historicity itself,
the fated personal entanglement with historic forces, as the
subject; the central conflict is between private and public or
historic and nonhistoric. Daiches sees the subject in one

5

kind of historical transition, and in what he asserts are (and I join Davie and Welsh in disagreeing) Scott's ambivalent feelings toward that transition from an age of heroic violence to an age of prudent civility. Thus the tradition is not a unified one.[16]

Its dangers are unified, however. Once Scott's subject has been defined as a vision of historic transition or conflict, fair considerations of his rhetoric vanish, for we are chained to a distinction between what is significant ("real") and what is conventional ("unreal") in Scott. We are obliged to assume that his narratives inevitably suffer (or deviate from their "idea") when they are nonhistoric, that conventional character and situation have neither aesthetic justification nor allowable thematic significance. This is to forget the truth in the important distinction derived by Pritchett from Hazlitt: history is not Scott's subject, although the "historical passion" was the "engine" of his "impulse."[17] To trace the outcomes of the impulse is to recognize that conventional characters and nonhistoric motifs have their functions. For most of Scott's protagonists history is a terror, a mysterious threat to meaning and stability, as well as a dangerous opportunity to find one's identity and place in a new and redeemed social order. The romantic world of the historic frequently is stabilized into the novelistic world of the comic. Having wandered naively into the first, the protagonist undergoes an ordeal of physical and moral survival which permits him to participate, chastened but redeemed, in the ahistoric reinstatement of the second. Thus, pastoral idylls (the end of *The Heart of Midlothian*) may represent escapes from history; conventional characters may serve as guides, foils, norms, or even symbolic unrealities. They may. The point is that the "essentializing" of Scott in terms of *a* subject – history or historic transition or historic determinism – prevents our even considering such possibilities. And until we seek to relate them to the shape and rhetorical evolution of the protagonist's ordeal in each comic romance, we cannot determine the several ends of Scott's historical passion.

The most recent account of the novels recognizes that significance and fictive convention cannot be separated, that subject and protagonist, however conventional, are bound together for better or worse. Welsh defines and interprets the hero, the passive hero, of the Waverley Novels; in his title he has significantly but deceptively dropped the question-begging adjective, though the question remains begged in his book.[18] His study belongs to the tradition of studies in heroes and hero types. His predecessors Thorslev (the Byronic hero and his genealogy) and Ridge (the hero of Sensibility's French Romantic cousin, the hero of Self-Consciousness) have compiled the archetypes and paradigms. The danger is clearly recognized by them: "It can of course be readily seen that the typing or classification of these heroes entails a great deal of oversimplification."[19] Their purpose is nevertheless accomplished, and one of the results is that we can distinguish between the passivity that the Waverley heroes (or some of them) share with the Romantic hero of Sensibility, and the unique significance which that passivity receives from its total mimetic and rhetorical context in a Waverley Novel. When, however, the same generalizing and deductive method is used on the many and various works of a single unreflective, undoctrinaire writer of historical romance, the danger is concealed. Welsh hopes his book will provoke a useful discussion, and the controversial character of his procedure together with the intelligence and lucidity of his argument guarantees that his hopes will be answered. The following chapters occasionally reflect a distrust of his method: abstracting a hero type; interpreting that type in terms of contemporary legal, economic, and politico-moral theory; and allowing that interpretation, together with a prejudicial image of Scott as Tory Gentleman journalist, to dictate interpretation of works of fiction. The meaning of a hero of fiction cannot be so easily and argumentatively abstracted from its mimetic and rhetorical context. Nevertheless, coming to Welsh's argument late in the drafting of my own more tentative essay, I have been forced by his original and challenging book to relearn much about my subject. Thus, however quarrelsome I may later seem on particulars, I am grateful to him in general.

My own attempt in no way seeks to reply to his argument. Yet it directs a basic question at his method. Waverley, Werther, Emma, Harold, René, and others all warn us how uncertain we are as to the meaning and normative function of the hero in Romantic narrative. Why this is so remains unclear. The mixture of lyric and dramatic impulses made "distance" a central problem to be solved for each narrative; new "projective" or "expressive" poetics mingled confusedly with the prevalent pragmatic justifications for fiction.[20] Whatever the cause, the problem is real. Have we, then, any a priori reason for believing the passive protagonist to be a static, uniquely normative element in a Waverley Novel? Would it not be better to test the passivity of the protagonist as a rhetorical device before interpreting it as a problem in cultural history?

Three observations pose a hypothetical meaning for his "passivity." Scott is not unique as comic romancer; the comic hero, suggests Northrop Frye, is "seldom a very interesting person: in conformity with low mimetic decorum, he is ordinary in his virtues, but socially attractive."[21] Second, the passive hero is hardly peculiar to Scott; the "hero of Sensibility," notes Thorslev, "is always passive, not acting but being acted upon."[22] Third, Scott held a lifelong moral objection to fatalistic passivity. In his journal he recognizes his own temperamental Stoicism: "From childhood's earliest hour my heart rebelled against the influences of external circumstances in myself and others."[23] How, then, might we fuse the stoic's insistence on moral autonomy, the passivity of the hero of sensibility, and the requirement of romantic comedy that the low mimetic hero be redeemed and reinstated in a new social stability into a tentative basic myth?

The protagonist, naive and without personal identity or status, inherits divided loyalties and is entangled mysteriously, as a result, with destructive or extralegal forces, forces either excessive or deficient in idealism. He becomes convinced that his entanglement implies an historic fatality. Through his awareness Scott conveys the "sense" Lukacs considers peculiarly his: a "deeper, more genuine and differentiated sense of historical necessity than any writer before him." The atmosphere of romance is skillfully transmuted into an "atmosphere of historical necessity," which, says Lukacs, "arises out of the very subtly portrayed dialectic between the effectiveness and impotence of a correct insight in concrete historical circumstances."[24] The climax comes at the moment when the protagonist fully recognizes the implications of his passivity and acts to assert his moral independence of the forces that have usurped his freedom of will. The act may involve a choice, a substitution of one guide or patron for another, or a shift of faith, a new belief that what had seemed fatality is actually providence. Often the act implies the subordination of some formerly inescapable idealism to a higher more flexible law of humanity. The act requires a new and mature prudence, it is true, but a prudence which serves not an old social stability but a new humanity, a humanity which permits the delicate adjustment between what Karl Kroeber calls "individual righteousness" and the "social lawfulness" on which a new social stability is to be built. No one has better described the subject of the Waverley Novels than Kroeber: they are all "an extended dramatization of the valuable diversities and complexities of mankind asserting themselves against laws too abstract, too rigid, too impersonal."[25]

Kroeber's summary may be explicated with the help of Lukacs. In characterizing the "historic" in the Waverleys, Lukacs bypasses the rather futile argument, recalled by Welsh with the formidable authority of Erich Auerbach, over whether Scott's historism is merely "atmospheric" or genuinely philosophical.[26] But the "manners" conception of Scott's historicity, says Lukacs, is wrong. Most distinctive in Scott's inventiveness is the organic relation of the vitally individual with the historically representative, the dramatizing of public crisis as operative in the most concrete human relationships – private, domestic, personal.[27] Because such relationships are analogous to political relationships, Scott emphasizes the parental or familial, rather than the erotic. In this inventiveness, technique and vision are one; the interanimation of public-historic and private-natural is what gives Scott's fiction its vital coherences, and at the same time the *problems raised* by that interaction become his major thematic concerns. Now the persistent effect of the interaction, as Scott dramatizes it, is to submerge human relationship in ideological struggle, to rigidify human response in the stereotype of ideal commitment. The problem to be worked out, then, is how to preserve or engender the human in the face of this disintegrative and petrifying influence. The solution is to find a common humanity, a law of mutual forbearance, a common language, which will allow reintegration without destroying ideological diversity.

Having tentatively recognized such a correlation of technique and concern, we can hypothesize an answer to one persistent question of Waverley criticism: the question of the function in the novels of the conventional domestic plot.[28] The function is actually three possible functions, and one question to bear in mind is whether the simultaneous and integrated presence of all three is a mark of superiority.

First, the domestic plot provides the inward – that is, the qualitatively human – dimension of history, which the late eighteenth-century historiographer insisted had been neglected to the detriment and falsification of previous historiography. Without a private plot, history lacks realized individual sensibilities; in Flaubert's *Salammbô* only Hamilcar's problematic relations as father give engaging human quality to a novel otherwise composed of wholly external, collective forces. In the second place, the domestic plot provides one pole for a dialectical or pendulous motion between public and private worlds and their conflicting demands. Thus is dramatized the characteristic Scott vision: the encounter of the historic by the ahistoric in human experience (Lukacs), and the working out of the public in terms of the natural or private to a point where "nature" is restored and the historic is stabilized or caused to recede. Finally, the private plot may serve as a metaphor or analogue to the public or historic. For example, the quest of the disinherited or fatherless son for his inheritance is the most familiar plot. And it is obviously serviceable as analogue to the public problem of historic transition and cultural continuity.

All of this is abstract. Any such attempt entails the risk of "essentializing." But at least this one is broad and general enough to suggest that no one subject matter is enough to

11

illustrate fully such a conflict or realize all the implications of such a myth. I shall begin, then, with Scott's most familiar subject matter – Jacobitism, and the alleged conflict in Scott between his loyalty to romantic lost causes and his prudential belief in bourgeois progress and enlightenment – what Mario Praz calls his Biedermeier side.[29] We can best realize the possibilities of such a subject matter for Scott through an evaluative comparison of the three Jacobite novels: *Waverley*, *Rob Roy*, and *Redgauntlet*. We must then face the fact that the two novels of highest reputation, *The Heart of Midlothian* and *Old Mortality*, belong instead to the Cavalier-Puritan group, sharing with *Woodstock*, *Peveril*, and *A Legend of Montrose* a different subject. This is the subject of opposing fanaticisms, of conflicts arising from fanatic commitments to opposing Laws or modes of communication; the dilemma is how to achieve humane reconciliation without losing prudence in cynicism or flexibility in relativism. We can next confront the "tushery" Scott, who, with the popular triumph of *Ivanhoe*, is alleged to have deserted Life to trifle in a never-never land of bookish romance. Here the subject whose possibilities are to be tested can be summarized as a problem: how to reconcile what is of timeless value in a decadent, quixotic chivalry with what is effective and humane in a new, sometimes flippant, sometimes selfish civility. The feverish, foolish dotage of chivalry is dramatized in three periods: Richard I and the Crusades; the late Middle Ages of Louis XI, Charles of Burgundy, Robert III of Scotland; the Renaissance of Mary Stuart, Elizabeth, and James I. Finally (and fourthly), there remain among Scott's relatively nonhistorical novels some of his best (and worst): his own favorite, *The Antiquary*; his most enigmatic, *St. Ronan's Well*; perhaps his artistic triumph, *The Bride of Lammermoor*. Considering these together, and recognizing that they share (with *Mannering* and *The Black Dwarf,* too) an historical theme – the declines, falls, and sometimes the redemptions of great houses – we can investigate whether Scott found here, too, some otherwise unrealized fictional possibility of his perennial concern: the problem of individual freedom and cultural continuity in historical change; or (to use Kroeber's words again) "the problem of cultural survival and fulfillment."[30]

Croce complained that there are just too many Waverley Novels.[31] One cannot blame the weary critic for seeking to save both Scott and himself by limiting his close attention to one or two masterpieces. Perhaps Ian Jack is right, that no service is done Scott's memory "by enthusiasts who find *Woodstock* as rewarding as *The Heart of Midlothian* and persist in prescribing *Ivanhoe* as a 'set book.' "[32] But how can we tell until we have tried *Woodstock* and *Ivanhoe,* or *The Abbot* and *The Fair Maid of Perth* (better books) on what appear to be their own terms? And this means avoiding many familiar traps, refusing to condemn the self-effacing Scott out of his own mouth, and trying not to defend him on grounds partly or wholly irrelevant.

SECTION ONE

THE QUIXOTIC
TRAGICOMEDY OF
JACOBITISM

1. WAVERLEY

EDWARD WAVERLEY, Scott wrote his friend Morritt, "is a sneaking piece of imbecility." To Trollope, *Henry Esmond's* admirer, Thackeray conceded, "Esmond was a prig."[1] The embarrassment with which two Romantic ironists publicly confront their protagonists provides an illuminating case study in the rhetorical problems of earlier nineteenth-century fiction. There is reason to suppose that upon viewing their protagonists with some objectivity, Thackeray and Scott were embarrassed by an unanticipated degree of sentimental involvement or self-reflection, an unexpected loss of ironic control or distance. The effect of recent inquiry into the backgrounds of Esmond's infatuation in Thackeray's relations with the Brookfields has been at once to explain the novel's curious intimacy and to assert its lack of objectivity.[2] The effect of *Waverley* criticism since Lockhart has been to imply the same lack. In Scott's case, however, it is noteworthy that shortly before turning to the completion of his fragment, Scott had looked back upon the earlier self that impinges on Waverley, and looked with a sustained and analytic objectivity while writing what became the "Ashestiel fragment" of autobiography.[3] The look was of use both to Scott and to his reader.

14

Consider how objectively aware he had become of the superficial gentlemanliness of his Cavalierism. In it there was "no real conviction" on his part, "arising out of acquaintance with the views or principles of either party."[4] More suggestive, even, are his reminiscences of early encounters with the ambiguous and tragicomic fact of the heroic idealism that *had* found its base in "real conviction" – more revealing, and most curiously parallel to an early encounter of which much has been made in Thackeray's life. Thackeray, not yet six years old, was on his way to England from Calcutta, and during a stopover on St. Helena, was taken for a walk. His servant pointed out the Great Man: "That is he; that is Bonaparte! He eats three sheep every day, and all the little children he can lay his hands on." This first view of the hero, argues Mario Praz, was to color Thackeray's "conception of heroism and superman-ism for the whole of his life."[5] The Marlborough of *Esmond* may well recall the image of Napoleon in his garden, with the added satiric perspective of *Jonathan Wild*.

If such images provide any legitimate stimulus for critical interpretation, then Scott's *two* formative encounters with past individual greatness are equally suggestive. Both encounters involved clients of his solicitor-father, and thus both were colored for Scott by his father's matter-of-fact dehumanizing legalism, of which the novelist later repeatedly made significant comedy. Scott's recollection of Invernahyle reminds one of Conrad's memory of his father: a figure of both fidelity and humanity, of wonder and common sense, a cool and effective leader in Edinburgh even as an old man, but an old man recalling an adventurous youth, dwindled into a client. The other client, Murray of Broughton, survived for Scott only in the symbolically complex memento known as Broughton's Saucer. The saucer survived as concrete reminder of the destroyed cup. The cup, hurled out the window by the elder Scott in a momentary revelation of his own hatred of infidelity, bore unforgettable testimony of the elder Scott's skillfully compartmentalized life and loyalties. Broughton, like Invernahyle, had survived the '45, but only by appearing as crown witness against many noble fellow Jacobites. Thus, Broughton could be discreetly served as a client, but never as a guest; and so Mrs. Scott's indiscreetly proffered teacup went out the window shortly after the traitor's use and departure.[6]

Both men had survived, one by cowardly infidelity; the other, Invernahyle, by two acts: the humane act of saving an enemy's life at Prestonpans, and the comic-pathetic one of hiding in a cave for weeks following Culloden. In *Waverley*, Invernahyle's two acts are divided between Edward and the man whom he ultimately reinstates and who becomes his *true* father, Baron Bradwardine. The saving of fidelity through a reconciliation of humanity and prudence contains, by implication, most of *Waverley* and perhaps most of Scott. One thinks again of Conrad: "Those who read me know my conviction that the world, the temporal world, rests on a few very simple ideas; so simple that they must be as old as the hills. It rests notably, among others, on the idea of Fidelity."[7] One recalls Crankshaw's suggestion that all his work, perhaps all of the Waverley Novels too, may be considered a fantasia on that idea.

But such conclusions are not to be reached through the juxtaposition of biographical anecdotes. The quest for Scott's well-hidden "secret life," in the manner of Edwin Muir, Sir Herbert Grierson and others, is rhetorical analysis in reverse. Lukacs's wise warning should be written at the head of every page that follows:

16

Biographical evidence of the individual instances which enabled Scott to become aware of these trends offers nothing of importance. . . . The less so, as Scott ranks among those great writers whose depth is manifest mainly in their work, a depth which they often do not understand themselves, because it has sprung from a truly realistic mastery of their material in conflict with their personal views and prejudices.[8]

An inquiry into that mastery is the only safe way to that depth.

Here, too, *Henry Esmond* is a useful companion. Thackeray acknowledged Scott as one of his "most important English benefactors," and *Esmond,* Gordon Ray argues, demonstrates Thackeray's singular competence to restore historical fiction "to the status that Scott had given it thirty-five years before."[9] Several writers claim to have found the plot of *Esmond* in the rakish Charles II's attempted seduction of the heroine of *Woodstock.* J. R. Moore properly sets aside such explanations as irrelevant to the "central situation" in *Esmond,* and then, less properly, traces that situation to *St. Ronan's Well.*[10] The similarity in plot – hidden legitimacy, in which the hero sacrifices the status of legitimacy to another – is undeniable. But the comparison proves once more that barebones plot comparisons, as Tolkien complained of *Beowulf* criticism, are critically misleading. What matters is how a plot is used in the total economy of a narrative. And if comparison is to be undertaken in these terms, *Esmond* warrants comparison with another Jacobite novel, another representation of history in fiction, another comic romance of the heroic loss and recovery of legitimacy, another fiction whose author found his protagonist embarrassing. Scott's *Esmond* is *Waverley.*

Their kinship is unconsciously demonstrated in a recent

17

account of the "unity of *Henry Esmond.*" G. J. Worth finds this strangely organized novel's unifying pattern in the form of the *bildungsroman,* which takes its young apprentice-to-life from Romantic idealism or quixotic folly through disenchantment in every area of experience, to reality and its mature acceptance.[11] The nineteenth century's classic example is *Wilhelm Meister's Apprenticeship:*

"The feeling of my ignorance in this respect," said Wilhelm, "often gives me pain; and I should thank you, worthy friend, if you would help me to get a little better insight into life. From youth, I have been accustomed to direct the eyes of my spirit inwards rather than outwards; and hence it is very natural that to a certain extent I should be acquainted with man, while of men I have not the smallest knowledge."[12]

This is the pattern which, for Worth, culminates in Esmond's rejection of the glittering, trivial Beatrix in preference for her retiring, pockmarked, mundane mother Rachel. "The protagonist," writes Worth, "through a process of trial and error, eventually attains stability and maturity."[13] This is unity, but it is not quite *Henry Esmond.*

Esmond as Aged Narrator's purpose in writing, after all, is to prove that he has been faithful *through life* to his childhood ideal, that the man-child as hero has proved uncorrupted by worldly fraud and cynicism. Worth's case demands that Rachel come at the end of Esmond's experience; but she has been there from the beginning. She is the ideal of his devotion even during his obsession with the false ideal, Beatrix. Worth's argument requires that Esmond go through a period of quixotic folly. But it is only as a child that Esmond worships Father Holt. The young man is no deluded romantic adventurer. Esmond courts Beatrix knowing her ambition and overweening vanity. His active Jacobit-

18

ism comes merely as a part of his courtship, never as a faith
or an ideology. Worth admits that Esmond when plotting
for the Pretender is no longer "the ardent enthusiast he had
been while living at Castlewood."[14] But then he had been a
mere child, with the ardor of a child.

If Worth seems not to have been describing *Esmond,* he
might easily have been describing *Waverley.* Such a reading
would have Waverley the young Man of Feeling, led by a
dangerous prevalence of imagination, a susceptibility to
quixotic folly in love and politics, through various entanglements to the brink of disaster. It is Waverley who defines the
turning point in his *bildung* as follows: "He felt himself
entitled to say firmly, though perhaps with a sigh, that the
romance of his life was ended, and that its real history had
now commenced."[15] It is Waverley who turns from the
chivalrous, anachronistic Fergus to the stolid but honorable
Talbot, and from the romantic dark Flora to the domestic
blonde Rose. Thus he is permitted to outgrow his imbecility,
survive his entanglements with passionate, destructive
forces, and become the proper hero, whose social reinstatement is a celebration of the survival of the status quo. Such,
at least, is the orthodox – and I think superficial – reading of
Waverley's apprenticeship. It is fairer to both novels to look
beyond such superficial differences to more significant and
real ones. The distinct forms of the two heroes' experiences
with romantic love and Jacobite politics will be clarified if
we concentrate on three shared motifs: the love conflict of
each hero; the nature of each entanglement with conflicting
political forces; and finally, the different articulations of the
same basic myth: the search of the disinherited son for
stability and identity, for an escape from the disorder of
history, through the achievement of child-parent relations
with his true ideals.

19

Both heroines express their authors' embarrassment. For Beatrix, Esmond is a prig; for Flora, Waverley is an imbecile – which for her means that his is an exclusively domestic temperament. None, I think, has accepted Beatrix as a reliable commentator. Some, unfortunately (notably, E. M. W. Tillyard and S. Stewart Gordon, both admirable interpreters of *Waverley*), are inclined to think Flora has the last word on Edward.[16] If so, here is a serious rhetorical flaw; Flora's tragically limited vision could not possibly allow her to judge Waverley fairly, and those who identify her view with the narrator's will make the same mistake. The thwarted romances in both books are attributable to human deficiencies in the heroines. The heroines' deficiencies are distinguishable in terms of the moral contexts of the books.

Flora was "precisely the character to fascinate a youth of romantic imagination" (149), and for Welsh she typifies Scott's dark heroine: the lady of passion, of hinted voluptuousness and long hair.[17] Scott does use contrasting heroines to suggest thematic alternatives; we had best postpone full discussion for the arrival of the most explicit example, Minna and Brenda in *The Pirate*. But to see how such a scheme misrepresents Flora's tragic deficiency we need only recall Frye's simplified statement of the motif. "The dark one," we are told, "is as a rule passionate, haughty, plain, foreign, or Jewish"; she is the "lady of pleasure," polar opposite to "the lady of duty."[18] But the danger which Flora represents, and what Waverley must reject or survive, is not a lawless surrender to life's pleasures, but a lawless withdrawal from them. Her idealism is self-petrifying, and the stone is temporarily precious in Waverley's quixotic eye. It gives her the rigidly cloistral character of some of Scott's other heroine-fanatics: she is the nun-bride of her political idealism; all her pleasures and passions are ideal, indistinguishable from duty.

Her competitor for Waverley's affections, Rose Bradwardine, is less the domestic than the private or personal counterpart to Flora. Naturally she is more moderate, more sociable, more modest, but this is no reason to reduce her to the condition of a heroine of propriety and convention. She is active as protector in Waverley's behalf. For her Waverley is valuable as an individual, not as a pawn in ideological warfare; she stands for concrete human loyalties, as opposed to rigid ideal commitments, in a world where the personal and the human win out. As we shall see, this is precisely the redeeming choice made by Waverley at Prestonpans. By his climactic assertion of moral will on behalf of the *positive* virtues for which Rose stands, he earns Rose, earns his role as her father's protector, and earns back his birthright, "Waverley Honour," redeemed from both opportunism and quixotic impotence.

Beatrix Castlewood is in competition with her mother, who, like Rose Bradwardine, represents the private, domestic virtues. But Beatrix is no fanatic idealist. There is no place in Thackeray's world for what is a basic moral conception in Scott. What in Scott is the tragicomic way historic or ideological commitments impinge on or destroy private humanity becomes, in *Esmond*, private life's self-preserving mockery of the vanity and inhumanity of public or historic reality. Beatrix's only devotion is to the cause of her own ambition; in this cause Jacobitism is simply a prime instrument. Beatrix is inhuman, hardhearted, as is Flora; but hers is a form of moral death more akin to that of Estella in *Great Expectations*. Beatrix and Estella are both damned by standards of humane feeling, "fallen" in sensibility or heart. Flora, like Diana Vernon in *Rob Roy*, is doomed by historic fatality (to which she surrenders herself) to the inhumanity of tragic quixoticism. Beatrix is not what she is from historic or ideological causes. Her character involves her with historic forces – her vain infatuation with James III causes the collapse of *his* hopes – but her tragedy, if it can be called one, is not shaped by those forces.

Nevertheless, both are Jacobite temptresses, and thus both are essential to the intertwining of public-historic and private-domestic experience in the books. The differences between them signify not just major thematic differences between the novels, but also structural dissimilarities in the two heroes' experiences of entanglement with history.

Of the historicity of *Esmond* Geoffrey Tillotson says that near its heart "lies much of the Stuart-Hanover conflict."[19] The same may be said of *Waverley,* but in a much truer sense. For in *Esmond* conflict is not translated into ideological terms and never becomes simultaneously ideological and personal as it is for Waverley. Tillotson describes Thackeray's "method of the historian," and cites the presentation of the Augustan rake Mohun as typical of the feigned historicity which gives *Esmond* its "air of the utmost veracity."[20] Veracity in *Esmond* is undeniably a remarkable achievement, accomplished by a period style, a texture of circumstantial allusiveness, the casual presence of specific actuality in a felt definiteness of milieu. *Esmond* does what Scott may have thought he was doing as Miss Edgeworth's disciple, but was clearly not doing in *Waverley* (he later did it in the "manners" panorama of the *Nigel-Kenilworth-Peveril* kind). But what, in fact, is the function of such a brilliantly realized milieu in *Esmond?* The answer may be collected from two statements: first, Charlotte Brontë's complaint that the first two volumes were much overloaded with history; second, J. Y. T. Greig's observation that the "main plot is entirely independent of history."[21] A fair appraisal of *Esmond* would find both exaggerated. But for our purposes Greig is essentially correct in noting that the Jacobite conspiracy is distracting and unprepared for, the main part of the story independent of this historic intrusion. *"Henry Esmond,"* he says, "is not an historical novel with a love story thrown in; it is a love story of a peculiar kind cast into an historical setting."[22]

The participation of Mohun epitomizes the uncertainty. He causes the deaths of Esmond's patron and of Beatrix's Jacobite suitor the Duke of Hamilton. Hamilton's death murders Beatrix's hopes, and Jacobite hopes as well, during Queen Anne's declining months. Mohun is Marlborough's man; thus his role in both private and public catastrophes fuses personal animosity and historic conflict. But only his *role.* Test his characterization against what Lukacs says of Scott: "Scott's unequalled historical genius shows itself in the individual characteristics which he gives his leading figures so that they really concentrate in themselves the salient positive and negative sides of the movement concerned."[23] Mohun as character is not historic in this sense. He is part of Thackeray's antihistoric satire of pretense and fraud in public history and great men, satire much closer to the eighteenth-century "historism" of Voltaire, Glubbdubdrib, and *Jonathan Wild* than to the historisms of Scott, Stendhal, and Pushkin, however these may differ from each other. Mohun's villainy, like Beatrix's inhumanity, is not defined in terms of historical-ideological conflict, for Thackeray's novel acknowledges no such terms. Even the leading Jacobite, James III, as Trollope says of him, is simply "such as Stuarts were, and only walks across the novelist's canvas to show his folly and heartlessness." He simply contributes to the story's chief effect: "a melancholy conviction of the vanity of all things human."[24]

The historicity of *Waverley* is accomplished in part by the avoidance of such actualities, except as symbols, and it is the displacing of the actual in the direction of ideological symbol that gives Scott's world of history its romance quality. Charles Edward, for one chief example, is an important focus for the complex fidelities and hostilities of his friends and foes, but as a character he is insignificant. If *Esmond* is historical only in the circumstantiality of milieu, in *Waverley* the historic is the locus of colliding spheres of value or antipathetic traditions. This has been said in a number of ways, never better, perhaps, than by Karl Kroeber: for Scott, "history was process. He was the first artist to conceive of history as the organic evolution of competing styles of life."[25] And thus history becomes a mode of experience, a process of individual ordeal caused by personal involvement in the collision. Part of the experience of collision is the felt impingement of the past – any past – on the present – all presents. In *Waverley,* 1745 is not a past but a present, of the type Scott was invariably to choose for illustrating how a past could rise again to condition and perhaps redeem a present. Such a threat and such a possibility become in *Waverley* and elsewhere central to the protagonist's ordeal of personal development, as he is forced to play mediator between divided and warring segments of his own lineage. Such is the very different role of history in what might be called Scott's *Esmond.*

To see some of these major differences more concretely, contrast with Thackeray's Mohun, Scott's Fergus MacIvor. Fergus is part of Waverley's personal experience and part of Scott's complex and realistic analysis of the historic cause that was Jacobitism. He is dangerous, dishonest, quixotic, Machiavellian, heroic. He may be explicated in terms of several of Thorslev's classes of Romantic hero types. But for the Author of Waverley he is at once a diagnosis and a commemoration of Jacobitism. His relationship with Waverley is simultaneously personal and public. He is an essential foil to Edward; both are studies in romantic quixoticism, yet their pairing and its plot consequences articulate Scott's analysis of Jacobitism itself, its complex and shifting motivation, its fatal tensions and instabilities, its tragic and comic features. When Fergus and Edward fall out over a minutia of honor, it is part of the plot, part of Waverley's experience as protagonist, but also part of the delineation of Jacobitism's hopeless instability.

In both novels Jacobitism fails. In both, the heroes are permitted to survive their entanglements, and in surviving establish themselves as redeemers of their respective lineages. Their entanglements, I have suggested, differ markedly, and hence their survivals must also differ. The climactic differences may best be seen by recalling the basic myth: the search of the disinherited son for stability and identity in true paternal relationship. In each case the hero's dangerous, disillusioning involvement with history is bound up with the mystery and/or the ignominy of his parentage. In the absence of true parentage each is misled by several false guides acting *in loco parentis*. Each must be a dutiful son, yet at some point assert his own will, in a sense become his own true father. Neither can return to a prior stability, since no such stability survives except as redeemed or recreated by the hero.[26] As Esmond and Waverley win their dynastic identities, they also realize their freedom from all that is degenerate or ignominious in the past. They literally escape from history and become heads of reinstated lines.

It is well known how Esmond does so, by the peculiar Oedipal ritual of destroying his adopted parents' marriage, by bringing in the smallpox and ruining Rachel's beauty. Thus Rachel is saved from vanity; and in his final winning of Rachel, Esmond escapes from history that is just vanity.

25

His marriage and removal with his mother-sister-wife to Virginia is a gesture of antihistoric defiance. He redeems his lineage by removing it to a new and pastoral land. He has earned the place and the redemption by being true to his "mistress" and to the innocent fidelities of his own childhood, by choosing in her the true over the false, the real over the vain, love and paternal protectiveness over ambition and worldliness.

Waverley's survival, like his involvement, is otherwise. We are customarily told that he simply outgrows his Jacobitism. He recovers his sound judgment; he recovers his propriety.[27] His survival embodies the victory of the unheroic future over the heroic past. "Jacobitism," says Daiches, was used by Scott to "symbolize at once the attractiveness and the futility of the old Scotland."[28] But who dies in *Waverley?* The two deaths that matter most in Edward's development from romance to real history are those of two Machiavellians: Fergus the Jacobite and Richard Waverley, Edward's despicable, opportunistic Hanoverian father. Both have been false fathers; both have used Waverley as pawn rather than human being. In this role Fergus's foil is Bradwardine, who repeatedly, and with good reason, refers to Edward as his son.[29] Fergus cannot be saved; Bradwardine, representing what seems attractive and futile in old Scotland, is not only brought back from the dead (rescued from his cave), but fully reinstated in his barony. The reinstatement is accomplished through Edward's sale of his opportunistic father's property and marks the climax of Waverley's marriage to Bradwardine's daughter. Thus Waverley, having emerged from criminal involvement to redeem his own lineage, establishes "Waverley Honour" in a new land, and in Bradwardine preserves or resurrects what is of permanent value in the "lost Past." The protagonist has saved the father and his lands and married the daughter. On the new marriage is founded a new social stability. The Mythos of Romance has fused with the Mythos of Comedy.

The question remains, how has the protagonist earned his survival? Any attempt to interpret Edward's victory must focus on what Gordon calls "the crucial point of the ac- tion – the Battle of Preston [pans]," where Waverley "acts for the first time on his initiative," and acts to save, not destroy.[30] This is not, however, a simple awakening from unsound judgment. As Edward recognizes the extent of his involvement and asserts voluntary control over his fate, he sums up his problem in a metaphor which the whole shape of his ordeal has made literal: "I am the very child of caprice" (334). His helpless entanglement has made him so, and his own "passion for the wonderful" (237) has in- creased his susceptibility. To describe the quality of his experience, two words are used interchangeably: "romance" and "dream." Of the dreamlike aspect of his experience Waverley is constantly aware. But his dream is not to be cured by waking.

Scott, says Welsh, "frequently compares the hero's bewil- dered experience of a romantic world to a bad dream."[31] But the comparison is Waverley's. And "bad" is inaccurate; the words are "strange, horrible, and unnatural" (291). Gordon argues that "throughout the novel dreams are used to signify the unreal, the 'romantic' in Edward's character as opposed to his real and awakening character."[32] Not quite so: his experience and its world are dreamlike, but all too real; he is experiencing the disintegrating interpenetration of romance and reality. That deeds of archaic violence "should be familiar to men's minds, and currently talked of, as falling within the common order of things" is what seems to him "like a dream" (93). His honorable prospects are what have passed away "like a dream." Lost in a strange land he wishes in vain to awake "from what seemed at the moment a dream, strange, horrible, and unnatural" (291). The dream is appropriately set in a darkness which, far from remaining mere setting, becomes for him the darkness of isolation and alienation. His family seal is mysteriously lost. Even language is abolished; for a long time he is "secluded" from the "social intercourse of question and answer" (246). Strangers speak to him in "very significant" but mysterious manners which he cannot interpret (105). A Gaelic bard sings of him in a song he cannot understand (135–36). He is almost killed during a hunt when the command to throw himself down is given in a language he does not know. Through this darkness of lost identity he is led by one strange guide after another: the lunatic Gellatley, the silent Highland girl, the devious Callum Beg. This, of course, is the "strangeness of his fortune, which seemed to delight in placing him at the disposal of others, without the power of directing his own motions" (244). The solution, however, is not simply "waking up."

Like his heirs in *Rob Roy* and *Redgauntlet,* Waverley has no choice but to surrender himself "to the full romance of his situation" (100) – to the darkness and passivity, that is, whence he must learn the meaning of his involvement with history. His self-surrender is an act of will: "Waverley agreed to be guided by his new friend" (222). "And with this resolution of being guided by circumstances, did our hero commit himself to repose" (337). His self-commitment to repose and romance is no mere aberration, but rather a step toward a fuller reality. Welsh has part of the truth here: "the romance, of course, is not over," he argues, when Waverley awakens, because the "history" is to be "an equally imaginary construction."[33] Of course it is equally imaginary, but distinct from romance nonetheless. "The dénouement of a typical romance is too good to be true"; so is the dénouement of a typical comedy, and it is impertinent to consider any romantic comedy as a tragedy *manqué*. Waverley awakens from the necessary passivity of his dreamlike ordeal to a sense of his moral identity.

The climax begins when, utterly alienated from traditional ties, he swears fealty to Prince Charles and thinks he has at last interpreted his relation to his own lineage. Ironically this beginning of self-assertion leads directly to its own repudiation. At this point, clearly signaled by the reappearance (after a long absence from the narrative) of his "true" and benevolent Jacobite father Bradwardine,[34] he begins to rediscover his individual humanity and assert control over his own destiny. Thus, the dawn that breaks for him on the Battle of Prestonpans marks the morning of his "real history." First, in coming upon an old tenant dying on the battlefield, he realizes his traditional responsibility as a Waverley. Then follows his humane and courageous defense of Colonel Talbot against the Jacobites, and with this act begins his alienation from his new cause and the process leading to his own survival. As proof of a more humane fidelity, the act transcends the historic accident of commitment to a cause.

From Talbot, another foil to Fergus, Waverley learns enough of his own heritage and its true values to free him from the counter-spell of Fergus. But to say with Davie that "Colonel Talbot is a more admirable representative of the unheroic English than Waverley"[35] is to miss the point of Waverley's ordeal. Talbot is a bigot; Talbot learns humanity from Waverley. Prince Hal must awaken from the dream of Eastcheap, but he has achieved a fuller humanity as a result of the involvement. Waverley's experience is the broadest,

29

his humanity the most attractive and fruitful, in the book. It is through Waverley's marriage, the ultimate symbol of reconciliation, that Talbot and Bradwardine end in amicable rapport. And whereas Talbot can only reject the doomed Fergus in a way which the narrator himself finds brutally old-fashioned, Waverley stands by him to the end.

On the episode of Fergus's execution hinges my argument that Waverley's commitment to the romance world of historic involvement is not just technically, but also thematically necessary, a morally constructive ordeal. It might be enough to point out that without it he could not have emerged at last as Bradwardine's "son" and protector. But his participation in Fergus's death makes the same point more vividly. Gordon, who feels obliged to exclude these moving scenes from his "unified design," has already recognized their relevance when he notes that "although Waverley loses enthusiasm for the cause, he does not lose sympathy for its advocates, nor admiration for the idealism and selfless loyalty which the cause inspired."[36] Waverley has recognized the central distinction singled out in Kroeber's fine phrase: "the Waverley novels are an extended dramatization of the valuable diversities and complexities of mankind asserting themselves against laws too abstract, too rigid, too impersonal."[37] To put it simply, he discovers in his own ordeal the distinction between ideology (or "history") and humanity (or "nature"). The discovery makes it inevitable that his loyalty to Fergus survive his falling out with Fergus's Jacobitism. As the novel evolves its moving distinction between the flaws of Fergus the Jacobite and the nobility of Fergus the doomed man, so Edward must accompany Fergus almost to his death, be fully reconciled with him, suffer for him, and inherit Fergus's timeless value in his future role as protector of the Sons of Ivor. Without this final act of humane loyalty to Fergus, Waverley could not deserve to be Bradwardine's protector. Without his imprudent involvement in the rebellion, he could have become heir to neither. As heir to both he realizes his own identity as a Waverley, and would thus seem most perfectly to embody the Author of Waverley's vision of a reconciling humanity that may heal ideological division, conquer the terrors of history, and establish a vital continuity to transcend loss and change.

If Goethe meant something more or less like this when he said that *Waverley* implied in advance all Scott would do, then one may agree with him. But a consideration of two somewhat inferior Jacobite novels suggests that Jacobitism as a subject could not suffice for the full realization of such a vision.

2. ROB ROY

Does *Rob Roy* "challenge comparison" with *Waverley*?[38] Its conception is wholly different. *Rob Roy* does not center on the '15 as *Waverley* does on the '45. It does not focus a conflict of loyalties on a scion of an important house, who is forced to experience and to try to redeem his divided heritage. From the title the legendary bandit seems to be hero. Rob Roy's kinsman Nicol Jarvie is, however, the book's most vividly realized character; and recalling Ian Jack on Scott and the "historical picturesque,"[39] one recognizes in the counterpointing of Rob and Jarvie the novel's basically "picturesque" conception. The lack of an underlying narrative conception can be argued from the lack of meaningful proportion. Plausible defenses have been made of the plotting, the balancing of halves, the marshaling of characters. Nevertheless, as focused and proportioned narrative, *Rob*

Roy is inferior to *Waverley,* and perhaps to *Redgauntlet.* The usual comparison with *Waverley* is invited on the assumption that *Rob Roy* is a return to an earlier theme after several departures, a rewriting of *Waverley* for 1715.[40] This is not the case. Jacobitism is at the center of *Waverley;* it is the focus of the book's pervasive conflicts of value; as a political movement in history it is of central interest. The major characters have their historicity and participate in the picture of the event. What part can Jacobitism play in *Rob Roy,* a novel of family conflict and pride, akin to intervening novels such as *Guy Mannering* and *The Antiquary?* Welsh argues convincingly that the connection between Jacobite conspiracy and the misfortunes of the house of Osbaldistone is merely asserted.[41] The titular character serves as a Jacobite agent, but his role in the conspiracy is questionable. The Highland grievances that led to the '15 are not those that turned Rob Roy into an outlaw. He and his wife may represent the "heroic" Highlands, but their heroism has little to do with loyalty to any one king or system. In *Rob Roy,* as in *The Black Dwarf* and *The Bride of Lammermoor,* early Jacobitism is included without providing a thematic center.

The role of Jacobitism in *Rob Roy* is blurred. For one thing, the central confrontation between Rob Roy and Jarvie has no real connection with the Jacobite cause. It represents the friendly and humane conflict of burgher and freebooter, the mutual distrust of commerce and adventure, or Credit and Honor. Another cause of blurring is the fact that Diana Vernon, the central Jacobite in the novel, is only superficially attached to a cause; she is rather the embodiment of family honor, or of a pathetic kind of self-destructive idealism independent of the rise of Jacobitism. Rashleigh Osbaldistone, the other arch-Jacobite, contributes to the uncertainty. He is Fergus with neither the ideological significance nor the tragic grandeur. He is a villain of opportunism and revenge – in a sense, he is the less attractive side of Helen MacGregor (Rob Roy's wife), who also lives for vengeance. His only loyalties are to himself. As a result of these factors, the hero's involvements are with individuals; his encounters with them are morally, but not politically or historically significant.[42] Appropriately, his entanglement with the Jacobites is commercial, since the crime of which he is suspected is theft, not treason, and since his only interest in the Highlands is the recovery of his father's assets. Thus, Jacobitism is thematically incidental.

Or is it? It might be argued that the book provides an economic analysis of the Jacobite uprising. Scott has used a primarily economic estrangement between father and son in dramatizing the effect of fiscal intrigue on political or ideological causes. Unfortunately the struggle among the Jacobites between Money and Honor is blurred by the interference of Rashleigh's personal motives. His design is to create rebellion out of financial desperation, and he is thwarted by Diana and her father, representing Jacobite honor. If it were their quixoticism which drove Rashleigh away and thereby doomed the rebellion, we could find in the book a consistent disillusioned view of the economics of political idealism. But Rashleigh is angered instead by his failure to win Diana, and this personal motivation confuses the Money-Honor conflict.

It remains a principle of thematic structure, however. Davie notes the early disagreement of Frank and Diana over figures of heraldry weighed against figures of arithmetic – the heraldic versus the commercial calculus. He complains that its implications are never worked out.[43] But if, as appears, it is virtually the same as the Honor-Credit

33

conflict, then it is given new development in the book's second half. First there are the financial intrigues of the Jacobites. Then Frank, presumably bound to the credit side, proves his honor, wins Diana's support and the interest of Sir Hildebrand, and thus inherits family seniority. Meanwhile, the Jarvie-Rob Roy exchanges have developed the same conflict, and their reconciliation has prepared the way for the marriage of Frank and Diana. Thus there is no failure to further the implications of the initial disagreement. The failure of thematic structure is, rather, a lack of focus. As Welsh writes, "The action seems inchoate because there are too many sources of interest, no one of which commands the whole."[44]

Take, as a challenge, the most ardent defense of the book's bifurcated structure. E. M. W. Tillyard sees in the halves a significant balance. The novel has a lovely shape in that "Part Two" is a thematic repetition, with richer circumstance and stronger emphasis, of "Part One." Each has its city-country contrast; each its need for reconciliation. In the first half reconciliation between the Osbaldistone brothers is unlikely. In the second half the opposing principals are themselves possessors of the reconciling principle: Rob Roy and Jarvie have a common humanity, forbearance, tact. Such are the lines of Tillyard's brief sketch.[45] But this shape excludes more than it organizes. Only a small part of the first half is about the Osbaldistone conflict; another small part is about Sir Hildebrand and his boorish sons. The first half is mainly about the father-son conflict, the machinations of Rashleigh, Frank's mysterious involvement in crime, the Frank-Diana relationship, and the Rashleigh-Diana relationship. This is the stuff of which the plot is made, and we cannot neglect it to fasten for plot on a parallelism which has little specific articulation.

The two conflicts in the first half which beg for resolution in the second are the two I have cited: Frank and Diana, and Rashleigh and Diana. In the first, Frank represents commercial prudence (temporarily lost in "poetry"), Diana honor, family pride. But both also represent undisciplined youth and fancy; Frank does not "stand by the principle of Credit,"[46] so the conflict is unreal. The Rashleigh-Diana conflict is potentially the tragic division in *Waverley* between Flora and Fergus: the two rebels – one composed of cloistral honor, the other of Machiavellian ambition. In *Waverley* the failure to resolve this conflict signals the doom of the cause; in *Rob Roy* the failure is lost in the personal motives of Rashleigh.

A further objection to the Tillyard hypothesis is its implication that Frank is not central in the second half. Rob Roy and Jarvie are vividly dramatized, but Frank is still there. His decision to leave Diana and set out in quest of his father's commercial salvation marks the beginning of the second half, necessitating a coherent narrative movement linking the halves, and not simply the pictorial symmetry Tillyard calls the plot. Potentially there is such continuity: Rashleigh and Diana remain the forces contesting for Frank's commercial sonship. But Part Two as Frank's search and Part Two as it focuses on Jarvie and Rob Roy are only superficially the same. Only on the plot level can Frank be said to affect the conflict and reconciliation of Rob Roy and Jarvie. His affairs bring them together and lead them into a situation where they rediscover their mutual affection and tolerance. Frank almost becomes the reconciler when he realizes that Jarvie has been insufficiently aware of Rob's feelings (340). But by contrast, a reconciling and compassionate humanity is the essential acquired wisdom of a Waverley who can love Fergus and admire Talbot at the

35

last. To such wisdom Frank has no access (nor does he have need for it), and the mutual forbearance and respect binding Jarvie's commercial civility and Rob Roy's freebooterism have little effect on the continuing problem of Frank's power to save his father. While there is genuine hope for reconciliation between Jarvie and Rob, none can take place. But while Jarvie and Rob Roy sadly recognize they can never inhabit the same world (such is the novel's climactic honesty), Frank's obstinate father hastily accepts a scapegrace Catholic Jacobite for a daughter-in-law (such is its final implausibility). No search for symmetry can circumvent this obstacle.

Not that all complaints of asymmetry are fair. For the most recent instance, Davie's argument that the book breaks up into half novel and half romance, while it recognizes the formal crux in many Waverley Novels, is unfair to this one. The opening chapters, we are told, introduce "an analysis, in historically realistic terms, of the state of English society in the first half of the eighteenth century." Then Scott, we hear, having found his hero "fit for nothing else," shifts into the realm of "high romance."[47] To take first things first, the nostalgia of a young man leaving Augustan London and the grotesque picture of country life in the North Country Hall do not add up to realistic social analysis. We are concerned with the Morris robbery and Frank's mysterious implication, hence with Rashleigh, Diana, the clerk, the Jacobite justice, and Campbell. All this is romantic enough. As for the second "half," it is scarcely a half. We are in Glasgow, in church, in Jarvie's house, in the College yards, in jail – there is more social realism here than at Osbaldistone Hall. Then we go to the Highlands and see rank poverty, brutality, barbarism. This is no high romance. The picture of Highland life is more informed by realistic economic analysis than the picture of life at the Hall.

There are more genuine reasons for finding the later chapters romantic. After Jarvie's long dinner-table disquisition, the narrative pace does quicken, and perilous adventure prevails. The sense of danger becomes stronger, and to say, with Welsh, that it remains purely in the realm of the potential is simply to point out its essentially romantic quality.[48] Rob himself is anything but a figure of high romance; he is a shrewd, pathetic outlaw. But the emergence in crucial situations of such vital and even archetypal elements as Rob, Jarvie, and Helen MacGregor, together with the emergence of the quest, the son's pursuit of his father's enemy, and an exotic wilderness for setting – all of these provide displacement sufficient to suggest a more significant reality than is apparent in the earlier chapters.[49] And thus, any attempt to measure the success of *Rob Roy* against its failure must focus on the late emergence of these principal elements, and on their significance for the book as a whole.

To return, then, to an observation made earlier, the central opposition of Jarvie and Rob Roy is only superficially related to the political differences that split the Osbaldistone family. Jarvie's Hanoverianism and Rob's Jacobite fooling are quite incidental. Rob would have the same problems if he were a Hanoverian. As a Campbell he actually is one, though he stands to profit by the strife when it comes. Rob, in Welsh's phrase, "has too many sources of interest." If all the novels are about law, then a novel whose titular hero is a semilegendary outlaw ought to be comprehensively typical. But Rob as archetypal outlaw receives strangely little attention, especially when one compares the attention given Ratcliffe in *The Heart of Midlothian*, or even Ranald MacEagh in *A Legend of Montrose*. Again, if *Rob Roy* were an economic tragedy of backward areas, of the destruction of Highland civilization, then Rob and his wife would be central, and Rob's significance as Jacobite outlaw would be more sharply defined. Jacobitism's appeal as an outlawed traditional humanity hostile to commercial avarice would provide thematic unity. But Jacobitism and Die Vernon's Honor are not symbols of humanity. The humanity that cherishes civility and prudence while it deplores avarice is the province of Nicol Jarvie. Any attempt to find the book's thematic structure must recognize that in Jarvie are embodied literally *all* of the values on whose behalf the book appeals. Any attempt to see the same ultimate division of appeal as may be found in *Waverley* – among, say, Bradwardine, the MacIvors, Talbot, Waverley himself – seems doomed.

Daiches and Davie, for example, committed in different ways to the thesis that *Rob Roy* weighs the old against the new, are forced to find Jarvie the new and Rob the old.[50] The book contains evidence to support such a view, but, because the book is not consistently articulated in theme, it also contains enough to refute it. "Rob Roy," we are told, "represents the old heroic Scotland."[51] Not at all. He is an ex-drover driven to outlawry by the avarice of a new order. No one represents "the old heroic Scotland." True, Frank sees in Highland pride and ceremony the essence of a romantic way of life. But there is little of this in Rob himself, except in his contempt for weavers and other bourgeois. Otherwise, he has been a good cattle drover, a good but fair businessman, and now he lives by blackmail and as a paid agent of the Jacobites. Since this isn't the old heroic anything, the novel's theme can scarcely be the "sense of the necessity of sacrificing heroism to prudence, even though heroism is so much more attractive."[52] The most attractive thing in the novel is Jarvie's combination of prudence, flexibility, and a humane love of life. The moment of starkest heroism is also Jarvie's, when he stands up to Helen MacGregor. Were it possible, then, to see the novel as one in which (as Davie says) "Scott tries again to strike a balance between the old and new,"[53] and were Jarvie to be seen as the full embodiment of the new, then Davie would surely be right in arguing that Scott tips the balance recklessly, and so admires the new that the old gets much less than justice.

But the old-new opposition is even less simple here than in *Waverley*. Jarvie's prudence is not a new force in history, but an old humanity, just as the commercialism of Frank's father is explicitly interpreted as the old adventurousness of the heroic merchant-speculator (6–7). The Osbaldistones of the Hall may be treated with "savage contempt," but it is not for being old. Their barbarity is not in their oldness. The father was in the past a better man, but his responses to historic events have cut him off from life, and barbarity in the present is the result. He doesn't represent an old way of life any more than Garschattachin does. Diana Vernon is the book's loftiest, most attractive Jacobite, and it is absurd to define her in terms of old versus new.

There are, to be sure, in all of these characters divergent attitudes toward the strength and significance of familial and cultural tradition. The adventurer prides himself on ignoring or defying it; the Dianas act in its image. But who speaks most of his father in the book – who is its most dutiful son? Nicol Jarvie. He is what he is because his father the deacon was what he was. He is truer and closer to his past than Rob Roy is to his. He is a local antiquary *con amore*, like the Whig, Jonathan Oldbuck. It is natural, then, that the book's most significant alliance, the relationship between Rob Roy and Jarvie, is rooted in kinship, in shared tradition, and represents traditional humanity at its best.

39

Thus the book's thematic vitality and coherence are crucially dependent on the significance of Jarvie, and that significance defies neat definition. The problem recalls two other early novels, *Guy Mannering* and *The Antiquary*, whose central elders have some of Jarvie's vivid complexity of attitude toward Tradition and Progress. It is not surprising that all three invite essentially the same critical – or anticritical – approach.

Those taking this approach would make of Welsh's valid stricture that "there are too many sources of interest, no one of which commands the whole" the compliment that the book is too big with Life to be confined to any single theme. Edgar Johnson, for example, reverts to this traditional praise when he defines its purpose as "the rich evocation of human characters."[54] Daiches pays little attention to the demands of thematic coherence and proportion and finds that characters achieve "life" when they dramatize Scott's ambivalent sense of old versus new. I am too committed to the premises shared by Welsh, Davie, and Dorothy Van Ghent to separate vitality from significant form. But I wonder whether the acceptance of such premises demands that we find Nicol Jarvie too big for the book, that, in Davie's words, he has "too much vitality for the good of the book as a whole"?[55]

To begin with, we are told that Jarvie has a "Dickensian exuberance," which inevitably implies a Pickwickian irrelevance. Dickensian exuberance, I take it, is a mythic energy of self-defining behavior in a character remarkable for eccentricity, for individuating habits and gestures so predictably indulged that the character seems quite isolated from both "world" and thematic significance.[56] If this is so, then Jarvie is not Dickensian. He is not predictable, not grotesque, not isolated; he converses with prudence and kindly tact. Virtually every individuating attitude or habit relates him to the logic of theme. If this is not as true of other elements in the book, the failure is in them.

The book is about mutual forbearance, tact, respect for the prejudices or ideological rigidities of others; it is about these humane ideals from the very first, when father and son, failing to observe them, are estranged. It is about the loss of such ideals throughout the Osbaldistone Hall portions, where both Frank and Diana are terribly lacking in compassion, and Rashleigh and Frank have an absurd fight (114). Contrast the later fight at Aberfoyle, dominated by the presence of Jarvie (267–68). It is he who embodies the antidote. Much of his vitality or "intensity" comes from the ways he acts upon his belief in such ideals, and his healthily pragmatic modes of reasoning in favor of them. All of his vitality works to the furtherance of those ideals in the novel. How, then, can he be "too much"?

The problem is structural. The book is conceived in terms of the kinship of Jarvie and Rob Roy. But Rob is present (though in disguise) almost from the very first, and so, when Jarvie does appear half way through, his emergence seems abrupt and causes a sense of disproportion. Jarvie serves as guide-patron of the second half. Diana serves in the same capacity in the first half, and one could make the same charge about her – too vital for the good of the book – were it not for the greater propriety and better pacing of her emergence in the earliest chapters. Like Jarvie, she controls Frank's experience for a part of the book; hers is a whole way of seeing the world of that experience, just as his is. Hence, she must seem peculiarly vital. And if Frank is to become aware, once he has sacrificed Diana, of the possible heroism and humanity of commerce, Jarvie must seem persuasively vital too. The fact that this awareness does not develop, the fact that Jarvie's thematic relation to Frank's father seems inadequately articulated, and the *resultant* fact that Jarvie's dramatic centrality and persuasiveness seem disproportionate – all these are not faults of Jarvie's vitality, but of the book that is not coherently formed around that vitality. The original flaw is the failure to realize Frank's significance as protagonist.

Frank becomes neither representative nor symbolic: his poetry is undefined. His late "poetic" responses to picturesque scenery serve comically to distinguish him from the unpoetic Jarvie. But poetry as a viable alternative to, or even a significant aberration from, his father's commercialism is never adequately defined. Welsh argues that "The point of *Rob Roy* would be gravely mistaken if we imagine Frank Osbaldistone to be a poet."[57] True, but the point requires that he vaguely suppose himself to be one. And the flaw is the utter failure of poetry to color or condition Frank's performance as narrator.

Indeed, all of the uncertainties or disproportions which mar the book come to rest on the chief technical uncertainty: Scott's apparent failure to recognize the possibilities of his first-person narrator.[58] The old man-young man cleavage might have given Frank considerable vitality; could have dramatized the historic quality, the pastness, of events; would have permitted an irony effective in the definition of value conflicts. But it is only in the opening chapters that Scott seems to have thought about these possibilities.[59] Once he has ceased thinking about them (precisely the same cessation flaws the different experiment of *Redgauntlet*), Frank might just as well not be narrator. Hereafter Frank as narrator is undramatized; and, because the later consciousness loses all definiteness, the earlier Frank has little separate existence, little of Waverley's growing awareness of the mysterious shaping of his destiny. The narrator seldom expresses the impact on his earlier self of events. Welsh cites exceptions to this – notably when, during Rob Roy's escape from the troops, Frank says he "was immediately awakened to the sense of my situation" (324). His sense registers only the immediate, practical circumstances, however, and nothing as significantly generalized as what Welsh calls "the anxiety of the hero of society."[60] Thus, the protagonist fails to achieve either the experiential or the dramatic reality his central position demands, and the formal possibilities of the novel remain unrealized or unfocused. *Waverley* and most of *Redgauntlet* provide revealing contrasts.

Donald Davie's distinction between Edward and Frank is helpful. Whereas some critics call Frank a weak character, Davie suggests that Waverley is the weak character strongly presented, while Frank's weakness is in presentation.[61] I am not sure what such a distinction means in rhetorical terms. Nevertheless, it is true that Frank is not morally weak. His only weakness of character is the obstinacy which estranges him from his father and provokes the fight with Rashleigh. But while he deplores his own obstinacy, it becomes no moral theme; for he is mocked for his poetry, and the two are not clearly related. He is sufficiently audacious to handle most situations, sufficiently insensitive not to be thrown off guard or robbed of his freedom of will. He lacks any powerful sense of his own plight and thus differs sharply from Waverley and Darsie, for that matter from Nigel and Roland Graeme and Peveril. The fate he occasionally mentions is only the result of his own obstinacy, his father's, and Rashleigh's cynical exploitation of both. Thus there is in his situation no poignant sense of involvement with historic forces or with mysterious agencies, none of the mysterious "romance of situation" felt by many other Waverley heroes. The suggestion that half way through, Scott shifted from novel to romance because he found he had a hero fit for nothing else,[62] misrepresents romance and fails to recognize that Frank is even worse fitted for the romance than he is for the novel.

What Frank's consciousness contains of the sense of the "romance of history" is limited to what has rubbed off on it from the fatalistic self-awareness of Diana Vernon. It is she, after all, who provides the book with its waif or pawn of history. In this she resembles Flora, Rose, and many other Waverley heroines, dark, light, and mixed. In the case of Edward Waverley no rubbing off is necessary. He himself is involved by dint of who he is, and the key to his identity is held by history. His choice between Flora and Rose provides the symbolic climax to his involvement; and whether or not one admires his choice, one never questions the inevitability of the marriage. One questions it in *Rob Roy*. For one thing, of course, Diana has no rival, and Frank's only choice is the temporary one between hopeless courtship and loyal sonship. For another, the obstacle to their love is ambiguous: for a while it is the conflict between Commerce and Honor, for a while it is her fateful commitment to her political ideal, which bars not just a commercial swain, but all earthly love. Thus there is no clear preparation for the final reconciliation as a symbol. The prospective wedding rushed in for finale may be interestingly compared with the expanded conclusion to *Great Expectations*. The union of Pip and Estella is defensible, at least, as a logical consequence of the painful humanizing of both. Frank and Die have undergone no comparable transformation, and thus the significance of the final match is even more dubious than its probability.

Once again the problem seems to lie in the lack of a significant shape for Frank's experience. Frank exists emotionally and morally in a very few patterns of engagement

and response. There is his tie to his father. From the outset
we expect that he must learn to understand his father, since
the narrator-Frank does, and the protagonist-Frank did not.
But he never learns, unless we simply infer that he learns
indirectly through engagements with surrogates or counterparts. Diana, for example, is the exact opposite of his father.
But in order to understand his father through the contrast,
he must discover the limitations in her perspective. He
never does, though he thinks he does when he thinks she
has fanatically surrendered his affections to her ideal (335).
But if Diana suffers, like Flora, from the rigid inhumanity of
the withdrawn idealist, the elder Osbaldistone is even less
flexible and humane than she, so there is no real contrast to
learn from. Likewise, Sir Hildebrand is too dim and too
gross a caricature until his death scene to provide an educative contrast, and anyway, Sir Hildebrand, though in a way
a more admirable father than Frank's, never becomes for
Frank an alternative to his own father. The only means by
which Frank can truly realize what is worthy of respect and
affection in his father is Jarvie.

Jarvie's appearance is perfectly placed to invite such an
interpretation. As soon as Frank chooses to be a son in
preference to a rejected suitor, he sets out for Scotland. This
decision is his "Prestonpans"; it commences his period of
greatest danger, but it also wins him his Talbot – his
reliable guide, the idealization of his father. We have every
reason, then, to expect that through the father-son relationship of Frank and Jarvie, Frank's understanding of his
father and his familial identity will be established. Jarvie
invites this expectation not just by expressing his love of
commerce, but also by indicating his judgment of Frank's
father. All he can really accomplish, however, is to make
Frank more critical of his father as Frank comes to realize

Jarvie's own humane goodness. Davie complains that the contrast between Frank's father and Jarvie is not maintained.[63] Its maintenance would have been to little avail. Frank's father, we gather, should and could have learned humanity from his forced dependence on Jarvie to patch up his affairs. But it seems that the patching up wasn't really important after all, and that the father had only to worry about the safety of his son. Thus the reconciliation of father and son is unrelated to the counterpointing of Osbaldistone and Jarvie. The virtual nonexistence of Osbaldistone throughout the middle chapters, except as the alluded-to father for whose plight Frank feels responsible, leaves the contrast unarticulated. Meanwhile, its very promise is lost in the counterpointing of Jarvie and Rob Roy.

There is another significant counterpart to Jarvie, whose role, in this novel of "too many sources of interest" and no dramatic center, indicates a final, easily overlooked possibility for thematic coherence. Johnson observes that Andrew Fairservice is set off against Jarvie. Davie, on the other hand, finds that Fairservice "has no part to play in the logic of theme, so far as this can be discerned."[64] An examination of his principal function discloses another side to that logic, which, though not sufficiently prominent to organize the novel as a whole, provides it with considerable added interest, and in so doing defines a prevalent theme of better Waverley Novels.

Fairservice represents all that can be held despicable in the Scottish character. He serves in the first half as an anticipation of the second, for he is waiting to go home, he hates England, and he deplores the Union. This in itself isn't enough to justify the narrative space he takes up. His position as gardener, although it gives him an outside vantage point useful in plotting, also lacks significance. As his unattractive features accumulate, it becomes clear that he provides contrast for almost every good feature of every sympathetic character in the novel. The problem of Fairservice's hatefulness is the problem of the narrative as a whole: lack of focus. One is persistently conscious that Fairservice is coward, hypocrite, and bore; hence, one misses more important features of his villainy. As a smuggler and a thief, he might have emerged as contrast to Rob Roy. But Rob's outlawry is thematically undeveloped. So Fairservice remains instead the kind of legal corruption Rob hates in the Lowland character, and thus an element to justify Rob's bitterness and his wife's vengefulness.

More important is the fact that Jarvie hates him too. From Jarvie's point of view – and Frank's – his specific evils are those of an evil guide and a gossip. As guide or servant, he is dangerous in his service because he is a travesty on loyalty. As gossip he is consistently dangerous in his undisciplined speech. He is selfish, a self-righteous spreader of ill-report. As such he is the most immediate threat to Frank, whose chief mystery is the way ill-report clings to him: he is suspected of crime, mistaken for a criminal, identified with outlaws, all suspicions providing substitutes for his actual misdemeanor against his father. For Jarvie, Fairservice's undisciplined speech is a crime against humane civility. Fairservice is the defiler of words, and as a result one who uses language in such a way as to *divide* men. He repeatedly endangers the good fame of Frank, of Diana, of England. As the party approaches Aberfoyle, he is sternly warned not to speak (257–59). When they are taken prisoner by redcoats, Fairservice immediately starts talking. At the end his words cause two deaths. Jarvie's whole prudence operates on the precept of not giving offence in speech, on the belief that language prudently used is a delicate and effective instrument for human reconciliation. "Whisht, sir! – whisht! it's ill-scraped tongues like yours that make mischief atween neighbourhoods and nations" (254), he mutters to Fairservice. Thus the omnipresent danger Frank faces is identical with the chief threat to Jarvie's ideal of humane civility.

This shared danger provides the second half with a unifying interest. But as a problem to be extensively dramatized, language as a social threat and possibility belongs more properly to other novels. From it, for example, *Redgauntlet* derives a thematic richness and coherence unequaled in *Rob Roy*. If this final Jacobite novel also falls short of *Waverley*, it may well be that the "matter" of Jacobitism proved too narrow to sustain such thematic possibilities.

3. *REDGAUNTLET*

From its early reputation as what one Blackwoodian called "an inferior kind of *Waverley*," *Redgauntlet* has come a long way to be considered Scott's *Antony and Cleopatra*, his *Don Quixote*, the most "vital" and "powerful" dramatic investigation of his supposedly ambivalent feelings about the old versus the new.[65] The recent enthusiasm, though one may not share it, is not hard to account for. *Redgauntlet* can be seen as the Author of Waverley's return (1824), after four years of flirting with exotic pasteboard, to his true subject. Since Lockhart, it has been popular to use it in psychological excursions into the dynamisms and emptinesses of Scott's imagination. It has uniquely autobiographical elements: Greenmantle, Scott's father in Saunders Fairford, the young advocate's picturesque entry into Edinburgh professional life.[66] For Daiches, the book is the "most adequate 'objective correlative' for his feelings about

48

Scottish history and for that complex attitude toward the relation between tradition and progress which explains so much of the workings of his mind and imagination."[67] But this is relevant only to parts of the book. And the book's parts are too easily detachable.

Those still committed to the view that a Scott novel is an anthology of brilliant parts find reason for joy in Wandering Willie's Tale, in the pre-Dickensian portrait of the foggy law's delay in the case of Peter Peebles, and in the scene supporting the Daiches interpretation: the tragicomic spectacle at the end when the Hanoverian general walks unnoticed into the Jacobite cabal, invites those assembled to go home and behave more prudently, and proves by his calm unconcern that Jacobitism is no longer a live issue. These are great and significant parts. But a fiction must stand or fall by its total economy. This test, which *Waverley* passes admirably and *Rob Roy* evades, *Redgauntlet* impressively essays and ultimately fails.

The failure seems strange because the first half gives rich promise of success. The falling-off point coincides with the reversion from epistolary or journalistic to straight narrative (236), as if the narrator, wearied of his method, had failed to recognize its thematic implications. The falling-off point also coincides with the emergence of Jacobitism as central problem. Once again, as in *Rob Roy,* a formal failure suggests the inadequacy of the subject once its possibilities had been fully realized in *Waverley.*

Take the epistolary beginning. The method seems implausible, yet functions admirably. *Redgauntlet* is, from beginning to end, a novel about friendship, and the exchange of letters between Allan and Darsie permits a full dramatic definition of their bond. The book opens with Darsie's facetious complaint that the absent Allan is a traitor to the cause of friendship, and Allan's determined behavior throughout the book is to demonstrate the falseness of the charge. Urging Darsie to come home from dangerous Dumfriesshire, he appeals to their vows of friendship. When his friend needs help, Allan throws up his first court case to go to his rescue, and ultimately Darsie reciprocates: each sacrifices his "interest" in a hopeless cause – Allan in the case of Peter Peebles, and Darsie in the Jacobite intrigues of his uncle Redgauntlet – to the safety of his friend. Darsie's chief attribute is his genius for making friends, and thereby acquiring would-be guides and protectors. Of these, the most interesting and important is a Friend – the admirable Quaker, Joshua Geddes.

The central position throughout much of the novel of an appealing Quaker is proof of Scott's thematic awareness. Any praise of the novel should focus on Joshua's role, for he is not simply a complex and sympathetic depiction of what was for Scott a potentially comic religious extremism, but more, the chief exponent of the novel's governing values. When, after Darsie's capture, he fades from view until the end, he takes with him much of the book's promise of ultimate unity. The Byronic Jacobitism of Redgauntlet which takes his place seems a digression rather than a fulfillment.

Joshua's central significance may be summarized. He is a Friend, a pacifist, a kindly guide, a spiritual father to Darsie. He is direct counterpart to the melodramatic Redgauntlet in his quiet courage, his combination of peaceableness and friendship with a devotion to plainspeaking and prudent commerce. Finally, he is a man who holds in contempt the wild pride of heritage, the obsessive concern with family tradition and honor, embodied in the cynical Redgauntlet. He may be seen as antiromance personified; if we utilize the

Daiches romance-progress antithesis, he, more than Allan or the elder Fairford, is the embodiment and validation of the new and progressive vision. But such a reading does credit neither to Joshua nor to the thematic complexity of the novel. Like Jarvie's, Joshua's significance warrants careful definition. Unlike Jarvie, Joshua is as much out of place in the post-Jacobite world as Redgauntlet himself.

Like most of Scott's distinctive characters, Joshua is dramatically defined by his traditional idiom, that which gives him at once his individuality and his representativeness. But as with Jarvie, language for Joshua is not just a behavioral idiosyncracy. It is a moral problem, and his basic moral attitudes concern language. In what we have seen so far of the Author of Waverley's world – in Waverley's dark isolation among those who speak an unknown language; in Jarvie's anxious concern with the conciliatory power of prudent speech – the narrative texture of repeated encounters between strangers, between representatives of opposing cultures or ideologies, makes language a constant problem. Conflict or misunderstanding between high and low, Scot and Englishman, Lowlander and Gael, lawyer and layman, pedant and pragmatist, Kirkman and Covenanter invites dramatization in terms of hostile idioms. It may well appear that the subject matters most rich in the opportunity for such confrontations provided Scott with his most congenial occasions for significant fiction. Such confrontations threaten the historic survival of what is valuable on both sides. Survival depends on reconciliation, and the search for reconciliation proceeds mainly through the search for a common language,[68] or at least for the linguistic flexibility and the tact (Jarvie's code) which make conciliation possible.

Wittig recalls that the tragedy of "The Two Drovers"

results from men's acting "in ignorance of each other's prejudices."[69] Such, for Scott, is invariably the threat to reconciliation. The kind of action which most vividly embodies the threat is speech. For all his sectarian jargon, Joshua Geddes is the ideal speaker, for whom speech is to convey the truth, yet keep the peace. Joshua's position in the novel, dramatizing friendship as subject and language as problem, reveals the genius for fusing character, historic type, and moral theme which makes Scott thoroughly impressive when he succeeds.

Joshua contrasts his own people with the public world: "Thine own people do not," he tells Darsie, "as we humbly endeavour to do, confine themselves within the simplicity of truth, but employ the language of falsehood, not only for profit, but for compliment, and sometimes for mere diversion" (53). His difficulties in the novel derive from his faith in simple language, from his refusal to "swear unto the truth of his words, which thing he might not do without sin, seeing it is written, 'Swear not at all'; also, that our 'conversation shall be yea or nay'" (246). His only human deficiency – one which makes him a less prudent conciliator than Jarvie – is in the literality with which he adheres to his code. Once he denies Darsie a piece of cake previously rejected because Darsie is "taking his word again" (66).

Joshua as plainspeaker is unique in his combination of simplicity and forthrightness with an equally strong determination to be peaceful and conciliatory. Others deviate from his ideal in different directions. Herries Redgauntlet, the cynical old Jacobite, has his own kind of bluntness, which Darsie himself contrasts with Joshua's. Allan's father has his ideal of simplicity in legal discourse. Allan's maiden plea before the court, on behalf of Peter Peebles, is aggressively clear and direct in cutting through years of legalistic obfuscation. Peter himself, in his tattered extravagance of legal jargon, is otherwise: "Speak in form of law," he commands, "or I sall bid ye gude day, sir" (208). Verbal indirection is not so easily remedied.

The Quaker's ideal of plain speech is mildly quixotic in a world of studied ambiguity such as Scott's post-Jacobite Scotland. Here, civility is essential to humanity, and civility is that kindly ambiguity of utterance by which men of good will but of opposing prejudices manage to respect ideological diversity. In this world, Joshua's opposite is Provost Crosbie, a publicly loyal Hanoverian with a Jacobite wife and a faith in conciliation. He is far less admirable than Joshua, yet his assurance to Allan that he is a plainspoken man eloquently summarizes the Author of Waverley's urgent faith in a reconciling humanity of view and utterance:

Well, now, you see one may love the kirk, and yet not ride on the rigging of it; and one may love the king, and yet not be cramming him eternally down the throat of the unhappy folk that may chance to like another king better. I have friends and connexions among them, Mr. Fairford, as your father may have clients; they are flesh and blood like ourselves, these poor Jacobite bodies – sons of Adam and Eve, after all; and therefore – I hope you understand me? I am a plain-spoken man [264–65].

Try as he will, however, Provost Crosbie is far from being a plainspoken man. His impulse is always to find some prudent mode of indirection. His comparison of himself to the elder Fairford is justified; the elder Fairford, too, is "particularly cautious to use all the conventional phrases which the civility of the time had devised as an admissible mode of language betwixt the two parties" (145).

Plain speech is qualified in another way. The book's two most colorful minor figures illustrate the social meaning and moral utility of linguistic eccentricity. Nanty Ewart, a divinity student forced to flee as a seducer, has turned pirate and smuggler. Wandering Willie, the Redgauntlet family minstrel, is now a displaced and blind wanderer. Nanty's speech is a picturesque contrast between the vigorous and flamboyant idiom in which he recounts his wild career, and the precision and economy of utterance with which he directs his ship and crew. He is effective when occasion demands, and his linguistic flexibility is related to his kindliness to Allan. Wandering Willie's idiom is best known in his famous tale. Darsie encounters him while retreating temporarily from the monotony of life in Joshua's little Eden and is at once struck by a "something odd" in Willie's speech, a suggestion of mental disorder (101). In him, as in Nanty, linguistic disorder symbolizes mental instability resulting from social disorientation. In both, however, as in Scott's rhetorically extravagant gypsies, the disorder is accompanied by a wisdom and/or humanity not available in Joshua's Eden. Willie's "extravagance of language" is frightening, even while laughable. His tale, suitably oracular for the story of a descent into hell, recounts a plainspoken confrontation of the devil himself. But Willie also lends the novel its most interesting mode of linguistic indirection. Darsie's kidnapping makes communication in Joshua's terms impossible. But when Darsie hears Willie's voice outside, he recalls Richard I and Blondel, and there ensues a long dialogue of traditional lyrics in which Darsie indicates his plight and Willie gives him hope of deliverance.

The novel provides other dramatic approaches to the problem of language: characters who never keep their word; those for whom speech is a game of concealment; the need for a password before conversation can begin. Climactic is the fact that the conflict between the Pretender and his supporters is caused by linguistic failure. Redgauntlet had failed to let the Chevalier know the intense prejudice of his supporters against Charles's mistress. Once more a pathetic breakdown is the result of men's conversing in ignorance of each other's prejudices.

The problem of civil and humane speech is accompanied by, and related to, another thematic strain. Daiches notes the novel's concern with "the mutations of heroism" and cites the disagreement between Darsie and Allan over the nature of courage.[70] The question is raised before Joshua's appearance and outlasts his major participation in the novel. Allan raises it in the second letter, contrasting his own natural or constitutional courage with Darsie's "intellectual courage, highness of spirit, and desire of distinction" (15). Darsie having mocked both Fairfords on this count, Allan returns to the attack with the definition Daiches quotes:

You impeach my father's courage! I tell you he has courage enough to do what is right, and to spurn what is wrong – courage enough to defend a righteous cause with hand and purse, and to take the part of the poor man against his oppressor, without fear of the consequences to himself. This is civil courage, Darsie; and it is of little consequence to most men in this age and country whether they ever possess military courage or no [40].

Allan's own behavior is fearless enough, but his definition proves narrow. A more sophisticated definition is offered by Joshua in self-defense when his nonviolent resistance to Redgauntlet is mistaken for cowardice:

Nay, say not cowardice, my friend, . . . since thou knowest there may be as much courage in enduring as in acting; and I will be judged by this youth, or by any one else, whether there is not more cowardice – even in the opinion of that world whose thoughts are the breath in thy nostrils – in the armed oppressor who doth injury than in the defenceless and patient sufferer who endureth it with constancy [51].

Darsie learns to confirm Joshua's view "that there was as much courage in sufferance as in exertion" (71), and Joshua later expands on the idea of courage as "doing and suffering, as becomes a man, that which fate calls us to suffer, and justice commands us to do" (174) at a time when Darsie proves his own courage standing by Joshua against overwhelming odds.

Other ideas of courage are alluded to. Darsie's father is recalled as the antithesis of the "bleezing braggarts," "the bravest fellow of them all" (254). Nanty, refusing a drink on encountering danger, says, "No Dutch courage for me: my heart is always high enough when there's a chance of fighting" (304). According to the dynastic fatalist Redgauntlet, the Redgauntlet courage "ever kindles highest on the losing side" (425). But Joshua's courage is far different. And Darsie, to whom he has been a true guide or counselor or Friend, has every reason to follow his ideal of plain-speech, truth, peaceful courage. Strangely enough, Darsie never loses his inclination to remain silent rather than speak the dangerous truth, to hope that the situation demanding courageous self-assertion may be avoided. Thus the all-important relationship between Darsie and Joshua leads nowhere, and the novel's complex thematic development of the ideas of courage and simple, humane speech is unresolved or allowed to evaporate.

Darsie has another mentor in courage whose counsel also seems ignored. Daiches wisely insists on Wandering Willie's close link with the "main theme of the novel,"[71] but the interpretation of that linkage requires a fuller exposition of theme. Daiches emphasizes the tale's concern with the violent, heroic Scottish past and its filtration through Willie's "shrewd and unromantic mind." But there is nothing intrinsically "romantic" about this tale of a villainous land-lord and a lost rental receipt. The heroism of going to Hell to recover such a receipt is scarcely in need of filtration. A miserable devil of irascibility such as the Redgauntlet Steenie goes to find is no more adequate as an "objective correlative" for romantic feelings of past heroism than his descendant, Darsie's uncle. To attribute the antiromantic quality merely to the narrator is to confuse the fantastic with the elegaic. Moreover, this tale introduces the Redgauntlet lineage in terms of its degeneracy and mean diabolism. The founder, Sir Albericht, for all his devotion to the Bruce, was murderer of his son and founder of the family's doom. The past supposedly yearned for here is a heritage of avarice and crime.

The tale's positive implications, however, are quite rele-vant to the novel's persistent themes. The story recounts a just man's descent to Hell for evidence to prove his right to his tenancy, to justify himself. It becomes a parable of courage and prudence combined, in the manner of Nicol Jarvie, or Joshua Geddes. Steenie is calmly courageous enough to confront the devil, and too shrewd to accept any of the devil's offers. Far from objectifying some lost past, the tale is a parable for present action. Steenie's confronta-tion of an earlier Redgauntlet in Hell explicitly anticipates a confrontation scene between Darsie and his uncle, when Darsie must face the devil and demand back his birthright, refusing the devil's offers. To this scene the entire novel builds up. The scene never occurs. Darsie hopes it may be avoided, partly because he fears that it may lead to violence. The confrontation, like the public conflict which fizzles into General Campbell's jocular offer of general amnesty, is lost in Redgauntlet's final concession that the cause is dead and that the family curse must disappear since his nephew has obviously been on the winning side.

How, then, has Darsie won back his birthright? How has he earned the recognition and redemption of his heritage? The answer is that with various types of guidance into danger, he arrives there without either the taint or the temptation that marks Edward and Frank, waits for rescue, and comes out again with our expectations for him blunted.

He begins promisingly enough. His sense of a mysterious and fateful alienation, his wonder as to his true lineage and his real fidelities, make him poignantly equal to Waverley as an exiled wanderer between conflicting worlds. His friendship with Allan is vitally important as his sole identifying human bond; otherwise he is a "lone thing in this world," "affected with a sense of loneliness, the more depressing that it seems to me to be a solitude peculiarly my own" (4). His peculiar solitude derives from the utter mystery of his name, from "a painful sense of his own unknown origin" (147). At crucial points in this novel of many aliases, he tries to identify himself by identifying others. But the mystery of names is part of the mystery of language itself, and he is answered: "What is other folks' names to you . . . who cannot tell your own father and mother?" (184) "My life," he feels in consequence, "is like the subterranean river in the Peak of Derby, visible only where it crosses the cele-brated cavern. I am here, and this much I know; but where I have sprung from, or whither my course of life is like to tend, who shall tell me?" (74) His wanderings into danger are a quest for this information. He is blinded by a fatality to linger in the neighborhood of danger, because there is where he is likely to discover the answers (168). Having been led into danger by his benevolent impulse to help Joshua, and having then been kidnapped by his uncle, he again justifies his indifference to the loss of freedom as a fatalism that alone can lead him to the illumination he seeks (189).

Meanwhile, his friend Allan sits in Edinburgh accusing him of quixotic folly, of a dangerous prevalence of imagination, of a "wildfire chase of romantic situation and adventure" (15). "All that happens to thee," charges Allan of Darsie's dread of the mysterious Laird, "gets a touch of the wonderful and the sublime from thy own rich imagination" (39). The exchange of letters becomes a study in contrasting imaginative and commonsense modes of vision. Moreover, Allan adds to the charge of romanticism an equally harsh attack on Darsie's lack of will, his passive attendance on Fortune to solve the mystery of his identity. He mocks Darsie's "peerless destiny," and boasts of his own modest lineage, his willingness to "reconcile myself to my destiny" (14), to accept his father's will, become an advocate, and make his own name, rather than wait for Fortune to disclose a brilliant heritage. He urges Darsie, then, to view things as they are, return to the workaday world, stop wondering who he is. Allan is the epitome of Welsh's "hero of prudence."

Why, then, is Darsie the "passive hero"? There are inherent contradictions in Allan's plea, and there is also the basic refutation of his charges by the outcome of Darsie's passivity. For one thing, Allan can reconcile himself to his destiny only because he knows who he is, and surrenders his will to his father's. For another, he does not make a name for himself; when he travels, his father's name goes with him as guardian. More important, Darsie's mode of writing does not suggest the Quixote, and his mode of seeing, his imaginative fatalism, is fully borne out. What Allan opaquely insists is just a romance of the mind becomes what Conrad called the "romance of reality." Darsie's sense of the sinister is validated when it turns out that the mysterious

Laird is *not,* as Allan contemptuously suggests, just an "old crossgrained fisherman" (41). The novel seems working toward a full justification of Darsie's imaginative mode of vision and of his behavior by leading him to the knowledge he seeks and to the dangerous commitments that knowledge implies.

Darsie's "passivity," then, demands an explanation radically different from Welsh's. Conceded that "the sympathies of both Scott and his reader" are aligned with "the passive Sir Arthur Redgauntlet (Darsie Latimer)." But then, the "center of activity" in *this* Waverley Novel cannot be the "resistance to romantic energies,"[72] for Darsie's imaginative passivity *is* a romantic energy. His defiance of Allan's commonsense prudence is closely similar to Waverley's willed commitment to his fate. Their curiously negative actions, far from being the conventional prudence or timidity described by Welsh, are more akin to the "wise passiveness," the mixture of alertness and somnolence, of creativity and openness, described by Wordsworth and Keats. Darsie is the imaginative hero which Frank as poet never becomes: his creative decision to remain passive recalls the metaphor of the water insect on the "surface of rivulets" in the *Biographia Literaria,* the reconciliation of active and passive powers in the mind's creative act. This is not to turn Scott into a philosophical Coleridgian, but simply to suggest the positive Romantic significance of the wilful and imaginative passivity of this Waverley hero, and perhaps of Waverley himself. At least it leads Darsie to the knowledge he seeks. Moreover, his prevalent imagination permits him to live up to Joshua's ideal of courage and gives him the delicacy and tact to converse with strangers without "unwittingly infring[ing] upon some of their prejudices or peculiarities" (52). Finally, his imagination never supports self-deception.

60

For, in speaking of himself, he lives up to his vow to keep to truth and simplicity (167).

His imaginative passivity leads him, too, into the danger of being forced by his uncle to accept the "tyranny of the past," the doom which, according to his uncle, accompanies his revealed identity. At this point, however, Darsie ceases to be a Redgauntlet and his ordeal becomes quite different from Waverley's, and for that matter from Frank's. Edward knows too well who his father is. The mystery of his fate is the mystery of his involvement with the ideological conflict which has corrupted his heritage. Frank knows his lineage, and our concern is with the moral complexity of his self-alienation. Both must undergo the ordeal of romance, of implication and presumed guilt, in order to come to the full realization of their heritages. Darsie's romantic nature simply leads him to his discovery. His imagination has nothing to do with the discovery itself, which is purely intellectual; that is, he never imagines himself morally or emotionally implicated. For him, the Jacobite conspiracy is simply a personal danger which he must avoid or survive. Hence, his search for identity, which begins as a profoundly felt personal need, fizzles out on the level of mere plot revelation.

Unfortunately, the same thing may be said of his spiritual or moral growth. The orphan's quest for his name, or the outcast's search for his true father, is obviously, as Davie has noted, the conventional plot most useful to Scott. To relegate Scott's use of such a basic myth, as does Daiches, to "those outward trappings of fictional technique" which Scott borrowed from conventional fiction because "these plot patterns are really quite unsuitable to the kind of exploration of the relation between tradition and progress which Scott is carrying out" is to be fair neither to the

61

Author of Waverley nor to literary judgment.[73] To discard as bad or inconsequential, as Scott enthusiasts often do, the elements they consider conventional is to fail to recognize the conventional nature of all fiction and, more unfortunate, to fail to see how organic and meaningful Scott's conventions often are.

The representative situation in the Jacobite novels depicts a young man seeking to discover and reconcile the discordant elements in his own heritage. The young man becomes, in his imaginative quest, the "objective correlative" for the Author of Waverley's desire to plot the historic survival of what is humanely precious in a time or milieu of violent and corrosive historic transformation. For the mythic critic the young man's success is generated through comic romance: an ordeal of alienation, followed by dangerous service in behalf of an impotent ruler or leader, culminating in marriage to the leader-ruler's daughter (in myth, a niece will do as well), and the forming of a new social stability around the marriage. The heroine has frequently to be saved not just from the political or ideological impotence of her parent, but also from her own ideological monasticism or rigid idealism. The archetypal vision might see in her the *anima* imprisoned,[74] released only when the protagonist makes his climactic choice in favor of life, exerts his individual will in favor of the vital human particular, or the personal fidelity, against the rigidity of ideological commitment, or the tyranny of the past. But the historical critic need only see that for the Author of Waverley, as Scott confronted imaginatively the disordering effects of historic transition in his own epoch, the chief problem was how to secure a vital continuity in change. For such a problem, the plot of the estranged son's search for a true father is the most fruitful of fictive symbols.

Waverley must redeem his heritage from its split between degenerate opportunism (Richard Waverley, and on a more ideal level, Fergus) and naive, eccentric romanticism (his uncle, and on a more ideal level, Bradwardine). He does so by reconciling, in his own ordeal and through his actions as mediator and protector, what is of humane value on both sides. Frank Osbaldistone must come to terms with the prosaic – the mercantile, the civil, the prudent – of his heritage. He never quite does so, but it is clear that he could do so only through his involvement with a substitute parent, Jarvie, who is himself a magnificent reconciliation and a preemptor of Frank's role. Darsie, too, has his sequence of guides and mentors: his prudent guardian, the elder Fairford; his necessary but ominous guide, the Laird (his uncle), who saves his life twice; his self-appointed spiritual guide, Joshua Geddes; the blind Wandering Willie, who, metaphorically at least, leads him to Hell and tries to lead him back. In his search Darsie thus confronts various alternatives, the most plausible being Joshua, Redgauntlet's direct opposite. Having confronted them, however, Darsie experiences no dawn of Prestonpans. He has become nothing significant; he has performed no act of moral self-assertion. His one sacrificial gesture is his effort to aid and defend Joshua, and this is the act, ironically, which places him in his uncle's power and thus opens the way to the discovery of his identity. But this is the climax to the book's first half. Thereafter he piles up information but does nothing more. Allan, presumably refuted as judge when Darsie's imaginative passivity proves valid, now becomes the heroic agent, and the initial theme of friendship replaces the motif of Darsie's search.

"The lost-father archetype," writes Davie, "is of no artistic value whatever, until it is placed in a context in which its symbolic overtones are meaningful, in which the search for the father can become the search for the birthright, for the source of true authority to which allegiance can rightfully be given."[75] Darsie's search begins promisingly enough. But thematic development loses its shape, and the question of Darsie's allegiance is lost in the suspense of his survival. *Redgauntlet* ends as "an inferior kind of *Waverley.*"

Jacobitism is of importance in two other novels: one a supposed failure, *The Black Dwarf;* the other a masterpiece, *The Bride of Lammermoor.* In both, however, Jacobitism is domesticated into the misfortunes of that cultural continuum symbolically so important to the Author of Waverley, the ancient noble house. The question of the effect and value of such assimilation may be left for the final section, while we consider two other general questions. (1) *The Heart of Midlothian* holds its reputation (quite unduly) as Scott's single triumph. From Lockhart to Welsh, *Old Mortality* has had its ardent admirers (I am assuredly one). Does the reputation of these novels identify a subject matter more rich and congenial than Jacobitism for the kind of serious fiction the Author of Waverley was best fitted to create? (2) Was the turning, with *Ivanhoe,* to a more remote or exotic historicity really an unfortunate break, or rather a necessary new departure in a continuity, an uncovering of new but related possibilities in structure, symbol, and theme for the fictional plotting of historic survival?

SECTION TWO

OPPOSING
FANATICISMS AND
THE SEARCH
FOR HUMANITY

THE Scottish novel comes into its own when the dominating religiousness of the culture precipitates in the form of conscience (whether or not specifically theological) – intensely scrupulous conscience whose demands strain unbearably the individual psyche and the relations of family, parents and children, persons and community."[1] So writes David Craig, for whom the Scottish fiction of religion is a far more significant expression of the Scottish people than "imitations of history and local life." He makes his case convincingly. But it scarcely provides a suitable foundation for a fair appraisal of the Author of Waverley. For him, an "imitation of history" may "precipitate" in the form of a fearful encounter with "intensely scrupulous," disintegrative ideological or political commitment. If Scottish fiction and religious experience, however powerfully dramatized in *Adam Blair, Confessions of a Justified Sinner,* and *Weir of Hermiston,* are truly inseparable, then we must conclude that Scott's is not Scottish fiction and go on from there.[2] I suspect, however, that the views of Daiches and Kurt Wittig are needed to correct the narrowness of Craig's conception.

Even Scott's admirers found his indifference to religion difficult to deny. The famous deathbed plea to Lockhart to

65

"be religious" proves nothing, whether or not Lockhart made it up (and that certainly remains unproved).[3] But Lockhart himself, the author of *Adam Blair* (some say of the *Confessions* as well), confessed later to Croker how striking was the absence from Scott's life of religious awareness. Carlyle had some such lack in mind when he complained of the spiritual emptiness of the Waverley Novels. Walter Bagehot explicitly refers to Scott's deficient "treatment of men's religious nature."[4] There are various explanations. Scott's Edinburgh and Melrose background was remote from covenanting shrines and battlefields. His was a generation too old for the religious revival which affected Lockhart and other earnest young Turks whose arrival in Edinburgh the Enlightened Henry Cockburn so deplored.[5] It is when Scott uses the materials of Scottish religious fiction that we can see most clearly his kinship with the Edinburgh Enlightenment. But any attempt to argue that the "Golden Age" of Hume, Ferguson, Mackenzie, Burns, and the young Scott is *not* an essential manifestation of the Scottish people is, to say the least, partial.

As for Craig's remarkably persistent failure to be "interested in" or to "believe in" Scott's characters, it is clear that his admitted disappointment at fiction's failure to respond appropriately to social change prejudices his literary judgments. One who cites Dickens and Disraeli as examples of what Scotland lacked has little reason to reject Scott's characters as "heavily caricatured."[6] Certainly he fails to document his charges that Scott's fiction lacks significant internal coherence. This is why Craig so perfectly illustrates Tillyard's complaint that "readers of Scott have oversimplified him and have read his best work too much influenced by the inferior, that they have not been sufficiently prepared for surprises, and that they have sometimes taken him not as he comes, but as they have decided to think he will come."[7]

"We must grant the artist his subject, his idea, his *donnée*," said Henry James. Scott's *donnée* for the fiction of religious conflict is described in a letter to Lady Louisa Stuart: "there are noble subjects for narrative during that period full of the strongest light & shadow, all human passions stirr'd up and stimulated by the most powerful motives, & the contending parties as distinctly contrasted in manners & in modes of thinking as in political principles."[8] The impulse is initially historical, the terms those of picturesque psychological contrast and social and political contention. Religious motivation is subordinate to political and moral: this is the *donnée*. In what terms, then, should we judge "what he makes of it"?

1. *OLD MORTALITY*

Scott claimed to be "complete master of the whole history of these strange times" and stood on the "truth" of his delineation.[9] Scholar-critics from M'Crie to Craig charge him with caricature in *Old Mortality*.[10] There is ample evidence that Scott found some justice in this – if not in the compassion with which he treats Davie Deans, then certainly in the more cautious and searching Puritan characterizations of later novels. The delineations of Mark Everard and even of Cromwell himself in *Woodstock* reveal greater care for human credibility and less for picturesque color. Scott's prefatory references to the painstakingly drawn Bridgenorth of *Peveril* indicate his awareness that Bridgenorth is "faintly traced" by contrast with his more "vivid" antecedents in *Old Mortality*.[11]

But let me attach the question of "truth" to the larger question to which it belongs. What has Scott made of the Cavalier-Puritan subject matter? Has such a matter provided him with an opportunity not matched by Jacobitism to project his vision of human relationship – the forces of separation, the obstacles to reconciliation, the hope for cultural and humane survival in "strange times" of ideological violence? We may best begin with *Old Mortality,* and with a testing of Craig's general judgment that "the surface of various themes is touched in passing, but they are not embodied through and through in every detail of the particular drama or fable."[12] Then we can compare *Old Mortality* with a later study of the dilemmas of moderatism in "strange times," *Woodstock.* There will then be much to learn from two relative failures in the same area, *Peveril of the Peak* and *A Legend of Montrose.* In conclusion, a new appreciation of *The Heart of Midlothian* may be possible.

In *Old Mortality* and *The Heart of Midlothian,* little attention has been paid to the titles, to the leisurely introductory strategies they signal, and to the full structural revelations of their meanings. Both are "Tales of My Landlord," both are transmitted by the pedantic Jedediah Cleishbotham in the compilations done by his assistant, young – now dead – Peter Pattieson. We are thus set, gradually, at greater and greater removes from those "strange times." Pattieson's first manuscript recounts his walks after school, describes the graveyard of the antiprelatist martyrs, and narrates his encounter with their itinerant caretaker, "Old Mortality." Pattieson is a perfect child of the graveyard school, echoing the melancholy dead young poet of Gray's Elegy. Pattieson, long since dead himself, fills his account of Old Mortality with his own melancholy sense of imminent death and tells us Old Mortality is himself long since dead. Old Mortality's

task of contending with the inevitable decay of the memorials is thus projected in the elegiac sense of death following
on death, and in the strong *memento mori* impression
conveyed by the whole introductory chapter. The compila-
tion itself, left by a dead youth in an account of a dead old
pathetic fighter against decay, recounts "the manners of that
unhappy period" which have all passed away, as they must
"in this valley of darkness, blood, and tears" (11). Thus the
title denotes a narrative frame and a thematic concern with
historic mutability different from that in the Jacobite novels,
as well as from that to be revealed in the novels of decadent
chivalry.

In theme, the book evolves through significantly different
attitudes toward Old Mortality – death and the value of
mortal life. Naturally, to the extent that all Waverley
Novels envision the persistence of the dead past in the
present, all their characters live in the presence of the dead.
But it is particularly striking that we should be introduced to
the protagonist of this novel through the eyes of Lady
Margaret Bellenden, for whom he is identified as the son of
her dead husband's dead enemy. Later Morton relives his
dead father's dilemma and finally, in the Enoch Arden-like
ending of the novel, earns his right to come back from the
dead. The theme of Old Mortality is everywhere; it appears
in the book's most memorable speeches and reflections.
There is Morton's Hamlet-like soliloquy upon examining
the dead Stewart's pocketbook after the first battle (214).
Best known is Claverhouse's speech on death (309), but
this one is followed by the measured, eloquent curse of the
dying Mucklewrath, himself the figure of mortality come to
pass judgment on the doomed Cavalier (309–10). Inviting
comparison with Claverhouse's is that of MacBriar, at his
trial, expressing the same contempt for life (326–27). And

as the returned exile Morton relives his earlier experiences in the splendidly organized final portion of the novel, the very landscape becomes a metaphoric means for a final sounding of the *contemptu mundi* note (377–78), whose persistent sounding suggests the "Be absolute for death" of *Measure for Measure,* the play which was shortly to exert so curious and important an influence on *The Heart of Midlothian.*

Sharing the contempt are the two halves of the picturesque conception on which the book is built. Claverhouse and Burley are leaders of opposing extremes. Yet they are equals in their contempt for life and in the brutal application of that contempt to ethical law. Claverhouse himself recognizes their kinship when he concedes that they are both fanatics (313). The meeting of extremes in Claverhouse and Burley is the central paradox in a complex and clearly managed structure of degrees and kinds of fanaticism. It is fitting that they end as allies. Their shared fanaticism is, as Claverhouse recognizes, manifest in their equal willingness to take life. When, at the moment of such recognition, Claverhouse attempts to distinguish between them on the grounds that they spill very different kinds of blood, Morton gives the answer which the entire book gives. The distinction, he says, is "too nice" for him. "God gives every spark of life" (313). Thus Morton aligns himself with those for whom each life is valuable against those for whom all life is contemptible.

Thus, too, he identifies the law for which he stands in a book whose concern with law is even more specific than its concern with mortality. For all of Welsh's curious attempts to force Blackstone into Morton's mouth, it is not *property* rights that Morton opposes to the fused extremisms of Claverhouse and Burley. Their final joining does, as Welsh suggests, "underline" Morton's "stature," but it is not on account of his "passive and loyal" submission to civil propriety.[13] When, during their first dialogue in Morton's uncle's barn, Burley and Morton argue the law, it is ethical law, and Morton speaks out on behalf of the same law of natural humanity to which he appeals in his argument with Claverhouse. With Burley he invokes "those feelings of natural humanity, which Heaven has assigned to us as the general law of our conduct." "It is natural you should think so," answers Burley; "you are yet in the dungeon-house of the law" (45). Morton's is clearly an absolute beyond "the right of property"; he is far more than "a sore-beset defender of the British Constitution."[14]

Burley speaks for the law that divides men and submits the "feelings of natural humanity" to the dogmatic divisions of "true faith." A comparable dogmatism is expressed on the comic level by Lady Bellenden, who finds absolute law in the most trivial behavior of the late King during his breakfast at Tillietudlem (105). The book contains many arguments on points of law, but those between Morton and Burley are crucial, and in these, it is true, Morton espouses the position of the due-process constitutionalist. When Burley urges that the justice of Archbishop Sharpe's murder be judged in and for itself and not by reference to its perpetrator, Morton answers with the premise of vested authority (199). When Morton writes his self-justification to Major Bellenden, he consistently, as Welsh notes, opposes lawfulness to capricious tyranny and violence (230–31). But the need for lawfulness is solidly based in the premise that only social order provides for the practice of "those feelings of natural humanity . . . the general law of our conduct" (45). The speciousness of Burley's radical alternative is vividly dramatized when, at the end, Burley the scorner of "the dungeon-house of the law" cynically uses legal contrivances to exile the Bellendens from Tillietudlem forever and place it in the hands of the legalistic trimmer Olifant. This, we shall see, is the point of the final issue over possession of Tillietudlem; it is not simply a concern with property rights which, says Welsh, "supplants the political issues" and cheapens the novel.[15]

The general law of natural humanity, opposed by both Claverhouse and Burley (as well as by Lady Bellenden and Olifant) with fanatic legality or legal brutality, acts without distinction on the assumption that "God gives every spark of life," that life belongs equally and preciously to all men whatever their divisions (313). Such a conception of humane law transcending all divisions in the interests of life is defined by significant differentiation on the folk level of the novel. The parallelism of Morton's adventures to those of his servant Cuddie encourages us to expect in Cuddie's attitudes counterparts to those of Morton. Cuddie acts from his own conception of natural law when he rifles a corpse on the battlefield. For him this is part of the natural sagacity of self-preservation. Pillaging "comes natural" (210). The only real distinction for Cuddie is between the living and the dead; thus, in his Falstaffian way, Cuddie might easily be confused with Morton in his alignment with life – and Old Mortality – as transcending all other distinctions. But the same might be said of Bessie Maclure. It is she who provides the climactic expression of Morton's general law, she in whom he sees that law vividly manifest when its validity needs such confirmation for him. The fact that she is one of what Claverhouse calls the "clowns" and Morton is "gentleman" – the distinction of which Welsh claims Scott makes so much[16] – has no meaning in the light of the humanity they share. She has lost her two sons on the Covenanter side in the Battle of Loudoun Hill. After the battle a wounded Cavalier comes to her hut, and she conceals him from the Covenanters and nurses him back to health. When Morton asks why she did so, she replies simply that further death would not "hae brought my Ninian and Johnnie alive again" (382). To the laws and fidelities of faction and division she has opposed the law of humanity.

If the book simply contrasted the two laws, it would achieve thematic coherence, as it does, but that coherence could scarcely be dramatically compelling. The choice of laws is a problem because the times are strange; ethical distinctions are blurred by history. The lawlessness of the times invites inhumanity. To the desperate query, Is there no law? Claverhouse's ominous reply is, "I think I could find one" (113). The times justify his law of division and death. From the outset, the book stresses the strangeness of the times – "that unhappy period" (10), it is first called. Claverhouse and Burley "are the characters formed in times of civil discord" (112). Claverhouse's appeal is in character: "These are not times to sacrifice to the dotage of greybeards, or the tears of silly women, the measures of salutary severity which the dangers around compel us to adopt" (131). The choice of laws becomes, then, the dramatic problem of whether the law of humanity can survive the apparent malevolence of history. It is in terms of this problem that Morton's heroic ordeal and personal survival must be understood.

Welsh properly insists on the "tortuous predicament" of Morton and the genuine "tension" dividing his allegiance.[17] More orthodox interpreters – Craig is one – hold that Morton is a "lay-figure . . . in whom the author's reason and moderation are vested."[18] Grierson, who lamented that Scott's heroes never really take sides, insists on the similarity of Morton's position to that of Waverley;[19] Morton's predicament clearly compares in reality with Waverley's, as Frank's and Darsie's do not. But to leave it at that is to ignore important differences between two subject matters. Morton survives his outlawed involvement by appeal to the same moral law that saves Waverley. But there the parallelism ceases.

Morton's problem is different. Waverley's moderatism is not part of his moral significance because he is not caught between opposing fanaticisms. Morton's moderatism is essential to his whole problem. It may not be fair to make the contrast in Welsh's terms: "The involvement of Waverley in the Stuart rebellion of 1745 is accidental and melodramatic in contrast with the involvement of Henry Morton."[20] But their involvements are profoundly different. Waverley's derives from his mysterious alienation. The Jacobite is cut off by anachronism, by decadence or illegitimacy; Waverley is isolated by his father's cynical opportunism, Frank by his father's philistine obstinacy, Darsie by mysterious orphanhood. Morton's involvement is the reenactment of his heroic father's career; this fact alone makes his ordeal essentially different. Waverley's plight is in part the result of a failure of language, an inability to understand. Morton's results in part from his heroic willingness to declare himself unequivocally to both extremes, Claverhouse and Burley, during times when moderatism is suspect and isolated. Those who find his moderatism facile or opportunistic ignore such actions; his moderatism is an active faith. He is neither passive nor opportunistic nor motivated by propriety in his loyalty to Evandale, his devotion to freedom of conscience, his concern for Edith, or his determination not to betray Burley. His moderatism is grounded in his sense of a general law of natural humanity. As a result his ordeal is by no

74

means simple or predetermined. We can best examine it with reference to three of its facets: moderatism's reputation for indifference or noncommitment, moderatism's problem with language, and Morton's survival.

The opening defines the precariousness of the times. To say, with Craig, that the description of the wappenschaw, or the country festival of ceremonial games, shows Scott to be "more interested in exactly what wappenschaws were like than in the historical bearings of his characters"[21] is to miss its whole significance. The Restoration government is seeking to end divisions between Cavalier and Puritan by imposing revived manners, hateful to Puritans, on Cavalier and Puritan alike. The effect is to create explosive situations in which precariously new solidarities are jeopardized. The image of precariousness here invites comparison with the opening episode of *Peveril of the Peak,* Lady Peveril's dinner for Royalist and Roundhead in celebration of the Restoration. At the wappenschaw, however, there is every sign that life and gaiety will ride over old divisions and carry the day. Yet there is a note in the proceedings both ominous and absurd. The Cavalier side, to lend full support, must preserve traditional appearances; Lady Bellenden lacks men to fill her quota in the games. Thus, into the armor of mock chivalry must go such barrel-scrapings as the moronic Guse Gibbie, with the effect (and possibly the recollection) of Dryden in Virgil's armor in *The Battle of the Books.* The Popinjay almost ends in disaster when the idiot Guse Gibbie, his visor slipped down, rides blindly full tilt with lowered lance at the coach of the Duke (24). Such is the day's comic ending; such, too, is a powerfully grotesque symbol of the precariousness of the whole absurdity, the blind violence of the times.

Morton participates in the Popinjay. We see him only

through Lady Bellenden's prejudicial recollection of his dead father. We hear that he lives a dull life with his miserly, prudent uncle, who is fearfully uncommitted. From the beginning Morton is caught between two extreme alternatives: active commitment in his father's name, and cold prudence or miserly noncommitment after the manner of his uncle. Grierson's characteristic complaint that Scott's heroes ought to have been committed is thus built into the thematic logic of Morton's ordeal.

Such is our preparation for the opening of that ordeal: Morton's abrupt entanglement with Burley. When Burley demands his help and protection, Morton seems the ideal hero of piety and prudence. Burley accuses him of joining the timeservers and forgetting his father's example (49). Morton, letting Burley hide in his uncle's barn, tries to have it both ways. This effort is the essence of his ordeal throughout. The strange times make such attempts dangerous, isolating, and even morally dubious.

In the ensuing chapters Morton gives the impression of which Scott's critics complain. Initially, the "current of his soul was frozen by a sense of dependence, of poverty, above all, of an imperfect and limited education." The times have added "an air of indecision and of indifference; for, being attached to neither of the factions which divided the kingdom, he passed for dull, insensible, and uninfluenced by the feeling of religion or of patriotism" (123–24). To find an artistic deficiency, then, in Morton's apparent coldness and indifference is to be blind to the fact that this reaction to Morton is an essential feature of his plight. His problem is, how can the humane man survive morally in times which make humanity look like something else? When he seeks to declare his reasonability to the sympathetic Major Bellenden, Bellenden despises him for being "rebellious in cold blood, and without even the pretext of enthusiasm" (231). The Covenanters feel a growing distrust of him as a latitudinarian and secularist, a "Gallio" who trusts "in the arm of flesh" (243). The impression Morton gives of being a remote and lay figure, often terribly abstract, is perfectly consistent with the narrative delineation of his plight in a world of extremists. He seeks to react reasonably and humanely; his humanity and reasonability are mistaken for indifference. Only Evandale understands his plight, for he shares it; and at the end, when Claverhouse needs help, Evandale inherits the plight. It is now Evandale who must face the charge of detachment.

This dilemma is further dramatized on comic folk levels. The analogies suggest how easily the prudent humanity of Morton and Evandale may be confused with callousness or opportunism. I have mentioned Cuddie's natural law of pillage. Cuddie's "parallel actions," observes Welsh, "subvert the precarious ambivalence of the hero by caricaturing it."[22] For "subvert" I would substitute "intensify," and recall that Cuddie's subversions receive their *coup de grâce* on the same level in Bessie Maclure's humane indifference. Jenny the maid and her lover Cuddie supply just one example of the folk wisdom that is really callous shrewdness. Morton's uncle is similar, suggesting the threatening closeness of such attitudes to Morton himself. But the comic analogy receives its most explicit articulation in a world of chorus characters and a minor scene. The fourth chapter presents a relationship strikingly parallel to that of Morton and his uncle. Neil Blane, widower of the widow of the landlord of the howff (and thus an expert in prosperous survival), turns over to his daughter the job of waiting on customers of all factions. His instructions are addressed squarely to the novel's problem in its most callous formulation: how to survive through indifference and disengagement. Jenny's mother was "civil to the customers, and had a good name wi' Whig and Tory, baith up the street and down the street" (27). Jenny is to be "civil to a' the folk," to make no distinctions and sell more ale when her customers are thirsty from disputation. Such is one kind of moderation with which Morton's is dangerously confused. Such, too, is the sort of detail with which to throw out the charge that the Waverley Novels invariably lack intense and cumulatively rich coherences.

Morton's plight is realized too in the novel's concern with language. The novel offers no hopeful note comparable in linguistic flexibility and prudence to Nicol Jarvie. The picturesque contentiousness of the times is repeatedly presented as a "virulent strife of tongues" (203). The rigid zealot uses language to raise walls, create disorder. "You speak well," says the shrewd Burley to the fanatic MacBriar, "but not wisely; your own ears have heard this night in council how this scattered remnant are broken and divided, and would ye now make a veil of separation between them? Would ye build a wall with unslaked mortar?" (194) The infernal disorder of the Covenanters is symbolized in its grotesque diversity of idioms. Even Burley is against communication with all enemies, as "the accursed thing which God hateth" (49). He at once finds Morton's timeserving manifest in his language. But he is opportunist enough to recognize the need to persuade Morton; and when Morton indicates that the Covenanters' language is lost on him, Burley agrees to speak "in the worldly language of that carnal reason which is for the present thy blind and imperfect guide" (194). It is fitting, then, that the moral precariousness which makes a genuine plight of Morton's moderation should be shown in his language.

In the idiomatically colorful world of factional violence,

the humane, reasonable man must seem to speak in an abstract, formal, coldly detached way. There is, I realize, a danger here of explaining away the style Scott shares with other early nineteenth-century practitioners of a neo-Johnsonian flaccidity. It is easy enough – most critics do it – to find devastating illustrations. However, we must at least grant the Author of Waverley the possibility that an uncomfortably wordy or colorless artificiality of English may be functional, and neither the accident of nationality nor proof that Scott was free of convention only when his characters spoke in colloquial dialect. When Morton seeks to communicate with fanatics of both sides, his predicament is vividly shown in the problem of his language. When he soliloquizes – when, for example, he expresses his weariness "of seeing nothing but violence and fury around me – now assuming the mask of lawful authority, now taking that of religious zeal. I am sick of my country; of myself" – his humanity is clear (50). For brief moments Morton finds the tongue with which to express his own zeal, his devotion to a humanity that repudiates fanaticisms under whatever mask.

The times, however, tie the search for humanity to the reestablishment of civil order. From the beginning Morton seeks to avoid or silence the language of disloyalty and danger (35). Language is the thing that may at any moment cause an outbreak of violence. In illustration, Cuddie's mother Mause serves as counterpart to Burley. Just as Burley's persuasions entangle Morton, so Cuddie must leave home because of Mause's "clavers," because her fanaticism will not shut up. It is like trying to silence Andrew Fairservice in Rob Roy, with the significant difference that Mause's babble, however ludicrous, may be mistaken for heroic integrity in the world of the Cavalier-Puritan novels. Mause agrees to put a lock on her tongue. But when the troops arrive, it is Morton who speaks out. He has tried in vain and on humanitarian grounds to avoid the "useless risk to which he would expose the family," to master an idiom of prudent indirection (72). To combine prudence and humanity and yet express his own moderatism, he resorts to an incredibly involuted syntax. When the effort fails, he speaks out courageously, and Mause's subsequent outbursts get him carried off to prison as Burley's accomplice. He speaks out again to Claverhouse; to both Claverhouse and Burley he declares himself on behalf of the law of humanity; his letter to Major Bellenden is still another brave act. Each courageous utterance only serves to isolate him more. He seems indeed to be reliving the divided commitments of his heroic father, and would seem doomed to die the same death.

He does not. As usual, Scott reveals the degree of his significant command of his materials by the success with which he plots his hero's survival, physical and moral. The rhetorical crisis in his effort to bring it off is, of course, the scene which has troubled critics since Adolphus: the trial scene in which the hero looks on at the torments of others with his own pardon in his pocket.[23]

The traditional criticism of the scene is facile. To it there are at least two answers. First, it is inevitable and proper, in the moral terms of the novel, that Morton should survive, not by historic accident, but by moral worth. Second, he does suffer for his involvement, to a lesser degree in being forced to look on helplessly at the torture of others, to a greater degree in the whole course of his exile and final return. Why is his survival proper? He has committed himself, to a degree Waverley never does, to active leadership in military rebellion. He clearly belongs to one side, Grierson's complaints to the contrary notwithstanding. His commitment is not, like Waverley's, based in error. Nor is he, like Cuddie, saved simply by deceit, by keeping his mouth shut. He is literally saved by influence. And in Scott's world of *realpolitik,* far from being an opportunistic substitution for "right," influence is actually a confirmation of "right," as we shall see in Argyle's protection of Jeanie Deans. For the Author of Waverley, right must be realized in terms of personal loyalties, not in terms of abstract justice. Morton is saved by the personal intervention of Claverhouse, who makes it clear that he is repaying the personal debt of Morton's selfless preservation of his friend Evandale.

Welsh is curiously uncertain about this justification. Initially he finds the whole rationale in Morton's rank as gentleman: "It is hard to find any other grounds for his rescue." Then he decides that Claverhouse's "interest has two sources," allowing one to be Morton's generosity to Evandale. Finally, he finds the class distinction uppermost in Claverhouse's own speech (313), which clearly stresses not the difference between Morton and the "clowns," but the difference between Morton's "generous principles" and the bloodthirstiness of "crazy" fanatics.[24] Claverhouse is now acting in accordance with the general law Morton has invoked. True humanity is manifest in a sense of personal loyalty that transcends ideological commitment: here is the pervasive Scott theme. The mutual loyalty of Morton and Evandale is grounded in their shared moderatism, and that moderatism means not that they believe less in their respective causes, but that they believe more in the law of humanity. Morton proves worthy of survival, of the personal interest that engineers that survival, by his humanity to Evandale, just as Waverley survives through his humanity to Talbot. Claverhouse, otherwise indistinguishable from other fanatics, holds personal loyalty as the loftiest of ideals,

81

although for him it is an hereditary ideal rather than a natural one. Burley exploits Morton by an appeal to a personal loyalty inherited from his father. The same law, cynically invoked at the beginning, threatens Morton's survival, and sincerely implemented at the end, confirms that survival. Later, when Evandale himself sacrifices security to go to Dundee's aid, his sister defends him by psychologizing the law: "You must be aware, my dear Edith, how often family connexions, and early predilexions, influence our actions more than abstract arguments" (346).

Thus Morton survives. But he must stand by and watch MacBriar's torture and his heroism. Scott gives MacBriar his full measure of heroism, as he does Fergus in *Waverley*. Those who find Scott's Covenanters uniformly grotesque contrasted, for example, with Stevenson's and Hogg's, should look closely[25] at MacBriar's final performance (326–27). His speech is free of jargon, formal, but rhetorically impressive. The narrator remains utterly objective, but he allows two crucial, equally true comments to be made. Morton, who has made his own violent attempt to intervene on MacBriar's behalf, is struck by the "firmness and gallantry," the self-devotion and heroism of the man and regrets that such qualities are mixed with the "fiercer features of his sect" (327). Claverhouse, whose own fierce contempt for life seems now to have been humanized by his association with Evandale and Morton, replies to Morton's admiration: "You mean," he asks, "his resolution to condemn you to death?" (327) The deficiency in MacBriar's heroism is that it has its basis in a deathlike rigidity, a contempt for life. It is a striking irony that Claverhouse, formerly a sharer in this contempt, must be the one to remind Morton of the implications of such heroism.

Like all of Scott's crucial scenes, this one is morally

complex. Morton survives, just as Jeanie Deans succeeds with the Queen, by a mixture of courage and humanity and shrewdness and good luck. To resent such a mixture is to deny Scott his own brand of moral and political realism. It would be strange if the modern reader, so ready to make a mystique of Stendhalian "duplicity," were intolerant of its mild variant in the Waverley Novels.

Morton's real ordeal is yet to come. MacBriar has gone triumphantly to death. Morton must win his way back to life, and for the final fifth of the novel the reader is forced to undergo the ordeal with him, although not in the resentful way suggested by Welsh. In a sense Welsh is right: the book at this point "succumbs to the stock material of fairy tales – but with the important result that the denouement overflows with thematic significance." But fairy tale matter replete with such resonances is to be defined and judged as romance, and Welsh, cataloguing improbabilities that "destroy the narrative illusion," is surrendering to a doggedly novelistic set of expectations.[26] One may disapprove initially of the curious mixture of novel and romance so characteristic of the Author of Waverley, but to read him sympathetically, one must be prepared to recognize such shifts of mode and judge them individually. The climax of Morton's ordeal, like that of Waverley and Frank, takes him into a romance world. The effect of the shift may be to lessen historical probability, but it is also to increase greatly the intensity of the reader's sympathy with Morton and to give the whole work a thematic completeness equaled by few of the novels.

The ordeal proceeds at a leisurely pace. Morton, after a lapse of years, returns as one assumed dead, seen as a ghost, unrecognized. He is a wretch struggling with wishes for death (361). The funereal melancholy of the Old Mortality frame prevails as the dead man revisits his life, and it is the persistence of the unifying mood that suggests to the reader the shift to romance. Morton actually changes into his old clothes and relives the opening scenes of the novel (372). He learns of changed times. On the spot where he and Burley first met, he reflects on the strange mixture of ill-fortune brought on by his humanity to Burley (377–78). At this moment of bitterness he meets Bessie Maclure (379), another whose humanity has transcended even her suffering, another, like Morton, thought unnatural because she sacrificed ideological fidelities to natural humanity. Her function is to confirm him in his faith. But it is also to help him meet Burley once more, and this repetition of his initial encounter brings the novel full circle. She is a sybil to direct him to the infernal cave where Burley hides. In seeking Burley, Morton is trying to carry out his final humane act, for Burley, having sadly degenerated Satan-like into the manipulations of stolen deeds and legal contrivances, has placed Tillietudlem in the hands of the arch timeserver Olifant. To rescue the deed, Morton, like Wandering Willie's grandfather, must face the meanest of devils in his own hell. This means risking his own life, sacrificing all claim to Edith, trying to save Evandale once more. It means retracing all the steps of his own ill-fortunes to the point of being cut off once more – quite literally this time – alone with the demonic Burley. Once more escape is cut off; but this time, at the brink of the cliff, he takes his leap for safety (397–98). The leap is literally and symbolically his leap back to life. It is his final refusal to fight, his own daring evasion of evil, his refusal to betray or take action against his father's preserver. He thus survives his own death.

What follows is the destruction of the obstacles in his path. I shall not now argue the plausibility, although I think it can be argued, with which both Evandale and Olifant are cleared out of the way. There is logic, it could be said, in the loss of Evandale as the anachronistic Dundee's follower. There is logic in using the shrewd, opportunistic Cuddie for the death of the far more despicable Olifant. The necessary clearing away is handled with more grace, we shall see, than the improbable but logical killing off of Sir George at the end of *The Heart of Midlothian*. I am concerned far more with Welsh's complaint that the final struggle for Tillietudlem is a melodramatic cheapening wherein "the threat to property gradually supplants the political issues," and Morton emerges at last as the defender of private property.[27]

If what I have said is valid, then of course the political issues are basically moral issues, and Olifant's role is far other than simply to be the "craven enemy of property." Rather, he is the book's extreme example of amoral survival and its most devastating comment on the fanaticism of Burley, whose pretensions end in union with Claverhouse and dependence on the legalistic opportunism of Olifant. Moreover, Morton's efforts to save Tillietudlem arise out of his personal devotion to Edith, not out of any abstract devotion to property rights. But the question of Tillietudlem's survival should not be examined with reference to *Old Mortality* alone.

By the end of *Old Mortality*, Tillietudlem has come to symbolize far more than private property. It has served as a locus of cultural continuity. It has been a haven and a fortress for Cavalier manners, for personal loyalties both admirable and absurd; it has represented the birthright which Morton has gone to Hell to redeem. It has become for the Cavalier-Puritan subject matter what Tully-Veolan is for Jacobitism. Perhaps by this time, certainly by the time of *The Heart of Midlothian* with its ambiguous titular focus on an ancient prison, Scott seems to have realized about himself what Coleridge noticed: that his imagination was essentially topographical; that its true "engine" was less a sense of history than a sense of *place;* that a house would serve most naturally as the symbolic focus for many of his narratives. This is as true for *The Heart of Midlothian* as, in different ways, it is true for *Kenilworth.* We have seen how the climax of *Waverley* is inseparable from the significance for the Author of Waverley of the redeemed "house." In the final section we shall place his most pervasive attitudes and themes in conjunction with the imminent falls of houses and the plotting of their survival. But almost nowhere else among the novels is an ancient house more fully realized as setting and symbolic center than in *Woodstock.* The question of Tillietudlem's redemption may be clearer once we have considered this other house.

2. *WOODSTOCK*

Old Mortality is significant and impressive fiction in spite of what Craig and others have proved to be an exaggerated delineation of the Presbyterian temperament. In *Woodstock* and *Peveril of the Peak,* in Everard and Bridgenorth, Scott made up in large measure for his sins of caricature. The question remains: did a truer, a more subtle and compassionate analysis of the Presbyterian temper, assure Scott of a superior novel? A comparison of *Woodstock* and *Peveril* suggests that the question is aesthetically meaningless. *Woodstock,* while lacking the scope and energetic diversity of Scott's "histories," is among his most mature and effective novels. *Peveril,* perhaps the longest and the most richly varied of his historical period pieces, is a dazzling failure.

Woodstock's Everard marks a striking advance in rhetorical sophistication on the Covenanters of *Old Mortality*. But *Peveril's* Bridgenorth is Scott's most subtly and compassionately rendered Presbyterian, and Bridgenorth cannot save the novel from getting lost in its own multiple possibilities. From the fact that *Woodstock* is the later, more deliberately wrought novel of the two, one might infer that Scott learned much from his failures, were it not for the fact that even later, in *Anne of Geierstein*, he repeated the *Peveril* sort of failure.

Evidently *Old Mortality* was conceived in a sense of the possibilities for violently picturesque contrast of opposing fanaticisms. From such a sense came the memorable vignettes of the sleeping Burley, Burley in council, Burley at bay in his infernal cave. The mode of tragic picturesque prevails in the descriptive style. The relative lack of such picturesque intensities in *Woodstock,* one suspects, explains why John Buchan attributes to the novel "the charm of a wise and mellow philosophy" and yet claims that it "rarely touches the deeper springs of life."[28] The former is true enough. The latter suffers from an Arnoldian prejudice in behalf of "high seriousness," which in its elegaic melancholy *Old Mortality* might seem better to appease. *Woodstock's* mode is relatively mundane and comic. Resultantly, there is less striving for picturesque effect, and in commentative detachment a better opportunity for fairness to the Presbyterian temper.

The basic situation is that of *Old Mortality*. The good man is the moderate Presbyterian, dedicated to humane conciliation, committed to liberty of conscience, weary of factional violence. Morton's "I am weary of seeing nothing but violence and fury around me" speech (50) has its close counterpart in Mark Everard's "Gracious Providence, where is this to end? We have sacrificed the peace of our families; the warmest wishes of our young hearts; to right the country in which we were born, and to free her from oppression; yet it appears that every step we have made towards liberty has but brought us in view of new and more terrific perils" (68). In both cases, as in *Waverley,* the hero pays for his final alliance with the antitraditional side by reinstating his "traditional" elders in their ancestral house – Tully-Veolan, Tillietudlem, Woodstock – and serving as their heir and protector. But first, Everard, like Morton, must survive his entanglement with opposing fanaticisms; and his success in plotting such a survival depends on the breaking down of the tragic divisions among men caused by a lack of mutual forbearance, by a failure of communication between fanatic idioms.

Can personal reconciliation transcend ideological division? The question is dramatized in various spheres in *Woodstock,* and the answers are various. One of the formal excellences of the book is thus apparent: its wealth of significant parallelisms. Mark Everard's customary role is that of mediator. The dilemma he faces is more immediately historic than Morton's, and he is already implicated when we encounter him, making unnecessary in *Woodstock* the mechanism of involvement needed for Morton and the Jacobite heroes. We attend at once to Everard's problem, as moderate, of making peace with extremes: first with Cromwell, then with Charles, then with Cromwell again. His own relationship with Roger Wildrake is the most obvious example of mutual forbearance, grounded in perfect candor, between ideological enemies. In the domestic sphere he must work for a reconciliation with his Cavalier uncle, the father of his future wife, the old Ranger of Woodstock. The search for a reconciling humanity goes on in social and professional spheres as well. The Royalist park-keeper Joliffe and the Cromwellian soldier Tomkins had been friends in boyhood; their hope for reconciliation ends in sudden and violent death. The most moving of all, the reconciliation most precarious and yet most poignant, is that which rece-ments the ancient friendship between the Anglican priest Rochecliffe and the Presbyterian minister Holdenough. Both are realizations of the compassionate but comic vision which dominates the book, and Holdenough is Scott's most sympathetic Presbyterian cleric. The two old friends are reunited as prisoners awaiting death at Cromwell's hands. Warm reminiscence quickly turns to heated theological debate. Then, suddenly, comes a reminder of the death that is imminent, and ideological division is lost in "repentant kindness," "generous shame," and mutual affection (444).

Holdenough serves as counterpart to the moderate Ever-ard in the book's total marshaling of Puritan types. During the long scene when he first tells Everard of his tragic separation from Rochecliffe, the complexity of the later scene is anticipated. Divisive zeal alternates feverishly with reconciling humanity, and perhaps nowhere does the Au-thor of Waverley bring a character more movingly to emo-tional and reflective life than here, when Holdenough perceives himself fluctuating between a stern nobility of judgment which is habitual and a humane and humble self-awareness which will not be denied. Almost in spite of himself he is reconciled to Everard, as later to Rochecliffe: "Take my hand, Markham – take my hand hastily; for the old Adam is whispering at my heart that it is a disgrace to hold it extended so long." The recollection of his supposed loss of one dear friend forces him to deny his own severe pride: "And surely I, who have by one unhappy exhortation to battle and strife sent the living to the dead, and, I fear, brought back even the dead among the living, should now study peace and goodwill, and reconciliation of difference, leaving punishment to the Great Being whose laws are broken, and vengeance to Him who hath said, 'I will repay it' " (209). Such reflective complexity of consciousness may be peculiar to the later novels; *Woodstock*'s immediate successor, *The Fair Maid of Perth,* is unusually rich in it. At least it seems remote from the strongly colored picturesques of *Old Mortality.*

Even the extreme Cromwellian, the soldier who usurps Holdenough's pulpit, is endowed with a complex humanity unenvisioned in the Covenanters of the earlier novel. His sermon is a masterpiece of imitative rant, but it never approaches the impenetrable jargon of the Mucklewraths (8–11). When forced to fight old Sir Henry, he is moderate and humane, although supercilious in his peculiar idiom. His final scene as a "fanatical voluptuary" far outreaches mere hypocrisy and delineates the remarkable consequence of superimposing on a rustic rake the casuistical jargon of the most libertine of the Levelling sects. It ends in a moment of pathetic dying repentance still "in character" (360–63).

But the historic figure which evidently provided the novel's generating impulse is Cromwell himself, claimed by Buchan with plausibility to be the best portrait before Carlyle's.[29] Cromwell's influence in *Woodstock* is pervasive from the beginning. Seven chapters prepare skillfully for his appearance. Our expectations are shaped by his messenger Tomkins and deepened through the soul-searchings of his officer Everard. But it is in the swashbuckling, clownish Cavalier Wildrake that we actually enter his presence. Wildrake, hating Cromwell at a distance, goes as Everard's messenger. Cromwell is at Windsor, the setting of Charles

I's burial. The lengthy meeting is in three parts, chiefly taken up with dialogue, showing Cromwell the individual through his strangely confused mode of speech with its clausal mazes sometimes wholly unintelligible. The initial portrait is moderate and insistent on Cromwell's sincerity. The dramatization that follows differs sharply from that of Burley; a sense of historic and dramatic individuality prevails over a taste for the psychological picturesque, and the more subdued delineation is at once more convincing historically and more probable mimetically.

Buchan's allusion to Carlyle, however, reminds us that the Author of Waverley by no means fails to recognize the charismatic quality in Cromwell. Indeed, as Everard ponders the utility of a great man as a stabilizing factor following a revolution (70), one senses the influence of the gigantic labor precisely contemporary with *Woodstock*, Scott's *Life of Napoleon*. With Napoleon in mind, the choice of Wildrake as present perspective allowed Scott to dramatize his response to the Cromwell phenomenon with complex authenticity. The dialogue is given its emotional quality through Wildrake's responsive presence. Wildrake is inclined to scoff and finds he cannot; he is ready to hate the murderer of Charles (especially at Windsor Castle), but finds himself stunned by the spiritual force of the Protector:

As the Cavalier looked on his dark and bold countenance, agitated by inward and indescribable feelings, he found his own violence of spirit die away and lose itself in fear and wonder. So true is it that, as greater lights swallow up and extinguish the display of those which are less, so men of great, capacious, and overruling minds bear aside and subdue, in their climax of passion, the more feeble wills and passions of others; as, when a river joins a brook, the fiercer torrent shoulders aside the smaller stream [98].

91

But the charismatic or Napoleonic figure coexists with the mean and unstable one. The room at Windsor where Wildrake and Cromwell meet displays a portrait of Charles on the wall. Through such a device, Scott forces Cromwell to confront his late victim in Wildrake's presence. Under such pressures the slippery and unstable Cromwell is always prone to collapse into incoherence. It is this Cromwell who appears in the second and third scenes with Wildrake, and it is he who returns at the climax of the novel.

Thus we encounter the novel's major structural problem. Having spent such time and skill dramatizing and interpreting Cromwell, Scott has no further occasion to introduce him until he abruptly appears in the book's final quarter. His importance in the novel is slight, comparable to that of Charles Edward in *Waverley*, although his influence on the fate of Woodstock is persistently strong. We must look elsewhere for the real subject of the novel.

It is not even to be found in Everard himself, or in his ordeal as representative moderate. Too limiting a recollection of *Old Mortality* is misleading. To be sure, Everard is essential to the action. In the first half he is instrumental in restoring Sir Henry to Woodstock, making himself the moving force of a kind of reconciliation in his own divided lineage. In the second half he becomes the fugitive Charles II's romantic rival, almost his executioner, finally his guardian. So important are Everard's actions that he is the "active hero" that Morton and his Waverley kin never become. Moreover, he is characterized with fairness and urbanity as a dedicated Presbyterian struggling with the problem of Cromwell. He is a vigorous spokesman for "modernism" when he responds to old Sir Henry's melodramatic lamentations over the death of chivalry with this impassioned defense of his own religious principles: "they are no less sincere than your own, and thus far purer – excuse the word – that they are unmingled with the bloodthirsty dictates of a barbarous age, which you and others have called the code of chivalrous honour" (53). The three chapters that follow this first appearance all develop his characterization, balancing lengthy reflective passages against lively dialogue with Wildrake. While the reader sees Everard from within as a complex and admirable man, he also sees the truth in Wildrake's accusation:

You have practised sobriety and hypocrisy from your hanging sleeves till your Geneva cassock – from the cradle to this day – and it is a thing of nature to you; and you are surprised that a rough, rattling, honest fellow, accustomed to speak truth all his life, and especially when he found it at the bottom of a flask, cannot be so perfect a prig as thyself [59].

This sophisticated irony, lacking in the presentation of Morton, is matched by the plausible complexity of the man. Wildrake rightly defines the limits of Everard's moral independence. And when Everard wrestles with the devils or ghosts that infest Woodstock, we are confronted with a convincing mixture of scepticism and credulity. He is, in a word, subject to none of the charges made against Morton – that he is too liberal and detached to be historical. Yet his humanity and liberality justify his central function as mediator. And still, in other ways he is an essential agent and nothing more.

As title and subtitle indicate, the novel's central problem is not his. The title suggests the crucial significance of the house, and the juxtaposition of title and subtitle hints at various symbolic relations between the fate of the house and the fates of its Cavalier proprietors. But consider the subtitle first: The Cavalier. Cavalierism as a spirit and an historical problem is differently embodied or expressed in three major figures, just as in *Old Mortality* it persists differently in Claverhouse, Bothwell, and Evandale. Each of the Cavaliers in *Woodstock* reflects differently on the novel's definition of Cavalierism as a problem. Sir Henry Lee is the embodiment of old Cavalier manners, and as such is presented with a carefully controlled mixture of respect, sympathy, and amusement. Roger Wildrake, a rather Falstaffian bridge between old and new, illustrates the utter decadence and/or disorientation of old Cavalier "virtu" in the new order. The fugitive Charles II is the selfish, witty, hedonistic new Cavalier. For the first half of the novel the problem is the restoring of Sir Henry to Woodstock; for the second half it is the restoring of Charles to his own Cavalier values as embodied in the restored Sir Henry and Woodstock. The historic Restoration follows as fitting end to this symmetrical two-part preparation. Everard's vital function as mediator connects the halves: it is his role to reconcile Sir Henry to his place as Ranger of Woodstock and to save Woodstock for its traditional tenants from Cromwellian extremes; and then it is to adjust the new Cavalier to this restoration and in so doing to save the new Cavalier from his own worst self. If, as has been claimed, *Woodstock* is among the best constructed of the Waverleys,[30] its significant unity will be found in this structure, not in the plot of attempted seduction or the suspense of Charles's flight from Cromwell.

Let me argue first that Sir Henry is the Cavalier of the subtitle. This is *prima facie* probable, and besides, biographical facts make it tempting to find in Sir Henry the book's moral and emotional center. It is demonstrably erroneous to claim, as Buchan does, that the book "bears no mark of" its author's "sad preoccupation" at the time he was writing it.[31] It was begun in November, 1825. The Lockharts left for

London on December 5. On December 18 came the first clear sign of the financial disaster that would shatter Scott's Abbotsford dreams. He was at work on *Woodstock* when the final news came, and he went on working at it during the long winter evenings of January in the city, part of his family having permanently "flitted" to London, the rest lonely and tensely unadjusted to the calamity. It was a time to lament the loss of a great house and the glorious recollections and anticipations associated with it. It was a time, too, of intense and unusual introspection for Scott. He had just begun his journal,[32] which he would write in daily and then turn to his other writing, with predictable effect in the direction of simplicity and intimacy. One is not surprised to detect a personal authenticity in Sir Henry's mourning for the lost house: "There is a feeling in nature, affecting even the instinct, as it is called, of dumb animals, which teaches them to fly from misfortune" (46). Or this:

Nephew, I do not shrink before my changes of fortune. I shall wear coarser clothes; I shall feed on more ordinary food; men will not doff their cap to me as they were wont, when I was the great and the wealthy. What of that? Old Harry Lee loved his honour better than his title, his faith better than his land and lordship. Have I not seen the Thirtieth of January? I am neither philomath nor astrologer; but old Will teaches me that when green leaves fall winter is at hand, and that darkness will come when the sun sets [149–50].

Nor is one surprised to find an unusually careful narrative procedure when one recalls Scott's anxious conviction that this book "had to be good."

Sir Henry's role in the novel may be enhanced by his giving expression to Scott's immediate feelings, by his serving to translate them into the book's terms as feelings for the old world of Woodstock that had died with Charles I. But his conception and moral development are independent of such function. The old knight seems to derive from a complex of literary recollections. Sir Henry, himself a "humorous" devotee of Shakespeare, identifies himself in self-pity with Lear. But his devotion to Shakespeare is part of his naive and foolish passion for the "former age," and this obsession recalls the type of humorous old man Scott knew in the neo-Jonsonian Restoration comedy of Dryden and Shadwell. These, each with its appropriate tragic or comic or pathetic judgment, are operative in the delineation of Sir Henry. He is pathetic when forced to relinquish his house, or when he tries to resist by fighting Tomkins. He is guilty of tragic folly when he allows a quixotic fidelity to come before his daughter's happiness. He melodramatizes his sense of betrayal, thinking himself Lear (52), but does not recognize the logic of his own analogy when Everard charges him with being an unnatural father. The charge translates the terms of Lear's folly into Scott's characteristic antithesis of natural human bonds and abstract or ideal loyalties: "Hold up your head, fair Alice," says Everard, "and tell your father he has forgotten nature in his fantastic spirit of loyalty" (51). When Sir Henry persists, Everard responds with his strictures on "the wild spirit of romantic chivalry" as "bloodthirsty dictates of a barbarous age," and leaves with, "We may meet in a better time, when your heart and your principles shall master the unhappy prejudices by which they are now overclouded" (52–53). Thus, saving Woodstock is dependent on saving Sir Henry's good nature, his heart, from his fantasy and his prejudices, his fanaticism.

But this problem is subordinated to Everard's attempts to wrest Woodstock from the less admirable fanatics of the opposing side. And by the time uncle and nephew meet again, Sir Henry has already softened considerably. He is restored to the house shortly afterward, and during the second half of the book he exists primarily as a problem for those who would save Charles from Cromwell, Alice from Charles, and Charles from himself. His naïveté and irascibility now make it necessary to keep him in ignorance of the King's presence. The resultant emphasis on the old knight's absurdity is typified in a Drydenesque episode of cross-misunderstandings. Everard and the disguised Charles fight in the forest over the King's attentions to Alice. Everard thinks he is fighting the disguised Rochester. Sir Henry arrives to halt the fight, thinking he has exerted his own authority and not recognizing the King. The quixotic absurdity of the old knight is played up in the description of him on horseback, and Everard and his antagonist share an amused smile at Sir Henry's expense (296–300). Yet the novel ends with the restored Charles, having learned to outgrow his cynical amusement at Sir Henry's Cavalier humors, acknowledging the old knight as his spiritual father (461). Thus, having struggled with his own nature, and having served as a source of humor in the disguise-intrigue chapters centering on Charles, Sir Henry achieves central importance for others. The "humorous" Cavalier, like the "humorous" Jacobite Bradwardine, ends as a potent symbol for characters in search of a genuine moral vision. One is reminded of the emergence as moral norms of the humorous innocents of Sterne and Dickens.

No comparable case can be made for the centrality of the second Cavalier to whom the subtitle might refer. Yet Wildrake, of the three, is the clearest example of the historically representative character, the "man of his age," for which Lukacs praises Scott. Wildrake's versatile participation in the novel's development gives him unique importance, and his reckless and sometimes ludicrous embodiment of the Cavalier spirit complements and qualifies the impression given by Sir Henry.

We have already noticed two effective uses made of Wildrake, illustrating his unique rhetorical value: his function as the critical friend of Everard to control whatever charges of priggishness may be directed at the hero; his usefulness in the effective dramatic interpretation of Cromwell. His other significant contributions are to both plot and theme. His Cavalier manners make him a companion for Sir Henry; and in at least one important scene, they act out together the manners of the old Cavalier in the disguised presence of the new Cavalier, who must learn respect for them. The birdlike qualities suggested by his name (and noted by him) make him a suitable emissary. It is Wildrake who, for all his frivolity and instability, manages to warn Woodstock of Cromwell's approach and to allow Charles to get away. But his most significant actions as emissary are those which mark the significant parallelism of the novel's halves. It is Wildrake who recalls each exiled or estranged Cavalier to his true domain: Sir Henry to Woodstock, and Charles to England.

If one Cavalier is central to the novel, then, it is ultimately Charles, but his restoration is to be understood through its complex parallelism with the earlier restoration of Sir Henry to Woodstock. The preparatory restoration of Charles at Woodstock is no mere suspenseful game of saving the fugitive's life and the heroine's virtue. It is rather a test to see if the fugitive is the proper and adequate vehicle for establishing a continuity of true Cavalier values. Just as Sir Henry's is an education of the heart to subdue romantic quixotry in the interests of restored natural affection, so

Charles's is an education of the heart to a respectful affection for the old Cavalier ways, however anachronistic and humorous they have become. The libertine-sceptic learns what is of permanent value in his Cavalier heritage. When, at the time of his restoration, Charles stops his progress to London to acknowledge Sir Henry as his "father," he is acknowledging this education.

It begins with a pair of disguises which symbolize Charles's uncertain relation to the monarchy. First Charles is disguised as an old woman, a fortune-teller, corrupting prophecy in the libertine interests of the seducer. Then he appears, with full dialect, as the ugly, vulgar son of a dead follower of Montrose. The effect here, too, is to put the fugitive King in the role of comic relief and decadent vulgarity. We are struck by the Lees' earnest devotion to the Stuart house and the devious and selfish frivolity of the King disguised in their midst. This contrast provides the organizing principle of the entire episode – its significant irony – and this forceful incongruity becomes the instrument of Charles's education.

Examples of irony are numerous. Shortly after "Louis Kerneguy" arrives with Sir Henry's son, Wildrake and Sir Henry, two old Cavaliers, reenact the loyalty and valor of their fellows in the wars in the undisclosed presence of one who should be recognizing his own heritage in such values, but is incapable of doing so. The scene makes clear, too, that as long as Charles remains in disguise he will remain in constant danger of involvement in petty battles – that, in short, assuming his true nature is a prerequisite to survival at Woodstock, even though it risks his discovery by Cromwell. A scene making the same point is one in which Louis is importuned by Sir Henry to "tell us a little, Master Kerneguy, about him we love most to hear about – the King."

"Louis bent his eyes on the ground," we are told, "and seemed at first uncertain what to answer" (270–71). He saves himself, perhaps from the perils of self-recognition, by calling on Sir Henry's son for the description. Albert gives a factual enough account; his sister Alice cries "For shame!" and proceeds to paint her own admittedly ideal picture of the monarch, as "every loyal heart in the kingdom ought to believe him" (271). Charles experiences some embarrassment, for "in some cases, exaggerated or unappropriate praise becomes the most severe satire" (273). He has entered upon the educative process which can end only when he recognizes a personal imperative in the idealistic visions of the Lees.

Meanwhile, his immediate response is lust for Alice, virtually the cynic-libertine's self-destructive desire for the good. He resigns himself to hiding at Woodstock, agrees to put up with the boring humors of the old Cavalier for a chance at his daughter, and refuses to believe in the spectacle of virtue before him. All his efforts at seduction fail. Alice repeatedly confronts him with the ideal Charles of her faith. The climax comes when Charles's life is imperiled in the duel with Everard. Alice now knows the real identity of her pursuer. To save him she risks her whole future with Everard, and Mark assumes he has lost her. Charles now, temporarily, has selfless action thrust upon him, is forced to admit the reality of virtue, discloses his identity, places his safety in Mark's hands, and reflects in surprise on his own virtue in words which anticipate whimsically the final thoughts of Sidney Carton: "Wilmot and Villiers, and Killigrew would laugh at me, did they hear of a campaign in which neither man nor woman had been conquered. But, odds-fish! let them laugh as they will; there is something at my heart which tells me that for once in my life I have acted well" (350). While Scott could scarcely imply that the historic Charles's education of the heart had been either complete or profound, he allowed this flighty humanitarian to last out the book, and saved the older sensualist for *Peveril of the Peak*.

For this Charles, the salvation of the heart through recognition of the reality of goodness is the chief of the wonders for which Woodstock is famous. Just as there is something supernatural in the recovery of the old house for Sir Henry, so in the parallel second half Charles has his own experience of the house's supernatural qualities. The novel's structural symmetry again calls attention to the title and suggests that we look finally to the house for the book's symbolic and thematic center.

Woodstock is haunted.[33] What happens or threatens to happen there is ghostly reenactment; the book's parallel halves are linked by a pair of ghost stories, both comic in atmosphere, yet ominous. Woodstock is a symbol of monarchy, of Cavalier tradition, and the ambiguous mood of its hauntedness evokes ambivalent feelings for the threatened traditional fidelities it symbolizes. The house is haunted by a Just Devil, and from this central fact derives a texture of seriocomic diabolism. The texture is controlled by a mock-Gothic sophistication recalling *Northanger Abbey* but with an added historical authenticity (even Everard cannot conquer his superstitious fears) and serious symbolic implication. Old Sir Henry Lee makes a joke of the devil: "As to old Harry – why, you might as well see the *Devil*. You take me, Master Kerneguy: the Devil, you know, is my namesake – ha – ha – ha!" (301). But the diabolical possession of Woodstock is no joke.

The devil is in everyone's mouth, but everyone identifies the devil of Woodstock differently. "I have seen the Devil," says Wildrake of Cromwell, "and have, as thou sayst, got a warrant from him" (103). The association with Wandering Willie is relevant. For a warrant to save Woodstock seems to require appeal to one devil or another. To keep Woodstock for the Commonwealth, the Commissioners must "lay the Devil" (113) that has arisen on behalf of its Cavalier tenants. All sides see in the struggle for Woodstock "fiends to be combated – incarnate fiends on earth, and raging infernal fiends under the earth" (158). The moderate Presbyterian Holdenough, who pleads with Everard for the house's total destruction, sees a real diabolism on all sides. The "Devil's brats," for him, are sectaries, and the growth of sects "has brought up the Evil One even upon the face of the earth" (110). The dire result is an "infernal tumult," for "surely nothing on earth could so much resemble Hell as when men go thus loose in mortal malice on their fellow-creatures" (200). There are demons of both parties at Woodstock: "This night will try whether the devil of the sectaries or the devil of the Malignants shall prove the stronger. O, sing jubilee, for the kingdom of Satan is divided against itself!" (405)

When, therefore, the local Royalists "summon up" the haunts of the Just Devil to frighten away the Commissioners – "for men say, for certain, it was the Devil came down bodily among them and made them troop off" (212) – they unwittingly invoke a real diabolical threat. Depending on traditional devils for the restoration of Woodstock to the Lees is analogous in danger to depending on Charles for the Restoration of a Cavalier monarchy. Sir Henry is ill-advised to take comfort in his beloved Shakespeare's tag: "the Prince of Darkness" is a gentleman who "never interferes with those of his own coat" (212). His folly is vividly symbolized in his first act as restored tenant of

Woodstock. The house cistern, he triumphantly complains, has been polluted by the Cromwellians. "I will taste no water from the cistern out of which these slaves have been serving themselves," he tells his daughter. "Fetch me down a pitcher from Rosamond's spring" (213). Woodstock's other royal ghosts are thus recalled, and Sir Henry, having recovered his nature as a father and his place as a Cavalier, now blindly sends his daughter into a new danger.

Alice goes to the well and meets Charles, disguised as a fortune-teller. Charles, at once the seducer, drops a gold ring in her pitcher. "Nay, we must look to that," warns Sir Henry, "for it is like to be a charm, and we have enough of the Devil's ware about Woodstock already" (222). The analogical succession is clear. Having rid itself of one demon, Woodstock has taken on another: the demon of libertine scepticism that possesses Charles. The warning note has sounded from the beginning in allusions to the ghostly mystery of Rosamond's Tower, but now the threat materializes as the possibility that Woodstock's restoration will end in a tragic reenactment of the Rosamond legend which haunts the place. The Royalist machinery of Halloween trickery gives way to the ominous warning of mythic repetition. The folk-legend "wonders" of Woodstock give way to the real "wonder" which saves Charles from himself. Folk legend and superstition are thus woven together into a symbolic texture, and that symbolism has its focal reality in the house itself. *Woodstock*, like *The Bride of Lammermoor*, illustrates what truth there is in the single condescending footnote F. R. Leavis grants the Author of Waverley: he was "a kind of inspired folk-lorist."[34]

The house in *Woodstock*, then, has symbolic centrality: its diabolism is both dangerous and corrective; its wonders are initially fanciful but ultimately real. The house meanwhile functions as setting, and does so in a way unusual in a Waverley Novel. Its role both as setting and as symbolic prize in an historic struggle makes unnecessary the customary strategy of connecting the forces and events of public history with private natures and destinies. The house belongs to both simultaneously, links public and private destinies, embodies political and ideological relations in domestic ones, focuses the problem of the vital continuity of value on the problem of the survival of an ancient house. Spatial concentration is uniquely possible because the struggle for Woodstock serves so well as microcosm for the larger struggle. Spatial concentration, meaningful symmetry, and symbolic density make *Woodstock* one of the Author of Waverley's most impressive works of art.

3. *PEVERIL OF THE PEAK*

Scott's other Restoration novel is for Grierson "the most complete failure of all the novels before the final breakdown."[35] The usually sympathetic Buchan makes most of the negative judgments that can be made of the book, but illustrates none of them.[36] Why is it a failure, and what can be learned from its failure? It is pointless to substitute for critical judgments a catalogue of the difficulties under which it was written. The idea that Scott was "not at home" in this period is either ambiguous or irrelevant or both;[37] it is, after all, roughly the period of *Old Mortality*. For Scott the editor-biographer, it is the age of Dryden, a fact one often recalls while reading this most Drydenesque of the Waverley Novels, a Spanish-plotted extravaganza on the intrigues and absurdities of the Popish Plot. Nor is the delineation of the shifty Charles, if indeed it is inadequately historical, enough to account for the failure.

The novel has portions in which the Author of Waverley is at his best. The failure, as we have increasing reason to believe is generally the case with a Waverley failure, is formal. A formal failure is a failure of focus and coherence, of sustained and operative recognition of governing thematic implication. Lockhart recognized the point of *Peveril's* deficiencies: "The post-haste rapidity of the Novelist's execution was put to a severe trial, from his adoption of so wide a canvass as was presented by a period of twenty busy years, and filled by so very large and multifarious an assemblage of persons, not a few of them, as it were, struggling for prominence."[38] The struggle depicts a never-conquered formal uncertainty, and the formal uncertainty makes of the midpoint shift which this novel shares with *Woodstock, The Heart of Midlothian, Rob Roy,* and others, a fatal caesura. The novel does and then does not belong to the Cavalier-Puritan group: it is and then is not about the problem of reconciliation in the face of opposing fanaticisms, is and then is not a fictional plotting of the survival of humanity in the face of divisive laws and languages.

The opening contains materials essential to such a novel. It shows Scott at his best in large historic episode. The fragility of the humane bond between Cavalier Peveril and Presbyterian Bridgenorth is put to a severe test by Lady Peveril's valiant attempt to give a dinner of reconciliation for all the people of Martindale to celebrate the Restoration and bear witness to their renewed solidarity. The dinner becomes a group study in the tragicomic divisiveness of men, stating on a large scale the tragic "Two Drovers" theme that men ordinarily act in ignorance of each other's prejudices.

105

The mutual forbearance of Peveril and Bridgenorth is quickly thereafter shattered by the reappearance of old loyalties and fanaticisms in the form of Lady Derby. The ensuing tragedy of thwarted reconciliation is focused on the separation of the children, Julian Peveril and Alice Bridgenorth, who grow up into a Romeo-Juliet plight, with an important difference. Julian is transferred from his own moderate parents to the arrogant and bigoted Lady Derby; Alice is placed by her unsuspecting father in the charge of the Countess's equally devious and vengeful enemy, Ganlesse-Christian. It is the adoptive parents who precipitate the pathetic separation and who embody the book's opposing fanaticisms.

By the end, the lovers have survived their adoptions, their parents' divisions, and their own involvement in the Popish Plot. The Countess herself concedes that "they love each other like lovers of the last age." Their marriage permits the usual symbolic consolidation of estates, and is the kind of climactic marriage in which Daiches recognizes Scott's ultimate symbol of reconciliation. But by the end of *Peveril* the Countess's allusion to "lovers of the last age" (565) is more accurate. Their love is at last not a union to transcend fanatic oppositions, but a stability capable of withstanding the total instability of the "new age." Between these two possible resolutions, the novel is divided and thematically confused. All it can say as a whole is that the traditional conflict between fanatic loyalty and natural humanity, dominant through the first half, loses its meaning when moved into the new world of Restoration trimming, frivolity, and disguise. The Isle of Man interlude provides some sort of connecting link or transition, it is true. As setting it has dual significance: as the dark place of fanatic and vengeful conflict; as the "old world" of little cultural change, withdrawn from the mainland of intrigue and new disorder. But it cannot function simultaneously as both symbols. And the presence of such a connective link simply underscores the disunity.

It appears that Scott began without a clear notion of how to combine his familiar thematic interest in the plotting of humane survival with his broad impressionistic delineation of the Popish Plot. Evidently, he often began without such a notion, and acquired it as he worked. Here one suspects he found equally strong and divided interests and lacked the patience to restrict his narrative scope and allow for their proper integration. The opening timetable is symptomatic: after the initial picture of the precarious bond between Peveril and Bridgenorth, we come to a chapter (the tenth) which opens with a jump of five years and closes with a jump of "many," transporting us at last to the Isle of Man, where the action proper finally begins.

It begins in such a way as to find its center in the complex and shifting relationship between Bridgenorth and Peveril's son Julian, who meet as father and suitor of Alice. Julian's suit subjects him perilously to Bridgenorth's uses. By insisting that only a "son" to him can receive Alice's hand, Bridgenorth entangles Julian in his own political intrigues. His appeal recalls Burley's appeal to Morton. Both men insist that the times call for unusual action. Bridgenorth, by nature kindhearted and humane, convinces himself and tries to convince Julian that "the seared wood is the fitter for the use of the workmen; the hardened and the dried-up heart is that which can best bear the task imposed by these dismal times" (108–9). The times call for the awakening of torpid spirits. As Morton is accused of disinterest or coldness, so Julian is charged with an unnatural lethargy. Ironically, the man who says the times call for hard hearts accuses Julian of hardness in failing to respond. Julian's reaction is indirect but predictable. He imagines himself the mediator; for once Scott treats the mediatorial impulse itself as a form of youthful quixotry. By entering public life Julian romantically believes he can win fortune and influence, be in a position to save Bridgenorth (as Waverley had Bradwardine, as Everard would Sir Henry), and thus fulfill his dream by winning Alice. But if Julian is dangerously naive, so is Bridgenorth; and in this novel it is the older man's ordeal of disillusionment that provides the chief interest.

Bridgenorth is an unusual rhetorical experiment for Scott. It entails winning cumulative sympathy for the character responsible for deliberately entangling the hero in a criminal political commitment. Burley alone would seem comparable, yet sympathy is never the word to use for one's feelings for Burley; perhaps only the intricate rhetoric of Fergus MacIvor's affective manipulation is really similar.

At the outset, as widower and bereaved father, Bridgenorth has already suffered much, and Sir Geoffrey Peveril's boorish behavior serves to win Bridgenorth further sympathy. His true affection for his daughter remains his most prominent trait throughout. Although Alice herself warns Julian that her father would sacrifice all human loyalties to his principles, we see increasing evidence that, even against his own political interests, he is strongly attached to Julian. In his long scenes with Julian as spokesman for moderate Presbyterianism, he is both convincing and affectionate. When Julian is captured by Bridgenorth's own allies and accused of alliance with the Papist Countess, Bridgenorth frees him. From this point on Bridgenorth is in almost constant contrast with the intriguers and drifters of all factions; and our admiration grows with the apprehensiveness with which we watch this naive man move into the unprincipled London world. For the man who intrigued to draw Julian into danger has himself become the naive victim of others whose interest it is to misunderstand him, and his own danger is increased by the human affections he has previously sought to subdue as earthly: "He even confessed his fears, that his partial regard for Alice's happiness might enervate his efforts in behalf of his country; and Christian had little trouble in eliciting from him a promise that he would forbear to inquire after her for some time" (344). His eyes are not opened to the truth until, when it is nearly too late, Julian saves Alice. Thus the moderate, driven to extremism, himself becomes the tragic center of a conflict between nature and ideological fanaticism, only to find the conflict itself dissolve in a world of unprincipled men masking as fanatics.

Julian's experience lacks this dynamic Waverley-like center. Julian differs from both Waverley and Morton in that his entanglement implies no ideological commitment. He even differs from Osbaldistone and Darsie Latimer in that his entanglement can be blamed on no quixotic weakness in himself. He is effectively used as the experiential center of the novel, but plays little part in its moral dialectic except in so far as his naïveté leads him to long for effective participation in public life. But because misleading influences make false parental claims on his loyalties, his adventures become perforce something of a mysterious search for his own birthright. As he leaves the Isle of Man to enter his public career, he does so directed by two opposing influences, both of which seek to sacrifice his personal trust to the cause of a political ideal. Both have appealed to him as a son. Says Bridgenorth, "he who would be my son must first show himself the true and loving child of his oppressed and deluded country" (196). Says the Countess a few pages later, "Go, my dearest son – for to me you should be dear as a son. . . . Am I not your mother; and are you not discharging a son's duty?" (208) Both are half sincere, and both are guilty of corrupting a natural loyalty in the interest of an ideological faction; this, and not Welsh's "hostility to property,"[39] is clearly the fundamental villainy in the book.

Julian sets forth to London and the Countess's Catholic agents with his true sonship much in doubt. The chapters ensuing – the romance of the bewildered youthful idealist's wandering across the strange, perilous mainland of experience to London – are among Scott's most effectively romantic. The romance continually verges on allegory. Julian's choice of roads seems fated but unknowable; his guides seem to know all about him; his experience is dreamlike in its arbitrary shiftiness. His recognition of the mysterious fatality that attends him is stated in terms Waverley might have used for his own dark journey. His guide has urged him to seek advice:

"And from whom or where can I obtain it?" said Peveril. "I wander in this country like one in a dream; so much a few months have changed it. Men who formerly occupied themselves with their own affairs are now swallowed up in matters of state policy; and those tremble under the apprehension of some strange and sudden convulsion of empire who were formerly only occupied by the fear of going to bed supperless. And to sum up the matter, I meet a stranger, apparently well acquainted with my name and concerns, who first attaches himself to me whether I will or no, and then refuses me an explanation of his business, while he menaces me with the strangest accusations" [246].

Perhaps no other single statement in the novels more perfectly sums up the ordeal of romance to which the Waverley hero is characteristically subjected upon entering the world of historic experience.

The nature of the world Julian enters is embodied not, however, in the opposing fanaticisms of the Countess and Bridgenorth, but rather in his two chief guides, one benevolent, the other malevolent, both unstable or capricious to a point of grotesqueness. The two characters seem absurd to the casual reader: the villainous Ganlesse-Christian and the exotic, ubiquitous gypsy mute, Scott's Mignon-ondine, Zara-Fenella.[40] Their absurdity is quite functional. Their multiplicity of names, their variety of disguises, their colorful instability of behavior all make them appropriate symbols in the book's vision of the mad and spectacular world of the Popish Plot. Ganlesse is at the center of Julian's dreamlike ordeal, boastfully changing costumes, voices, and characters, mocking Julian's prudence and sincerity: " 'Sincerity!' said the stranger. 'A child's whistle, with but two notes in it – yea, yea and nay, nay. Why, man, the very Quakers have renounced it, and have got in its stead a gallant recorder, called hypocrisy, that is somewhat like sincerity in form, but of much greater compass, and combines the whole gamut' " (243). Julian, awed by Ganlesse's "boldness and freedom" of speech, "thought he discovered in this man's manner a wild and reckless frankness, which he could not but connect with the idea of sincerity in the present case" (246). In a time when informers and false witnesses are everywhere, Ganlesse the man of many voices is an epitome. Zara-Fenella, hopelessly in love with Julian, as unstable as the man who is finally and appropriately identified as her father, is deaf and cannot speak at all. Both suggest how *Peveril* (1823) prepared the way for the treatment of the problem of language in *Redgauntlet* the following year. Both prepare the way in this novel for major thematic developments in the London chapters, for both become closely involved with the main historical figure of those

111

chapters and serve as perfect symbolic counterparts for him.

Scott's Buckingham is conceived in the light of Dryden's "Not one but all mankind's epitome" and thus serves the novel as the historic and symbolic epitome of the age of the Popish Plot. While such grotesques as Fenella and Ganlesse-Christian might seem distractingly out of place in the densely historic world of the later chapters of *Peveril*, actually they are metaphorically akin to Buckingham as the human symbols of it. And one might well add to the list lesser grotesques such as the dwarf in Julian's cell, Sir Geoffrey Hudson, a pathetic-comic Cavalier spokesman of the old school; and the gross, spiderish prison official who assigns Julian to his cell, memorable as a Dickensian macabre in a Waverley Novel:

this man's features, surly and tallow-coloured; his limbs swelled and disproportioned, his huge paunch and unwieldy carcass, suggested the idea that, having once found his way into this central recess, he had there battened, like the weasel in the fable, and fed largely and foully, until he had become incapable of retreating through any of the narrow paths that terminated at his cell; and was thus compelled to remain, like a toad under the cold stone, fattening amid the squalid airs of the dungeons by which he was surrounded [392–93].

The vision of a grotesque, topsy-turvy theatrical world is supported by an appropriate iterative imagery, which replaces the prevailing imagery of "the hardened and the dried-up heart" (108) when the book's search for humane reconciliation is lost in the later search for stability and survival. It is anticipated in the early characterization of Fenella, whose impulsive and passionate waywardness make her similar to Effie in another book concerned with the disciplined heart and its aberrations, *The Heart of Midloth-ian*. Fenella's waywardness (181) links her to the repeated imagery of a rudderless ship adrift (224–25), most fittingly used for self-description by the one in whom instability and drift are finally concentrated, the Duke of Buckingham. Buckingham postpones stability to the time "when age (touching his forehead) shall make this same weathercock too rusty to turn with the changing breeze. But as yet, while I have spirit and action, let it whirl like the vane at the mast-head, which teaches the pilot how to steer his course; and when I shift mine, think I am bound to follow fortune, and not to control her" (435). Fenella is suitable as *genius loci* of Buckingham's establishment. She is also the genius of the capricious destiny (212) which eventually leads Julian to employ the same imagery: "whether he contemplated the interests of his love, his family affections, or his friendships, all seemed such a prospect as that of a sailor who looks upon breakers on every hand, from the deck of a vessel which no longer obeys the helm" (399).

Such is an appropriate plight for one doomed to entangle-ment in the world of the Popish Plot, for the world itself is repeatedly seen as a storm. The Countess sees it so when directing Julian to her coreligionists for advice: "None can tell so exactly how the wind sets as the pilot whose vessel is exposed to the storm" (213). The situation is "an awful tempest," and the King, "with his usual selfish prudence, truckles to the storm" (205). Julian's father asks God to keep him "good and true to church and king, whatever wind shall bring foul weather!" (275) Buckingham complacently predicts that he "will keep his own steerage-way through shoal and through weather" (336). The imagery is not abundant, and the novel is obviously not to be read as a pattern of iterative imagery. But its recurrence does contribute logically to the world of instability and drift which the Buckingham half of the novel envisions.

Scott's awareness of the imagery's structural importance is implied in his introduction of another, logically related pattern of imagery, no less conventional, but nonetheless meaningful. Julian, having separated from Alice and set out for the mainland, muses on the separation and his prospects:

"Constancy," he repeated to himself – "constancy." And, as if in coincidence with the theme of his reflections, he fixed his eyes on the polar star, which that night twinkled with more than ordinary brilliancy. Emblem of pure passion and steady purpose – the thoughts which arose as he viewed its clear and unchanging light were disinterested and noble. To seek his country's welfare, and secure the blessings of domestic peace; to discharge a bold and perilous duty to his friend and patron; to regard his passion for Alice Bridgenorth as the loadstar which was to guide him to noble deeds – were the resolutions which thronged upon his mind, and which exalted his spirits to that state of romantic melancholy which perhaps is ill exchanged even for feelings of joyful rapture [219–20].

When next the image of the polar star as guide or beacon to constancy at sea appears, it has become the beacon that traditionally shines forth from the battlements of Martindale Castle, is known as Peveril's Pole-star, and is given various interpretations by tradition, all implying the vital permanence and continuity of the Peveril house, not as property, but as humane patriarchal stability, as domestic locus and emblem of true political value. As Peveril approaches and sees the beacon unlit, he sees in the darkness the end of his race. When it is relit, the enemy of the Peverils himself sees in it a sign "that Heaven intends to work great things by your hand, so singularly has that augury followed on" Peveril's prediction that "if the light of our house be now quenched, God can rekindle it in His own good time" (276). The rekindling is accomplished ultimately through Peveril's perseverance, his ability to hold with constancy to his star. The nature of his perseverance is defined here at the outset of his adventures in the "storm."

It is seen clearly and familiarly in his Waverley-like gesture of choosing to reject his dangerous guide, to plot his own direction and assert his own will. The devious Ganlesse-Christian urges him to come straight to London: "You may see already," he says, "that I am no ordinary person, but a master-spirit of the time" (260). He is precisely that. His guidance involves helpless surrender to the times and to their spirit of grotesque instability, and as such it marks for Julian the logical climax to the influences of the Countess and Bridgenorth, who have called him fraudulently in the name of parental duty to surrender himself morally to the times. This is what Julian rejects when he rejects Ganlesse as guide: " 'I understand not your threat,' answered Peveril, 'if a threat be indeed implied. I have done no evil – I feel no apprehension; and I cannot, in common sense, conceive why I should suffer for refusing my confidence to a stranger, who seems to require that I should submit me blindfold to his guidance'" (261). This self-assertion is the point at which he turns aside from his romantic sense of mediatorial mission to warn his ineffectual father Peveril. The assertion places his loyalty to a natural bond above less authentic, more ideal or timely interests, and signifies in recognizably Waverleyesque terms his ability to keep his moral bearings amid the storm world of London and the Plot.

In this chaotic world, however, Peveril's virtue and humanity – and his house, the historic continuity in whose name they are held – survive by no unambiguous means. As usual we must look to the plotting of Julian's moral survival for the novel's ultimate test of vital coherence. The problem is that of *Old Mortality*: how, in a world of social and moral instability, in times of ideological violence and hard hearts, the moderate, the man of humane prudence, can survive. It is pointless to expect from *Peveril of the Peak* the coherent and inevitable resolution of *Old Mortality* or *The Heart of Midlothian*. Formal control is inadequate; the emphases are too many and unstable. If Fenella's improbability is defensible on grounds of her symbolic place in Buckingham's world, her importance to the plotting of the Peverils' survival is not. Her ability to play the providential Ariel, penetrating walls of town house and prison alike, has no real thematic connection with her symbolic instability. Thus, one is finally distracted by her crucial importance. Moreover, Julian's reunions with his father and with Alice should be meaningful for thematic resolution, but either they are not or they are unable to make their meanings apparent in the face of the plot's exhausting complexity. The marriage and joining of estates should signal the triumph of reconciliation, but instead it simply represents the survival of a stable and virtuous relationship. The problem of reconciliation, though it is solved here, has lost its central importance. In these ways and others, in the ways of significant formal resolution, the novel as a whole fails. And because it fails, its elements seem uncontrolled and unassimilated, hence unreal.

While saying what can be said on *Peveril's* behalf, however, one should take note of the trial scene itself, with its devastatingly realistic statement on the problem *Peveril* shares with *Old Mortality*. We know already how dependent the survival is on the amorous caprice of Fenella. We learn later how dependent it is on Charles's chance encounter with one who reminds him of his debt to the Peverils. But in the trial scene the Peverils are saved merely by what the stately dwarf Sir Geoffrey Hudson calls "a marvellous conjunction of circumstances" (497) – that is, by the fact that the storm of the Plot is ebbing, and Titus Oates is becoming tiresome. The judge is treated satirically by all as one who, "sagacious in the signs of the times," has begun to "see that the tide was turning" in Court favor. "His conduct, therefore," to revert to the imagery noted before, "during the whole trial, resembled the appearance of a vessel about to go upon another tack, when her sails are shivering in the wind, ere they have yet caught the impulse which is to send her forth in a new direction" (478). Peril thus ends in a mixture of wise humility and ludicrousness. Sir Geoffrey Peveril, on the verge of new violence with Bridgenorth, must be reminded by his dwarfish counterpart Sir Geoffrey Hudson, who is both wise and ludicrous, that his prejudice and anger should be lost in gratitude for his recent providential liberation. The whole episode warrants comparison with the crucial scene often slighted in *The Heart of Midlothian*. Jeanie's interview with Queen Caroline in the presence of the humane, politic Argyle makes a quite similar ironic observation on the mixture of justice, humanity, prudence, and caprice in the survival of the humane and the virtuous at such stormy moments in history.

Peveril the failure may thus provide illumination for a new reading of *The Heart of Midlothian* the success.

4. A LEGEND OF MONTROSE

The relative failure of a shorter, earlier novel, *A Legend of Montrose*, is also illuminating, but in different ways because

117

it fails differently. *Montrose* is the kind of failure over which Waverley critics most often take basic issue. Any assessment must begin and end with the charge, familiar since Jeffrey, that Dalgetty is "too big" for the book, just as, according to the same critics, Jarvie is "too big" for *Rob Roy*. The defenders are those who worry little about proportion in a novel's economy. They include the curiously similar Buchan and Daiches, for whom Dalgetty is great because Dalgetty is "alive," and in him the book "lives."[41]

As mercenary soldier and Scots pedant, as the man of more verbosity than humanity whose loyalties are strictly professional, he is bound to be one of the most interesting character conceptions in the Waverley Novels. Here, as in comparable cases, a character conception is interesting insofar as it embodies those problems of historic experience which to the Author of Waverley were most perplexing and urgent. But any character conception acquires full imaginative meaning only in and through its narrative context. If *Montrose* "lives" only in Dalgetty, or if he is "too big," the reason may be the book's failure to develop the implications of his character, or it may be that his importance undercuts or confuses the narrative's real concerns without resolving them.

Dalgetty is the type of character who, like Jarvie in *Rob Roy* or Burley in *Old Mortality*, ordinarily enters the protagonist's experience as a problem, guide, or norm. He may be a blocking character or an educative force or both. The reader knows him as a significant element in the protagonist's ordeal. In *Montrose,* though he had his moderate protagonist ready-made, Scott chose instead to move Dalgetty into the experiential center of the novel, even though Dalgetty, by his humorously static nature, by his fixed limits of vision and response, cannot be said to be

118

capable of experience at all. Dalgetty is a guide used as a central observer. To judge him as hero is as much of a mistake as to judge Reuben Butler as hero of *The Heart of Midlothian*. To recognize such distinctions is to understand better the problem of making Jeanie Deans the hero of a novel.

But first, what has Dalgetty to do with the potential meaning of the structure to which he has been added? The germ of the story is the historical murder of Menteith by his devoted friend and fellow supporter of Montrose, Stewart of Ardvoirlich – in short, a tale of abrupt violence between devoted friends. "Our subject," Scott wrote later in the Introduction, "leads us to talk of deadly feuds" (139), and in Scott, a feud between clans or individuals is a study in the tragic inhumanity of conflicting fanaticisms. The murder is fated; fatality for Scott is historic, and in the Cavalier-Puritan context historic fatality works through inheritance of fanaticism. Thus the murder of Menteith becomes an account of how a close natural bond is destroyed by tragic fanaticism, or by the sudden precipitation of an inhuman fidelity to an impersonal ideal.

The murdered friend, who survives in Scott's version, is the Cavalier moderate, the Evandale, the Julian. Like Julian, Menteith survives his involvement with extreme Cavalier forces and ends as mediator in his marriage to the daughter of his moderate Presbyterian counterpart, Sir Duncan Campbell. He and his father-in-law, both wounded, retire from partisan violence to the security and stability which the marriage represents. The familiar pattern of the Cavalier-Presbyterian novels is apparent, but its specific articulation is sporadic. Montrose is no Dundee; he is not the extreme form of Menteith's ideology. His presence in the novel has little thematic significance. Characteristically,

Scott shows greater interest in Montrose's fanatic Presbyterian opposite, the Duke of Argyle. Moreover, the fanaticism of Menteith's friend and would-be murderer has no political or ideological significance; it is purely dynastic or domestic. Nor has his fanaticism any necessary connection with his attempt to murder Menteith.

The would-be murderer, the fictional Ardvoirlich, is Allan M'Aulay, brother to the chief of the M'Aulays, supporters of Montrose. While stressing his Highland peculiarities, the narrator nevertheless describes them in terms of a Lowland analogy and thus early introduces the image of fanaticism:

An air of gloomy severity, the fruit perhaps of ascetic and solitary habits, might, in a Lowlander, have been ascribed to religious fanaticism; but by that disease of the mind, then so common both in England and the Lowlands of Scotland, the Highlanders of this period were rarely infected. They had, however, their own peculiar superstitions, which overclouded the mind with thick-coming fancies as completely as the Puritanism of their neighbors [175].

So we hear from Menteith of the grim vendetta which has produced Allan's "disease," the history of the M'Aulays' feud with the outlaw band known as the Children of the Mist. Allan's uncle had been murdered, his head brought to the M'Aulays' dining table. His sister, Allan's mother, never fully recovered from the shock, but brought up her son for merciless revenge. Thus he has come to represent in extreme form the heir whose whole identity is a fanatic projection of ancestral inhumanity.

His enemy Ranald MacEagh, chief of the Children of the Mist, is an interesting variation of Rob Roy. Like Allan he lives only for revenge; too old now to achieve it himself, he trains his grandson Kenneth in the same bloody cause, doing to him what has been done long since to the tragic Allan. Ranald is given vigorous and eloquent speeches in defense of fanatic vengefulness, unequaled in *Rob Roy*. Asked in prison what he would do to save himself, he replies, "I would do what a man might do and still call himself a man." "Do you call yourself a man," he is asked, "who have done the deeds of a wolf?" "I do," he answers.

I am a man like my forefathers: while wrapt in the mantle of peace, we were lambs; it was rent from us, and ye now call us wolves. Give us the huts ye have burned, our children whom ye have murdered, our widows whom ye have starved; collect from the gibbet and the pole the mangled carcasses, and whitened skulls of our kinsmen; bid them live and bless us, and we will be your vassals and brothers; till then, let death and blood and mutual wrong draw a dark veil of division between us [263–64].

In this he is like Allan, his opposite. But the point at which their likeness is most meaningful is law. On law they share a view we have seen shared by the opposing fanatics of *Old Mortality*, Claverhouse and Burley. Theirs is a rigid clan code, a law defiant of humanity. It is illustrated first by Allan, who extricates his brother Angus from a foolish wager and thus saves the M'Aulay honor by arranging his retainers about the dinner table as living candlesticks, as men become absolute in their sacrifice of humanity to fidelity: "not one of these men," he announces, "knows any law but their Chief's command. Would you dare to compare to THEM in value the richest ore that ever was dug out of the mine?" (181) MacEagh's death speech is comparable. It is as moving a declamation as any in the Waverley Novels. It celebrates the absolute freedom of the outlaw in heroic tones and rhythms and pours contempt on those who, "Saxon in their souls," value herds and flocks more than honor and freedom. Yet it ends by invoking the same law as that by which Allan lives. "Farewell, beloved!" says Ranald to his grandson, "and mayst thou die like thy forefathers, ere infirmity, disease, or age shall break thy spirit. Begone! begone! live free, requite kindness, avenge the injuries of thy race!" (345)

Such is the novel's feud between opposing fanaticisms. On the one hand, it is only casually connected to the political-ideological feud of Montrose and Argyle, to which it provides no parallel. On the other, it has little to do with Menteith's moderatism. For a time near the conclusion, to be sure, it plays the role played by the Edward-Fergus rivalry in *Waverley*. It comes to represent the dreadful instability, generated by divisive fanaticism, which makes the Cavalier cause (or its descendant, the Jacobite) a lost cause. Montrose finds himself in the position of Charles Edward. The furtherance of his own historic conflict with the house of Argyle leans precariously on forces incapable of reconciliation among themselves. Of this precariousness the outbreak of violence between Allan and Menteith is only a late aggravation. It is nothing more. To realize the poor management of this novel's economy one has only to make two speculations: (1) what kind of meaningful coherence could have been effected had the Menteith-M'Aulay friendship-rivalry been centrally developed as the Waverley-MacIvor friendship-rivalry had been; or (2) what meaningful coherence might have been articulated had Menteith become morally implicated in the conflict of Allan and MacEagh? Neither is done. Menteith matters only at beginning and end. The novel is not his but Dalgetty's experience. The mediatorial force in the war of opposing fanaticisms is not Menteith's moderation, but Dalgetty's pedantic, mercenary anti-idealism.

Dalgetty touches all the book's opposing forces. But being by nature incapable of moral implication, he never interrelates the forces he touches, in a personal search for reconciliation, as the representative Waverley protagonist does. The truth in the traditional charge against *A Legend of Montrose* may be interpreted thus: Dalgetty is "too big" for the book because he is neither rhetorically nor thematically suited to be its personal center.

He is, to be sure, its center in a variety of ways, which may be seen in his relationships with the principal characters of the book. His first encounter is with Menteith, who urges him to join Montrose's army as a paid officer. Menteith seems prudent and reasonable enough to know that an army needs its mercenaries. But while Montrose can accept this need as a fact of life, Menteith cannot, and for him Dalgetty remains one who "knows neither honour nor principle but his month's pay, who transfers his allegiance from standard to standard at the pleasure of fortune or the highest bidder" (174). For the Falstaffian Dalgetty, honor is to be tested against convenience; war is war, and all causes are to be looked upon sceptically.

"Loyalty" is your password, my lord; "Liberty," roars another chield from the other side of the strath; "the King," shouts one war-cry; "the Parliament," roars another; "Montrose for ever," cries Donald, waving his bonnet; "Argyle and Leven," cries a south-country Saunders, vapouring with his hat and feather . . . good watchwords all – excellent watchwords. Whilk cause is the best I cannot say. But sure am I that I have fought knee-deep in blood many a day for one that was ten degrees worse than the worst of them all [167–68].

His professional anti-idealism is an immediate rebuke and a provocation to any whose fidelities are more than contractual. Thus he is treated with everything from quiet contempt to active hostility by all those committed to any causes whatsoever. Only Montrose sees him merely as a "man of the times," necessary to the carrying on of a military enterprise. Montrose's pragmatism is vindicated at the expense of Menteith's idealism.

We begin to sense this when, having been confronted with Dalgetty's professional ethics, we meet his opposite in Allan M'Aulay. Whereas M'Aulay is fidelity carried to the extreme of fanaticism, Dalgetty is fanaticism's antidote. His loyalty is utterly free of fanaticism; he even serves as a shrewd mediator, although for strictly professional reasons. Yet Dalgetty is and is not a normative character. At the last, his contractual loyalty proves reliable, while Allan's strong, personal devotion is not, and Allan is seen as the destructive, disloyal force. An ironic logic determines, then, that in a book concerned with different kinds of loyalty, different grounds for loyalty, and the problem of determining their relative value, Dalgetty should receive Montrose's own horse as replacement for his own, and name it "Loyalty's Reward" (329). From the point of view of the judicious Menteith, Dalgetty remains despicable. But Dalgetty, when offered double salary by Argyle to betray Montrose, answers by attacking Argyle. And the most extended and emphatic manifestation of Dalgetty's capacity for loyalty is seen in his curious relationship to the outlaw MacEagh.

The bond between prudent mercenary and heroic outlaw is a rather grotesque variant of the Jarvie-Rob Roy kinship. But in the latter case the bond between such extremes signifies possible reconciliation, possible coordination of the values that they represent. A genuine sympathy between Jarvie and Rob is morally meaningful. In the case of Dalgetty and MacEagh, it is true that both expound a

radical independence, and both radical independences signify the breakup of stable traditional fidelities. The outlaw
lives strictly for self and family against both historic factions.
The mercenary lives strictly for self and professional name
and is available to both factions. But while their bond is
logically interesting, it remains humanly accidental, leading
nowhere. Fittingly, Dalgetty's final attempts to unite Ranald
and his traditional enemy M'Aulay under Montrose come to
nought. For this fanatic conflict is abruptly subordinated to
the sudden hostility between M'Aulay and Menteith, and
Dalgetty's mediatorial role loses whatever significance it has
acquired.

If Dalgetty's role as normative character is unsettled, his
role as itinerant observer seems unsuitable. At the outset we
expect to trace the problem of Dalgetty's professionalism
through its assimilation into Montrose's army together with
the contrasting idealism of Menteith. Instead, Dalgetty is
abruptly separated from the Montrose world and sent off on
an absurd errand to the Argyle country. The narrator's
purpose is to use him as an entertaining military observer of
enemy territory and of Argyle *chez lui*. His escape with
MacEagh permits him also to witness the wild customs of
the Children of the Mist. The effect of his observations is
consistently comic, and the comedy always focuses on his
own limitations or humors. In Dalgetty as observer, professional anti-idealism is minimized. Stressed instead are his
scholastic pedantry and his modern views of archaic mili-
tarism. In these views he is comic; in his pedantry he is a
bore. And in both there seems little connection with his initial significance – his anti-idealism, his strictly professional
loyalty.

If Dalgetty as observer is inappropriate, Dalgetty as historical symbol is unintegrated. As a "personage proper to the

125

time and country" (142), he would seem the type of character for which Scott has been most highly praised. "Scott's unequalled historical genius," writes Lukacs, "shows itself in the individual characteristics which he gives his leading figures so that they really concentrate in themselves the salient positive and negative sides of the movement concerned."[42] But the representative strains of Dalgetty's character are haphazardly joined. "The ludicrous combination of the *soldado* with the Divinity student of Marischal College," as Francis Jeffrey saw, "is entirely original."[43] The mixture may be lifelike, but of no historic significance. Pedantry as divinity student and pedantry as soldier are related without being jointly related to his charming and jovial anti-idealism. Moreover, comparison with a much lesser character – the divinity student turned swashbuckler, Nanty Ewart of *Redgauntlet* – reminds us that the author's enjoyment of his Falstaffian pedant is never translated into significant experience for Menteith, the protagonist of a new order, as for example MacIvor, Bradwardine, and Talbot become elements of Waverley's growth. There remains a large gap between the narrator's enjoyment of Dalgetty and the pattern of response and assessment in other characters. And thus Dalgetty's central position remains inexplicable.

In the unsuitability and the disunity of Dalgetty as observer, mediator, and symbol we can learn much of the nature of a true Waverley success. His pedantry as a military man becomes a kind of subjectivity, defiantly impervious to the value or mood of what he sees. His observations must, then, differ radically from those of other protagonist-mediators. Through them, unfamiliar scene and person acquire animation by being observed with the mixture of dread and fascination and baffled wonderment which, for the Waverleys seeking to fathom their mysterious destinies, animates everything observed. The mystery of their involvement is a necessary phase in the process of romantic self-discovery. Dalgetty is involved simply by choice, a choice professional, not moral. His mediation is professional, not ethical. His comic interest as a character can never really be fused with the moral interest awakened by the adventure in which he is central.

Is the failure inevitable with the transferral of the center of the "excursion" novel from the responsive mediatorial moderate to the static, representatively historical character type? Or is the failure simply in Dalgetty? The question calls for additional evidence. The exceptional nature of Dalgetty points to the more interesting exception of Jeanie Deans and implies that the alleged disproportions and discontinuities of *The Heart of Midlothian* may usefully be seen in the light of her exceptional nature as central character, as the static and exemplary, rather than the progressive and projective hero.

5. *THE HEART OF MIDLOTHIAN*

Every critical interpretation, however formalistic its protestations, is the creature of presupposition and anticipatory recollection – a truth attested to by recent discussions of "Scott's most significant piece of work," his "most comprehensive study of moral themes."[44] My purpose has been to challenge their shared postulate (it is never a demonstration) that *The Heart of Midlothian* is the only "live" Scott, to take as my point of departure the admirable heterodoxy of Tillyard, Lukacs, and Davie. But the way to accomplish my purpose is not to declare the inferiority of

127

The Heart of Midlothian. While in some ways overpraised, it has rarely been praised as a complete work of art. And each partiality gets stuck on the same formal crux: the economy of the post-trial chapters.

The *"Measure for Measure* school" has part of the truth. The novel invites consideration as an ambiguous analogue to the play in hanging a precarious balance of justice and mercy on a crime involving sexual license.[45] Any novel provoking comparison nowadays with *Measure for Measure* suffers for its unwitting presumption. Burkean and Christian Humanist alike make of the novel a parable of Law versus law versus instinct; P. F. Fisher, in one of the finest essays ever written on Scott's historical imagination, risks losing the novel in general reflections on Providence and Divine Law.[46] The philosophers of history make it a tragedy of historical determinism, then drop it like a hot potato when historicity recedes and romance enters to carry us off to a West Highland Arcadia. Daiches fits it to his "problem of heroic action" in a new, unheroic world.[47] Davie leaves it as an inferior analogue to Pushkin's *The Captain's Daughter.*[48] Welsh joins Mrs. Van Ghent, Mayhead, Craig, and others in finding it a novel of moral urgency and depth that went wrong.[49] Presupposition, ubiquitous, is inescapable, but regrettable nonetheless.

If we must have a frame of expectancies, why not one provided by the Author of Waverley himself in the other novels of divisive fanaticism, of cleavages in society caused by conscientious rigidities, the other projections of the difficulties of adjusting the strenuous ideal demands of an ultimate vision of Law to the personal demands of one's natural humanity as father, sister, friend? The other "Puritan" novels provide a necessary familiarity with the subject, and also supply structural and rhetorical clues.

Montrose warns us that when the moderate Cavalier or anti-Cavalier recedes into minor importance and some sort of extremist – Jeanie may be taken for one – becomes central, we should expect significant deviations from the Waverley pattern. Jeanie is no prudent or passive hero of society. Before we are through with her, her role has become mediatorial, and her mediatorial destiny has taken her on the romantic excursion suffered by other Waverley mediators, to win at last, for her and her dependent elders, a new and more humane stasis remote from history. But this is a later development. Likewise, the unimportance of Menteith in *Montrose* prepares us to deal with the unimportance of Reuben Butler in *The Heart of Midlothian*. In both cases control of the mediatorial function has been transferred, as in the "House" novels, *Mannering, The Antiquary, St. Ronan's Well*, to powerful providential agents, Montrose and Argyle.

Peveril prepares us to consider the relation of the "problem" of these novels – how to preserve humanity amid conflicting fanaticisms – to the typical second-half excursion. And this means expecting without prejudgment the transition from analytic novel to archetypal ("conventional," "theatrical") or projective romance, the world of gypsies, outlaws, and other "naturals." It suggests we watch carefully for the symbolic and thematic in such a world and in such a mixture of grotesques. The father-daughter relationship of Ganlesse-Christian and Fenella has its counterpart in the Meg-Madge connection, and both belong to the organizing principle of parental relations. Madge and her mother, Staunton and his father, directly linked in the "improbable" chapter of Jeanie's excursion in search of humanity, are logical elements in the full exposition and judgment of Effie's reckless, unfilial nature and Jeanie's dilemma. Most important, *Peveril* suggests another implication of the mid-way shift of worlds. It suggests that an issue, having reached its climax unresolved midway, may thereafter be moved into a new and different world where its original significance is either lost (as in *Peveril*) or seen in new terms, as in *The Heart of Midlothian*. Such a possibility is suggested when we find in the Peverils' trial an analogue to Jeanie's queen-scene and reconsider Effie's trial scene from the point of view of its later counterpart.

Finally, *Woodstock* urges that we grant the Author of Waverley his right to such a midway shift, to multiple climaxes, to a new beginning, as it were, with an ostensibly new center, a new suspense, even a new major character if he can justify them, make of them an appropriate resolution. In the case of *The Heart of Midothian,* this is the temporary concession even the most enthusiastic of interpreters seem unwilling to grant.

It is customary to acknowledge that in Jeanie's initial dilemma, as it is realized in early chapters, Scott is for once "sufficiently mastered by a theme" (Mayhead, 266) to dramatize coherently and movingly a "very nice question of rational principle" (Welsh, 128) in a treatment of law that "trembles at several points on the verge of a wider significance" (Pittock, 477). But alas, Scott the "conserva-tive" was "uncomfortable when confronted with an unsettl-ing ethical problem" (Fisher, 103). He avoided negotiating between opposing ethical commitments, and hence, the "moral pattern of the Waverley Novels takes the shape of an excursion, not an effort to resolve moral conflicts that Scott does not believe in resolving" (Welsh, 133–34). Having pledged to explore such conflicts, Scott "refuses to explore them in the concrete terms of aesthetic structure – presum-ably because he does not know that they are there" (Van

Ghent, 120). Blindered with "his comparatively simple 'prohibitions,'" Scott "cannot . . . follow out his significances right through the plot that embodies them" (Craig, 224). After the trial of Effie, then, we are confronted with "deadwood" (Craig, 217), with the "pressure of popular taste" (Mayhead, 267), with Scott's contractual obligations to his publisher and his "financial needs in building Abbotsford" (Van Ghent, 114–15). Such a riot of intentional fallacies and psychological irrelevance confuses questions of material motive with those of aesthetic value only at the risk of making of *Rasselas* and *In Memoriam* pawn tickets for a funeral and a honeymoon, and of sending such hacks as Shakespeare, Dryden, and Dickens to ignominy along with the lowly Author of Waverley and his fellow philistine Trollope. We begin by applauding Mrs. Van Ghent's insistence that a best novel cannot be a best half-novel,[50] and go on to deplore the way she and others have prejudged it.

There is no question about it: the novel divides in the middle. Jeanie is presented with rationalizations for "resolving" her dilemma by adjusting the conflicting demands of Law and law, Truth and truth. She refuses: she cannot accept them. She accepts the fact that she is determined by personal and hereditary code to deny her ability to make the adjustment in the terms proffered. The sun may shine and the rain fall, as Butler reminds Deans, on the just and the unjust; Jeanie's refusal to play sun or God strikes some as an act of severe pride. It is, rather, an act of theological humility and of moral and political realism. In its entirety the book says that her dilemma is not to be resolved speculatively. The actual human problem – the fate of Effie vis-à-vis the fate of many murdered infants – is what matters. Her dilemma is to be resolved in other ways at other levels of authority. The actual problem is historically fated to be inseparable from the historic accident of its connection with the Porteous affair. It is to be solved only by the kind of providential power or force which can manipulate the fatalities which have created it. The agents of such power are available to Jeanie only after she has refused to think herself capable of the adjustment and has, with an energetic faith in Providence and in the concrete humanity of political power, committed herself to her excursion, to the strangeness of her fate, and to dependence on human means for transcending the legalistic fanaticisms of both her father and the Saddletree world in behalf of a higher Law.

Of what significance, if any, then, is the nature of Effie's crime in itself? That depends on how we define it. Here an incautiously rigid application of the *Measure for Measure* analogy is quite misleading. The play evolves poetically in a dense atmosphere of diseased sexuality, and no such condition surrounds the narration of Effie's "sin." "The *real* 'crime' in Scott's novel," says Mrs. Van Ghent, "is also sexual indulgence – for Effie is guilty of no other." But, she complains, "never in the book is it even implicitly suggested that this *is* the crime." There is no other "structural motivation for Effie's long punishment"; yet we are given only "an absurd obscuration of whatever meaning sexual indulgence on the part of a person like Effie might have."[51] Donald Davie concurs. To counterbalance Jeanie's strength, Effie, he conjectures, must be made

so extremely weak that her weakness cannot be motivated nor accounted for by any features of temperament or environment. And in fact Scott never even attempts to justify or explain this weakness, not by analysis nor (and this is more damaging) by any direct presentation. Effie's susceptibility, on which the whole action turns, is not even defined, not even described, let alone analysed or accounted for.[52]

Obviously those seeking an incisive consideration of Effie's sexuality will feel disappointed, not because the Author of Waverley is the wrong author to give it, but because it would be largely irrelevant to the novel. Those dismayed, with David Craig, that "Scott has not the moral nerve to let Effie escape retribution for her 'sin' "[53] had better recognize that her "sin" is a small element in her unhappiness. Those who, with Welsh, see the contrast between the sisters strictly in terms of some passional calculus – Jeanie the plain-jane civil blonde who "defers to rule," Effie the "dark heroine" who surrenders rule to passion[54] – had better recognize that she is neither dark nor heroic, and that the book makes little allusion to her passion because that is not the point.

The crime for which Effie suffers is a continuing one: it is her nature, as that nature is defined and judged in the context of the book. Fisher sums it up best when he refers to Effie as an improvident, fatal character with a "capricious lack of integrity."[55] Effie herself concurs. Near the end, when she is the dazzling, secretly miserable Lady Staunton, her sister is struck by her self-possession in sustaining a fictitious role. "I daresay you are surprised at it," Effie replies "composedly," "for you, my dear Jeanie, have been truth itself from your cradle upwards; but you must remember that I am a liar of fifteen years' standing, and therefore must by this time be used to my character" (505). Secrecy is the legal cause of her conviction; secrecy is later accompanied by hypocrisy, fraud, and terror of discovery. Her life is a lie; she is socially false, and "the outworks and bulwarks of fiction and falsehood" (485) are founded on the earliest tracings of her capricious untruth. The "natural happy emotion" Craig finds admirable[56] is from the outset colored

133

by petulant wilfulness. Her "guileless purity of thought, speech, and action" (95) is tainted by "a little fund of self-conceit and obstinacy, and some warmth and irritability of temper" (96). She is an "untaught child of nature, whose good and evil seemed to flow rather from impulse than from reflection" (97), in a fictive world where such "nature," egoistically insistent on extreme freedom, ends in caprice, fraud, and barrenness.

The novel, moreover, must allow us to see it end there. Were the book to stop where many say it should, Effie's meaning would be far from complete. In her late letter to Jeanie, she is still the egotist; in their meeting we are increasingly aware of the excess of her "natural" vivacity, coupled with her ruthless disregard of the feelings of others (503–4). Her "natural irritability" (531) still makes her fitting companion to the reckless, melancholic Staunton and fitting mother to the fierce "Whistler." Her final confrontation with her son is an ironic gloss on Mrs. Van Ghent's complaint that Effie alone is endowed "with taste and passion and susceptibility to beauty."[57] Her "love of the picturesque" (511) takes this now mature "child of nature" deep into the woods near Knocktarlitie (509). The "nature" she finds is more picturesque than she bargained for and takes on the demonic character which Saint Leonard's Crags possessed for Jeanie when she met Robertson-Staunton there. The ragged gypsy boy, her own unrecognized son, is a "child of nature" too – the logical one to be born of the union of fatalistic recklessness and petulant, selfish vivacity.

It is important to realize that this is what the union is. Effie's devotion to Staunton is real enough; she loves him, she claims, as few women have ever loved (211). But it is a love for a false ideal, a theatrically unstable casuist; and repeatedly the book stresses that the source of her later misery is not her sexual sin but rather her devotion to this man, which she places above all other loyalties, duties, and truths. While she repeatedly endangers her own life to protect Staunton, she is grossly unfair to her sister – "I dinna deserve this frae ye, Effie" (213) – and it is after all she who, with Staunton's help, gives the reader the idea that Jeanie's refusal to lie is evidence of a stiff, indefensibly self-righteous temperament. Enough readers are convinced; few note that Effie herself makes a comparable and much less defensible choice. When she could save her own life, she remains silent; in vain she is offered "a commutation and alleviation of her punishment, and even a free pardon, if she would confess what she knew of her lover" (207). She "might have fled frae this tolbooth on that awfu' night wi' ane wad hae carried me through the warld, and friended me, and fended for me. But I said to them, let life gang when gude fame is gane before it" (214). It appears to be like Jeanie's kind of devotion and modesty, yet it is unstable and overly concerned with reputation. Caprice, lack of integrity, a selfish disregard for others, secrecy, a corrupting desire for social status, these are the qualities that make up the sin for which Effie's life is a punishment. Her crime is emphatically limited to child murder; the crime is presumed on the basis of her secrecy; it is her secrecy that most hurts the devoted Jeanie.

Where does the responsibility for Effie's nature lie? Pritchett insists that both sisters are "children of history."[58] Daiches argues that their differences attest to Scott's faith that history alone can never determine character: "Each is influenced by that aspect of history to which she is temperamentally most sympathetic."[59] Mrs. Van Ghent skirts the issue when she declares that the Cameronian training imposed by David Deans is nothing but local color.[60] Craig insists that "Effie is as much a natural, feminine reaction to severity and sobriety as Jeanie is its dutiful product."[61] The book insists otherwise. It blames Davie Deans for overindulgence and for a naive lapse of paternal authority. It blames him, too, for imposing his own special language and preventing natural domestic communication – and this blame he shares with his counterpart Saddletree. In both, fanaticism, religious and legalistic, is insuperably present as a special idiom, making natural discourse impossible;[62] both, therefore, serve *in loco parentis* to Effie, foster her impulse to secrecy. But Effie is also to blame when she seeks, out of shame and irritation, to remove herself from the inconvenient authority of her father and places herself under the equally naive supervision of Saddletree. In so doing she exchanges a situation in which she *might* communicate with her sister for another in which she *need* communicate with no one. The result of her petulance and caprice in removing herself from natural authority is the same as it is in the public area regarding the Porteous affair. When true authority becomes remote, the shell and the jargon of legality alone remain. Such is Edinburgh's plight with its royalty and parliament gone south, and such is the plight to which Effie commits herself in substituting Saddletree's house for her own. One person is clearly not to blame, and this is the person who inherits the full legalistic dilemma thus created.

That dilemma is not fairly to be stated in abstract terms as simply the problem of adjusting "truth" to "Truth," or "the valuable diversities and complexities of mankind" to "laws too abstract, too rigid, too impersonal."[63] To find, with Robin Mayhead, only an "ironic probing of the nature of justice"[64] in *any* age is to refuse the book its concrete concern. First

136

there is the individual element of Jeanie's natural devotion to truth. Second there is the complex of circumstances which make evasion of an admittedly extreme law impossible or ineffectual.

As for the first, too much has been made of Jeanie's truth-telling as historically conditioned reflex. Jeanie cannot tell a lie to save her sister's life, we are repeatedly told, because her tongue is bound by generations of Cameronian ancestors "who, after the civil war, waged wars of logic and turned a none too logical theology into a strait jacket of scruples."[65] This is true neither to history nor to the book. Jeanie has no "generations of Cameronian ancestors"; she has a father, and he proudly considers himself a Deanite. It is her sister's advocate who refers indiscriminately to "the peculiar tenets of these people" (226). True, she has been "educated in deep and devout reverence for the name and attributes of the Deity" (237). But she differs even from her father, in crucial ways: in practical humanity, in active providential faith. Her "love of and veneration for truth" are called "almost Quaker-like" (278), recalling not the garrulous and argumentative Deans but the mild and humane Joshua Geddes of *Redgauntlet*. With him she shares a devotion to the sacredness of human speech. Faced with the dilemma created by the confrontation of an inflexible legalism with an inflexible moralism, Jeanie's truth has no language to use. The word with which she answers the court's crucial question reminds us not of Isabella, but of another Shakespearian heroine, also caught in the face of impossibly conflicting demands with no adequate language. Asked what her sister told her, Jeanie replies, "Nothing" (240). She has no more choice than Cordelia; to say more would be to resort to the facile humanitarian untruth thrust upon both by the spokesmen of opportunistic flexibility. Cordelia's humane lie

137

would not have solved Lear's arrogant blindness; Jeanie's would not solve the problem of Effie's nature or of a cruel and fictional legalism. Jeanie knows this through her absolute faith in law.

Welsh strives to fit Jeanie into his pattern of the proper social hero; nowhere is the pattern more of a misfit. The attempt requires that Jeanie be ultimately social in her loyalties, that her "moral perception" be "fully committed to human as well as divine law."[66] The passage he quotes in support – Jeanie's speech to Robertson at Muschat's Cairn – makes clear, as a matter of fact, that compared with Effie, Jeanie is impervious to social pressures (159). It is Effie whose "loyalty extends first to society": her shame and secrecy and fraud prove it. Society for Jeanie is not "a collective resistance to individual passions."[67] It is a complex of appeals to her to solve the dilemma of its own legalism by compromising a higher Law. Its cowardly voice is heard in the words of the reckless outlaw Robertson and those of the benevolent fatalists of the law, Sharpitlaw and Middleburgh. The legalism of Saddletree and the outlawry that seeks to evade it are interdependent. Sharpitlaw must use Ratcliffe; Robertson, the leader of the Porteous mob, is unwitting accomplice of the helplessly abstract legalism of the Saddletree world. From all this world of social law Jeanie is set apart; as Fisher puts it, "The moral legality of Jeanie Deans is a divine legality distinguished from that of Saddletree by reason of its Source."[68] Far from committing herself, as Welsh claims, to the letter of the law, it is she alone that upholds its spirit and refuses to triumph by manipulating a mere legalism: "her clear and unsophisticated power of discriminating between good and evil instantly rejected an interpretation so limited and so unworthy of the Author of the law" (206). It is not that Jeanie alone thinks the law good or necessary. There is general agreement on this, even among benevolent people, as necessary to prevent child murder. But she is almost alone – the judge is the only other spokesman for the view – in holding that humanity is not served by evasive untruth. And so, temporarily, she becomes not the heroine of propriety, but the heroic fanatic, temporarily replacing the moderate protagonist of other Waverley Novels.

Reuben Butler, of course, is the mediatorial moderate in the tradition of Everard, Morton, and the rest. As he is displaced by Jeanie as narrative center, we become aware of the complexity the book shares with *Old Mortality*. For here, too, we are made aware of the apparently small distance between a truly humane prudence and a cynically reckless relativism masquerading as humane prudence. Butler speaks on behalf of tolerance and reconciliation, but so, too, does Robertson-Staunton. To arguments presented by such a spokesman, Jeanie can only reply with a temporary rejection of the "humanity" he and much of society urge upon her. It is to Robertson-Staunton that Jeanie gives her oft-quoted answer that she "canna . . . make that true which is false," that she fears not man, but God, who "will know the falsehood" (158–59). Her ultimate decision isolates her from every sort of social appeal; nowhere in social or domestic reality is anyone able to understand her refusal in the proper terms. It is highly significant, though usually overlooked, that Jeanie, supposedly the product of her father's conscience, makes her decision in spite of the conviction *that even her father* would have her do otherwise: "A sister's life, and a father pointing out how to save it! O God deliver me! this is a fearfu' temptation" (205). Such is her isolation. The decision is made regardless, and it is peculiarly her own.

But what is the decision? When Jeanie testifies, her thinking has already taken her beyond the dilemma which binds her father and Effie's other well-wishers. It is no longer what she had anticipated: that "she was to be dragged forward into the court of justice, in order to place her in the cruel position of either sacrificing her sister by telling the truth, or committing perjury in order to save her life" (204). She now knows that Effie must be saved, and by her; but the opportunistic way is not the way for humanity to triumph over divisive, abstract legalism. The intuition has come initially on her return from Muschat's Cairn. She hears her father praying, and the effect is a "strong confidence, that while she walked worthy of the protection of Heaven, she would experience its countenance." The words describing the revelation are significant:

It came, as she described it, on her mind, like a sun-blink on a stormy sea; and although it instantly vanished, yet she felt a degree of composure which she had not experienced for many days, and could not help being strongly persuaded that, by some means or other, she would be called upon and directed to work out her sister's deliverance [185].

It is this intuitive conviction that carries her through the trial, not a stern self-righteousness or social propriety. Note the emphatic difference between Jeanie and her father the morning of the trial:

The secret of this difference was, that Jeanie's mind had already anticipated the line of conduct which she must adopt, with all its natural and necessary consequences; while her father, ignorant of every other circumstance, tormented himself with imagining what the one sister might say or swear, or what effect her testimony might have upon the awful event of the trial [217].

140

She has emerged as more profoundly humane than her father. But from this moment on through the trial, we see Jeanie only from without; we are given no further image of vacillation or anxiety. We are left, then, sure that in refusing to lie, she is convinced another means, a human means demanding worldly virtues but not requiring the violation of divine law, will offer itself. The hint comes directly.

It comes, appropriately, from an allusion to the Porteous affair (254), and we are brought back to the second contextual delimitation of Jeanie's dilemma. The topical historicity of the Porteous affair plays a complex role in her problem. The entanglement of Effie's crime with the Porteous execution through Robertson-Staunton's role in both is merely the arbitrary plot inception of a rich network of implications. Mayhead and others stress the relevance of the mob's action to the novel's concern with the conflicting demands of true justice.[69] For our purposes, the important connections are three. First, the allusion to Porteous is, ironically, a reminder to Jeanie that king and queen grant pardons, though the outcome of the first pardon makes the second unlikely. Second, the Robertsonian-societal way of circumventing legalism is precisely the same in each case, and in each case Robertson is spokesman: he would lead the mob to kill Porteous, using outlawed means to see "true" or "natural" justice done; he would have Jeanie lie, use outlawed means, for the same end. When Jeanie sees the casuistry in his appeal, she is also rejecting the rationale of the intensely "lawful" outlaws that executed Porteous. Reuben Butler's helplessness as the mob's chaplain perfectly anticipates Jeanie's helplessness as legalism's scapegoat. The mob in its scrupulous lawfulness during its outlawed action is a perfect metaphor for the legalism that scrupulously observes its forms and mouths its idioms while expecting Jeanie to save it from the human consequences. Third, the Porteous affair is a specific condition of Effie's plight and Jeanie's dilemma, providing the Author of Waverley with his characteristic way of saying that such a dilemma is never to be resolved speculatively. Effie's plight is the function of two conditions: increase in child-murder to such an extent that humane authorities are determined to use the extreme law to discourage it; anger in the English court against Scotland on account of the Porteous execution, administered by Effie's lover, which makes her pardon unlikely. Since Effie's plight is the function of historic particulars, her survival must be plotted accordingly. Far from failing to resolve the book's dilemma, Jeanie alone recognizes the human means required.

The grounds on which she justifies her expedition are, in fact, her faith in the human reality of authority: "It's but speaking to a mortal man and woman when a' is done," she says of addressing the King and Queen. "And their hearts maun be made o' flesh and blood like other folks', and Effie's story wad melt them were they stane" (279). The voice she could not use in untruth can be used eloquently and shrewdly in an appeal for humanity. A letter won't do, for "we *must* try all means" and "writing winna do it: a letter canna look, and pray, and beg, and beseech, as the human voice can do to the human heart" (280). The heart will speak its own language. The heart that had seemed stonily unmoved by Effie's plea will show itself wisely humane, just as the prison of the title, the Heart of Midlothian, proves to possess humanity beneath its forbidding exterior. This revelation is completed only with the second great scene which serves as a response to the first. The book's two climactic scenes – Effie's trial and Jeanie's interview with the Queen – must be recognized as the logical succession in which the entire book finds its thematic center.

142

Remarking on likenesses between *The Heart of Midlothian* and Pushkin's *The Captain's Daughter,* Donald Davie singles out "the parallel which is too conspicuous to be missed," the similarity between Marya Ivanovna's interview with the Empress, and Jeanie Deans' interview with Queen Caroline. "The two scenes have too much in common," says Davie, "to leave it in doubt that the Scott episode was Pushkin's model in an unusually deliberate and immediate way."[70] The claim neglects ways in which Pushkin's scene more closely resembles Amy Robsart's appearance before Elizabeth in the gardens of Kenilworth, or Nigel's confrontation of James I at Greenwich. It does concede the chief difference: Pushkin's scene has no Duke of Argyle. The lack is crucial and helps us to recognize the significance of Argyle's role in the final chapters. But he is just one of the many complicating ironies in the Scott scene without parallel in the Pushkin.

Jeanie, having adhered fanatically to her code of truth-speaking, triumphs with the Queen through an eloquence combining humane compassion and diplomatic shrewdness. Her code still declares its presence: " 'No, madam,' answered Jeanie, happy that the question was so framed that she could, with a good conscience, answer it in the negative" (390). But whereas the languages in the book have so far been divisive, leaving the good person with only "nothing" for reply, here Jeanie manages to speak a language that can reach the Queen, just as previously she has happened upon the talisman of a common language with Argyle. What makes the feat remarkable and gives its narration its wonderfully suspenseful ironies, is the need to use two languages in perfect balance: the "language of the heart" and the language of diplomacy. In maintaining the balance, Jeanie does far better than her guide Argyle thinks possible. To the Queen he expresses the hope that "if your Majesty . . .

would condescend to hear my poor countrywoman herself, perhaps she may find an advocate in your own heart
more able than I am to combat the doubts suggested by
your understanding" (387). But having invoked the language of the heart, he cannot help but attempt to direct the
appeal in accordance with the language of diplomacy. Ironically, he forgets the extent to which the Queen is still
susceptible to human appeal. Jeanie's allusions to unnatural
parents and violators of the seventh commandment hit
home. The Duke is caught in utter surprise, and Jeanie,
with truth and prudence, succeeds far better than he thinks
possible. The result is a triumph of ironic vision, marking
Jeanie's victory over the dilemma of the trial.

But the vision sees a further condition of Jeanie's success
in the Duke himself. His powerful interest at the court of
Caroline and George is essential. Just as Morton survives by
Claverhouse's influence, so Jeanie's shrewd humanity
triumphs through Argyle's. To see influence as Scott's *deus
ex machina,* however, is to miss the point. Morton won
Claverhouse's influential support by his "generous principles." Jeanie wins Argyle's through a more complex set of
appeals. Thereafter, Argyle embodies the hope for reconciliation toward which the book moves. It is Jeanie's triumph
to bring into play the force for which he stands; Argyle, says
Fisher, "is the vehicle of a miracle which the persistent faith
of Jeanie Deans has effected."[71] To see the outcome, we
must have the final chapters, the final pastoral image of a
new world in which Butlers and Deanses are reconciled in
marriage and progeny, and where the demonic forces loosed
by Staunton and Effie are finally dissipated.

Far from being *deus ex machina,* Argyle's emergence as
resolution of Jeanie's speculative dilemma is prepared for by
the entire book. To see how is to recognize the novel's most

comprehensive and significant coherences. Fisher distinguishes Argyle as the man of Providence. He is also the man of traditional loyalties, and the landlord of active humane concern. He is the good paternalist in a world of ineffectual parents – Deans, old Dumbiedikes, Meg Murdockson, Staunton, even Effie herself.

Historic fatality having linked Jeanie's dilemma and Effie's plight with the Porteous affair, the problem must be resolved by a force that can deal with such historic particulars, that can subordinate historic fatality to other powers – the powers of personal and national loyalty, and of humane concern. The initial appeal to Argyle is grounded in personal historic loyalties. Argyle owes help to one who comes in the name of Reuben Butler's ancestral loyalty to Argyle. Thus, Butler's background, which serves in the world of Davie Deans as a divisive force, becomes for Argyle just the opposite. In other ways, too, the divisiveness embodied in Davie Deans implies social and linguistic conciliation in Argyle. Jeanie's historic fate is to be the child of Davie. By committing herself to that fate, yet preserving a natural humanity, she earns the protection of Providence, and Argyle as providential agent supersedes the divisive heritage of Deans. As Deans is the center of the first half of Jeanie's experience, so Argyle is the center of the second. As Jeanie fails to communicate with her father, so for Argyle her Scotch tongue is an emblem of all that makes her humanly precious. We see, then, as two parts of the same phenomenon Jeanie's efforts at speech, the trial and the interview, and the characteristic importance to the Author of Waverley of speech as a moral and social act.

Argyle is not just the antidote to Deans. His other chief role, that of landlord, is also anticipated by sharp contrast in the older Dumbiedikes. The novel is framed in pastoral

145

images. In each pastoral situation, the problem is how to reconcile opposing fanaticisms – Deans and Butlers. Old Dumbiedikes is the first landlord to provide a setting, but he does so only at the point of death, and it doesn't last. At the beginning Butler's ancestry is the obstacle; at the end it leads Argyle as landlord to accomplish what old Dumbiedikes was too limited and eccentric to do. Thus, much of the early book anticipates the necessary later role of Argyle.

But perhaps the most interesting connective link between the first part and Argyle is also the least obvious. Jeanie's earlier protector, Ratcliffe, is the outlaw in service of the law, with loyalties transcending legality. His complex role is an essential link between Jeanie's earlier dilemma and her later triumph with Argyle. First, he clearly anticipates Argyle's interest in his demonstration of Jeanie's capacity for engaging the hearts of the most unlikely people, forcing lawyers, magistrates, outlaws, dukes, queens, to discover their own humanity. Second, he is the one who refuses to take the law too seriously. His reflections on the helplessness of the law, recalling Pompey and Escalus in Act II of *Measure for Measure,* his insistence that the law's bark is "waur than her bite," that "the auld jade is no sae ill as that comes to" (139) – all provide a hint that legalism will be transcended and suggest that he is an instrument by which the law may be made more adaptable to human realities. His disillusioned prudence, grounded in a healthy attachment to life (it is fitting he should try to seduce Jeanie as well as help protect her), finds its match, on a higher level, only in that of Argyle. Third, it is from the realization of Ratcliffe's survival that Jeanie gets her determination to make her trip (256). And while Ratcliffe as turnkey swears Effie will never escape, *he* is the one who sends Jeanie to "Scotland's friend" Argyle and provides her with protection en route.

His loyalties transcend his prudent involvement with the law; Jeanie carries his letter as well as Butler's, and through it Ratcliffe's influence in the outlaw world protects her until she comes under the protection of Argyle's influence in a higher, but perhaps not essentially different world of court politics. That protective influence carries her safely through the romance – Fisher rightly sees it as a purgatorial[72] – world of the pilgrimage as surely as any other Waverley hero moves through the same kind of romance world with an invisible but human protective influence. It is appropriately in this romance world that she confronts the logical connection between the mad, pathetic Madge Wildfire and the reckless, theatrical Staunton. She survives the incursion into romance, as the other heroes do, through a mixture of natural worth and the prudent use of human means.

Finally, Ratcliffe is symbolic proof of the truth of the novel's titular paradox. The prefatory discussion between Peter Pattieson and the barrister plays wittily on the traditional name of the Edinburgh Tolbooth. "The metropolitan county," observes Pattieson, "may, in that case, be said to have a sad heart."

"Right as my glove, Mr. Pattieson," added Mr. Hardie; "and a close heart, and a hard heart. Keep it up, Jack."
"And a wicked heart, and a poor heart," answered Halkit, doing his best.
"And yet it may be called in some sort a strong heart, and a high heart," rejoined the advocate [8].

Just as the ostensibly close, hard heart of Jeanie is proved strong and high, so she proves somewhat the same of various unlikely people, even the Tolbooth's jailer. Ratcliffe has a conscience – "a'body has a conscience, though it may be ill wunnin at it" (172) – and a heart: "And what is that I am

147

doing now?" thought Ratcliffe. "But I'll hae nae wyte of Robertson's young bluid, if I can help it" (180). The prison, as Fisher wisely notes, has a variety of functions, replacing as symbolic and traditional landmark the ancestral house at the center of *Waverley, Old Mortality, Woodstock,* and numerous others to be noted. It is symbol of traditional law and order, center of the historical event, "the outward and visible sign of the theme itself." It is the "stark emblem" of "the negative aspect of the law."[73] But, in the transactions within its walls between Ratcliffe and Jeanie, it stands revealed as a sign that the search for humanity will overcome the prediction that "naebody's nails can reach the length o' Lunnon" (37), that the grim prison can provide "new pages of the human heart" (10), and that those pages and the reconciling they record will survive even the now vanished old Heart of Midlothian itself.

Where does such a reading leave *The Heart of Midlothian* relative to other Waverley Novels? In the realizing of the ordeal of personal involvement in historic crisis it cannot approach *Waverley* or *Old Mortality.* In narrative economy and imaginative unity, not just *Old Mortality,* but also *Quentin Durward* and *The Bride of Lammermoor* may be superior. Significant thematic coherence is achieved possibly more explicitly with the commanding question of historic fatality in *The Bride,* the question of loyalty in *Durward* and *Kenilworth,* the question of courage in *The Fair Maid of Perth.* But while its coherences and proportions must remain controversial, and while its exemplary protagonist must continue to have a static and ambivalent effect on many readers, the foregoing discussion has, I hope, shown ample cause why it remains among the most impressive of the novels.

Where does it leave our concern with the Cavalier-Presbyterian subject matter? On this no conclusive word may be spoken until we have considered the remaining areas. It is safe to say that the Enlightenment humanitarian side of the Author of Waverley could find in no other area a subject more congenial than the one shared by *Old Mortality, Woodstock,* and *The Heart of Midlothian.* But while the Enlightenment humanitarian remained a part of the author of *Ivanhoe,* *The Fair Maid, The Bride,* he stood sometimes in the ambiguous presence of the fatalist for whom historic survival might not always be so providentially plotted.

SECTION THREE

THE HISTORICAL PICTURESQUE AND THE SURVIVALS OF CHIVALRY

THE distance from *The Heart of Midlothian* (1818) to *Ivanhoe* (1819) seems huge. It is smaller, however, than critical orthodoxy recognizes. *Ivanhoe's* inferiority is not to be explained in the simple categories customarily imposed: Scots versus non-Scots, recent versus remote, "reality" versus "tushery" and "pasteboard." That most of the early novels came from "living memory" and most of the later ones from "bookwork" has been claimed, and the exaggeration implies a naive misrepresentation of the creative process. Even were it not exaggerated, the claim would be irrelevant. The "life" of fiction is not to be judged genetically, but pragmatically and rhetorically. The "life" of *The Abbot, Durward,* and *The Fair Maid,* while it may differ from that of *The Antiquary, Rob Roy,* and *Montrose,* is less doubtful.

It would be pointless to attempt to show that some later Waverley Novels are superior to some earlier ones, though that proposition is often implied in what follows. My purpose, rather, is to recognize, in the novels of more remote epochal reconstruction, not merely a freshly marketable commodity, but a distinctively new subject matter. Ian Jack properly stresses the importance for Scott of the concept of the picturesque; he insists on the ideally picturesque character of the eighteenth century, yet his most significant illustrative quotation is from the introduction to the Renaissance *Fortunes of Nigel*, and his most convincing citation of picturesque structure is *Quentin Durward*.[1] The quest for the historical picturesque, for the animating principle of social and moral contrast, found a new imaginative freedom in the very remoteness of the new subject matter, in its susceptibility to a more freely symbolic rendering. Thus the symbolic contrasts of Richard and John, of Burgundy and Louis, of Elizabeth and Mary, provide controlling picturesque structures for most of the books discussed in this section. And each structure is focused on the moment of crisis which determines the survival of one member of the pair. All of the critical moments, with their animating polarities of historic-symbolic character, have in common a concern with the same process: the decadence of chivalry, and with the same question: is there a spirit, are there essential values, in chivalry whose historic survival would be desirable?

For Scott, chivalry is romantic Cavalierism and Jacobitism in a more remote, more abstract, and perhaps, paradoxically, a more permanent form. Scott examined it first as the motivating impulse of the Crusades, and we had best begin with the Crusader novels as a group, though they extend from *Ivanhoe* (1819) over several years to *The Betrothed* and *The Talisman* (both 1825) and to *Count Robert of Paris* (1831). We can then turn back to the new departure that followed directly on *Ivanhoe, The Monastery* (1820), and view the line of Renaissance novels – Scott's most remarkable achievements in historiography – through *The Abbot* (1820), *Kenilworth* (1821), and *The Fortunes of Nigel* (1822). Finally, we can examine together the renderings of medieval France and Scotland – *Quentin Durward*

(1823) and *The Fair Maid of Perth* (1828) – and their claims to be considered the most effective of the entire group.

All of these are the novels taken least seriously now. They will never be taken seriously until close critical attention determines whether they are worthy of notice. Yet, they are so numerous and dense that our scrutiny must be more selective than hitherto. The compromise must seem somewhat arbitrary.

1. IVANHOE AND OTHER CRUSADERS

For generations of juvenile enthusiasts it was easy to see in *Ivanhoe* only the quintessence of chivalric adventure. The critical reader now finds it difficult to account for such blinders. Recently we have been reminded of the book's stringently antichivalric attitude, one more expression of the Author of Waverley's "anti-Romanticism."[2] But a book subject to such contradictory interpretations must be more complex than either extreme has recognized. If the book conveys a complexity of attitude which it fails to control, we may at least hope for a further articulation of that complexity in the later Crusader novels.

All four books provide ample passages which unequivocally damn the reckless inhumanity of romantic chivalry. The most bitter in *Ivanhoe* appear at strategic points. At the end of the tournament, the climax of the novel's first third, appears the narrator's sharply ironic recapitulation:

Thus ended the memorable field of Ashby-de-la-Zouche, one of the most gallantly contested tournaments of that age; for although only four knights, including one who was

152

smothered by the heat of his armour, had died upon the field, yet upwards of thirty were desperately wounded, four or five of whom never recovered. Several more were disabled for life; and those who escaped best carried the marks of the conflict to the grave with them. Hence it is always mentioned in the old records as the "gentle and joyous passage of arms of Ashby" [119–20].

The theme is dramatically stated during the bloody siege of the castle, when Rebecca asks of Ivanhoe's chivalry if possession by "a demon of vainglory" brings "sufficient rewards for the sacrifice of every kindly affection, for a life spent miserably that ye may make others miserable?" (275)

The Betrothed portrays an England left by its quixotic Crusading rulers to disorder and decay, and thus gives full expression to the same critique of chivalry. Its spokesman for Rebecca's general position is the Jarvie-like burger, Wilkin Flammock, who, when asked by the departing constable to care for his betrothed during his absence, replies: "Let those who lost the Holy Sepulchre regain it, my lord. . . . If those Latins and Greeks, as they call them, are no better men than I have heard, it signifies very little whether they or the heathen have the country that has cost Europe so much blood and treasure" (198). Later, to his daughter, he defines his attitude: "This is one of your freaks, now, of honour or generosity; but commend me to prudence and honesty. Ah! Rose, Rose, those who would do what is better than good sometimes bring about what is worse than bad!" (239)

In *The Talisman* we are shown the diseased state of chivalry itself, in the decline of its pretentious idealism, in the poisonous rivalries that surround the arrogant imprudence of a Richard much less Romantic than his ancestor of *Ivanhoe*. The hero, Sir Kenneth, is by contrast guilty only of reckless naïveté:

153

Sir Kenneth had full leisure to enjoy these and similar high-souled thoughts, fostered by that wild spirit of chivalry which, amid its most extravagant and fantastic flights, was still pure from all selfish alloy – generous, devoted, and perhaps only thus far censurable, that it proposed objects and courses of action inconsistent with the frailties and imperfections of man [133].

His teacher, Rebecca's counterpart, and like her an oriental humanitarian healer, is the noble Saladin, whose function in the tale may be defined as at once a critique and a transcendence of the "wild spirit of chivalry." The counter-pointing throughout of Richard and Saladin reaches its climax when the Soldan rejects the King's earnest plea for single combat – "half smiling at Coeur de Lion's affectionate earnestness for the combat" (313) – in the name of political and social responsibility; and in his voice humane prudence more effectively repudiates chivalric folly than at any point in *Ivanhoe*.

Finally, in *Count Robert* and his quixotic amazonian wife, the "wild spirit of chivalry" appears to have dwindled into an inconvenient joke. Count Robert's critic is Hereward, the Saxon guard, for whom Robert is "a wild knight-errant, incapable of being influenced by anything save his own wayward fancy" (127). Hereward's efforts to aid Robert are constantly being opposed by Robert's own knight-errantry: "not even the extreme danger of my lady," he vows, "shall make me break through the rule of a fair fight." The indignant but amused Hereward promises to "arrange matters according to thy pleasure, so that thou findest out no more fantastical difficulties; for, by my word, an affair so complicated in itself requires not to be confused by the finespun whims of thy national gallantry" (255–56).

All four Crusader novels, then, seem to regard chivalry as

a mixture of heroic folly and dangerous imprudence, confirming the pejorative suggestions of Scott's "Essay on Chivalry" (1818), that the institutions of chivalry, however pure its theory, often and soon deteriorated – "love into licentiousness," "spirit of loyalty or of freedom into tyranny and turmoil," "generosity and gallantry into hare-brained madness and absurdity"; that the ends were too often the carrying of "every virtuous and noble sentiment to the most fantastic extremity" and "that indifference for human life, which is the usual companion of intolerant zeal."[3] But this is to oversimplify all four books. A safer method is to replace the spokesmen for chivalry and antichivalry in their narrative contexts.

An abstract view of *Ivanhoe* would find in Richard and Rebecca spokesmen for opposed extremes, with loyal, hapless Wilfred of Ivanhoe somewhere between. It is typical of the kind of complexity to which the Author of Waverley often commits himself that the antichivalric Rebecca is the most Romantic conception in the book, while her chivalric opposite Richard is one of the least. Rebecca's memorable orations are easily interpreted, but her meaning in the story is only to be worked out in terms of the various shifting relationships to which she belongs.

The first is defined in the early linking of Saxon and Jew under the heading of the disinherited. Isaac and Cedric, like Robin of Locksley, are representative of defeated, disinherited lineages. Both are mocked and persecuted by Norman chivalry. Both are fanatically dedicated to their cultural pasts. Both admit defeat at the end, Cedric by accepting his son and his son's Norman king, and Isaac by leaving England. Both by virtue of their tragic commitments to lost heritages are tempted to sacrifice their natures as fathers. Ivanhoe and Rebecca share the plight familiar to Scott protagonists: the pathos of disinheritance and divided loyalties, the imperative to be loyal to fathers whose bequest is fanaticism and alienation and yet to transcend their fathers' commitments in the interests of an enlightened humanity. Ivanhoe's dependence on Rebecca is an encounter with his own plight in a more exotic form, and at the climax of his helplessness he must prove himself by repaying his debt to her.

Scott's readers were distressed that the complex bond between Ivanhoe and Rebecca did not end in marriage.[4] The obvious reasons may be insufficient but they should be recognized. Rebecca's unspoken love for Ivanhoe is ultimately part of the tragedy of her alienation. A sudden romantic reciprocity between Ivanhoe and Rebecca at the end would require a thorough revision. She remains a victim, sees herself an "unnatural child," "who forgets the desolation of Judah, and looks upon the comeliness of a Gentile and a stranger" (277). The conflict between Ivanhoe and his father focuses throughout on the love of Ivanhoe and Rowena. Welsh is considerably ingenious to account for Rebecca's rejection[5] in terms of Scott's later comments, which do indeed seem contradictory: (1) Rebecca's nobility would be cheapened by the attainment of her wishes; (2) Rebecca's "passion" for Ivanhoe was "rashly formed or ill-assorted" anyway (xviii). However interesting Scott's later observations may be, they have little bearing on our reading of the novel. The novel's facts are plain. Rowena may be less interesting, but she is stunningly beautiful, and Ivanhoe is from the outset deeply in love with her.

Rebecca's place in Ivanhoe's experience is complicated by her pursuit by Brian de Bois-Guilbert, and in turn by the sustained hostility of Brian toward Ivanhoe. For Ivanhoe,

Rebecca is not an object of romantic devotion, but a paragon of humane gentleness and skill. This role is climaxed when, during the siege, she becomes an eloquent castigator of chivalry. Thereafter she is the prisoner of Brian, and our main question is whether she will accept Brian. To interpose Ivanhoe at the point of her rejection of Brian would be to confuse the question; moreover, an abrupt courtship with Ivanhoe after Brian's intense passion would seem anticlimactic at best in a novel given to anticlimax. Her passionate involvement with Brian during two-thirds of the novel makes any but the present pathetic resolution inconceivable.

Marriage in a Waverley historico-political romance symbolizes fruitful cultural reconciliation and continuity. The impossibility of the union of Brian and Rebecca is as meaningful as the inevitability of the union of Ivanhoe and Rowena. Each suggests a new beginning, but in the Waverley context a new beginning is made possible only by the discovery of a viable continuity. The Brian-Rebecca union implies no continuity; it is too "new." Ivanhoe's feelings for Rebecca, we hear, are conditioned by the prejudices of his time; Brian claims to be free from such prejudices, but his dissolute nihilism implies that this is freedom gone to excess, freedom utterly negative or destructive. Only on such a nihilist basis could the union of Brian and Rebecca be built. The process of reconciliation and fruitful continuity which culminates in the union of Ivanhoe and Rowena thus requires, however tragically, the sacrifice of Brian – however valid his freedom – and Rebecca – however valid her humanity. A marriage between Wilfred's Saxonism and Rebecca's Judaism would be hugely appropriate in a Disraeli novel but meaningless in *Ivanhoe*.

There is, finally, Scott's rhetorical problem of how to give Brian the effect his significance demands without utterly starving Ivanhoe's proper role. They must be seen in counterpoint, not as passion versus propriety, but as related but distinct attitudes toward tradition and freedom: Brian's egoistic and nihilistic, Ivanhoe's selfless and faithful. To make Ivanhoe Brian's rival in love would be to lose Ivanhoe's separate significance altogether, to remove even the slight insulation that at present saves poor Ivanhoe from oblivion. Such insulation, I take it, is the point of their several indecisive battles. At the beginning Wilfred has been victor in past skirmishes. At the first tournament he defeats Brian, yet in victory he is seriously wounded and remains incapacitated for the remaining two-thirds of the novel. When he meets Brian in the final battle, Brian is fighting against his will, and Ivanhoe is almost too weak to sit on his horse; the effect is a travesty of chivalric jousting. No one can win; the outcome is wholly symbolic. Ivanhoe makes his sacrificial gesture on behalf of Rebecca's humanity; Brian, through a chivalric form of old Krook's combustion-syndrome (see *Bleak House*), dies of his own internal disorder. Providence in history saves one as worthy, rejects the other as self-destructive.

It is notable, however, that during this final encounter the chief agent of this providence in Ivanhoe's earlier perilous survivals is kept out of the picture. Such may be the only way to save the titular hero from oblivion. Or it may be the way of indicating that whereas Wilfred survives, Richard ultimately does not. Whatever the motive, the effect climaxes the structural evolution of our second of the book's "most absorbing" characters, Richard Coeur de Lion.

Richard's role is, for most of the way through, positive and constructive. P. F. Fisher has noted that his is a distinctly providential role as against the fatalism of John.[6] That role is confused by the late introduction of the theme of Richard's reckless knight-errantry, which is later to become the central problem of *The Talisman*. Studying the structure, one suspects it occurred to Scott only late in the writing of *Ivanhoe* that central to his vision of Crusader chivalry was the problem of Richard and his heroic, feckless romanticism, a problem he later dramatized in the Burgundy of *Durward* and *Anne of Geierstein*. Consider Richard's emergence in the book's total structure.

The book is symmetrically designed in three equal parts, each reaching its climax in a great military spectacle: the first the Ashby tournament; the second the liberation from the castle of Front-de-Boeuf; the third the trial by combat of Rebecca. The introductory chapters are skillfully manipulated to draw together all character groups for the tournament: Cedric and the Saxons; Brian and John's Norman gang; Isaac and Rebecca. The problem of seating at the tournament provides a preliminary sketch of the cultural animosities that fragmentize the world of the novel. Ivanhoe is present only as the mysterious palmer; because we don't know his identity, he remains wholly external – ironically during the only part of the novel in which he is physically active and impressive.

The same paradox is almost true of Richard. He does not appear until he fights as the mysterious Black Knight during the second day of the tournament. Here he is effective but reticent, serving only as a providential agent to save Ivanhoe. He then disappears until the scene of his jovial midnight feast with Friar Tuck. Our impression here is of a flexible, fun-loving, heroic fighter; the friar sees in him "a man of prudence and of counsel" (153). He combines the best of chivalric *virtu* with natural humanity and a love of life; he is alert, always ready to act as providential protector of other characters, as he proceeds to do in leading the forces

of liberation against Front-de-Boeuf's castle. We are still
admitted to none of his private reflections; his identity
remains implicit. But his meaning in this second or central
third is clear, and this is the part during which the novel's
thematic interests most clearly and effectively emerge.

Indeed, the combination of structural craft and thematic
richness makes the middle third of *Ivanhoe* equal as narrative to anything in the novels. And throughout, Richard as
character is paramount, just as Richard's significance is the
triumphant resolution. It opens in transition from the tournament through a severely critical portrayal of John and his
followers, who have just received word that Richard is on
his way home. Richard's domestic enemies are thus facing
the crucial question of what to do. If the novel were to
become antichivalric delineation of Richard as imprudent
knight-errant, the theme would surely appear here in a
contrast of John and Richard. But no mention is made of it.
The problem is simply that John's followers despise him;
that John himself is again and again made ineffectual by
petulance and levity. It thus seems inevitable that the
novel's historic climax will be the confrontation of Richard
and John, and that John's forces will quickly disintegrate.
Indeed, they begin to disintegrate at once. At the time John
summons them to York, his chief supporters, De Bracy, Bois
Guilbert, and Front-de-Boeuf, go off in pursuit of their own
selfish, romantic ends to kidnap Rowena, Rebecca, Isaac,
and Cedric. Thus the image of John's faction is consistently
one of imprudent and divisive selfishness, in immediate
contrast with the image of the Black Knight in the company
of Friar Tuck and Locksley's crew.

There is another side to this contrast. The same middle
section supplies the first significant delineation of Richard's
other opposition, the diehard Saxonists. While this force is

more affable or moral than that of John's Normans, it, too, suffers from divisive rigidity. Cedric, recognizing his disinherited son in the wounded victor Desdichado, becomes torn between conflicting impulses: "Nature had asserted her rights, in spite of the patriotic stoicism which laboured to disown her" (164). Rowena defines the alternatives open to him when she warns "lest what you mean for courage and constancy, shall be accounted hardness of heart," to which, complicating the thematic problem, he replies, "thine is the hard heart, which can sacrifice the weal of an oppressed people to an idle and unauthorized attachment" (164). We think of unnatural – i.e., "Jacobin," ideologue – parents in Jacobite and Cavalier novels alike when we are told of Cedric, "The restoration of the independence of his race was the idol of his heart, to which he had willingly sacrificed domestic happiness and the interests of his own son" (167). For his son he has substituted the absurd Saxon Pretender Athelstane the Unready, and the ludicrousness of the artificial bond is symbolic. Cedric is too unnatural, Athelstane too concerned for animal nature. His only interest is food and drink (191). When they are attacked in the woods, Cedric is too ready to fight, Athelstane not ready enough. Together they embody the hapless imprudence and disorder of Saxonist fanaticism. Such is Richard's other opposition. Against both, he, with natural vigor and good sense, with firm allies in the natural good (the woodsmen of Robin of Locksley), is sure to prevail.

His victory is assured by the internal chaos of Front-de-Boeuf's castle, a chaos articulated with striking formal precision. Leading up to the siege is a carefully paralleled sequence of four simultaneous scenes, each terminated by the same winding of the attackers' horn. First is the comic scene in which Cedric's faith in Athelstane receives ludicrous comment when Athelstane delivers his defiance with his mouth full. Then come Front-de-Boeuf's cruel threats to roast Isaac alive unless he pays a huge ransom, a fate to which, when he learns Rebecca has been given to Brian, Isaac heroically submits himself. Third is Rowena's haughty rejection of De Bracy's "jargon of a troubadour" (204), an hauteur shattered when she hears she can save Ivanhoe and Cedric only by submitting to De Bracy. His offer softens her, her resistance softens him, and both are more natural for the encounter. Climactically comes Brian's first attempt to win Rebecca, and already Brian is so captivated that he vows to share all with her. In each scene, then, a reciprocal humanizing, a comic or pathetic restoration of nature, takes place. The battle continues the process.

The battle itself is densely and meaningfully rendered through two parallel scenes. In each, a woman, nursing a wounded man, recounts to him what is going on outside in the siege. In the first, the true healer Rebecca preaches peace and reconciliation to Ivanhoe throughout her narration. In the second, her hideous counterpart, the Saxon sybil-hag Ulrica, vengefully torments Front-de-Boeuf, telling him she has set fire to the fuel magazine under the room. She literally roasts the dying man alive, as he had sworn to do to Isaac, and destroys herself in the same fire. In scorning her for having lived *par amours* with the Norman conqueror, Cedric, she charges, had burst the last tie which united her to her kind (239). Thus, all in the castle have participated in the inhumanity or unnaturalness which the disorder signifies. All suffer a humanizing, however slight or however destructive, before the providential force of Richard and Locksley sets them free. Nor is it an accident that even Cedric is forced to escape from the castle disguised in a friar's habit smuggled to him by his jester; for in this ludicrous disguise he is forced to learn a humane duplicity, a wise prudence.

Ivanhoe's role in the educative process has been suggested. He is forced into passivity; he is forced to hear hatred and contempt expressed for his romantic chivalry. Moreover, he is forced to interpret his helplessness, to make the kind of comment the hapless Waverley protagonist often has wrung from him: "It seems as if I were destined to bring ruin on whomsoever hath shown kindness to me" (263). But such fatalism is a dangerous spiritual error.[7] Rebecca warns him he has misjudged the purposes of Heaven and defies his temporary fatalism with her own providential faith, as later she does with the irrevocable fatalist Brian. "Thou and I," says Brian, "are but the blind instruments of some irresistible fatality, that hurries us along, like goodly vessels driving before the storm, which are dashed against each other, and so perish." "Thus," she replies, "do men throw on fate the issue of their own wild passions" (386). Like Richard she plays a providential role; like him she seems herself to be beyond the protection of Providence.

In all of this education in Providence and humanity Richard appears to have nothing to learn. His education is of a different kind, and it continues through the middle third and on into the final section. In answer to Cedric's offer of reward, the Black Knight replies, "Cedric has already made me rich . . . he has taught me the value of Saxon virtue" (306). Later he justifies his desire to attend Athelstane's funeral as a way to "see your Saxon kindred together, Sir Wilfred, and become better acquainted with them than heretofore. Thou also wilt meet me; and it shall be my task to reconcile thee to thy father" (390). Richard is thus fully engaged, not just in fighting as Locksley's ally, but also in educating himself to the realities of his divided

163

nation, to his own role as reconciler and leader of a united England. He is thus the moral and political center of the book and the fitting object of Ivanhoe's fidelity.

Abruptly, however, at the end of the book's second third, our image of Richard is distorted by warnings that Richard is irresponsible. The first hint is seen in his extreme fearlessness before the gates of the besieged castle. Later, the note is sounded by John's follower Fitzurse: "Such is indeed the fashion of Richard – a true knight-errant he, and will wander in wild adventure, trusting the prowess of his single arm, like any Sir Guy or Sir Bevis, while the weighty affairs of his kingdom slumber, and his own safety is endangered" (330). Of course, Fitzurse is no reliable judge; and so far, the Black Knight's anonymity allows us no chance for assessment through an interior look at Richard. But in the final sixth of the novel, the narrator builds his case emphatically. Richard refuses to let Ivanhoe accompany him and sets out alone with Wamba the jester to "play priest or fool as I shall be most in the humour" (390). Sensing danger, Ivanhoe, who progressively assumes the role of prudent counselor, sets out after him. The point of the image of Richard here is unmistakable: "the whole gesture and look of the champion expressed careless gaiety and fearless confidence" (394). Shortly, Wamba tricks him out of Locksley's horn and saves his life in spite of Richard's determination to seek no help. The now judicious Ivanhoe sounds the theme fully: "Why – oh why, noble Prince, will you thus vex the hearts of your faithful servants, and expose your life by lonely journeys and rash adventures, as if it were of no more value than that of a mere knight-errant, who has no interest on earth but what lance and sword may procure him?" (408) Shortly, "Wilfred bowed in submission, well knowing how vain it was to contend with the wild spirit of chivalry." The narrator is thus justified in interposing his own full statement: "In the lion-hearted king, the brilliant, but useless, character of a knight of romance was in a great measure realized and revived; and the personal glory which he acquired by his own deeds of arms was far more dear to his excited imagination than that which a course of policy and wisdom would have spread around his government" (409). Richard was forced to recognize and resign himself to his dependence on two good counselors – Ivanhoe and his grave advice, Locksley and his prudent trickery. Thus, his positive function in the novel has, by the time his identity is revealed, become lost in the "anti-Romantic" interpretation of his historical character, whose late introduction is both anticlimactic and confusing.

There are other anticlimaxes which confuse the world of conflict in which Richard's reconciling humanity is the central force. There is the outcome of Athelstane's death, presumably the dying out of the Saxon cause and the occasion for Richard's bid for unity with the Saxons. Here Scott committed what he later thought the unpardonable sin of bringing the doltish Athelstane back to life.[8] This is actually a happy sin; it makes the same comment made by the end of *Redgauntlet*. The Saxon cause does not die a rigidly heroic death; it hangs on with a pathetic and foolish life, and Cedric can sustain no more pretenses.[9] Throughout, Athelstane has been a dull fool, a devastating comment on Cedric's dreams. For him to be mourned as the death of heroic Saxonism would be completely illogical. His coming back to life is a proper touch, but it undercuts Richard's serious funereal plea for new unity.

The other anticlimax is the late introduction of the Grand Master of the Temple, Lucas Beaumanoir, who arrives to clean up his Order in England and almost to burn Rebecca as a witch. His late arrival seems a serious formal flaw. Yet his role is logical enough. He provides an ecclesiastical counterpart to Cedric in his rigid inhumanity, and in his defeat the hopelessness of the other lost cause of chivalric monasticism is dramatized. Bois Guilbert's life and ambition are threatened by Lucas's presence. He strains to transcend his fatalistic cynicism and prove his devotion to Rebecca, but ambition and pride win out, and his mysterious death (which is "unreal") is a counterpart to Athelstane's "death" (also unreal). He is destroyed as he becomes morally alive, and his death demonstrates the hopeless instability of monastic chivalry just as Athelstane's return to life dramatizes the absurdity of fanatic Saxonism. For all this, Lucas is essential. But it is Lucas who provides Richard's ultimate opponent. John is kept out of the final picture, after all; Richard's triumph is temporary.

With the resurrection and transformation of Athelstane and the defeat of cruel fanaticism in Lucas, the novel really ends. The final expected confrontation between Richard and John would be irrelevant to such late developments or would require a more extended consideration of the problems thus raised. Such a confrontation instead supplied the germ of a later better novel, *Quentin Durward*. Meanwhile, *Ivanhoe* concludes on its own positive note of reconciliation, with the clear suggestion that the courageous idealism which is an undying value of the chivalric spirit when combined with prudence and practical loyalty can transcend many of the barriers of fanaticism and selfishness dividing men.

The three later Crusader tales may be considered together as a complex gloss on the topic thus opened in *Ivanhoe*. *The Betrothed* is perhaps most interesting because most unusual in its complex psychological realism; *The Talisman* is for-

mally the most impressive; and *Count Robert* is the fullest
development of the thematic implications of *Ivanhoe*. In
each, the hero or heroine undergoes an ordeal which is at
once a consequence of and a critical comment on the
fantastic idealism of the chivalric spirit.

The Lady Eveline Berenger's ordeal begins with the
quixotic death of her father, guardian of the Castle of Garde
Doloureuse on the late twelfth-century Welsh Marches.
The Welsh warlord Gwenwyn attacks the castle when his
suit of Eveline is rejected in favor of the middle-aged
constable, Hugo deLacy. To preserve his honor, Eveline's
father needlessly risks his life and is killed. The castle is left
in the capable hands of the antichivalric Flammock, and
salvation comes in the form of deLacy's cavalry. Eveline,
meanwhile, has made a solemn vow that she will accept as
her husband the one who comes to her aid. The thematic
problem of the novel receives its fundamental statement
when, upon seeing the middle-aged, blunt, ugly constable
for the first time, she tries to squirm out of her foolish vow
(100–101). She is encouraged by her realistic attendant,
Flammock's daughter Rose, who warns against betrothals
that oppose duty to inclination.

DeLacy, meanwhile, is also squirming. But the conflict of
inclination and duty in which an imprudent vow has placed
him is the conflict between his inclination to marry Eveline
at once and his vow that he will promptly join the Crusading army. Both participants in this star-crossed betrothal are
plausible and sympathetic persons. But the familiarity of the
January-May fabliau motif has sounded a warning; and
when, directly following the betrothal, deLacy reluctantly
leaves for the Holy Land, leaving his nephew Damian to
"watch out for" his lady, we expect the inevitable.[10] The
proud, wilful Eveline seems with the purest of intentions to

167

rush on her fate and realizes too late the "intricacies" in which her foolish attempt to subordinate inclination too much to the ideal of duty has placed her (240).

She is finally tricked – she tricks herself – into taking the wounded Damian into the castle. Her rationalizations on this occasion give her an unusual and charmingly ironic complexity for a Waverley heroine (234–36). Flammock warns that such generosity to Damian is the dangerous quixotry of a "damsel-errant" – "but commend me to prudence and honesty" (239). Wild chivalry is thus manifest in Eveline as the perilous self-deception of a kinswoman to Byron's Donna Julia. But in the evil consequences of her knight-errantry, Eveline's actions simply repeat the actions of those who have left her and England unprotected to go off on a quixotic Crusade. Such is the close and sustained parallelism between her domestic peril and the social plight of England. We recognize, too, a more general Waverley theme when we realize that all of her deserters are elders *in loco parentis* who lose their natural responsibility in the vows of fanatic loyalties. Her father has sacrificed his natural role to ridiculous honor and pointless death. Her great-aunt is a female Cedric who never forgave Berenger for stealing her Saxon niece and sees in their daughter Eveline a hateful adulteration of Saxon purity. Even her aunt, the abbess, haughtily rejects her and deprives her further of protection. Thus, in Eveline's ordeal, the Crusade is the central symbol or instance of the fanatic idealism which distracts human beings from their personal loyalties. And she discovers the same imprudence in herself.

The ordeals of Kenneth in *The Talisman* and of Hereward in *Count Robert* are closer to the familiar Waverley pattern. Each is caught in a web of conflicting loyalties to dubious authorities. At the outset, each is guilty of a rigid fidelity. Kenneth, in his initial scenes with Saladin, is a superstitious bigot; the Saracen already shows himself to be typical of Scott's heroes of humane prudence, skilful in forbearance, careful not to speak or act in ignorance or neglect of another's prejudices (19–20). Kenneth thus begins an education in humane reasonability at the hands of Saladin. But Kenneth's loyalty to Richard involves him in the defense of Richard's dangerous rashness, while his closeness to Richard makes him an ideal tool for those who seek Richard's destruction. He plays squire of low degree to the royal Edith only to hear that Richard seeks to marry her to Saladin. Finally, he is a Scot, and Richard is at odds with the Scottish king. His ordeal becomes critical when, as guardian of Richard's banner, he is lured away from his post by a message from Edith and returns to find the banner gone. Thus, the recklessness of Richard and his own rash susceptibility to the appeal of chivalric romance place Kenneth's life and honor in jeopardy. His only course is to work for a set of interdependent ends: to save Richard from his enemies and from himself, to save Edith, to redeem himself. Only the guidance of the antichivalric Saladin makes success possible.

In a better, earlier novel Hereward would have been one of the most energetic of Waverley heroes. As a mercenary in the imperial guard of the Eastern empire, he is in the position of Quentin Durward; he too is the exiled remnant of a vanquished lineage. He is what Ivanhoe might have been a century earlier – a proud, bitterly vengeful Saxon: "All was laid desolate by the command of the victors. . . . The fire has destroyed the church where sleep the fathers of my race; and I, the last of their line, am a wanderer in other climates, a fighter of the battles of others, the servant of a foreign, though a kind, master, in a word,

169

one of the banished – a Varangian" (81). When the Norman Crusaders arrive at Constantinople, he sees in their
coming only the chance for revenge. When the most wildly
chivalric of the Franks, Robert of Paris, insults Hereward's
master, the Emperor Alexius, Hereward sees his vengeance
at hand. But Hereward and Robert quickly find common
interests and join forces against the decadent, hypocritical
Greeks. Hereward's task now becomes to save Robert and
his wife, his hereditary enemies, from palace conspiracy, and
at the same time uphold his trust to the unworthy but
humane Alexius, without losing his own simple dignity and
honor as a loyal Saxon. His ordeal is made the more
agonizing by the Hellenistic corruption of Constantinople.[11]

His Saxon fiancée reminds him "of things that passed in a
far different land, where faith and honour are not empty
sounds, as, alas! they seem but too surely to be here" (252).
Yet in this land of no faith and honor, caught between
fantastic chivalry and its opposite, Hereward combines the
shrewdness and energy of the natural manipulator with the
forthright honor and courage of a Jeanie Deans or a Henry
Wynd and manages to survive his ordeal. "My highest
ambition," he tells the emperor coldly, "is to merit the
epitaph upon my tomb, 'Hereward was faithful'" (263).
His success is attested to by the fact that both Robert and
Alexius recognize his fidelity and put complete trust in
him. "If he is false," observes Robert, "there is no faith in the
hand of nature, for truth, sincerity, and courage are written
upon his forehead" (234). "I cannot tell," reflects the
cynical Alexius with astonishment, "there is in that man's
looks and words a good faith which overwhelms me; and,
what is almost incredible, my belief in him has increased in
proportion to his showing me how slight my power was over
him" (264–65). Thus, in surviving his own ordeal, Here-

ward has provided a touchstone and an educative force for the more extreme characters whose hostilities have created his ordeal and forced him into the mediatorial role. Such would seem to have become the role of Ivanhoe by the end of the earlier book, but Scott could not have known it as long as Richard remained central mediator.

The three ordeals seem to be the same ordeal of prudent nature plotting to survive its encounter with the wild spirit of knight-errantry. But such a reading oversimplifies. To be sure, the chivalric extremists are deficient in prudence and "nature." But the evil principle is to be found in their opposites, those deficient in idealism, or those in whom – Brian de Bois Guilbert, for example – a naively excessive idealism has turned into its opposite, a reckless cynicism or fatalism, recalling Flammock's warning: "Those who would do what is better than good sometimes bring about what is worse than bad!" (239) The evil principle is the "seducing spirit," the "acute and depreciating spirit," of Goethe's Mephistophilis, which Scott said he preferred to the more "elevated" evil principles of Byron and Milton.[12] Consider the agents of villainy in the three books.

Hugo deLacy's quixoticism is part of the unnatural quality of his betrothal to the young Eveline and therefore dangerous. But what causes evil is that his absence leaves his selfish, ne'er-do-well cousin Randal free to seek his own destructive ends. Randal plays the Iago needed to realize the dangers of Hugo's January-May marriage; Randal, the sower of disbelief, the tempter, the evil manipulator, the man of many disguises and no real loyalties or disciplines, is the negative force liberated by the absence of true authority – akin to the John who flourishes during Richard's knight-errantry in *Ivanhoe*. Randal has his logical ally in the minstrel Vidal, the professional cynic who, asked to sing of

171

the truth of woman, sings a long *lai* of Tristrem and Ysolte, providing a warning analogue to the potential rivalry of nephew Damian and uncle Hugo. Vidal emerges as the spiritual destroyer, the nihilistic Mephistophilis, who strives to turn Hugo's doubt and grief into despair and violence. *The Talisman* has two nihilistic evil-doers to exploit Richard's chivalric excesses and thus to flourish on the moral disease into which the Crusade has fallen. Conrade of Montserrat and the Grand Master of the Templars share a hatred for the Crusade and its leader. Conrade is a voluptuary, selfish, ambitious, the complete anti-idealist. The Grand Master is cruel as well; Conrade sees him as a devil he has raised (113). Together they foster disorder, arouse Richard's natural rashness, and seek to destroy faith – Richard's in Kenneth, Kenneth's in himself. The Grand Master's final desperate act is to murder his wounded ally before Conrade can confess and win salvation; he is thus the ultimate mocker of faith and its instruments. He alone is beyond even Saladin's compassion, and Saladin's single violent act is to kill him (298, 310).

The destructive anti-idealist in *Count Robert* is the cynic philosopher of many disguises, Agelastes. Agelastes plots to destroy the Crusaders through exploiting their idealism: they "must be acted upon," he counsels, "by very different motives, if we would make ourselves masters of their actions and the principles by which they are governed" (171). It is he whose croaking augurs ill fortune "like the raven from the blasted oak on the left hand" (213). Of him Hereward says, "With the mask of apparent good-humour, he conceals his pandering to the vices of others; with the specious jargon of philosophy, he has argued himself out of religious belief and moral principle" (217). He is common enemy to

172

Hereward, Robert, and Alexius, who find unity in opposing his destructive influence. Yet it is he who most forcefully condemns the follies of chivalry. He mocks the quixotic countess for "laying aside the character of a mother and a wife, and adopting that of one of those brain-sick female fools who, like the bravoes of the other sex, sacrifice everything that is honourable or useful to a frantic and insane affectation of courage" (296). The reckless lady replies with Scott's most memorable celebration of chivalric glory: "One hour of life, crowded to the full with glorious action, and filled with noble risks, is worth whole years of those mean observances of paltry decorum in which men steal through existence, like sluggish waters through a marsh, without either honour or observation" (296). His answer seems the book's ultimate statement of antichivalry. That it is put in the mouth of the single unpardonably evil person in the book, the proud, selfish philosopher who is with emphatic symbolism killed by an ape-man (299), suggests that the book is no simple, unequivocal critique of chivalry.

In all three books the most attractive characters constructively oppose an extravagant knight-errantry in the name of humane prudence. But all three suggest, too, that prudence and common sense alone are inadequate responses to evil. In Ivanhoe they are subservient to his devotion to Richard and his willingness to sacrifice his life for Rebecca. Flammock seems convincing as shrewd protector of Berenger and his daughter, but then Flammock selfishly retreats from his trust, refuses the service asked of him by the departing Hugo, and in so doing recommends the youthful Damian for his place as Eveline's protector. Such selfish folly puts Flammock's prudence and loyalty in a strange light. Even as he warns his daughter against freaks of honor, he is refusing to save Eveline from temptation. Flammock's plausible anti-chivalry is not much more trustworthy than that of Agelastes.

It is clear, too, that Hereward by himself, however shrewd and sensible, must remain the mercenary servant of a decadent emperor. It is through transferring his loyalty to Count Robert that Hereward regains his freedom, and ultimately his betrothed and his homeland. The process of reconciliation between Saxon and Frank – the central thematic impulse when the book manages to define one – moves toward the definition of the complex ideal embodied in *Ivanhoe* in the group of Wilfred, Richard, and Locksley. The point of projecting dual heroes in *Count Robert* becomes apparent as the two men, fated to be enemies, recognize their kinship. Robert suggests his worth by seeing in Hereward "something in thy face of candour as well as sense." The narrator acknowledges that the two "had a stronger resemblance to each other in their dispositions than probably either of them would have been willing to admit": "Chance, therefore, had made a temporary alliance between two men the foundation of whose characters bore such strong resemblance to each other that they were only separated by a course of education which had left rigid prejudices on both sides, and which prejudices were not unlikely to run counter to each other" (215). Chance appears to have been providential. Meanwhile, the accidental allies are in the classic "Two Drovers" situation and must work out, with tact and forbearance, a common language offensive to neither. Hereward's is the major contribution, for he has the requisite tact and restraint. He is determined that Robert "shall be ruled by calm reason while I am with you" (226–27), yet he learns to manipulate without openly defying the "fine-spun whims of thy national gallantry"

(256). From his long-lost and newly-found Saxon fiancée he learns the pattern of reconciliation; for Bertha is attendant on the quixotic countess, loyal, tolerant of her excesses, yet still devoted to her own Saxon traditions. Ironically, the process of reconciliation between Frankish Robert and Saxon Hereward is climaxed in a ritual duel. Robert fights in defense of his wife's honor; Hereward performs his final act of loyalty to Alexius. As is the case between Ivanhoe and Brian, neither really wins. Or, Robert wins but then saves his friend Hereward's life, and Hereward becomes his servant, accompanies him on the Crusade as a devoted Sancho, and is ultimately "restored to a country which I have never ceased to love over the rest of the world" (375).

Such is the more conclusive analogue to the search for cultural survival in *Ivanhoe*. Prudent honesty and humane realism enter the train of an idealistic spirit which is saved from the disastrous consequences of its own excesses by its ability to recognize the worth and attract the devotion of its humbler, shrewder servant. Chivalry undergoes a modification which renders its true value stable and permanent. The same outcome is realized through the similar bond of Richard and Saladin in *The Talisman*, the most complete work of art of the four.

In Scott's single thorough study of the Crusades as an historical and a political fact, the chief providential agent and moral arbiter of the book is the Saracen emir. Hazlitt admired him as Scott's "most dashing and spirited" character.[13] This he may be; but he is not the "dark hero." To say (with Welsh) that he is "the one romantic character in the Waverley Novels about whom Scott has no reservations at all" is to slight his role as spokesman for antiromantic attitudes. Welsh's reasoning at this point is elusive.[14] I fail to see how Saladin illustrates that "courage and generosity" are, for Scott, good but not "moral" qualities; I fail to see how Scott's inability to "accept the notion of spontaneously generated ethics" requires that Saladin dwell "far away in the east." For Saladin is a moral hero before he becomes a political ideal; and his morality of courage and generosity is *natural*, not "artificial and social." *The Talisman* enacts the symbolic transferral of the power of the Saladin politico-moral ideal from a mythical or utopian East – in no way the real society of the Muslim empire – to a politically sick Europe. The force of Saladin is not to reject a sick chivalric idealism, but rather to humanize and stabilize it; to see it as a potent force in man's search for humanity and enlightenment.

Saladin's first appearance as Sheerkopf illustrates that he has already been influenced by the chivalric spirit of his enemies. He intends to save the Richard he admires from a variety of sicknesses. Already, Richard finds Saladin more honorable than his fellow Crusaders. In short, the conciliation is well underway, as it is not in *Robert* or *Ivanhoe*. The purpose of the story is to test its full meaning and value.

Saladin's first appearance tells us more. It shows him possessed of the forbearance and tact which Kenneth, and more spectacularly Richard, do not yet possess. The absence of such virtues has turned the moral and political idealism of the Crusade into a moral and political disease. Our first image of the camp gives clear notice that Scott sees in the Crusade the kind of phenomenon he had studied in other radically idealistic political movements – the Jacobites, the Covenanters, the Cavaliers of Montrose or Dundee. Richard is feverish and ill. Richard recognizes, as we do, that the sickness of the king signals the sickness of his society, even though Richard's is an illness of moral excess, while in his allies "It is a cold palsy – a dead lethargy – a disease that

176

deprives them of speech and action – a canker that has eaten into the heart of all that is noble, and chivalrous, and virtuous among them – that has made them false to the noblest vow ever knights were sworn to" (65). The analogy of spiritual to physical illness is made explicit when we are told that upon Richard's illness "and the disadvantageous circumstances in which the Crusaders were placed, the national disunion between the various bands united in the Crusade, began to display itself, just as old wounds break out afresh in the human body when under the influence of disease or debility" (71). Into this picture comes the shrewd but humane healer Saladin. The fact that Kenneth has brought him, has in a sense become both his patron and his apprentice, is what makes Kenneth the book's hero. Saladin is the ideal for whose workings Kenneth must risk much, and whose true influence he must assimilate.

The value of the ideal and its efficacy are implied by the most obvious fact of Saladin's development: the sequence of his disguises. The disguises signify his various talents. More important, they are the means by which he functions as a providential force for health and wholeness in the face of disorder and bigotry, the disease prevalent in the Crusaders' forces. His disguises partly signify – as, say, in a Shakespearian comedy or a picaresque novel – the duplicity that permits a humane flexibility. It is necessary to Saladin's ultimate moral ends, the spiritual testing and proving of both Richard and Kenneth, their redemption from the disease, that he operate as an unknown force and not in his true and potent identity. Thus, in his disguises, Saladin resembles Shakespeare's "duke of dark corners" who must partly withdraw from the moral arena while his protégés discover and freely work out their salvations.

Salvation demands of both Richard and Kenneth that

177

they recognize true worth and value when they encounter it in the disguised Saladin and that they put absolute trust in his truth and power. Such is Kenneth's act when, in despair, he commits himself wholly to the hands of Saladin (the physician) and goes off as his slave. Such, too, is Richard's act when, as the Crusaders peaceably approach Saladin's camp for the climactic trial by combat, they are met by a volley of arrows and spears. Richard's faith in Saladin's honor and humanity is put to its climactic test; the reckless, impetuous king restrains himself, refuses to lose his faith to a contradictory appearance, and it turns out directly that the arrows are headless, the spears pointless, the volley purely ceremonial, a disguise, a final test of faith (284–85).

But this cannot occur until Kenneth, too, the loyal but rejected follower, has become Saladin's instrument for the protection and redemption of Richard. To do so, Kenneth has necessarily taken on Saladin's machinery of disguises. He returns to Richard as a Nubian slave. The disguise permits him to be at Richard's side when the king is attacked and to receive the poniard's stab meant for Richard. What follows is an important, an extraordinarily symbolic, act in Richard's redemption. When his yeomen refuse to suck the poison from the Nubian's wound, Richard unhesitatingly does it himself and, as we later hear, by so doing discovers that the messenger's blackness is only disguise-deep! (221) There follows the trial wherein the Nubian's dog, injured during Kenneth's fateful watch and subsequently healed by the talisman of the emir, also plumbs disguises, identifying Conrade as the thief of the banner and thus of Richard's and Britain's honor. Thus, Kenneth has participated in Saladin's efforts by disguise, and another test is passed by the ability to see through masks to moral truth.

But Kenneth, like Saladin, has been in disguise from the

178

beginning. The secret of his real identity has provided a further test of Richard's ability to recognize true worth and honor through disguise and to separate true nobility from the appearance of rank or birth. And this is a test of the proud Edith as well as of her kinsman Richard. Again, as with the "Tristrem" *lai* of *The Betrothed,* an interpolated song – a ballad of the "Bloody Vest" – indicates the thematic motif (273–76). The ballad implies that if Kenneth proves himself as a knight or squire of "low degree" and Edith humbles herself in the admission of his true equality in worth (Saladin is spokesman for the view that this *is* true equality [309–10]), then Kenneth will shed his disguise and emerge a princely figure. He emerges as prince royal of Scotland, whose fidelity to Richard under trying conditions now makes possible a reconciliation between England and Scotland. Once again disguise is used in the providential work of social healing. The finale symbolizes reconciliation in marriage. The Soldan, who has prudently denied the book its chivalric climax in single combat, sends the talisman as a wedding gift and thus, through Kenneth who has earned the role, he sends his healing power to Europe.

The talisman itself becomes merely an antiquarian relic. But its full significance warrants more serious attention. Early in the book it is a token of redemptive magic. When the physician pleads with Richard to save Kenneth's life, he does so by insisting that the healing virtue of the talisman and his own healing powers will cease unless the day sees one more life saved, that he has touched an unclean animal and cannot do it himself (a patent pretense), that therefore the continued usefulness of the talisman as humane power must be assured by Richard himself, who must save Kenneth's life (181–83). Richard gives in, passes his first test, and the power is saved. The token finds its true use as a healing power for humanity and becomes the means by which Richard's spiritual ills are healed. Thus, through its healing encounter with Saladin and his talisman, chivalric idealism has been humanized and stabilized and made accessible as a permanent source of value to European culture.

Such an outcome obviously need not mean that Saladin must be converted and brought back to Europe as philosopher-king, any more than the influence of Rebecca in *Ivanhoe* requires that she be personally included in the conventional social arrangements which terminate that novel. In both, a talismanic healing power permits the historic survival of chivalric idealism and generosity. If this is more sharply articulated at the end of *The Talisman*, it is because the latter solves its fictional problems with more skill and assurance than the other three tales of the Crusaders. But the four together work out a significant statement about the values and risks of quixotic idealism and the virtues needed to humanize and stabilize it. And such a statement is at once familiar and new to the reader of the Jacobite and Cavalier-Presbyterian novels.

2. THE RENAISSANCE
RECONSTRUCTIONS

We have neglected the aspect of *Ivanhoe* which most concerned Scott: its historicity. Such neglect is not crucial. It is ironic that the era of Scott's world fame as historical romancer opened with one of the least "historic" of his romances.[15] In the tales of the Crusaders, remoteness and strangeness make truth and wholeness of milieu as irrelevant as they are unattainable. The Dedicatory Epistle to *Ivanhoe* attests to Scott's awareness that the very feasibility of this new application of the Waverley method was in doubt.

The results have been variously interpreted to prove that his conception of history was, from a Romantic point of view, antihistorical in the Enlightenment tradition of Hume, Diderot, Gibbon. In "Vico and Aesthetic Historism," Auerbach defines such a tradition in terms of its persistent belief that Nature and History remain distinct, even hostile, as contrasted with the Vico-Herder "organic conservative" premise that Nature is in historic process.[16] Such a premise, Welsh insists, Scott could not share (neither, really, could Burke),[17] and he quotes in support the Waverley *loci classici*: the heraldry metaphor from the first chapter of *Waverley* and the uniformity-of-passions text from the Dedicatory Epistle to *Ivanhoe* (xxv). Even if it were safe to rely on such passages, the passages as quoted would be misleading. The Waverley "heraldry" metaphor clearly belongs, as Donald Davie has argued, to the seven early chapters. The book as completed, years later, was conceived of as a companion piece to *Castle Rackrent*, as an attempt to save local, ephemeral sentiments and manners from oblivion, an impulse remote from the motivations of the Philosophic Historian.[18] The quotation from the *Ivanhoe* dedication stops short of important qualifications. Scott is distinguishing between passions, which are "natural" and uniform, and sentiments and manners, which *derive from* the passions and therefore, "however influenced by the peculiar state of society, must still, upon the whole, bear a strong resemblance to each other." These are substantial qualifications, and Scott's illustration is significant, for it concedes only basic resemblance and allows for considerable cultural difference, if not psychological particularity: "Our ancestors were not more distinct from us, surely, than Jews

181

are from Christians. . . . The tenor, therefore, of their affections and feelings must have borne the same general proportion to our own" (xxv). In *Ivanhoe*, Scott took considerable pains to portray and account for the differences in the case of Isaac and to create in Rebecca a strong awareness of them.

But to the charge that Scott was "of the Enlightenment" and therefore no true historicist in the modern sense, there are two answers, one philosophical, the other pragmatic and aesthetic. First, it is naive to make a categorical either-or classification on the expectation that an unphilosophical, somewhat erratic artist, vaguely in touch with Hume, Robertson, and Gibbon, but also with Montesquieu, Ferguson, the German Romantics, and Burke, would plump himself categorically in Enlightenment or counter-Enlightenment. Indeed, Dilthey, and after him Cassirer, long ago challenged as Romantic myth what Cassirer calls "the popular error concerning the unhistorical and antihistorical spirit of the eighteenth century,"[19] the idea that there was a monolithic Enlightenment antihistorism available to Scott or anyone else. The more pragmatic objection to the charge is that if *Ivanhoe* is primarily ahistoric, then so is all fiction. Without some assumption of basic uniformity, neither history nor art is possible. Goethe and Hegel, supplying Lukacs with an essential term for his admiration of Scott, both observed that all art or poetry is grounded in "necessary anachronism."[20] Such is the element in Scott's portrayal, the "living, continuous relation between Scott's themes and the present . . . the many living links which make it possible for us to experience even the distant Middle Ages,"[21] to which Sainte-Beuve alludes in his critique of Flaubert's *Salammbô*, the romance wrongly cited by Grierson as the classic of the *Ivanhoe* genre.[22] *Salammbô* is a striving to depart radically from the historicity of *Ivanhoe,* as is, in the opposite direction, Bulwer Lytton's *Last Days of Pompeii.* A brief comparative note on these two departures may suggest the idea of fictive historicity implicit in *Ivanhoe.*

Flaubert's intention, a consciously escapist one, was to evoke in massive particularity the material fact of ancient Carthage. Immediate material density is the predominant, even exclusive, effect. The milieu is utterly remote and yet utterly concrete. Lytton was motivated by the same compulsion, though without the conscious escapism, to "archaeological authenticity."[23] Lytton accomplishes this end, to be sure, by radically different methods, by a guidebook matter-of-factness, a fullness of allusion, that is not sensuous at all, but rather, "notional."[24] Lytton's monumental externality is directed explicitly at a later reader by an archaeological historian *quâ* narrator; hence, the reality, as solidly independent of human inhabitants as Flaubert's, is neither immediate nor concrete. By contrast with both, Scott's evocation of material setting is thin and generalized even when he most nearly approximates the ponderous and scrupulous inanimate particularity of Lytton in, say, *The Talisman* and *Count Robert.* But as the Epistle to Dryasdust makes clear, *Ivanhoe* is determinedly anti-antiquarian and makes no comparable attempt at the materializing of milieu (xxiii–xxv). It evokes no quotidian circumstantiality after the scene of the initial night in Cedric's hall, and even there the description functions strictly as "manners" typification. *The Betrothed* goes further, but even here the depiction of the castle provides a social emblem of human solidarity, of ethnic conciliation; while the Saxon hall of Eveline's cruelly fanatic great-aunt appears strictly as an evocative element in Eveline's ordeal. Lukacs is fair, then, in his contrast: whereas in Flaubert (and I would add Lytton) there is little

183

organic relation between objectified milieu and psychological or moral impulse, in Scott material facts are realized almost purely as integral parts of dramatized sentiments and manners.[25]

The historicities of Flaubert and Lytton differ most significantly from the historicity of *Ivanhoe* and *Waverley* in the projecting of psychological pastness. *Salammbô* belongs at one extreme. Desiring an imaginative retreat from the sordid ugliness of modern life and realizing that he could in no way reconstruct the psychology of ancient Carthage, Flaubert simply excluded all but a basic inhumanity, scarcely distinguishable from brutality. The exceptions are in the emergent father-daughter and father-son bonds of Hamilcar Barca and his children; and here, as Sainte-Beuve noted, the result was merely a mythologizing of the psychology of *Madame Bovary*.[26] Otherwise the human participants are best described as appetitive hordes led by divine brutes. At the opposite extreme, Lytton is the shameless anachronizer, the nineteenth-century utilitarian conceiving his Pompeiians in terms of their philosophic attitudes, making them parade with intellectual pretentiousness before a Belascoesque backdrop, and citing satiric analogies between their behavior and Regency manners.

Between these extremes, the conception of historicity in *Ivanhoe* would seem to be more useful. For Lytton, the link for the reader between past and present is to be found in surface accidentals and a timeless pettiness:

It is not without interest to observe in those remote times, and under a social system so widely different from the modern, the same small causes that ruffle and interrupt the "course of love," which operate so commonly at this day; – the same inventive jealousy, the same cunning slander, the same crafty and fabricated retailings of petty gossip. . . .

We should paint life ill if, even in times the most prodigal of romance, and of the romance of which we most largely avail ourselves, we did not also describe the mechanism of those trivial and household springs of mischief which we see every day at work in our chambers and at our hearths. It is in these, the lesser intrigues of life, that we mostly find ourselves at home with the past.[27]

For Scott, the link must be psychological and this means "throwing the force of my narrative upon the characters and passions of the actors" – those passions belonging to all men – and upon "that extensive neutral ground," the ground *between* historically unique past and historically unique present, the "large proportion, that is, of manners and sentiments which are common to us and to our ancestors, having been handed down unaltered from them to us, or which, arising out of the principles of our common nature, must have existed alike in either state of society."[28] There is a principle of selection here. The choice of similar or unaltered manners is a deliberate artistic one and is not necessarily reflective of a philosophical assumption of invariable uniformity, such as Scott is alleged to have shared with Hume. Indeed, *Count Robert* contains ample satiric criticism of the Enlightenment philosophical historian in the treatment of the pompous moralist Anna Comnenia; Agelastes' dream of placing her and himself, historian and philosopher, on the imperial throne may be read as a mockery of the Gibbon ideal.

Ivanhoe, then, is historical as *Waverley* and its heirs are historical: it defines an epoch in terms of a critical tension of cultural patterns, "sentiments and manners"; it chooses patterns formative of the present; it dramatizes a problem of cultural survival analogous to such problems in modern revolutionary Europe; it embodies crisis and transformation

185

in timeless personal relationships so that, while dramatized in their own political-cultural terms, they are imaginatively grounded in familiar, natural problems of individual human experience. In *Ivanhoe* epochal reconstruction goes no further. Even in *The Talisman*, massively concrete in setting, the setting remains too spectacular and exotic, perhaps too symbolic, to be taken for a coherent past milieu. Had *Count Robert* sustained its promise, it would be an exception. But in its present state its dependence on archaeological particularity merely signalizes a marked failure of imaginative assimilation and at the same time calls attention to the danger inherent in the novels of epochal reconstruction to which we now turn.

When, following *Ivanhoe*, Scott turned back to the England and Scotland of the Renaissance and Reformation, he found materials less malleable than Saxon-Norman conflict in the age of the Crusades, new kinds of possibilities for historic reanimation. From *The Monastery* he learned a good deal; and fortunately he wrote about what he learned. One thing he had realized, it would seem from the immediate sequel *The Abbot*, was the enduring value of the Waverley pattern, for *The Abbot* is perhaps the most successful of the four and at the same time the closest adaptation of Waverley motifs and methods. *The Abbot's* Mary Stuart, called by Lukacs "one of the greatest feats of portrayal in world literature,"[29] led naturally to *Kenilworth's* Elizabeth the following year (1821), but this novel is an utterly new departure, and unique among the Waverleys. In 1822, Scott undertook a terribly ambitious manners panorama, in which the fiction remained a feeble excuse for a broad survey of Jacobean London. The chief artistic gains of *The Abbot* and *Kenilworth* seem to have been lost here. In fact, a glance at chronology shows *The Fortunes of Nigel*

186

(1822) bracketed by *The Pirate* (1821) and *Peveril* (1823), all three recklessly overambitious in scope. But then came *Durward* (later 1823), followed by *St. Ronan's Well* and *Redgauntlet* (1823–24), and the loss of control proved temporary, not again apparent until 1829 in *Anne of Geierstein*.

Whatever the four Reformation-Renaissance novels have in common, they do not share a single historical impulse. Each sets out from a different kind of historical "given": *The Monastery* from a spiritual cataclysm; *The Abbot* from a problem of loyalty to the ideal image of the persecuted Mary; *Kenilworth* from a mystery evocative of the socio-moral texture of Elizabeth's spectacular reign; *Nigel* from the character of the royal Scots goldsmith Heriot in the chaotic world of the Jacobean citizen comedies. Historicity is different in each and presents in each different problems.

Of the "given" of the first, Scott wrote:

The general plan of the story was to conjoin two characters in that bustling and contentious age who, thrown into situations which gave them different views on the subject of the Reformation, should, with the same sincerity and purity of intention, dedicate themselves, the one to the support of the sinking fabric of the Catholic Church, the other to the establishment of the Reformed doctrines. It was supposed that some interesting subjects for narrative might be derived from opposing two such enthusiasts to each other in the path of life, and contrasting the real worth of both with their passions and prejudices [vii].

The possibilities for picturesque confrontation in such a pair were to be augmented by exploiting the general "manners" contrast between the locale's two dominant social groups: the lay barons and their dependents (the Avenels) and the monastery tenants (the Glendinnings). But "much advantage could not be derived from this": "There were, indeed,

187

differences betwixt the two classes, but, like tribes in the mineral and vegetable world, which, resembling each other to common eyes, can be sufficiently well discriminated by naturalists, they were yet too similar, upon the whole, to be placed in marked contrast with each other" (xii).

As for the initial contrast between opposing personal responses to the spiritual cataclysm of the Reformation, it is not clear from Scott's comment which pair he thought central. If he meant the Glendinning brothers – and the contrast of their spiritual developments is the central structural fact of the novel – then it is strange he did not mention their close domestic relationship and the tragic poignancy of their divergence. In fact, the novel never brings the brothers into direct confrontation. The two "enthusiasts" whose "real worth" *is* contrasted in scenes of direct confrontation are not the brothers at all, but their spiritual guides, Subprior Eustace of the titular monastery, and the itinerant Reform preacher, Eustace's boyhood friend Henry Warden. But whereas Eustace remains important throughout and is the narrative's only individuated adult consciousness, Warden does not appear until past the halfway point as an accidental climax to Halbert's implausible conversion. Our first impression, then, is of disproportion and uncertainty.

The implausible elements are what concerned Scott, however, as he analyzed the causes of the book's failure. His later thinking reflects his concern for ways to pass the test of historicity as defined by Welsh, to convey, that is, "the full sense of the present as a concrete and particular environment."[30] The flaws, Scott finds, are three.

"The conclusion was brought about, not by incidents arising out of the story itself, but in consequence of public transactions, with which the narrative has little connexion, and which the reader had little opportunity to become acquainted with" (xviii–xix). The fusion of private experience and public destiny was incomplete, and this, for the master of such fusion, was an unusual failure. The abrupt intrusion of Murray's expedition, the invasion of English troops at the same time, seem mechanically interposed to extricate the author from his story. And as the author judges himself on this account, we get an unusual glimpse of the ideal of structural coherence to which he adhered. Incoherence is true to nature, he concedes; but the romancer's province is "artificial." His model is Fielding, who, "especially in *Tom Jones,* his *chef-d'oeuvre,* has set the distinguished example of a story regularly built and consistent in all its parts, in which nothing occurs, and scarce a personage is introduced, that has not some share in tending to advance the catastrophe."[31] Thus, "the more closely and happily the story is combined, and the more natural and felicitous the catastrophe, the nearer such a composition will approach the perfection of the novelist's art" (xx).

The ideal is potential in *The Monastery.* It is evident from the beginning that one brother must move into the political world of border conflict, and one into the monastery-centered battle against heresy. The novel must build to the confrontation of Eustace as monastic leader and Murray as secular force. But the process of realizing the ends is faulty. The difference may be seen through reference to a novel by a French disciple of Scott's, Prosper Mérimée. *A Chronicle of the Reign of Charles IX* is almost identical in epoch with *The Monastery* and focuses on two brothers in conflict, one a Huguenot, the other a Catholic opportunist in the Beyliste sense. Lukacs finds Scott and Mérimée dissimilar in philosophical basis. In Mérimée he sees a persistent Enlightenment dualism of empirical reality and

189

abstract general law. Mérimée is "more empirical than Scott, adhering more closely to individual features and detail; at the same time he draws more directly general conclusions from historical facts" than Scott. Thus, for Lukacs, Mérimée lacks Scott's "recognition of the concrete and complex intricacy of the historical process."[32] Mérimée himself concedes that "I love in history only the anecdotes, and among anecdotes I prefer those where I imagine that I find a true picture of manners and characters at a given epoch."[33] The result, as Lukacs sees it, is that the destinies of his characters are strictly private, that "there is no really organic link between the great historical event which Mérimée wishes to portray – the night of St. Bartholomew – and the private destinies of the principal heroes."[34] In short, Mérimée slights the ideal by which Scott found *The Monastery* deficient.

Lukacs is not fair to Mérimée. Our concern with the massacre of St. Bartholomew's Night is naturally focused on the brothers, whose affection easily transcends the public conflict as it does in *The Monastery*. The Huguenot brother's liaison with Diane de Turgis is played out under the shadow of a threatened renewal of violence, and she seeks repeatedly to convert him to save his life. Thus public and private intertwine. But Lukacs's main point is just. The public event remains external; its relation to the private destinies of George and Bernard conveys little understanding of the determining forces of the event itself. Whatever the failure in execution of *The Monastery*, the personal relations of Glendinnings and Eustace and Julian Avenel function as parts of the historic decline of the monasteries and of the social structure built on their power.

The real failure of *The Monastery* derives from the other two flaws Scott analyzes, the White Lady of Avenel and Sir Piercie Shafton. Both belong to what Scott calls "machin-

ery." The White Lady is an odd amalgamation of speculations in comparative folklore and Shakespeare's poetic supernaturalism. She is of the order of Rosicrucian beings added
by Pope to *The Rape of the Lock*. She is the banshee of the
Avenels. She behaves like a water nymph and converses in
lyrics derivative from Ariel's in *The Tempest*. Such a
mixture could only be odd. Yet Scott thought there was "no
great violence in supposing such a being as this to have
existed, while the elementary spirits were believed in"
(xiii). She is thus conceived of as part of an epochal
reanimation. The reader is to accept her as an independent
reality and yet share with the narrator a sceptical "modern"
view of the superstition which is alleged to have given her
"reality." Scott is uncertain how to create the historic reality
of superstition and at the same time to separate the "true
worth" of his characters from "passions and prejudices" that
are ephemeral, including superstition! Five years later, handling the Bahrgeist of Baldringham in *The Betrothed*, he
has solved the problem. Eveline unquestionably *sees* "the
vision fatal to my race" (128), but her mode of vision is left
in doubt, and we see it only through her reaction as later
described.[35]

Sir Piercie Shafton is a more surprising failure. He fails as
a character conceived in historical terms, whose function in
the plot becomes the activity of an individual embodiment
of historic forces. Shafton is an Euphuistic foppish Cavalier
whose conspiratorial involvement with North-country Cath-
olics has forced him to flee Elizabeth's England and take
refuge among the remnants of Border monasticism. His
chief characteristic is his Euphuistic speech, which fills
many long pages. Scott thought the failure due to Sir
Piercie's remoteness from the "neutral ground" of manners
and sentiments described in the Dedicatory Epistle to *Ivan-*

hoe. The absurd unnaturalness of Sir Piercie, then, would owe to the fact that, whereas "the manners of a rude people are always founded on nature" and therefore are accessible to sympathetic understanding, the follies of a civilized period, "when driven to extravagance, are founded not upon any natural taste proper to the species, but upon the growth of some peculiar cast of affectation, with which mankind in general, and succeeding generations in particular, feel no common interest or sympathy" (xvii). But this should mean the failure of Wildrake and Dalgetty, too. Shafton's failure is not as Scott suggests. And if we are to be fair to *The Monastery* in itself and recognize the major problems of historic reanimation in the group of novels, we must understand that failure.

His failure is one of tonal and historic irrelevance. His folly is social and linguistic, yet his central plot importance depends on his role in an ideological struggle to which his folly is unrelated. For Eustace, Edward, Halbert, and Mary Avenel, his presence is a serious problem, yet he himself can in no way be taken seriously, nor does he stand for any conflux of historic forces. He is the exception that proves the rule formulated by Lukacs: Scott individualizes his leading figures so as to concentrate in them "the salient positive and negative sides of the movement concerned," or so as to add to the total picture the "interaction between different levels of response" to the "major disturbance" that gives the novel its subject.[36] The importance of Sir Piercie as enemy to Elizabeth, suitor to Mary Avenel, and provoker of Halbert's social ambitions acts to confuse that "major disturbance" and Halbert's relation to it.

The introduction makes clear that both *The Monastery* and *The Abbot* were to be concerned with Halbert's brother Edward, the last of the abbots. From the beginning, Edward is more reflective and sensitive; from childhood he seems destined to defend the church in its decline. To him Eustace gives his chief attention, trying to draw him into the church, only to discover that he already loves Mary. Edward loves his brother, yet senses himself rejected by Mary and so hates his brother as a rival. In compensation he turns to the church, though in a frenzy of conflicting motives (254–56). His climactic scene is the book's most interesting. Halbert, having run off to join Murray's forces, is supposed dead. When it is discovered that he lives, Edward, who has sworn sincerely to avenge his death on his supposed slayer Sir Piercie, confesses that he wished Halbert dead: "I could hardly disguise my brutal and insane joy under the appearance of revenge" (307). Under the burden of this horrifying self-discovery, he turns to the church.[37]

A plot focused on Edward, Eustace, Edward's shrewd mother Elspeth, and Mary Avenel, and excluding the White Lady, the tedious Shafton, and the arbitrarily included military history would have served Scott perfectly. Auerbach argues that the scene between the Abbé and Julien Sorel overheard by Mademoiselle de la Mole is fully and concretely reflective of a particular moment – France on the eve of the Revolution of 1830.[38] *The Monastery*, as I have conjecturally revised it, would have supplied such scenes in abundance. Consider the position of the Glendinnings, fatherless after Pinkiecleugh, socially and economically dependent on the doomed monastery, faced with the power of the swashbuckling trimmer Julian Avenel and with the presence of the heretic protected by Murray. A novel in such a milieu, focusing on the rivalry of Eustace, the noble, kindly monastic, with Elspeth, the shrewd, energetic mother in her bleak tower, for a son who was to become the last of the abbots – such a novel could have been as profoundly and organically historical as anything Scott ever wrote.[39]

Partly, however, as a result of Shafton's importance, these possibilities are lost in the theme of the poor orphan's search for status in the new world of Reformation. Halbert becomes hero – Halbert, who can participate more actively in the forces of change, but in whom the relation of private destiny and public involvement remains inorganic. All of the book's inappropriate and implausible elements belong to the evolution of his role as heir of Avenel and lieutenant to Murray. His growing up begins when he invokes the White Lady in order to learn his destiny. She is the first of four causes of his development. The Ariel-like banshee bestows upon him neo-Elizabethan lyric prophecies, takes him to find the black book (the Bible in English) of the late Lady of Avenel, hidden in a Vathekian cave in the center of the earth, and thus he is made aware that he is destined to more than the inheritance of Glendearg and becomes restless. Then comes Sir Piercie, whose foppish condescension makes him violently defensive about his rank and crudeness of manners, leading to the duel which forces him to run away. Abruptly Halbert encounters the itinerant Reformer Warden; he is impressed with Warden's courage and faith, and we are to suppose that this and the black book suffice for the religious side of his conversion. Finally he joins Murray's conveniently available expedition and finds in Murray, himself a bastard and a self-made leader, one sympathetic to his own drive for status and power. Halbert's drive is historically appropriate. But the forces that produce it scarcely add up to a probable sequence of formative experiences. They all are presented as equally credible, yet all represent different kinds of historic and mythic reality.

The "reality" of *The Abbot* is also, like that of most of the

Waverleys, a mixture of modes, fusing history and romance so as to make one function in the operation of the other. Of the four Renaissance novels, *The Abbot* has perhaps least of "the full sense of the present as a concrete and particular environment." Yet the avoidance of a surface texture of epochal reality is essential to the fulfillment of the book's historic intent: the personal discovery of Mary Stuart as individual symbol and force. Of all the major historic personages in these novels, she is most impressive. For Lukacs this is because she "concentrates all the features which from the outset condemn to failure her *coup d'état* and flight."[40] But her impressiveness results more from the rhetoric of her presentation, from the romantic-realistic atmosphere of the personal adventure whose climax is her charismatic presence, from the intricate way the complex problem of Roland Graeme's freedom becomes entangled with her own.

She does not appear until the middle of the book (215–16), yet every element has prepared both protagonist and reader for her appearance. The opening is a unique mixture of romance and matter-of-fact. Halbert and Mary, now approaching middle age, are childless and anxious. In her lonely, mundane world, Mary longs for romance; and the arrival of the mysterious orphan, the boy hero from the Debateable Land, provides romance in the shape of the child she has never had. The orphan's destiny takes him to Queen Mary's prison at Lochleven. The lonely mother who rescued the mysterious child from her lake now has her lofty historic counterpart in the lonely maternal figure on another dangerous lake. Through Roland's youth we experience the phenomenon of Mary in varied roles as problem, as symbol of guilt, as romantic legend, as political obstacle, as political ideal; and finally, at the center of this fusion of historic reality, personal imperative, and romantic legend, we confront the woman, pathetic, noble, dangerously compelling, yet tragically aware of the fatality of her power.

The historic particulars of her plight, needing exposition, are masterfully translated into the dramatic particulars of her first scene. Roland has arrived to join her household as Murray's spy. His guides are Murray's messengers, come to browbeat Mary into signing abdication papers; her argument with them is as expositorially lucid as it is dramatically vigorous. The rest of the novel centers on her escape; yet it becomes her story without becoming any less the enactment of Roland's ordeal of hereditary loyalties impinging on a struggle for moral freedom. Mary's escape provides the climax of that ordeal. In turn, Mary is humanized and individualized through her concern for the young lovers, both fated to serve her, both finding their private destinies inextricable from her public fate. The humanizing only makes more urgent our sense of Roland's personal danger. Waverley's involvement with Charles Edward is superficial and inorganic by comparison. The focus on Roland's fateful experience of the dangerous romance and the persuasive reality of Mary in her remote island prison excludes almost all need for the particularizing of historic milieu.

The historicity of Elizabeth and her England in *Kenilworth* is realized by different means and with different effect. Both plot and texture are grounded in a mode of historicity not found elsewhere among the Waverleys. *Kenilworth* is recklessly anachronistic, confusing one Elizabethan decade with another, moving the death of Amy Robsart back and the maturity and fame of William Shakespeare forward. It is distractingly fictitious, yet unusually historical: fictitious in that it manifests a constant inventiveness; historical in that its materials are historic personages – Amy, her warder Foster, Leicester, Sussex, Walter Ralegh, Elizabeth herself. *The Abbot* introduces Mary in a romance world, in a romantic fiction, which is then endowed with personal actuality; *Kenilworth* places a whole social complex of actual personages in a real world, which is then made almost wholly fictitious. *The Abbot* ends with the historic catastrophe of Mary's public career; *Kenilworth's* anachronisms don't matter because the novel excludes the epoch-making events of Elizabeth's reign. In *Kenilworth* the socio-political conditions of which Auerbach makes much in *Rouge et Noir* are translated wholly into an all-pervasive moral atmosphere.[41] Human relations are those of servant and master on every level. Theme is stated and restated in an astounding variety of forms and motifs, as divergent answers are given to this question: what makes a true servant? or this question: is the servant a moral emblem of his master? or this: can the master who has invoked a "devil" ever free himself morally from that diabolical servant's power?

At the center of the problem is the proud, vacillating Leicester; at the apex of the pyramid of true and false servants is Elizabeth. The principal characters all acquire the same degree of psychological particularity, always governed by the normative implications of the "true servant" theme. There is no rhetoric of approach to the historic reality of one central personage, as with Mary or Charles Edward or Cromwell. Moreover, Leicester, Amy, and Tressilian, the central triangle, are not historically typical, not embodiments of forces in historical dialectic. They are more completely particularized than most Waverley characters; they are all equally accessible to the omniscient narrator's eye as they struggle with a moral dilemma that is at once timeless and peculiarly appropriate to a moral stylization of

197

Elizabethan political society: the striving for the freedom to choose between the spectacular unreality of public ambition and glory and the pastoral stability of contentment and true love. Thus, the question of historic or cultural survival scarcely arises in *Kenilworth*. The book's principals fail to survive, yet the tragedy embodies no such historical pessimism as is implicit in the tragic endings of *The Bride of Lammermoor* and *St. Ronan's Well*. Leicester is identified with a new speciousness, a new poison of moral unreality, contrasted with the old chivalric honor of Sussex. But in Leicester's downfall we are too aware of his moral dilemma as an individual to recall earlier hints of a controlling historical dialectic.

If King James of *The Fortunes of Nigel* seems the fullest, most vigorously participant of all of Scott's important historic personages, it is because James was as ready-made a Waverley "character" as if the Author of Waverley had invented him. This alone gives him a completeness and vitality independent of any historical milieu. The characteristics are historical enough: ponderous antiquarianism and scholastic lumber joined to vulgar, even slovenly informality; licentiousness and timidity; extravagance and meanness – in short, the colorful walking anomaly of "the wisest fool in Christendom." Give such a character kingly power and James's name and he becomes an appropriate center for the Jacobean age. Yet in the novel he seems an accidental center. Elizabeth is symbolic center of a sociomoral universe. Mary is focus and tragic victim of the forces which have turned her world to chaos. James's world shares his traits of meanness, materialistic and egoistic extravagance. But the world is neither cause nor effect nor symbolic extension of him. This is in part because *Nigel* lacks the symbolic organization of *Kenilworth* and *The*

Abbot, evoking the surface realism of the citizen comedies rather than, say, the prevalent moral symbolism of a *Volpone.*

But if *Nigel's* historicity seems inorganic, it is not inorganic in the way *The Monastery's* is. The situation of Nigel is inconceivable in any other epoch. The young Scot's inheritance is mortgaged to the hilt to support his father's generous loans to James. Nigel must enter a strange world and remind James of his heritage and of his debt. The world is economically as unstable as its king, and instability aids in the rise of the usurer, the gamester, and the projector to positions of power. But it is moral, not economic, decay which entraps Nigel. He becomes implicated in the final setting of the "beams of chivalry," the decline of fidelity and truth into cynical egocentricity.

Nigel is trapped into acquiring a reputation for meanness in gambling and thence moves downward through further falls of reputation. Among Waverley heroes he is *par excellence* the creature of reputation. He can participate in no ideological conflict, for he thinks of little other than the danger of appearing foolish. He is a generalized anxiety; hence, if, as Welsh argues, he is "actually one of the most complex of Scott heroes,"[42] they are an insipid bunch indeed. But he is atypically conventional and passive. The "transformation" Welsh describes is simply a development of malicious rumor spread by Dalgarno. Even the narrator is aware of Nigel's inadequacy, recalling his central position in the narrative with a mixture of boredom and irritation as, for example, in the openings of Chapters XXII and XXVII. His only activity is to attract to himself, usually because he is his father's son, numerous guides and protectors. Only in this activity does he acquire any moral reality whatsoever.

His initial downward step is embodied in a foolish choice

199

between alternative guides. If his fortunes are to acquire significant historicity, it will be definable only in terms of the characterization of these guides.

The first provided the idea for the novel. Recalling Jeanie Deans, Scott decided to venture an unheroic hero with "worth of character, goodness of heart, and rectitude of principle" – and no more romantic traits than these (vii). The reference, however, is not to Nigel, but to George Heriot, the prudent, wealthy, middle-aged goldsmith. Heriot belongs with Jarvie, Jonathan Oldbuck, the elder Phillipson, the benevolent Quaker Geddes, and other bourgeois figures of practical humanity and courage. His role is as surrogate father or spiritual elder. Heriot's own rise to the wealth and power of the King's goldsmith would provide a story appropriate to Jacobean London. But we do not see his rise; we see only his attempts to influence and protect the young Scots nobleman whose fortunes are largely controlled by other agencies. Moreover, his attempts abruptly terminate. Having taken initial steps in Nigel's behalf, Heriot is sent off to France on royal business and returns only to find Nigel in the Tower of London, to be taken in by reports of Nigel's disgrace, and to watch while others reinstate him. The only meaningful explanation is that Heriot is withdrawn because Nigel rejects this true mentor and guide in favor of a false one.

The false one nearly ruins Nigel's fortunes; if Nigel's secular fall and redemption are to have any historical significance, that significance should be implicit in the characterization of the false guide, Lord Dalgarno. And so, at the beginning, it seems to be. Dalgarno embodies the manners and sentiments that are evil or destructive in the new age. He is fop, rake, gambler, cynic, and follower of Buckingham and "Baby Charles." To get Nigel's ancestral estate as a hunting domain, Buckingham must prevent James from paying his debt and thus clearing the mortgage. Dalgarno thereupon sets out to destroy Nigel's reputation in order to prevent him from appealing directly to the King. His temporary success is founded on Nigel's passivity; the crucial effect of Nigel's passivity is to set him at a hopeless distance from James. In a soliloquy which might be spoken by most Waverley heroes, Nigel recognizes that he has become "a mere victim," "a thing never acting but perpetually acted upon." He has been "as passive and helpless as a boat that drifts without oar or rudder" (263) – and this metaphor becomes literal at the moral turning point in his fortunes, his moral self-assertion. Provided with boat and boatmen for an escape down the Thames, he asserts himself by forcing the well-meaning boatmen at gunpoint to do his bidding; he becomes the rudder of his own boat, turns to shore at Greenwich (315–17), and knowing "that he must now be sufficient to himself or be utterly lost" (326), he confronts James directly. For Welsh, this is simply the final proof of his utter propriety, his surrendering himself to proper authority.[43] Nigel does not see it, however, as surrender. In the book's terms, this is rather a self-assertion which frees the protagonist from his destructive passivity and forces upon the timid James a test of his own worthiness to survive. Our final affectionate but respectful image of James certifies that Nigel's assertion of moral will has effected more than just his own moral survival.

Dalgarno's chief role has been to prevent this appeal. For a while his efforts can be explained in terms of historic transition or conflict. He is the son of an old rival-friend of Nigel's father. Dalgarno and his father Huntinglen are introduced as a contrast of old and new manners in James's London as Sussex and Leicester serve in the Elizabethan

London of *Kenilworth*. We have been told that in such contrasts Scott identifies the old with the quixotically imprudent and the new with the mundane and sensible. Appropriately, the Introduction to *Nigel* sees the Jacobean period as rich in picturesque possibilities, a time to be conceived spatially in terms of the "foothills" of Lady Mary Wortley Montagu's metaphor, where rough manners give way to enlightened restraint, and remnants of chivalry momentarily coexist with the impulses of a new naturalism. Here the romancer is free to mix the improbable (turbulent, ferocious) in incident with the subtly differentiated and varied in character and sentiment (viii–ix).

Such is the historical picturesque. The prudent Heriot adopts it as a mode of comparison as he and Nigel leave Huntinglen's house: " 'There live,' he said, 'the old fashion and the new. The father is like a noble old broadsword, but harmed with rust, from neglect and inactivity; the son is your modern rapier, well-mounted, fairly gilt, and fashioned to the taste of the time – and it is time must evince if the metal be as good as the show' " (129). At times Dalgarno seems to offer Nigel an authentic modernism, to play the serious and reliable guide for Nigel's passage from the old and rigid world of Huntinglen to a new reality (150). His attack on his father's "old-world service" at court seems plausible enough:

Your prompt and uncourteous sword-in-hand attendance on the Sovereign is no longer necessary, and would be as unbeseeming as your old-fashioned serving-men, with their badges, broadswords, and bucklers, would be at a court mask. Besides, father, loyal haste hath its inconveniences. I have heard, and from royal lips too, that when you stuck your dagger into the traitor Ruthven, it was with such little consideration, that the point ran a quarter of an inch into the royal buttock. . . . This comes of old fashions [158].

But this is unusual. Dalgarno's manifest cynicism, foppishness, absenteeism, denial of responsibility for his servants – all these soon make clear that Heriot's delay in judging the "metal" inferior to the "show" is merely naive. Dalgarno's purpose embraces no new civility. It is to shame Nigel out of his scruples, to blunt his conscience and ruin his reputation. He can hardly serve as legitimate guide to the new. While licentiousness and cynicism might easily flourish in such an epoch, there is no reason to see Dalgarno as historically representative of a widespread shift of manners. The other "originals" said to be "of their time" – the dandified apprentices, the malicious cripple Sir Mungo Malagrowther, the burghers of the City – turn out to be reasonable and humane enough. Dalgarno as villain is increasingly isolated; even Buckingham and Charles finally reject him. Thus, Nigel's rejection of Heriot for Dalgarno and his consequent ordeal can hardly be defined in terms of historic transition. And thus, the densely particularized milieu remains separate from the central experience indicated by the title. The historic moment is there; but we cannot get into it, for it lacks a moral or psychological center. James himself remains too idiosyncratic and peripheral; Heriot removes himself for much of the book; Nigel is seldom used as observer or central consciousness.[44]

The more organic historicity of *Kenilworth* is due to the book's degree of moral and poetic unity. Emblematic iteration and socio-moral atmosphere are substantially fused into an ethos that surrounds and defines the single suspense of the Leicester-Amy secret. The controlling structural emblem is apparent in the focus on two sharply contrasted houses and significant movements between them: Cumnor Hall,

Amy's gilded prison as Leicester's secret wife; and Kenilworth, the place of ultimate theatricality. The places are poles of public glory and private truth between which Leicester is gradually torn to pieces; they are forces in the book's central psychological tension. Cumnor is a place of hidden gold, a seclusion whose value is contingent on utter removal from the world. The sumptuous apartments are a Palace of Art; a House of Busyrane:

The new and highly decorated suite of rooms were for the first time illuminated, and that with a brilliancy which might have been visible half a dozen miles off, had not oaken shutters, carefully secured with bolt and padlock, and mantled with long curtains of silk and of velvet, deeply fringed with gold, prevented the slightest gleam of radiance from being seen without [52].

Here, Foster plays guardian "dragon" over Leicester's "golden fruit" (79). To visit his hidden gold, Leicester can come from his world of spectacular falseness only in disguise; Amy, his "hidden gold," boasts of her ability to distinguish Leicester's true worth from the outer garments he can here dare to hold in disdain (65). Amy becomes increasingly dissatisfied, however, with the artifice of playing her true role as Leicester's wife in such unreal surroundings. As she becomes more insistent on public recognition, Leicester's reasons for avoiding it also increase in urgency, and both motivations lead the novel toward its climactic location, the utterly spectacular setting of Kenilworth, where, as in Elizabeth's court, "you will please remember that your blazonry must be *argent* and *or;* no other tinctures will pass current" (139).

The castle, in full preparedness for the theatrical pomp of Elizabeth's entertainment, is seen first through the sad, bewildered eyes of the fugitive Amy. The effect is of combined melancholy and fraud. When she first sees the "stately towers rising from within a long sweeping line of outward walls, ornamented . . . with many a banner streaming from its walls," she questions her own worthiness. "But her pride and generous spirit resisted the whisper which bade her despair" (294–95). A closer look casts the "princely splendour" in an odd light. "Gigantic warders" on the battlements are designed to represent the soldiers of Arthur. Some are "real men, dressed up with vizards and buskins; others . . . mere pageants composed of paste-board and buckram, which, viewed from beneath, and mingled with those that were real, formed a sufficiently striking representation of what was intended" (296). Ironically, Scott makes a moral emblem of the pasteboard theatricality of which his severer critics often accuse him. The garish unreality in turn makes an effective judgment on the equally pitiable Leicester and Amy.

Amy is one of the most complex of Scott's characters. She is pathetic and faithful, proud and vain. Her devotion to Leicester resigns her to the prison of Cumnor Hall; for a time she delights in playing her ornamental role in her own secret palace. Yet she comes to Kenilworth, a Disneyland of disguise and pasteboard, to claim a public reality as the Countess of Leicester. An actress by instinct, she refuses "obstinately to play the part assigned to her in the drama at Kenilworth" (248), wife to Leicester's servant Varney. When she appeals in the name of reality to Elizabeth, the logically ironic occurs:

Elizabeth naturally conjectured that the beautiful but mute figure which she beheld was a performer in one of the various theatrical pageants which had been placed in different situations to surprise her with their homage, and that the poor player, overcome with awe at her presence, had either forgot the part assigned her or lacked courage to go through with it [367–68].

Reality has no chance at Kenilworth. Amy is easily misrepresented as mad and spirited back to Cumnor to be imprisoned symbolically where Foster hides his own gold; she falls to her death through the trapdoor designed to protect that gold. Amy's tragic destiny seems, then, to move between two gilded artifices, one fraud and one concealment, and she herself is doomed to fall in the final revelation of falseness.

The obsession with gold provides another structural motif: the importance of alchemy and alchemists which figures literally and metaphorically throughout the narrative. From the outset, when Mike Lambourne (rogue, bravo, picaro) returns with a diminishing gold supply to find a new master who "may prove the philosopher's stone to me, and convert my groats into fair rose nobles again" (26), we are continually aware of alchemic aspiration and metaphor, and of master-servant relationships built on the quicksand of alchemic fraud. Varney promises Lambourne, enrolled now as servant to Leicester, "thou goest to a household where you have gold, as they say, by the eye" (83). Already in Leicester's service is the astrologer-alchemist Alasco, who promises him "gold, which promises power, wealth, dignity, all that the proud heart of man desires" (214). Leicester's rival and Amy's rejected suitor Tressilian acquires as his servant Alasco's runaway "canon's yeoman," the curious folklore figure Wayland Smith. The importance of Alasco and Wayland grows until the struggle between good and evil seems a struggle between good and evil alchemists for the survival of Amy, and even of Leicester.

Wayland's two roles as alchemist and servant connect the book's iterative imagery and its central moral theme. As good servant he is in increasingly direct conflict with Varney, the evil servant. They have many skills in common as actors and manipulators, and both are devoted to their masters. Varney's ends, however, are selfish, and Leicester becomes helplessly entangled in his servant's manipulations. Wayland is compassionate and as a result finds himself "engaged far deeper than he had expected in a train of mysterious and unintelligible intrigues, in which the actors seemed hardly to know their own course" (317). At times Wayland is the book's central consciousness and takes on the traits of the Waverley protagonist, anticipating the later smithhero of *The Fair Maid of Perth.* The conflict of Wayland and Varney embodies in plot the book's controlling concern with the moral problem of the evil servant.

The theme first appears in the lively, functional opening chapters with Lambourne's return. Foster recognizes in his old friend one who is "well qualified" for the service of Varney, and through him, Leicester. Varney instructs both in the nature of service to one like Leicester: "He has the more need to have those about him who are unscrupulous in his service, and who, because they know that his fall will overwhelm and crush them, must wager both blood and brain, soul and body, in order to keep him aloft" (48). "Know you aught of the requisites expected from the retainer of a rising courtier?" he asks Lambourne. Lambourne enumerates: "a quick eye, a close mouth, a ready and bold hand, a sharp wit, and a blunt conscience." "Thou mayest do me, and my lord, and thyself, good service," Varney concludes (81). Tressilian is "not altogether so secure of the fidelity of his new retainer" (145) and instructs Wayland very differently: "I advise you to practice no such knavery while waiting upon me. . . . [He is to] understand that to have such tricks of legerdemain practiced by one attending on me diminishes my honour" (149). Elizabeth is obliged to instruct her chief servants, Leicester and Sussex: "For, my lords, I tell you plainly, your follies and your brawls lead to strange disorders among your servants" (181). Capriciously she excuses Leicester and then judges the "truth" of his servant by the illustrious Earl's own word (188).

Again and again the book restates the moral interdependence of master and servant. Poor Amy finds in her attendant, Foster's daughter, the book's most exemplary faithful servant: "She hath much need of faithful service," says Wayland to Janet (236); and Janet's response is to place her "faithful service" above even her loyalty to her father and to help Amy escape. "Am I to lose thee? Is this thy faithful service?" asks Amy (266). The book's world consists wholly in relationships that raise this question and provide diverse answers. The most comprehensive and explicit answer is provided by the young Walter Ralegh. "What doth he with such attendants, then, as he hath about him?" he asks with reference to the claim that Leicester is honorable. "The man who raises the devil may be honest, but he is answerable for the mischief the fiend does for all that" (154). Varney is frequently likened to the devil, especially by Leicester himself: "Thank the devil, whose agent thou art. . . . Thou art a devil, Varney . . . but thou hast the mastery for the present: I follow thee" (196). The book dramatizes the paradox of the diabolical servant mastering his master. The initial instance, during which Lambourne blackmails Foster into presenting him to Varney's entourage, anticipates the most important instance. Leicester is increasingly passive in Varney's hands. His plight is evident from their first departure together from Cumnor. Varney is disguised as master; Leicester

208

forgets "his assumed character of a domestic" and rides ahead. "There goes fine policy – the servant before the master!" mutters Varney ominously (77). In later scenes, by skills Varney has inherited from his roguish antecedents Mosca and Iago, Varney "saves" his master by forcing Leicester into greater and greater dependence on his disguise.

The book thus achieves thematic and symbolic unity quite in keeping with its ornate, literarily derived theatrical texture, its recurrent images of false splendor, its formulaic figures of court gales, tempests, and tides of favor. Such is the poetic texture of its historicity. But the public pageantry enters into a heightening tension with the private awarenesses of Leicester and Amy. They are continually internalized for us; we watch them, both proud and ambitious, yet both longing for freedom, truth, and stability, as they experience the deepening unreality of pomp and power.

Amy is an Elizabethan, aristocratic variant of Effie Deans; the narrator's few explicit judgments depict her as the vain daughter of a too indulgent father. But her real capacities gradually render this judgment trivial. Her pride rises to heights of firm courage and candor; consider, for example, the scene in which she does speak out to Leicester, an incident immediately following the scene in which she could not speak to the queen except in contradictions (381–83). Her ultimate helplessness is Effie's in an ennobled form: she loves Leicester too much to endanger his public role, although that role is a lie which robs her of all reality. There is no way for her to save herself without destroying Leicester. Her sense of this plight builds in intensity throughout the narrative against a background crescendo of theatricality, the climaxing of Leicester's public role in the pageantry of the Kenilworth progress.

Leicester is equally complex. It is easy to find in him the

Mirror for Magistrates figure. But so dynamic are the fluctuations of his conscience that one can never predict when his impulses to truth and honor will win out, how long they will prevail, or if and how they may prove effectual. Such psychological dynamisms as these are in increasing tension with the formal pageantry of his public presence. Such is the narrative's movement: the intensifying contrast between the deepening truth with which the lovers recognize their impossible situation and the clamoring falsehood, which neither finds strength to deny, of Leicester's public glory. There is nothing like this elsewhere in the novels; its strengths differ from the strengths of successful novels in the Waverley pattern – *The Abbot, Quentin Durward.*

The Abbot is far less "literary," far more the personalizing of a dilemma of divided historic loyalties against the background of a crisis of cultural survival. The hero's ordeal, the fated inheritance of fanatic loyalty, his determination to be free, and his agility at role playing, at being true to his trust and true to the values that ensure his survival, is a full articulation of the Waverley formula. In addition, Roland remains perhaps the most complex and interesting of the heirs of Edward Waverley. Welsh sees only justice in Senior's early disapproval, and adds that Roland's "aggressive compulsion to stab people" would "intrigue the clinical psychologist."[45] So, even more, would his curious but repeated encounters with sexual ambiguity, with the charges of effeminacy leveled at the lady's squire, with the Seyton brother disguised as the Seyton sister. Whatever the conclusions of the hypothetical analyst, few individual moral developments in the novels can compare with Roland's. He grows from mystery and unpredictability as an orphan from the "Debateable Land," through juvenile recklessness and vanity, into humane fidelity, and finally to an earned stability worthy of survival. In his mixture of the thwarted, proud orphan, the witty lover, and the defiant rebel, he is Scott's closest approximation to the Byronic-Beyliste phenomenon of Julien Sorel.

Roland's dilemma is akin to Ravenswood's: how to realize his historic identity and at the same time assert his independence of its extreme imperatives. It is akin, too, to Darsie Latimer's: his origins are a mystery to him; the possibility of self-identification seems inseparable from the imperatives of hereditary loyalties. To be his historic self he must surrender his freedom to historic involvement and yet earn his individual right to survive that surrender. Ultimately, with the maturing of the idea of the freedom he seeks, he conceives of and acts upon an honorable duplicity which permits active personal loyalty to Mary Stuart and at the same time a growing ideological commitment to the forces that oppose her. Such a duplicity enables him, in spite of a willed participation, to escape the fatality which, as Mary herself sadly observes, attends on all her devotees. Like other morally dynamic Waverley protagonists, he survives by transcending the historic fatality which dooms his coparticipants.

The engineer of Mary's escape from the isle, George Douglas, is aided by Roland; yet for Douglas the consequences of chivalric devotion to Mary are alienation and death. Roland, superficially viewed in the contrast, simply falls short of such devotion and must be found inferior except by standards of prudence and flexibility. But this is to mistake the point of distinction. Roland's dedication is no less; but it is based in a free and reasonable commitment to the chivalric code, and it is held within personal limits. Throughout, Roland is scorned as a mere lady's page; by the end, however, this service and sustained attachment to the lady, and not her faction, save him from a fatal entanglement with the forces that support her rebellion.

What gives *The Abbot* its unusually coherent vitality is the way Roland serves simultaneously as central observer in the rhetoric of Mary's compelling delineation and as moral center of the book's historic experience. Contributing to this coherence are three complex parallelisms. First, his lively romantic pursuit of Mary's attendant Catherine Seyton is itself wrapped in the *Twelfth Night* mystery of Catherine's twin brother's female disguises, and this contributes to the mystery of Roland's fateful involvement with ambiguous, domineering women. Second, Catherine is as much a pawn of hereditary commitment as Roland, and thus, while their union seems appropriate, their love is imperiled by history, growing as it does in the compassionate but fateful presence of Mary. Third, Roland's obsessive concern with freedom, his determination to liberate himself from the obscure, yet powerful imperatives of the past, finds a sympathetic parallel in Mary's pathetic longing to be free of her prison. Roland seems fated to risk himself in behalf of her freedom in order to win his own.

The structure of his involvement is also the structure of his personal growth. Three stages may be discerned. The first leads from his mysterious appearance, through his alienation from Avenel and his reclamation by his fanatic grandmother, to his commitment to history as Murray's spy. The second traces the parallel growth of his romance with Catherine and his devotion to the royal prisoner. The final stage compels him to act in accordance with both attachments: Mary's forces collapse, she loses all freedom in flight to England, and Roland survives his involvement and attains his freedom from the historic fatality attending on

Mary. The stages amount roughly to three thirds of the book.

The first third shows the petulant, vain youth's false idea that he can be free by childish self-assertion. Ironically, when the boy is forced to leave the Castle of Avenel, he imagines himself free, and already the ambiguity of his freedom is couched in an imagery abundant throughout the book. The child, initially rescued from the lake, as he says, "like a hurt wild-duck" (93), earns by his petulance and vanity the accusations that he is simply a "foul kite, that would fain be a tercel gentle" (34), that he is a "cock-sparrow" that would "crow over" the whole household. When he is put out, "he is gone like a wild duck, as he came" (52), but his companion the falconer assures him that he may "soar the better and fairer flight for all this yet": "you are your own man, and may go where you will, without minding whoop or whistle" (64).

Ironically, he is reclaimed by his grandmother immediately, and her praise translates the prevalent bird imagery into implications directly hostile to his immature will to be free. She sees only that her "gay goss-hawk hath been well trained, and will soar high," but at her "whoop or whistle" (82). "Thou hast kept well," she says admiringly, "the bird in thy bosom" – indicating by proverb, as Scott's note tells us, that he has "preserved unstained his fidelity" to ancestral loyalties (70). Roland recognizes that his freedom has simply led to a new constraint and is determined to know the destiny she envisages before he commits himself: "I will be no reclaimed sparrow-hawk, who is carried hooded on a woman's wrist, and has his quarry only shown to him when his eyes are uncovered for his flight" (75). Much later, precisely the same figures are used tauntingly by Catherine's brother to describe Roland's moral growth. For whom "do you take me?" Roland asks. "For the wild falcon," is the answer, "whom a dog brought in his mouth to a certain castle, when he was but an unfledged eyas; for the hawk whom men dare not let fly, lest he should check at game and pounce on carrion; whom folk must keep hooded till he has the proper light of his eyes, and can discover good from evil" (291). Such is his grandmother's determination. She demands absolute obedience, and while he secretly determines that "I will not be all my life the slave of a woman's whistle, to go when she bids and come when she calls" (88), for the time being he can only wonder: "Am I for ever . . . to be devoured with the desire of independence and free agency, and yet to be for ever led on by circumstances to follow the will of others?" (82)

The first phase reaches a climax when, having become Murray's agent, Roland recognizes his surrender to the romance of history:

It did not diminish from, but rather added to, the interest of a situation so unexpected that Roland himself did not perfectly understand wherein he stood committed by the state secrets in which he had unwittingly become participator. On the contrary, he felt like one who looks on a romantic landscape, of which he sees the features for the first time, and then obscured with mist and driving tempest. The imperfect glimpse which the eye catches of rocks, trees, and other objects around him adds double dignity to these shrouded mountains and darkened abysses, of which the height, depth, and extent are left to imagination [185].

Few passages illustrate so vividly Scott's translation of the Gilpinesque vision of picturesque landscape into the romance of historic involvement. For the third time, then, Roland's loss of freedom makes him a lady's page, commits him to an effeminate passivity. But now, as he enters Mary's service, he is expected to sustain a duplicity whereby he can be personally faithful to Mary and yet true to Murray's trust: "the sum required of you," warns Murray, "is fidelity – I mean fidelity to myself and to the state" (204). It is the same absolute demand from a dubious authority which Quentin Durward is to receive from Louis. Durward, however, morally a simpler figure than Roland, resists the demand. In view of Roland's lively ambition, witty egocentricity, and determination to be free, we expect that he may sustain his opportunistic fidelity to Murray.

Yet behind it looms a prior fidelity, and his initial response is to resent both claimants and think only of personal survival:

It was quite evident that he had, through various circumstances not under his control, formed contradictory connexions with both the contending factions by whose strife the kingdom was distracted, without being properly an adherent of either. . . . It required very little reflection to foresee that these contradictory claims on his service might speedily place him in a situation where his honour as well as his life might be endangered [208].

But he is not the type to be apprehensive. Besides, the conflict gives him a degree of freedom: "None of them can say I have given word or promise to either of their factions; for they have led me up and down like a blind Billy, without giving me any light into what I was to do" (209). The hood ensures the hawk's moral freedom; he will wait to shape future commitments on the basis of direct experience of "this beautiful and unfortunate Mary Stuart" (209).

Throughout the book's middle third he watches Mary in prison. Situation and technique fuse: he is sent as Murray's spy and can therefore be our observer. It seems perilously inevitable, however, that the initial duplicity of the spy will be transformed in a youth naively chivalric into infatuated

215

loyalty to Mary. There are abundant, well-placed warnings. Roland himself is reminded, seeing Mary's isle, of the Castle of Avenel and struck (as we are) by the rhythmic coherence of his destiny: " 'I must have been born,' he thought, 'under the star that presides over ladies and lakes of water, for I cannot by any means escape from the service of the one or from dwelling in the other.' " The familiar impulse and imagery then reappear: "But if they allow me not the fair freedom of my sport and exercise, they shall find it as hard to confine a wild drake as a youth" (210). Mary herself becomes tenor of the same vehicle when Lady Douglas warns her son George: "She is like an isle on the ocean, surrounded with shelves and quicksands – its verdure fair and inviting to the eye, but the wreck of many a goodly vessel which had approached it too rashly" (243). The reader recognizes in the historic fate of Douglas the threat to Roland. Mary is a dangerously alluring isle, and Roland is warned against the songs of sirens (268). The most effective hint, though, is association with Rizzio. Led through the winding passages of Holyrood, Roland trips and nearly falls on a "low step." His guide reminds him ominously that, as the bloodstains indicate, this is where Rizzio fell (174). Such hints sustain our sense of Roland's peril through the novel's middle third.

Meanwhile, he remains unsure of his loyalty, his proper role; and for his increasingly conscientious efforts to discriminate, he earns the reputation – hence, the ordeal of Morton in *Old Mortality* – for "mere fickleness and coldness of spirit" (262). The dilemma of "contradictory claims on his service" (208) has worsened. Whatever he does, he is "exposed to suspicion on all sides for my mistress will consider me as a spy placed on her by her enemies, seeing me so far trusted by them; and the Lady Lochleven will never cease to suspect the possibility of my betraying her, because circumstances put it in my power to do so" (268). Under such moral pressure, the Roland who defies his grandmother at the second climax has matured. He now insists that

I have been treated amongst you . . . as one who lacked the common attributes of free-will and human reason, or was at least deemed unfit to exercise them. A land of enchantment have I been led into, and spells have been cast around me – every one has met me in disguise – every one has spoken to me in parables – I have been like one who walks in a weary and bewildering dream; and now you blame me that I have not the sense, and judgment, and steadiness of a waking, and a disenchanted, and a reasonable man, who knows what he is doing, and wherefore he does it! [296–97]

This is the familiar moment of post-romantic self-assertion for the Waverley hero. If Roland is to act in support of a traditional loyalty, it must be as a morally and intellectually free agent, not as one passive and blind in the toils of historic fatality. He determines to act by his own code; fidelity to his personal trust takes precedence over all other ties: "I like not that good service which begins in breach of trust" (302). Caught between absolutes of commitment and noncommitment, he comes of age morally when he recognizes the limits of his choice and freely chooses to act for the time being in accordance with traditional loyalties and codes: "I was bred a Catholic – bred in the faith of Bruce and Wallace – I will hold that faith till time and reason shall convince me that it errs. I will serve this poor Queen as a subject should serve an imprisoned and wronged sovereign" (308).

Paradoxically, the effect of self-assertion is at once to commit Roland, for he now "felt himself at liberty, without any breach of honour towards the family of Lochleven, to contribute his best aid to any scheme which should in future be formed for the Queen's escape" (329), and to give him a sense of freedom far more mature than that of the petulant boy of the early chapters. Through this final stage, then, the problem of freedom and its associated imagery of birds focus elsewhere.

Mary's thoughts of freedom are birds; the plot to liberate her is a bird; she is a fair dove pent up in a wretched dovecot (336, 337, 362). But as she realizes the fatal tyranny of her control over those who would free her, Mary sadly realizes that fate allows her no true freedom. Roland alone is now free of the fatality of her influence. He grows further and further away from Mary's devotees. His chief doubters on both sides are the spokesmen for extreme fatalism – Dryfesdale and Seyton, Catherine's brother. From their fatalist viewpoint, Roland's freedom, his willed autonomy, makes him unreliable. He is able, however, to convince both extremes of his trustworthiness. As the romance of the escape unfolds, and even Mary sadly enjoys the spectacle of herself as "princess of romance" with her knight and squire (372), Roland alone plays his role freely and rationally, and to him alone can Mary appeal for a fidelity based on reason and on personal humanity, a kind of fidelity she has not known: " 'O! Roland Graeme,' said Mary, in a tone of deep despondency, 'be true to me; many have been false to me. Alas! I have not always been true to myself!" (384) Her misgivings are confirmed, her nobility is undeniable, as she sees her fear that she must "drag into destruction with us every generous heart which makes an effort in our favour" (335), written in the dying features of George Douglas on the battlefield of Langside, where, comments a bitterly ironic narrator, "in the name of their sovereign, fellow-subjects on both sides shed each other's blood, and, in the name of their Creator, defaced His image" (414).

If the young Douglas dies, why does Roland survive? Roland is true to his personal code, to his devotion to Mary's person. There is no basis for his involvement in the final struggle to restore Mary to the throne. His remaining in personal attendance on Mary during the battle is consistent with the role he has chosen to play and with the fidelity she has asked from him and at the same time is the basis for his survival. Surviving are his mature, rationalized chivalry, his devotion to the doomed Queen; gone are his petulance and presumption. He has won control over his destiny, over the historic fatality that might have encompassed him, too, by realizing and affirming the crucial difference between personal humanity and fidelity on one hand and chivalric fanaticism on the other. We are reminded of Waverley and Morton. But Waverley's struggle with his own commitment to Charles Edward is superficial and abstract by comparison with Roland's, and Morton's struggle is more with conflicting ideas than with persons as compelling as Mary Stuart and the witty and alluring Catherine Seyton. As observer, Roland is uniquely dynamic; as lover, he is witty and even sexually responsive; as chivalric servant to Mary, he is energetic and self-aware. The suspenseful structure of his complex involvement with her in such a variety of roles makes of *The Abbot* a remarkably successful adaptation of the Waverley pattern to new materials with new implications.

3. CHIVALRY IN DECAY: THE COMPLEXITY OF LOYALTY AND COURAGE

We have seen a variety of novels pose the problem of whether chivalric values may be so stabilized and humanized as to be worthy of historic survival. The problem, basic to the Crusader novels, obviously must lose its focal importance among the other interests of the Renaissance novels. Besides, the era of Elizabeth and James could scarcely provide the most appropriate milieu for dramatizing the decline of chivalry. The most impressive of the romances of decadent chivalry, *Quentin Durward* and *The Fair Maid of Perth,* are more fittingly set in the times of Froissart and Malory, where chivalry persists only as a romantic memory, easily lapsed into cynical brutality, and feudalism is far advanced in weakness and decadence.[46] The late feudal, postchivalric world shared by the novels provides a grim setting for the historic testing of chivalric values. The question asked throughout *Durward* – is true fidelity possible for the chivalric aspirant cut off from his own lineage in a strange world of selfish tyranny and moral chaos? – concerns one such value. The similar question asked throughout *The Fair Maid* – is true courage possible in such a world? – concerns the other. Admirably formed and with vigorous, morally complex protagonists, the novels derive their chief virtue from their comprehensive thematic concern: one with the complex and elusive nature of fidelity, the other with the equally complex and equally elusive nature of courage. In both, the concern operates within limits set by the narrator's urgent pacifism.

Both novels refute the notion that the Author of Waverley saw heroic ages end only with the importing of the Hanoverians. The France thrown into chaos by the reckless feuds of Louis XI and Charles of Burgundy is more remote from romantic heroism than Rob Roy's Highlands and Redgauntlet's Borders. A sense of distance from the "reality" of chivalry is as poignant here as when Mary Stuart and her prison attendants play at being figures of romance. Playful, denigrating allusions to "old romaunts" abound in *Durward* (78), in the voices of realistic courage and destructive scepticism alike. The chivalry of the "romaunts" survives only as naïveté in a young soldier of fortune, and as a "romantic enthusiasm for the profession of chivalry" (162) in the foolish Lady Hameline of Croye, who is angrily aware that the days when "ten knights were slain in the lists" at the "great tournament of Strasbourg" are quite over, "and no one now thinks of encountering peril for the sake of honour, or to relieve distressed beauty" (203). Quentin's perilous adventure, like that of Browning's Childe Roland, is undertaken amid a scepticism which doubts its very reality.

The days of Bruce and Wallace are equally remote from the Perth of the prudent and jovial burgher Simon Glover. From his point of view, men of the heroic rigidity of the clan patriarch Torquil of the Oak are rare anachronisms, "giants in romaunts" (350). The historic clan battle which climaxes *The Fair Maid*, one of the strangest and most significant events in Highland history,[47] is a grim study in the incongruousness of chivalric convention in the Scotland of Robert III. A harsh feudal power, cynically attempting to order a chaotic world, forces two powerful clan federations to settle their differences, preferably by destroying each other. The result, with a bellicose Perth blacksmith preeminent on one side and a cowardly young clan chieftain fleeing on the other, is a mockery of chivalric ritual. A weak and gentle king, forced to support the expedient, but horrified by violence, cannot bear to watch. The battle, set on Palm Sunday, is a bloody travesty of romantic warfare and the fitting climax to a book which portrays both the awful futility of violence and the pale ineffectuality of pacifism in a chaotic world.

The narrator's sustained distance from romantic chivalry

221

thus travestied in both books is nowhere better exemplified than in the delineation of Burgundy, the last reckless personification of chivalric *virtu* and, as Louis's disloyal bondsman, the archviolator of the feudal order. Just as *The Fair Maid* builds up to the dreadful clan battle, so *Quentin Durward* is skillfully directed to the climactic confrontation of Burgundy and Louis, and their "summit conference" and "reconciliation" are as sordid a gloss on the decay of chivalry as the Perth battle is a grim and bloody one.

Burgundy appears only in the final third of *Durward*, but his destructive and problematic influence is present throughout. From the outset he is "the Bold," a figure of humorous passion, of rashness, of reckless wilfulness (6–7). In the final chapters he is "hasty," "impatient," "nay, the most imprudent, prince of his time," "frankness" coupled with "grossness," liable to explosions of passion (293, 297, 300). His temper, "though rough, fierce, headlong and unyielding, was not, unless in the full tide of passion, faithless or ungenerous" (309) – but such are the limits of the narrator's admiration. He is one whose passions were permitted "almost a free and uncontrolled dominion over his actions," whose "mind resembled a volcano in eruption, which throws forth all the different contents of the mountain, mingled and molten into one burning mass" (346). The narrator remains at precisely the same affective distance from both Charles and Louis on the few occasions when he draws them together for picturesque contrast. But intellectually he is drawn to Louis; the book's picturesque contrast remains for the most part in the background. Even in the final chapters Charles remains chiefly a foil, and the narrator slights the "exasperated and headlong passion" of Charles to follow Louis and the "deep workings of a vigorous and powerful mind" (300). Burgundy is more central in the novel which excludes Louis and finds its climax in Burgundy's death, *Anne of Geierstein*.

In scope, *Anne* is Scott's most ambitious novel, and it deserves fuller attention than we can afford it. Its protagonist is a middle-aged Lancastrian earl in disguise, one-time saver of Burgundy's life, devoted supporter of Margaret of Anjou, guest and then ambassador of the noble Republican Swiss, guest of René of Provence. Burgundy is at the center of this huge network of conflicting European forces; Louis does not appear; all roads of appeal, defiance, and conciliation lead to Burgundy. The Duke, still reckless and warlike, is seen through the concern and fidelity of his boyhood preserver Oxford ("Phillipson"). Oxford has come to beg Charles's support for Margaret and the cause of the fallen Lancastrians. Charles remains the last inflammable remnant of European chivalry; Oxford appeals to Charles's idealism. Charles recognizes that he is being asked for knight-errantry, and with a mixture of wistfulness and scorn reminds Oxford that "when thou and I wore maiden armour, such words as fame, honour, *los,* knightly glory, lady's love, and so forth, were good mottoes for our snow-white shields, and a fair enough argument for splintering lances" (319). But their lifetime has seen the fading of chivalry.

The wistfulness is insincere. Burgundy is playing power politics as animatedly as the rest. He is no heroic anachronism, but little more than the novel's chief exponent of violence and tyranny. As such he is unequivocally judged by contrasting norms of pacifist libertarianism, which bracket this huge narrative and give it significant unity. At the outset we encounter an idealized world of republican simplicity and patriarchal stability in the Geierstein of the Swiss Landamann, Arnold Biederman. At the end we are led to the fantastic, anachronistic Provence of Margaret's father,

223

the poet-king René, who is at an opposite extreme of chivalric folly from austere Geierstein, but who shares a devotion to peace and a justified fear of the rapacious Burgundy. Thus Burgundy is judged from widely divergent points of view, and at the same time he provides the novel's central problem, as Louis provides it for *Durward*.

The problem at the center of *Anne of Geierstein* (1829) seems to have carried over from *The Fair Maid of Perth* (1828), its immediate predecessor: is pacifism an adequate response to the tyranny and rapacity of Charles? If so, what kind, and with what tactic? A conflict of answers centers on Phillipson-Oxford's acquired conflict of loyalties. Phillipson sees in his new friend Biederman a mirror of ancient fidelity, integrity, and candor; and he promises, in support of Biederman's pacifism against the militancy of the younger Swiss, to become mediator with his old friend Burgundy. This difficult assignment he must carry out without jeopardy to his primary mission to Charles on behalf of Margaret.

Ultimately he fails to secure Burgundy for any cause. Burgundy has too many enemies; the secret Vehmic Tribunal of Westphalia has sworn his death. All Phillipson can do is accompany his old friend into the final disastrous battle with the Swiss. Neither he nor his son is forced to fight against Biederman. Phillipson survives, then, and the survival of his friendship with Biederman and the marriage of his son to Biederman's niece Anne suggest that the death of chivalric tyranny and violence in Burgundy may permit the carrying back to England of the pacifist, libertarian ideals of the Swiss. But for all Burgundy's importance as central problem, for all the depth and complexity of his characterization, he remains a flamboyant, individual anachronism at the center of a crowded, hasty narrative permitting no consistent definition of his role in an historic process.

Although he is less of a character in *Durward,* he plays an important role in the novel's controlled logic of theme. The problem is the nature and survival of chivalric fidelity, of honorable allegiance, in the world of Louis. The disorder of that world derives from repudiation of a chivalric bond on the highest level: Charles's denial of Louis. In this disruption of allegiance are the seeds of lesser disorders: the usurpations of the Wild Boar of Ardennes, the rebellions of the burghers of Liège, which flower so thickly that both pawns to history – Quentin and his fugitive Countess – recognize in desperation, as do father and daughter Glover in *The Fair Maid,* that there is "no corner of the world safe from oppression" (267). This brute fact is the "given" of *Durward* and *The Fair Maid;* their protagonists Henry Smith and Durward must then, however imperfectly, engage actively with this world. For Durward this means resigning himself to the destined loyalty that binds him to the Machiavellian Louis, and manipulating and surviving that bond by a mixture of duplicity and fidelity. In such a chaotic world, the problem is not how to live with the reckless, expendable evil of Charles, but how to survive with and through allegiance to the despicable, necessary evil of Louis.

The complexity of this allegiance reflects the complexity of Louis himself; his characterization provides the central force for the novel's extraordinary coherence. Scott's later introduction (1831) leaves no doubt but that "this remarkable person" is "the principal character in the romance" (xvii). But the introduction, insistent on Louis's gross and debased character, is hardly fair to his ambivalent centrality in the novel itself. For the narrator, Louis is a fascinating moral phenomenon and an inescapable historic force. We have seen the narrator's admiring reference to the "deep workings of a vigorous and powerful mind" (300). The opening chapter concedes that Louis's character, "evil as it

225

was in itself, met, combated, and in a great degree neu-
tralised, the mischiefs of the time" (2). The "time," then,
makes the problem of fidelity to Louis comparable with the
problems of conscience wrestled with by Jeanie Deans and
Henry Morton. The problem is dramatized in Quentin's
ordeal. There is no real alternative to Louis. Confronted
with the "headlong impetuosity" of an imprudent Dunois,
for instance, Louis is the author of peace and order, the
instrument of a higher order: "By the means of this monarch's powerful and prudent, though most unamiable character, it pleased Heaven, who works by the tempest as well
as by the soft small rain, to restore to the great French nation
the benefits of civil government" (4). In the skillfully
expository second chapter, Louis's smiling political realism is
set in contrast to Quentin's boyish taste for chivalric life
(21–22), anticipating at the outset the climactic confrontation of Louis and Burgundy. Louis's followers are, in their
diverse ways, reflections of him – mercenary, realistic, courageous. But they are also emblems of his indifference to
human life and suffering; and as such they serve to expound
another theme shared by the later romances and compel-
lingly developed in *The Fair Maid*: the theme of how the
prince's evil taints his followers, however admirable their
fidelity (54).

Once Durward is trapped into fidelity, we are able to see
Louis more closely through Quentin's unique point of
vantage (87–89) and to note his genius for policy, his
"piercing and majestic glance." In evidence, too, is his
superstition, exemplified in the "dozen of little paltry figures
of saints stamped in lead" worn in his hat band (88).
Quentin is present to hear Louis accuse chivalric idealists
such as Crevecoeur of reckless folly. Louis speaks for peace,
sordid eloquence in behalf of a cynical pacifism; yet Scott

allows Louis to make his case convincingly (98–102), and, whatever Louis's motives, the pacifism he expresses remains part of the book's truth. Similar scenes allow Quentin to observe, as well as to become implicated in, Louis's theatrical duplicity (120–23). But the climax of the preliminary exposition of the complex Louis, and with it the climax of the first third of a remarkably symmetrical narrative structure, is a scene at which Quentin must not be present. Chapter Twelve, "The Politician," shows Louis with his diabolical chief counselor Oliver the Barber. Their plotting prepares for the remainder of the book: they plot an intricate policy to trap Burgundy, exploiting, sacrificing Quentin as guide to the fugitive countess, and this development constitutes the middle third. The policy is to culminate in Louis's own ruse, his daring expedition to visit his dangerous and defiant vassal of Burgundy, and the confrontation makes the final third. The plotting and the ruse illustrate the extraordinary interdependence in Louis of shrewd policy, political daring, and superstitious recklessness. Finally, the scene climaxes the process by which Louis entangles Quentin's destiny with his own, forces Quentin's fidelity, by grounding Louis's initial interest in the young Scottish stranger in his own superstitious character. He had seen Quentin's image in a dream; upon Quentin's arrival, he had had the boy's horoscope cast, and "I have plainly learned, through his [the astrologer's] art and mine own observation, that, in many respects, this unfriended youth has his destiny under the same constellation with mine" (145). Ironically, while the book and its narrator mock Louis's superstitions, both translate the fatalism that is a part of Louis's character into the historic fatality which does in fact entangle Quentin's destiny with that of Louis.

In tracing Quentin's plight, the book's first third has

moved toward the same revelation, which, true to Louis's character, is in a *truer* sense true to the narrative's own rhetoric of connectedness and its theme of historic fatality. At the outset, his family dead in vendetta, his Scottish heritage cut off, his upbringing tainted like Henry's of *The Fair Maid* with violence,[48] Quentin is the exile in search of a new allegiance or, what is the same in a Waverley Novel, a new identity. He is the naive wanderer that Waverley and Osbaldistone and Latimer become. But his quest is more active, and in no other instance is the process of moral implication more skillfully managed. In making Quentin's fortunes merely instrumental, Scott's later introduction is unfair to his protagonist. As Quentin serves the narrator's exposition of Louis, his own entanglement with Louis as a man of destiny, an historic force, is perfected link by link.

The Waverley protagonist's quest for a new allegiance ordinarily embodies an ordeal of historic or cultural survival. But Quentin is more energetic, shrewd, even opportunistic – hence, morally more ambiguous – than his Waverley antecedents, and in this he resembles Roland of *The Abbot* and Henry Smith of *The Fair Maid*. He is a plausible representative of the vestigial chivalry whose historic survival has reached its crisis; he is bloodthirsty, naive, yet capable of generosity and kindliness. What makes his plight so moving is that among the several alternatives available, Quentin can find no place or person worthy of his allegiance. He is an involuntary mercenary, trapped by his mercenary uncle, by his nationality, by accident, by his own careless humanity (cutting down the hanged man), into choosing between death and service in Louis's Scots guards. The pathos of his search and the complexity of his plight are unequaled, for he must plot his survival through contriving to be simply loyal to an unworthy recipient of his fidelity, who is planning to destroy him.

228

It is difficult to imagine a metaphor for the intricate problem of political allegiance, as the Author of Waverley saw it in his own world, more useful than Quentin's plight. The young Scottish exile, intent on finding service where his chivalric idealism will permit fidelity, confronts first the disenchanted "Maitre Pierre," Louis in disguise. To him, the youth poses his questions: where to find service in a world of violence and thieves? where to find a master worthy of true loyalty? Louis is Durward's first guide through the strange, perilous country of his quest, and as Durward gives vent to boyish dreams of chivalry, Louis's amusement anticipates Durward's inevitable disenchantment. The process is complicated as Durward meets his Uncle Balafré, one of Louis's mercenaries. The meeting shapes his choice of a master. He seeks the greater chance for honor under Burgundy; his uncle mocks his boyish folly, praises Louis's policy, calls Burgundy "a hot-brained, impetuous, pudding-headed, iron-ribbed dare-all" (49). Such lessons seem likely to draw a shrewd youth into Louis's service. But the romantic part of his nature has already found its counterforce in the mysterious maid of the turret, the young countess. Romantic involvement with her may imperil Durward's very life under Louis; and his talk with his prudent uncle, in terms echoing other Waverley crises, has temporary effect: "It might have been expected that, when left alone, Durward would have again betaken himself to his turret, in order to watch for the repetition of those delicious sounds which had soothed his morning reverie. But that was a chapter of romance, and his uncle's conversation had opened to him a page of the real history of life" (52). But it serves Louis's policy to place Durward in the service of the lady, as it had served Moray's to use Roland. He will exploit Quentin's romantic side in his war of policy with Burgundy.

229

Durward's plight is indeed complex. His romantic nature ensures his devotion to the lady; his devotion to the lady becomes part of his new allegiance to Louis, a commitment anything but romantic. To protect the lady and himself, he must follow the spirit of Louis's instructions in such a way as to change their letter; and in preventing the fulfillment of Louis's designs, he is preparing himself to save Louis from his own policy. His chivalry and his prudence are put to as difficult a test as ever Gawain faced. Without Julien Sorel's fatal sexuality, he must have Julien's skill in the "politics of survival" if his chivalric values – loyalty, generosity – are to survive. In his triumphant emergence from his ordeal, he demonstrates the capability of humanizing and stabilizing the chivalric spirit, of ensuring its transmission through his own house redeemed, and even of using its power in the temporary pacification of the Burgundy-Louis feud.

The agility with which he grasps the intricacies of his plight makes him perhaps the most actively clever of Waverley protagonists. Such is the subject of the book's central third, the excursion portion so familiar a part of the Waverley pattern, so different in *The Fair Maid*, where the excursion is more a futile gesture of escape than an adventure into the perils of historic allegiance.

Durward's excursion is rich in controlled meaning, and, for a book of "adventure for boys," extraordinarily lacking in action. It begins in Quentin's romantic notion that he will be the lady's "successful guide through the hazards of her pilgrimmage" (149). It proceeds through moral mystification and disenchantment, raising the familiar Waverley questions: which is the true guide, and how true? It places the characters who struggle with the book's dilemma of fidelity in a no-man's-land of confused or delusive loyalties, linguistic uncertainty, and no satisfactory destination, no escape. It demands of them a flexibility in the adoption and rejection of conflicting uniforms, costumes, disguises (216–18, 232–33, 237, 239, 242). The setting is as much a Debateable Land as the Borders which produce Roland Graeme or contain the key to Darsie Latimer's identity. The scenes involve the travelers in discussion of what loyalties are possible in a wilderness where authorities are remote and ambiguous, and laws uncertain.

When Quentin and the ladies meet the gypsy guide provided by Louis, Quentin sets the problem: "I will question the man . . . and assure myself of his fidelity as I best may" (177). In what follows, Quentin is astounded to recognize that there *is* no conventional foundation on which to appeal to the gypsy's fidelity. The man has no religion, no nationality, no dependable livelihood, no home (178–79). In the political terms of a Waverley identity he is "unaccommodated man," Quentin's essential plight embodied, like Lear's in Tom o' Bedlam, in a moral-legal wilderness. But, like Ranald MacEagh in *Montrose*, the gypsy cherishes his liberty, the absolute freedom of political or cultural nakedness. "What is it that remains to you," asks Quentin, "deprived of government, domestic happiness, and religion?"

"I have liberty," said the Bohemian – "I crouch to no one – obey no one – respect no one. I go where I will – live as I can—and die when my day comes."

"But you are subject to instant execution, at the pleasure of the judge?"

"Be it so," returned the Bohemian; "I can but die so much the sooner."

"And to imprisonment also," said the Scot; "and where then is your boasted freedom?"

"In my thoughts," said the Bohemian, "which no chains can bind; while yours, even when your limbs are free, remain fettered by your laws and your superstitions, your dreams of local attachment, and your fantastic visions of civil policy" [179–80].

Quentin, trapped in a new allegiance to Louis's policy and superstitions and without other alternatives, has no answer; the book has supplied him with none. Confrontation with an eloquently defiant political "natural" is a crucial educative aspect of Quentin's excursion.

Moreover, he and the Countess Isabella are logically akin to the gypsy: neither has a stable home or a fidelity grounded in tradition or authority. Isabella's impulse, like that of the fair maid of Perth, is to withdraw from this chaos to monastic seclusion. Quentin's, as he recognizes that he is a man without a cultural identity, is to turn to his own humanity. One bond holds the group together. When Quentin asks the gypsy the crucial question again – the question with which the entire book confronts Quentin himself: "Canst thou be faithful?" – the answer is, "I can; all men can." Asked whether he *will* be, asked "what will bind thee?" – he answers, "kindness" (181–82). Quentin learns that his initial act of kindness in cutting down the body of the gypsy's brother, which imperiled his life and made his entanglement with Louis inescapable, has already won him the gypsy's fidelity in the only way it could be won. When the gypsy conspires with the ultimate in lawlessness of the region, the savage William de la Marck, Quentin overhears the gypsy demand the lanzknecht's oath that not a hair of Quentin's head will be harmed (193).

The "weary wilderness" which serves as setting for Quentin's excursionary ordeal verges, as do like settings in other later novels, on the allegorical. In the terms of political order and allegiance it is a Hell with its proper devil in William the Boar, enemy to every kind of order and humanity.

Louis's attempt to use the demonic force of William almost results in Louis's destruction. The radical burghers of Liege unleash the same force and find that the bestial once loosed cannot be controlled: "This De la Marck is a fury – a perfect boar in his nature as in his name" (243). His men are "monsters," "demons"; the festivity following their bloody conquest of the bishop's palace is "a scene of wild and roaring debauchery" (246).[49] Survival in the face of such forces requires of Quentin every kind of courage and shrewdness; and this climactic proof of himself, though not the last, is the decisive one. With the escape from the wilderness of Liege and the Boar, the excursionary middle third of the book ends, and it ends fittingly with the shock of returning reality.

The wanderers meet Burgundy's courageous and humane ambassador Crévecoeur. Crévecoeur challenges the very reality of the excursion, especially the romance of Quentin's self-proof. It has all been romantic role playing, he warns the youth (281–82); and though he remains one of the book's admirable characters, he also remains spokesman for antiromance. He is Quentin's Colonel Talbot, with the same worth and the same limitations. The excursion has by no means been mere romance. The reality of Quentin's survival, the humanizing and maturing of his chivalric virtues, these and other things prove Crévecoeur's antiromance views, like those of the antichivalry spokesmen of the Crusader novels, too limited. But, while Quentin has earned his role as instrument for the historic survival of chivalric values, he must pass a final test in coping with the intricate and absurd realities to which he has returned.

In his participation in the final third of the book, Quentin is reminiscent of Jeanie Deans. But *Durward* is a better formed book than *The Heart of Midlothian;* and appropriately, Quentin's is the more ambiguous task of saving, not a sister whose sin is venial, but a king unworthy of Quentin's fidelity. We recall the plight of the Saxon hero of *Count Robert*. Like him, Quentin, in order to free himself historically from an unworthy allegiance, must save his unworthy master. The escape from history is through history. Quentin aids in restoring a relative peace and order within which his own romance may be transferred to the real world and consummated in the twin finales of the Waverley pattern: marriage and the restoration of his lost lineage.

Such are Quentin's function and meaning in the book's picturesque climax, Louis's reckless excursion to Burgundy. The scenes between the rulers focus on the problem with which Quentin's experience has familiarized us. The effort to reestablish peace involves Louis himself with the same problem: can Burgundy be faithful? on what grounds can he appeal to Burgundy for good faith? what loyalty is possible – hence, what stability – given the cynical policy of Louis and the reckless self-aggrandizement of Charles? The entire problem of loyalty is underlined by the abundance of mercenaries, some of them capable of the fidelity of a Dalgetty, and by the confusion about whose mercenaries are guarding whom, or whether Louis's reliance on purchased fidelity is recklessness or a necessary evil (300, 318, 322). The question is complicated by the reader's realization that in disobeying Louis, Quentin has already saved Louis's life (307). But now Quentin also becomes chief witness in defense of Louis; and the demands placed on him as key witness are as difficult as those placed on Jeanie Deans. At Louis's trial, Quentin and the young Countess Isabella prove their skill in enlisting an honorable prudence in the service of pacification. Quentin has no illusions about the peace to be secured, and the reconciliation of France and

Burgundy is patently insincere and manifestly temporary. The rulers find a common foe in the bestial William the Boar, and this grim *realpolitik* provides the setting for the triumph of Quentin's bourgeois chivalry in marriage and reinstatement.

The book I have nominated as companion piece to *Durward* came five years later; and, while it belongs to the same moral and artistic maturity that produced *Durward,* its increased grimness, its harshly antiromantic severity in choice of protagonists and delineation of action, reflect a unique period of its author's later life.

The Fair Maid of Perth is the single, full-scale, energetically sustained fiction of a time of circumspection, disenchantment, and loneliness following the financial disaster (January 1826) and Lady Scott's death (May).[50] It is the time of the great "Gurnal" and the masterful short stories. The Author of Waverley had put off his disguise, and Scott had invented a new persona, the mild Croftangry and his Lamb-ish Canongate establishment, as more suitable for the tales to come. Scott was also looking back over all his novels, beginning to edit and revise for the complete edition, the "Magnum Opus."

Goethe certainly had none of this in mind when he rhapsodized over the book to Eckermann: "Das ist gemacht! Das ist eine Hand! Im Ganzen die sichere Anlage, und im Einzelnen kein Strich, der nicht zum Ziele Führte."[51] Goethe's praise for *The Fair Maid* appears to be directed chiefly at its structural unity on a superficial level. But even on this level it is instructive to note how the story evolved. Scott began with an incident and two characters, one dimly traditional, the other anonymous in history. The latter was a Highlander, the last of his clan's champions, who turned and fled the climactic duel; the former was a Perth "mechanic" who had taken the place of a missing champion on the other side. But the Palm Sunday massacre is only the climax, the final comment on a complex moral theme which has been explored through the deceptively simple romantic relationships of which the book is made.

The Maid, daughter of the burgess Simon Glover, is courted by three central male characters. Conachar, Glover's apprentice, inherits his Highland chiefdom just in time to lead his clan champions into the Palm Sunday duel and to destroy his clan and himself through his cowardly response to their absolute devotion. It appears from his journal that Scott was most interested in Conachar and in his novel attempt to win tragic sympathy for a potentially ludicrous figure.[52] But Frau von Goethe, for one, found another of the suitors most amiable – Scott's Scottish Prince Hal, the young Duke of Rothesay, dissolute son and heir to gentle, weak Robert III. The actual "hero" is the third, the burgess-mechanic Henry Smith, the armorer whose penchant for violence, whose ability to involve himself in bloody feuds with almost everyone, is the cause of much of the book's bloodshed. He is a good man of strong passions and questionable propriety and a far cry from the moderate caught in historic conflict and forced to divide his allegiance, which characterizes the central figure associated with the Waverleys. Welsh has a simple explanation for this: "The extenuating circumstance for Henry's behavior is not far to seek. His social class is responsible: he is an artisan, whereas the proper hero is a gentleman."[53] At this point, full-scale refutation of such a simplistic account should be unnecessary. Roland Graeme and Quentin Durward are far from "gentlemanly." Scott's really passionless, priggish heroes were few and early. Henry Smith and Conachar, like the "heroes" of many other novels (including *The Bride of*

Lammermoor and *St. Ronan's Well,* yet to be discussed), reveal Scott's own dissatisfaction with the hero type Welsh has ascribed indiscriminately to most of the Waverley Novels.

Moreover, Henry and his rival Conachar disprove the claim that Scott's characters never transcend the generic.[54] Both verge on the archetypal or mythic. The "Gow Chrom," the bandy-legged Smith, is a folklore progenitor of his line, a Scottish counterpart to Vulcan, a bourgeois champion of superhuman strength. His courtship of the rigidly pacific fair maid verges on the courting of Beauty by the Beast. His addiction to violence and his fame as armorer make him almost War personified, but ultimately it is his beneficent strength that must win beauty in a world of bloody disorder. Conachar is even more the figure of myth. Smith's rival, he is his opposite in destiny, doomed by clan prophecy to end his line. The last son of the Chief, born in the forest and nursed on the milk of the white doe, he carries the curse of mildness into his inheritance of absolute power. He is proud and afraid in a world where the good man's only alternatives are the brute strength of Smith and the life of monastic withdrawal desired by the maid whom all three court.

Catharine appears as rigidly decorous as conventional Scott heroines are alleged to be (we have seen exceptions already, and shall consider others), but her rigidity enters into what Davie would call the "logic of the theme"[55] as a function of the historical setting, which in turn causes the climactic developments of the story. She is indeed the Maid, persuaded by her Lollard mentor Father Clement that in a corrupt and violent world an inflexible, withdrawn unworldliness is the only desirable posture. When the heresy-hunt for Lollards begins, she must flee; and the Duke of Rothesay's enemies, trapping her in flight, use her to bait a trap for him, which leads to his pathetic and sordid death by starvation or violence in Falkland Castle. Her absence from Perth permits the misunderstanding which arouses the passionate jealousy of Smith, and thus makes of the Palm Sunday duel an even bloodier personal vendetta against poor Conachar. Against this background, the reconciliation of Smith and the Maid is a sober one at best.

That there is a reconciliation between children of bourgeois Perth is another departure from the Waverley pattern of cultural conflict in which a marriage signifies the possibility of cultural survival and renewal. The marriage here, a petty bourgeois echo of Manzoni's Renzo and Lucia, has its significance on a more abstract moral level, for it unites two extreme reactions to a world of evil and violence by modifying both. Buchan objects that Catharine "till the later chapters is too conscientiously noble, and her pacifism becomes a burden."[56] It is essential to the logic of the theme that the reader feel this way, just as he should feel it necessary for the man of war, through a surfeit of bloodshed, to learn gentleness and restraint. And when Glover, in an early chapter, tactlessly tries to play the agent of reconciliation by dragging Smith with bloody sword in hand into his daughter's bedroom, one should also feel that he has much to learn before he can deserve that role and win the reconciliation toward which the book moves.

Glover is a less colorful, more serious, nondialectal Nicol Jarvie with a complex literary heritage. Initially his seriousness is concealed by his evident kinship with Chaucer's Pandarus, his delight in forcing Smith into compromising situations with his daughter. The centrality of his paternal role becomes evident as we recognize the precision with which it is related to the novel's major themes. Glover is foster father to both Conachar and Smith. While Conachar's Highland foster father, Torquil, seeks in vain to make his charge a man of war, Glover is working in the opposite direction with his. The chaos of the novel's world is owing in large part to the fact that the parallel heirs to power, Conachar to his father's chiefdom and the Duke of Rothesay to his father's throne, are simply too weak to uphold their heritage. Thus Glover's role as parent is part of the total thematic structure. So, too, is the Jarvie-like role he plays as mediator between Highland and Lowland. It is his manifold usefulness in this role, as Lowland burgess dependent on Highland poaching for the materials of his glover's trade, that Goethe so admired: "Es entspringen daraus für das ganze Buch die günstigsten Verhältnisse und Zustande, die dadurch alle zugleich eine reale Basis erhalten."[57] But the book transcends Scott's customary Highland-Lowland contrast, and Glover's major thematic significance is realized only when, in two closely related scenes, he confronts his daughter's priestly mentor and her Highland suitor. Here he reflects on the nature of courage, which is what this study of war and peace is ultimately about – courage, and the conflicting demands of peace and honor upon both the coward and the brave man.

The distinction is no simple one. In allocating shades of cowardice and courage, Scott does exactly what the admirers of Manzoni, Stendhal, and others of his followers deny him: he wins sympathy and admiration for those who compromise or challenge conventional codes. It is not simply that he succeeds in winning sympathy for the impulsive, unpleasant Highland progenitor of Lord Jim, or even that he makes a hero of the good but bloodthirsty armorer with the mistaken desire for revenge, for he achieves parallel effect with minor figures. Conachar has his ludicrous counterpart in the bonnet-maker Oliver Proudfute, who first has our amused

sympathy for his garrulous and hypocritical martial boast-
ing, and then our shocked compassion when, in abrupt and
unsentimental transition from comedy to ballad-tragedy, he
is struck dead in the street. Proudfute has his opposite in the
apothecary-poisoner Dwining, whose life and death are out
of Websteresque nightmare. The contrast between them is
absolute: Proudfute is the lovable cowardly braggart, while
Dwining, who hides behind a pose of pacific timidity,
emerges as the most starkly brave character in the novel.[58]
He dies with Bosola's contempt for the pretensions of the
great whose destinies he has manipulated, with no sign of
fear, with one of the most eloquent, if bitter, speeches on the
nature of courage in the book (385–86). However hack-
neyed the comparison, there is something here akin to the
Shakespeare of Keats's idolatry, who had "as much delight
in conceiving an Iago as an Imogen."

The glover is not so brave a man, as his two statements on
courage reveal. The second, his account to Conachar, the
confessed coward, of his own involuntary military service,
reveals the moderate man capable of being pushed into
momentary bravery when the situation demands (340–41).
But the first reveals his Falstaffian contempt for martyrdom
to an abstract principle. It provides subtly differentiated
anticipation of the youth's confession, as Glover tells the
heroic but rigid Lollard priest: "I have no heart to be a
martyr: I have never in my whole life had courage enough
so much as to snuff a candle with my fingers" and indicates
he is quite ready to recant whatever heresy he may be
suspected of (322). The priest is "a great scholar, and a
great saint," says Glover to a friend, with a subtle irony for
which Scott is rarely given credit.

It is a pity almost he is no longer in danger to be burned,
as his sermon at the stake would convert thousands. . . .

But what would the burning of a borrel ignorant burgess like me serve? Men offer not up old glove leather for incense, nor are beacons fed with undressed hides, I trow?

Sooth to speak, I have too little learning and too much fear to get credit by the affair, and, therefore, I should, in our homely phrase, have both the scathe and the scorn [351].

Here we are close to a full statement of the theme variously stated in the later Waverley Novels, but nowhere more perfectly than in the words of an insignificant old man in *The Pirate*. Having unwillingly fought for Montrose, he remembers one Sir John Urry as an enemy and has to be reminded that Urry was on the same side, was captured with Montrose, and lost his head. He replies, "I believe you may be right; for he changed sides mair than anes, and wha kens whilk he died for? But always he was there, and so was I; a fight there was, and I never wish to see another!"[59] Who hath honour? He that died o' Wednesday.

Although the humane glover bears marks of Scott's memories of Falstaff and Pandarus, the true Falstaffian role, in this book built on echoes of *Henry IV*, is played by a less lovable character, the knight who is indeed his prince's pander, his mentor in libertinism, and his devoted follower, Sir John Ramorny. Ramorny's suffering and his revenge are too grim for Falstaff. What he keeps of his literary ancestor is the pathos of his master's rejection, and his master, a Scottish Prince Hal who is never wicked and never reformed, and who hence seems more plausible than Shakespeare's opportunist, pays for the rejection with his life. Ramorny is less the evil counselor than the scapegoat, and so cruelly is he treated that one scarcely blames him for his cruelty in return. At the outset, aiding the prince in a Valentine's Eve raid on the Maid's bower, Ramorny encounters the wrathful Smith and has one hand chopped off.

241

Thereafter that grim token of princely service haunts the book, is the butt of grisly jokes, lies at the center of the delineation of chivalric violence, and acquires the evocative force of a symbol, an emblematic device in the simple heraldic imagery which gives the book its metaphoric texture.

At the end of the deadly clan duel, Smith justifies his participation with the proverbial, *"I fought for my own hand"* (424), and the history of his violence comes full circle. Ramorny, his evil victim, going handless through the same history, justifies his deceitfulness with the plea of the powerless: "He that cannot right himself by the hand must use his head" (359). Ramorny and those like him who do evil in the name of their overlords, their "heads," are the "hands" who are punished when the heads are immune. "The hand is punished," observes Douglas, "but who shall arraign the head by whose direction the act was done?" (392) From the time of the initial act of amputation, hand and head are divorced, and the hand, engine of power and violence, takes on a grim life of its own, even as Ramorny's hand lives on in the action as a bloody threat to loyalty and peace: "Certainly I were best strike my right hand off, and nail it to the door of a church, that it may never do me discredit more." Dwining taunts the suffering Ramorny with descriptions of his laboratory, a world of "dead members" from which the apothecary learns to deal with the living (262). In the larger world of political disorder, amputation acts naturally as political imagery. The King's brother, persuading the King to send away his disgraced son, dwells on the prince's misdeeds, for "the chirurgeon must first convince his patient of the incurable condition of a shattered member, ere he venture to name amputation, though it be the only remedy" (249). The King is horrified: "Shattered and mortified member, my Lord of Albany!

amputation the only remedy!" (249) In fact, the amputation leads to the member's death, as the brother who should
be the King's hand fights only for his own, and the King,
possessed of heart, but lacking both head to govern and
hand to act, can do nothing.

The hand that represents the necessity and the threat of
action plays a significant role, also, in the two sordid murders. To discover Proudfute's killer, the burgesses arrange a
ritual of proof by bier-right, wherein the suspected persons
file past the body; they assume that "the antipathy which
subsists between the dead body and the hand which dealt
the fatal blow that divorced it from the soul will awaken
some imperfect life" (241), and the wounds will bleed.
Moreover, the prince, lured to his death in Falkland Castle
by the promise that the Maid will be his prisoner, enacts his
own absurd ritual by joining the symbolic hand to its related
emblem the glove in a travesty of sworn fealty. Disguised as
his own duchess, he permits the duped girl to kiss his gloved
hand "with much devotion and simplicity" (369). Early in
the book, Glover, in the course of celebrating his craft's
virtues, relates the glove and hand symbolism to the book's
theme:

Bethink you, that we employ the hands as pledges of
friendship and good faith, and the feet have no such
privilege. Brave men fight with their hands; cowards employ their feet in flight. A glove is borne aloft; a shoe is
trampled in the mire. A man greets a friend with his open
hand; he spurns a dog, or one whom he holds as mean as a
dog, with his advanced foot. A glove on the point of a
spear is a sign and pledge of faith all the wide world over,
as a gauntlet flung down is a gage of knightly battle [56].

"A glove is the emblem of faith," he repeats near the end;
"Catharine's hand is promised" (344). Throughout this tale
of St. Valentine's Eve, beginning with the loss of a hand in

the course of a deceitful effort to win one, the emblems of hand and glove are woven ambiguously. And here at Falkland, on the false hand of a foolish prince, the emblem of faith becomes a symbol of deceit.

This, like *The Abbot* and *Durward*, is the "Tushery" Scott, the weary, pasteboard romancer without any serious criticism of life to weave into coherent fictive structure. In some such terms Croce contrasts Scott with Manzoni,[60] and it is ironic that the book which serves thus admirably to refute his charge is so close to Manzoni's masterpiece – possibly a result of its influence. But Croce's judgment neglects form. And significant form, we have seen, is the signal achievement of the best of the later Waverley Novels. Comparison with the philosophically profound but formally indefensible analogue to *The Fair Maid*, *I Promessi Sposi* (1827), reveals that it is Scott who passes the Van Ghent test and Manzoni whose materials "carry on occasion the conviction of imaginative reality, but they do not cohere in a common rhythm for the mind; their juxtaposition does not *mean* anything."[61] Indeed, it was on the basis of Scott's formal achievements that Manzoni himself, for whom Scott was *l'Omero del Romanzo storico*, repudiated the very *art* which for Scott was uppermost: the *esprit romanesque*; the "effort to establish interesting and unexpected links between the various characters, to bring them on to the scene with others, to find events which at some time influence them all, and so in different ways all their destinies, to discover in fact an artificial unity which is not to be found in real life."[62] The words were written six years before *The Fair Maid*, but no earlier novel serves better to illustrate the formal achievement they define.

By 1827–28 the question of the historic survival of chivalric values had lost its vitality for Scott, had, perhaps, faded with the vanished eidolon of the Author of Waverley. Crystal Croftangry is a bourgeois persona; the new lineage of Henry Smith and Catharine Glover signals a new dialectic, a newly antiaristocratic continuity, reminiscent, it is true, of the new lineage begun by Jeanie Deans and Reuben Butler, but freed of the limiting ecclesiastical implications of their union. Smith is the survivor, like Quentin Durward, of chivalry's bloody decadence, the burgher who conquered the field and then his own violence. As such he represents Scott's last successful, and perhaps his most sceptical, word on the historic survival of chivalric values.[63]

SECTION FOUR

THE FALLS AND
SURVIVALS OF
ANCIENT HOUSES

1. *THE ANTIQUARY* AS
A MODERN TEST CASE

"An error of our boyhood reading of Scott is, I fancy, the easy assumption that Scott is primarily an historical novelist. There is more reason to think of him as a comic writer."[1] So says V. S. Pritchett. Now, it may be that no "historical novelist" is *primarily* that. But all I have written implies otherwise. All I have written simply confirms the view that in the Waverley Novels the ordeal of historical determinism, the human problem of historical change, the crisis of cultural survival, all are definitive themes and structures of the fiction. But Pritchett remains to remind us of those for whom the "representative best" of Scott is otherwise. To illustrate the essentially comic Scott, he recalls one of the least historical of the novels. What he says of it illustrates the unfairness of the choice, and perhaps the weakness of his position.

"I can read about half of *The Antiquary* and enjoy the flavours of what I read" – flavors redolent, Pritchett has already pronounced, of the *English* eighteenth century, and not limited, *mirabile dictu,* to the "grotesque" and "pawky" of "purely Scottish humour," but nourished by the red blood of Fielding and Sterne![2] The choice of *The Antiquary* has the sanction of Scott himself, for whom, Lockhart reports, it was "chief favorite among all his novels." It wanted the "romance" and "adventure" of its two predecessors, but found its "salvation" in its "nature,"[3] an eighteenth-century judgment reminiscent of Johnson on Richardson and Fielding. The pleasure Scott felt may have been due to his refusal to adulterate the rewards of the anecdotalist with strivings for artful unity. The advertisement is apologetic: "I have been more solicitous to describe manners minutely than to arrange in any case an artificial and combined narrative, and have but to regret that I felt myself unable to unite these two requisites of a good Novel" (v). Since then, those who love Scott, and those who scorn him, as a novelist who can't – or won't – construct, have found fair game in *The Antiquary*. To cite the supreme example, no one will forget the virtuoso piece of lecture-hall wit with which it provided E. M. Forster.[4] And perhaps no work of fiction *need* be defended against treatment of that kind.

Nevertheless, since *The Antiquary* provokes so many basic questions involved in Waverley criticism – the issue of history vs. comedy, significant form vs. artless miscellany, character and manners vs. conventional plot – it will be wise to consider it first in this concluding section, proceeding to a succession of its kin, books which also substitute for historic or cultural crises ostensibly domestic crises in the fortunes of ancient houses.

If *The Antiquary* were bad in the way Forster says it is, or anything but a grossly unfair specimen of Scott the artist, mine would be an exercise in futility. *The Antiquary* fails in a variety of ways, and the character of its failure illustrates the risks and possibilities of all the novels. Forster, considering only its slack story-telling,[5] does not understand its failure and ignores its potential success. Any story outline can seem contrived or capricious, provided only that the critic be unable or unwilling to recognize the organizing elements of the form to which the story belongs. Both form and formal integration of the story are, it is true, relatively vague in *The Antiquary*: such is the result of its major flaws. Nevertheless, both form and potential integration can be discerned.

Forster introduces Scott's story-telling during a discussion in which he names time sequence and time sense as primordial givens of story-telling.[6] Ironically he fails to notice what is most curious about time and time sequence in *The Antiquary*. The story "takes place" in the present, but its "present" is simply a stage for the recovery, the digging up from earth and from memory, of the past, the ancient past of Malcolm Misticot and the Battle of Harlaw, and the recent past of the hero's tragic birth. Ultimately, all that has force or reality in *The Antiquary* as story exists in a quasi-legendary past and ultimately survives in the folk memory of old Elspeth of the Craigburnfoot.

In Scott's conception the book was third in a series of fictional portraits of recent manners – *Waverley* of "sixty years since," *Guy Mannering* of the generation prior to Scott's, *The Antiquary* of the opening years of the new century (v). The story sets out from the Edinburgh of anti-invasion gentleman volunteers, ends with a false alarm of a French invasion; along the way reports sift in of anticipated French arrivals, of the villain's supposed dealings with the enemy, of the hero's being either a noble emigrant or a Napoleonic spy. But the effect is simply to remind us of the remoteness, and hence the imaginative irrelevance, of such a setting. And when at last the narrator attempts to ennoble the mysterious hero by abstract allusion to his heroic service in wars against the French, the attempt draws upon a source

248

that has no imaginative existence in the book, and it fails miserably. The mysterious Lovel vanishes halfway through; the heroic, dashing Major Neville arrives at the conclusion. We neither care for him nor identify him in our imaginative sympathies with the nondescript Lovel, even when told we are to do so.

The chief characters were to illustrate manners in that just-past decade. But as it turns out, the illustration of manners is, in almost every case, subordinated to the character's illustrative relation to the book's title. In this present romance of recovering the past, almost every character of consequence is an antiquary, and the book becomes a tragicomedy of conflicts among antiquaries with conflicting methods and values.

The first chapters dramatize, with extravagant leisureliness, the antiquarian humors of the titular figure, the Whig laird of artisan German descent, Jonathan Oldbuck. The dominant impression is of a pedantic collector with no evaluative discrimination or little human involvement in the past whose relics he collects. His folly is first defined in his encounter with Edie Ochiltree, royally sanctioned local beggar, as he is showing off the alleged site of Agricola's last battle to the credulous but bored Lovel. Edie breaks in on Oldbuck's fanciful conjectures to notify him that he "mind[s] the bigging" (recalls the building) of the earthwork just twenty years before (31). We are thus introduced to the comic team whose cooperation will dominate the novel, and their byplay marks the novel at once as comically concerned with the persistence and recovery of the buried past, the genuine and the fraudulent past, and its protection or redemption.

Oldbuck's dinner party introduces another antiquary, Sir Arthur Wardour. The conversation moves from the military frenzy of contemporary Edinburgh to the habitual argument of Sir Arthur and Oldbuck over the "Pictish question." The Celticist is pitted against the Gothicist, and the argument becomes one over whether Sir Arthur's Celtic authority was a gentleman, and then a fight between Oldbuck's "low" lineage and the romantic Wardour's noble ancestors. Even an idle dinner table *flyting* is thus a comic reenactment of ancient feuds. Whig and Tory invariably fight, are invariably reconciled, and continue to share the delights of their antiquarian humors.

Three more antiquaries emerge at the picnic among the ruins of St. Ruth's: the minister Mr. Blattergowl, possessor of the third of the parish's three remaining wigs; the fraudulent German adept, Dousterswivel, who claims the power to find the past's buried treasures; and Lovel himself, who enunciates a modicum of philosophy of history concerning true and false ways of remembering and preserving the past: "the events," he contends, "which leave the deepest impression on the minds of the common people"

were not such as resemble the gradual progress of a fertilising river, but the headlong and precipitous fury of some portentous flood. The eras by which the vulgar compute time have always reference to some period of fear and tribulation, and they date by a tempest, an earthquake, or burst of civil commotion. When such are the facts most alive in the memory of the common people, we cannot wonder . . . that the ferocious warrior is remembered, and the peaceful abbots are abandoned to forgetfulness and oblivion [151].

We also meet Oldbuck's Highland nephew Captain MacIntyre, who, like Sir Arthur, is foolishly and inflammably proud of his past and is thus its prisoner. All of these antiquaries are predominantly comic, and their adventures in mutual deception are comic, too.

The novel's second half abruptly changes key with the introduction of the book's tragic antiquary, old Elspeth Mucklebackit, who, hearing of the death of the Countess of Glenallan, feels her tongue loosed at last from the constraints of a fanatic loyalty to the Glenallans and reconstructs the grim past of that proud, doomed family. Old Elspeth stands at one extreme of a spectrum of antiquaries. For her the past is a hideous sin in which she is personally implicated, and for which her whole subsequent history is punishment. At the opposite extreme stands Oldbuck, too little implicated in the past, which is for him an indiscriminate collection of academic *curiosa*. The place of Edie Ochiltree, the debunker, the facile maker of legends (273), is evidently ambiguous and will require analysis later.

The abundance of practicing antiquaries has predictable effect on the present story sequence. The story sequence is completely subordinate to a sequence of recovery or retrospective narratives, and this has the effect of robbing the contemporary scene of all significance and value – except, of course, for the present question of different ways of looking for and dealing with the buried past. Moreover, the search must be somewhat arbitrary or capricious in form, must be marked with the "ragged ends" of which Forster complains.[7] Indeed, one difficulty is that there are not enough "ragged ends" just as there aren't enough in the retrospective crescendo of *Bleak House* or, from the same "realistic" standpoint, the ends are not "ragged" enough. What is needed for the recovery of the past, for the saving of its social orders, for the reinstating of its lost heir, seems ridiculously accessible. We wonder why it hasn't all been dug up before. Why now?

The answer points to the essential problem which these novels of "houses fallen, houses redeemed" have in common with each other and with more ostensibly historical Waverley Novels. At the outset of his ordeal of namelessness and ostracism, the lost heir, Lovel, hears a female voice singing a lamentation for fallen houses, which ends with an exhortation to redeem time:

> "Why sit'st thou by that ruin'd hall,
> Thou aged carle so stern and grey?
> Dost thou its former pride recall,
> Or ponder how it pass'd away?"
>
> "Know'st thou not me!" the Deep Voice cried;
> "So long enjoy'd, so oft misused,
> Alternate, in thy fickle pride,
> Desired, neglected, and accused?
>
> "Before my breath, like blazing flax,
> Man and his marvels pass away,
> And changing empires wane and wax,
> Are founded, flourish, and decay.
>
> "Redeem mine hours – the space is brief –
> While in my glass the sand-grains shiver,
> And measureless thy joy or grief,
> When TIME and thou shalt part forever!" [89]

Now is a time of crisis in the fortunes of two ancient houses. The Wardours are on the brink of economic, hence, social and political, disaster (385–86). The Countess of Glenallan has just died, leaving only a diseased and withdrawn son (antecedent to Roderick Usher), whose marriage she long ago opposed, and with whom the Glenallan line will die out. The rediscovery of the past, the reinstatement and legitimizing of one *lost* heir, who can marry and thus reinstate the other *disinherited* heir (Sir Arthur's daughter), saves both houses. Both, through the reimposition of value embodied in the heirs, are literally founded anew. The novel's myth is one of redemption in continuity, of saving the disinherited present from disinheritance and the ruined past from obliteration. Such a meaning, in a fiction peopled with antiquaries, does not guarantee a good novel, but it indicates the kind of significant unity we might expect.

The redemptive process is impeded by the past to which each house is prisoner, just as, symbolically, the well in the ruins of St. Ruth's is hidden by old rubbish, and the human reality of the past is, for Oldbuck, lost in the antiquarian clutter of his study. Each house is prisoner to its past in a different way. The Wardours are in trouble, to be sure, because of Sir Arthur's own folly. But Sir Arthur has inherited the real obstacle just as, in their novels, the Bertrams, the Mowbrays, and the Ravenswoods have inherited imminent ruin. It is the obstacle that now prevents the marriage of Lovel and Isabel Wardour: Lovel's supposed illegitimacy. "You know the opinions – prejudices, perhaps you will call them – of our house concerning purity of birth," says Sir Arthur to Oldbuck (111). He recounts his family's hereditary terror of an illegitimate usurper, its precedent in Malcolm Misticot, bastard son of the first Lady Wardour. "His temporary seizure of our property, and most unjust attempt to establish his own illegitimate line in the estate of Knockwinnock, gave rise to such family feuds and misfortunes as strongly to found us in that horror and antipathy to defiled blood and illegitimacy which has been handed down to me from my respected ancestry" (112). The expression of a mystique of dynastic Legitimism the year after Waterloo has sharp political overtones, and there is no reason to doubt the revelation of Scott's political ambivalence in the sarcastic retort of his Whiggish spokesman Oldbuck. He knows Sir Arthur's story, he says, and "I was telling it to Lovel this moment, with some of the wise maxims and consequences which it has engrafted on your family politics" (112).

Present crisis, then, is rooted in the past and its usurping illegitimacy. The instability of the house is reflected and aggravated by Sir Arthur's attempts, through Dousterswivel's fraudulent Rosicrucian mysteries, to dig up value from the past. The treasure, ironically, is found in the grave of Malcolm Misticot, where it has been placed by the family's savior, the "illegitimate" modern Malcolm, Lovel, with the help of Edie Ochiltree, who fabricates antiquities and legends to serve modern humanitarian goals. A comic parable of post-Napoleonic Legitimism indeed!

The present trouble of the Glenallans is rooted, too, in tragic prejudice. Theirs is a fanatic dynastic pride. A cruelly haughty mother has destroyed her son by letting him believe that the secret marriage she had sought to prevent was incestuous. As illegitimacy dooms the Wardours, so incest symbolizes the destructive, isolating pride of the Glenallans, which is turned to horrified withdrawal by the son, following the suicide of his alleged sister-wife. But this past turns out to be as fraudulent as Misticot's treasure or Agricola's earthwork. The marriage was neither incestuous nor fruitless; the heir reappears in the same young man feared as the nameless threatener of Wardour legitimacy. Through his discovery of identity and name, both houses are released from their slavery to fraudulent pasts.

What matters, then, is that the hero be identified and legitimized. The efforts to do so are made by others. There is little for him to do except provide an occasion, a focus for the center of the mystery. His presence in the first half is of external interest only and is externally delineated. He is a "gentleman," a straight man for Oldbuck's antiquarian humors. For the second half his presence is unnecessary.

Hence, we have neither occasion to experience his quest for identity, nor cause to interpret the qualities he embodies. His role as redeemer is simply that. He is the extreme among Waverley heroes in the discrepancy between the significance of his role and the insignificance of his character. He is an empty significance, and this is why the account of his fortunes and misfortunes seems abstract. At one point only are we given a brief interior view, a point marking a critical moment in his moral development. His response to the haughty Hector's challenge, his willingness to engage in the duel which forces him to flee, is judged as the youthfully imprudent subjection of "his calmer reason" to "the dictates of his offended pride" (180). He joins Hector in ignoring Edie's peacemaking and places himself outside the law of man and of Edie's "nature"; his subsequent hiding in a cave used by outlaws is a symbolic action reminiscent of other extralegal Waverley protagonists. But we have been prepared for no such significance here; this alienation is not a phase in a dialectic of reconciliation. Lovel then utterly disappears. The failure to provide, in his experience, a dynamic moral center is the cause of the book's lack of vital unity.

Yet Lovel's fortunes cannot be ignored. The essential characters and episodes are elements of his quest. For Scott, of course, as the retrospective analyst of the later introduction, this was not so. For him, the central importance of Oldbuck and Edie was explained when he had shown that they were "true" (vi–xiii). For us, their centrality will have to be assessed in terms of the interaction between character and function in the novel's quest.

Oldbuck and Edie share the role – Oldbuck primarily in the first half and Edie in the second – of admiring, guiding, and protecting Lovel. The qualities and attitudes in which

255

their guidance and help are grounded should provide meaning for Lovel's plight and his effort to save the fallen houses. Oldbuck is sceptical, pedantic, and prudent on the surface. The discrepancy between his façade and his reality derives from both Parson Adams and the Man in Black. He successfully manipulates present situations from behind an affected cynicism and academic detachment. "Oldbuck, beaten from the pride of his affected cynicism, would not willingly have had any one by upon that occasion to quote to him his favourite maxims of the Stoic philosophy" (309). He is actually capable of sincere sympathy with the sorrows of others, Glenallans and Mucklebackits alike. Edie, his affectionate tormentor, sums him up to his face: "I hae aye said ahint your back that, for a' the nonsense maggots that ye whiles take into your head, ye are the most wise and discreet o' a' our country gentles" (348).

Oldbuck, in the same vein, has earlier defended Edie to Lovel:

"That rascal, now, knows more old ballads and traditions than any other man in this and the four next parishes. And after all," continued he, softening as he went on describing Edie's good gifts, "the dog has some good-humour. He has borne his hard fate with unbroken spirits, and it's cruel to deny him the comfort of a laugh at his betters" [35].

Edie, too, is a pragmatic humanitarian. As Oldbuck judges dreams by whether or not they foster prudent conduct, so Edie assesses a legendary past by its usefulness in the service of the present. Edie's mendicant status is essential: he is independent and is jealously attached to his freedom. His is the "life of nature," and he serves as a norm of natural contentment and independence, especially in the eyes of the tormented Earl of Glenallan (265). His mixture of moral independence and wide and disinterested experience gives him his unique value as messenger, counselor, even arbiter (269). Thus he shares much with Oldbuck. Both are devoted antiquaries uniquely free of the past, flexibly at home in the present, morally and socially independent, committed to the humane use of the past in behalf of the present.

One aspect of their freedom is economic; both play normative roles in a novel about financial instability. Both are economically prudent, Oldbuck because he is somewhat "close"; Edie because he takes only what he really (i.e., naturally) needs. Edie is frequently offered economic security and always refuses it as a threat to his freedom; thus he is the perfect agent for Lovel's financial manipulations on behalf of the Wardours: "I am the fittest man in the haill country to trust wi' siller, for I neither want it nor wish for it, nor could use it if I had it" (399). And Oldbuck's closeness has evidently permitted him to be effectively generous at critical moments.

Their cardinal virtue is not, however, economic. For the nameless Lovel, it is rather their respect and affection for common humanity, their shared freedom from the romantic prejudices and follies that beset the Wardours and the Glenallans, their capacity to sustain an effective humanity in spite of misfortune or doubt or betrayal. Both have their temptations, and both suffer mildly for yielding to them. Oldbuck is too ready to detach himself pedantically from his own humanity, which comes back to haunt him in the person of his lost beloved's son, Lovel. Edie is too ready to indulge in playful lawlessness. For the tricking and beating of Dousterswivel he is punished with the accidental death of his accomplice, with imprisonment, and with the knowledge that he may not be able to help Lovel. But each of these minor flaws has its extreme counterpart in the major flaw of one of the fallen aristocrats. Wardour must learn stability, must escape the romantic recklessness that has brought his house to the verge of ruin. Glenallan must learn forbearance, acceptance of life. Both must learn the humanity that Oldbuck and Edie share, the humane sympathy that transcends distinctions of name and wealth and receives its ultimate test in the often noted and moving scene between Oldbuck and Mucklebackit (307–9). Both do learn; and thus the plight and the quest of Lovel occasion moral trial and redemption for two houses and their flawed masters, and Lovel is enabled at last to regenerate a foolish and decadent aristocracy through the guidance of natural prudence and common humanity. What, then, are the essential weaknesses of the book?

I have noted several in passing: a disproportionate display of the humors of the several antiquaries; the lack of vital unity consequent on the characterless and external conventionality of the heir-hero; structural disunity resulting from the abrupt introduction of the Glenallans and the consequent drastic shift of mood; the intrusive irrelevance of historical setting. But one weakness in particular is worth stressing as we move on. The triumph of *The Antiquary* is the saving of great houses. What would their loss mean? In their survival what threatened or lost values are redeemed, what alternatives avoided or displaced? These are the crucial thematic questions raised by such a structure. They are questions variously developed and defined in *Guy Mannering, St. Ronan's Well, The Pirate, The Bride of Lammermoor*. But they have little presence or force in *The Antiquary*.

2. *GUY MANNERING* (1815) AND *ST. RONAN'S WELL* (1823)

Both *Guy Mannering* and *St. Ronan's Well* have suffered from a futile concern with Scott's *ex posteriori* statements of intention. Such statements are useful as the glosses of a knowledgeable interpreter, but the novels should not be compromised with what an editorial Scott later said about them. Yet such statements do call attention to problems of intrinsic motive, to apparent shifts of intention in the novels themselves. For instance, Scott later claimed that a radical shift of topic had taken place early in the composition of *Mannering*. The original conception is described by Buchan in Godwinian terms as the intensive psychological portrayal of a seemingly doomed individual whose efforts at goodness are invariably disappointed by the interventions of some "malevolent being," and who is increasingly obsessed with his own fatality. The doomed individual's fatality was to be revealed in his crucial encounters with astrology. But astrology, says Scott in 1829, "does not now retain influence over the general mind sufficient even to constitute the mainspring of a romance" (xii) – which could mean either that the hero's credibility would be impaired by his credulity, or that the audience would be distracted by flagrant anachronism from a willing suspension of disbelief in such an agency. Scott's heroes are invariably too enlightened to make such an obsession likely. The astrologer's predictions are fulfilled, but his faith in astrology remains merely a humorous part of his own character and scarcely dents the consciousness of the fated man. The greater credibility of two comparable novels of dynastic fatality, *St. Ronan's Well* and *The*

259

Bride of Lammermoor, derives from the fact that in the first, fatality remains a strictly psychological force, while in the second it pervades every level of reality and is definable in terms both "enlightened" and "unenlightened."

At any rate, *Mannering* changed, and the new emphasis appears in the two characters whose genesis concerns Scott in the later introduction: Meg Merrilies, who, in her dealings with her declined lords and protectors, "possessed the savage virtue of fidelity" (xiv); and Dominie Sampson, tutor to the same house, who, in his inarticulate way, showed himself equally heroic in possession of the same virtue. In Mannering himself, half-serious astrology becomes part of a larger motive of loyalty to the house of Ellangowan, and thus part of the motive force for its preservation or redemption.

The claims of intention appended later to *St. Ronan's Well* signal no shift of purpose. But they suggest some uncertainty on Scott's part as to the form and character of the novel, and critics have befuddled themselves with the uncertainty ever since. He insists that the book is a new departure (1) in its domestic emphasis, and (2) in its location in "our own times." He humbly aligns himself with the gifted ladies of social fiction, including "Edgeworth, Austin, Charlotte Smith," and "reckoning from the authoress of Evelina to her of Marriage" (v–vi). There is no suggestion that Scott overlooked profound differences between the Misses Edgeworth and Ferrier on the one hand and Miss Austen on the other. He may have had in mind only a general classification which *could* include *St. Ronan's Well* without falsifying its essential differences from *Evelina, Emma,* and the like. Nevertheless, he characteristically joins his own disapproving critics and judges his novel in terms of the truth and subtlety of the social comedy of

260

"Well" society. [8] The reader, turning from such misguided criticism to the novel itself, is surprised to discover the real nature and place of that comedy in the larger context of a bitter struggle between decadent old and corrupt new. To go to *St. Ronan's Well* with Austenite expectations is to expect from Snopeses and Compsons the comedy one finds in Ivy Compton-Burnett.

St. Ronan's Well, like *Guy Mannering*, is the tragicomic portrayal of a dying ancient house in the context of a battle between old and new. The same initial contrast frames both. The stranger, young Mannering, is shown what he assumes is Ellangowan, and his romantic nature is at once captivated: " 'Why, my little fellow,' he said, 'this is a ruin, not a house?' " His boy-guide responds, "Ah, but the lairds lived there langsyne; that's Ellangowan Auld Place. There's a hantle bogles about it; but ye needna be feared, I never saw ony mysell, and we're just at the door o' the New Place" (5). In the initial view of St. Ronan's "auld place" we are shown an entire community in decay, a vision of indifferent nature devouring human obsolescence which anticipates Robert Frost:

a complete and commanding view of the decayed village, the houses of which, to a fanciful imagination, might seem as if they had been suddenly arrested in hurrying down the precipitous hill, and fixed as if by magic in the whimsical arrangement which they now presented. . . . On some huts the rafters, varnished with soot, were still standing, in whole or in part, like skeletons. . . . Nature, in the meanwhile, always changing, but renewing as she changes, was supplying, by the power of vegetation, the fallen and decaying marks of human labour. Small pollards, which had been formerly planted around the little gardens, had now waxed into huge and high forest trees; . . . while quantities of dock, and nettles, and hemlock, hiding the ruined

walls, were busily converting the whole scene of desolation into a picturesque forest-bank [3–4].

Mannering's romantic attachment to the Ellangowan ruin is
translated into restoration. But the best comment on the
nabob Touchwood's attempts to renovate St. Ronan's "aul
toun" is what happens to him as he is returning to his inn
one night at the peak of his zeal for restoration. He must pass
the door of Saunders Jaup, leader of "those who held out for
the practices of their fathers" (294). Avoiding Jaup's
defiantly still-uncovered sewer, he falls into a roadside
brook.

In both, restoration is linked to the discovery and reinstatement of a lost or illegitimate heir. A stability for the
present can be gained only through the recovery of a truth
buried in the past. As in *The Antiquary*, the past is knowledge and value when repossessed (1) by a paternalistic
agent of providence and (2) by an elderly woman with a
prophetic impulse to pronounce the doom of the new and
the redemption of the old. Since the two types are essential – the providential restorer and the prophetical bel-
dame – we can best define meaning and value in the books
by considering their specific representatives.

Neither Guy Mannering nor Peregrine Touchwood is a
Jonathan Oldbuck. Mannering has too much of the Wardour infatuation with name and birth, and Touchwood too
much of Edie Ochiltree. Yet all three place themselves *in
loco parentis* to the young heir-hero and play restorer of a
fallen house. All three are disinterested. Mannering becomes father-in-law to the restored house, but his own
wealth is assured regardless. Touchwood, a nabob like
Mannering, has long since refused to play heir to his own
foolish house-building father and has accepted and pros-
pered by a commercial code. But he remains a humorous

devotee of old days and can now indulge his humor as manipulator in the work of restoration.

The three obviously presented Scott with a unique fictional persona for wish fulfillment. The biographical critic would remind us of his divided inheritance – son of the shrewd city solicitor, grandson of the patriarchal Border, returning, a domestic literary nabob, to restore the Border barony. Buchan and Grierson have called Mannering Scott's truest self-portrait; comparable identification is implied by his own love of *The Antiquary*.[9]

Such biographical glosses are suggestive if they do not blind us to the detachment with which the three characters are treated, or to the distinct judgments made of them in their contexts. We have noted Oldbuck's comic shortcomings, yet as restorer he proves most admirable and effective of the three. Mannering and Touchwood fall short. Mannering's own romanticism must be cured by a wiser humanity if he is to serve as Ellangowan's restorer. Touchwood needs a cure for the opposite of Mannering's romanticism. He is too whimsical, too capriciously domineering; he has arbitrarily cut himself off from traditional values which Mannering too romantically accepts, and thus he is ineffectual as restorer. There are differences of role, too. Mannering has so much help – from Meg Merrilies, Dandie Dinmont, Pleydell – in carrying out his designs as restorer that he gradually loses his active part. Touchwood enters in the middle of his novel, achieves key importance toward the climax, then abruptly proves ineffectual. But Mannering's relative unimportance towards the end of the novel named for him is a symptom of that novel's shifting focus and of its sentimentality. Whereas Touchwood's ineffectuality is one of the most profoundly sad and honest revelations in all of the novels.

263

Mannering is seen first as the itinerant youth, like Waverley, Osbaldistone, and Latimer a romantically naive, yet enlightened young Englishman, wandering as if by fate into the dangerous, romantic potentialities of primitive Scotland. His presence at the birth of Ellangowan's heir seems to mark him as central consciousness. Yet he departs at the end of the fifth chapter, "for it is to another and later period of his life that the present narrative relates" (33). The older man returns to Ellangowan as restorer. But there are complications. We are asked to identify the romantic youth with the tragic product of a complex, bitter experience abroad. We hear of the experience only in summary. Only the effect on Mannering has a place in the novel. The result resembles *The Antiquary* and *St. Ronan's Well:* a somewhat thin present foreground, and a background of bitter past misfortunes. As in *The Surgeon's Daughter,* Mannering's misfortune occurs in India; the effect in both is to return the unfortunate to a British domestic stability after he is abnormally withdrawn from life.

The tragic nabob is a complex figure. Chapters Eleven through Twenty define the mature, withdrawn Mannering from a variety of viewpoints, and he becomes an unusually full or round character, a study in the dangerous humors of the romantic personality. Since his earlier departure the folk of Ellangowan have wonderfully assimilated a fantastic mixture of superstition and gossip into an orally transmitted legend of an aged astrologer. To his correspondent Arthur Mervyn, Mannering is the melancholy romantic, of keen feelings, lively imagination, wilfulness. To his daughter – also, says Mervyn, a romantic – he is an obstinate but fascinating tyrant, too fond of lineage and name. To the desolate Lucy Bertram and her devoted tutor Sampson he is a savior, an ancestor of John Jarndyce. His late wife thought him a petty tyrant "and read romances until she became so enamoured of the complicated intrigues which they contain as to assume the management of a little family novel of her own" (112), and she let him think himself an Othello. His Cassio, the cadet Brown, whom Mannering thinks he killed, knows him as a tyrant and the malevolent author of his misfortunes. We have, then, a complex delineation with the promise that Mannering will eventually be better understood and perhaps humanized. We have, too, the ironic situation in which Mannering, determined to reinstate the Bertrams, will be acting in behalf of a lost heir who is actually his past victim "Brown."

Mannering's humanizing does take place, but it is neither complex nor important. We wait for two scenes: (1) the moment when the father is finally humanized into an affectionate understanding with his daughter Julia; (2) the moment when he recognizes the lost Bertram in the supposedly dead Brown. Both scenes arrive. But they come as brief incidents in a veritable barrage of recognitions, narratively well managed, but so numerous that no single moment can be explored to any depth; no consciousness can be scrutinized in the narrator's rapid shift of focus:

The remaining part of the company would have formed no bad group for a skilful painter. Each was too much embarrassed with his own sensations to observe those of the others. Bertram most unexpectedly found himself in the house of . . . ; Mannering was struggling between his high sense of courtesy and hospitality . . . and the former feelings of dislike and prejudice . . . ; Sampson . . . ; Dinmont . . . [362].

Mannering's final humanizing comes in his reconciliation scene with Julia. His humor remains, however, and his daughter lets us see that we are now to regard him with affectionate forbearance. His complex melancholic despotism is hastily translated into a harmless crotchet – such is apparently one of the causes of the book's lightness of mood. His moral interest as a source of evil has been transferred to Hatteraick and Glossin; his moral interest as a source of good has become secondary to that of Meg, Dinmont, and even Pleydell and Sampson. Even his role as central reagent, experiential protagonist, has long since become Bertram-Brown's. Mannering remains only as a source of wealth and authority, and as a romantic foil to his rival Bertram-Brown.

Touchwood is managed with greater detachment and considerable rhetorical skill. When he is introduced half way through the later novel, he identifies himself at once as equipped to play providence, as a rich, whimsical sharer of Meg's hatred for the fraud and corruption of the "new world" of the Well. As he establishes himself as Meg's supporter, connects past and present through goading Cargill back into life, and shows increasing concern for Tyrrel and the Mowbrays and increasing power over the villain Bulmer, our confidence grows that he will indeed "fix everything up," prove Tyrrel's legitimacy, even save the Mowbrays. Our confidence is strengthened by his manifest kinship with other whimsical antiaristocratic manipulators in the novels: Jarvie, the good Quaker of *Redgauntlet,* Simon Glover of Perth, Heriot, Oldbuck. He is the antiromantic self-made man, at once mocker and protector of aristocratic values and romantic attitudes: an ideal comic persona for the Author of Waverley, nabob projector, epicure, benevolent despot. He must, we assume, play deus ex machina, and his late appearance encourages our assumption. But we notice, too, that as a bore and busybody he can make himself disagreeable to good and bad alike. His faith in his own providential powers troubles our optimism. The skillful placing of the revelation of his identity tells us the purpose of our well-managed uncertainty. In his tactless manipulations he is too late. Tyrrel will, we know, succeed; Bulmer will be exposed and beaten. The plot will fulfill its melodramatic promise; but its fulfillment will be as meaningless as, ultimately, Touchwood's manipulations are meaningless. What is of value is already lost.

The setting for the climactic revelation is the Mowbrays' decaying castle. Mowbray, wholly ruined, has just learned of his sister Clara's disgrace. A scene between them of imminent violence subsides into melancholy reconciliation and tragic resignation and produces one of the greatest dramatic images in all the novels, one which must have haunted Poe and Hawthorne, Dickens and Thackeray:

He held out his hand, and she placed, but not without reluctant terror, her trembling palm in his. In this manner, and with a sort of mournful solemnity, as if they had been in attendance upon a funeral, he handed his sister through a gallery hung with old family pictures. . . . The moon, which at this moment looked out through a huge volume of mustering clouds that had long been boding storm, fell on the two last descendants of that ancient family, as they glided hand in hand, more like the ghosts of the deceased than like living persons, through the hall and amongst the portraits of their forefathers [387].

Touchwood's arrival and disclosure at this point seem hideously anticlimactic. By contrast with this tragic tenderness, his arrogant, bland optimism seems both ludicrous and profane. And so it proves. Clara dies. Mowbray kills Bulmer. Tyrrel, having won, vanishes, never claiming his estate. Touchwood becomes significantly pathetic, "forming plans which have no object, and accumulating a fortune, for which he has apparently no heir" (426). Mowbray endures somewhat the way Jason Compson endures. Having played the Quentin to Clara's Caddie, he now withdraws to the opposite extreme, his character having throughout been complex enough to include both potentialities. Morally speaking, only Meg Dods endures – and she in a kind of hot-tempered rearguard action against inevitable decay.

Meg's role in *St. Ronan's Well* – to turn to our second type – is, in fact, to endure. Unlike the gypsy Meg of *Mannering*, she is less an agent than a symbol. Meg Merrilies, it is true, is remembered chiefly as the deliverer of one or two great set speeches. The speeches are rhetorically impressive and thematically essential,[10] but it is characteristic of *Mannering* that Meg's chief function should be as a busy agent in the exciting action leading to Bertram-Brown's reinstatement. It is she who knew of the boy's kidnapping, she who first recognizes him, she who is fated to save his life, and she who strides about the countryside saving him from a second kidnapping and bringing him to his other supporters. Of greater thematic import, it is she who saves him from her own outlaw world and gives him a purse of stolen gypsy wealth to finance his efforts.[11] But *Mannering* is primarily a tale – says Dinmont, "deil o' sic a story as yours, wi' glamour and dead folk and losing ane's gate, I ever heard out o' the tale-books!" (323) And the tale's chief interest is in the adventure through which the heir discovers himself and recovers his place. Hence Meg's role as agent is more important than her role as symbol of threatened values.

Meg Dods begins and ends in the same conception of fidelity. She is doggedly loyal, like Meg Merrilies, to a threatened way of life, deplores the disloyalty to that way in a powerful house to which she has also been loyal, and seeks to save the exponents of that way from its destroyers. Ultimately she can only *be* loyal; she is helpless to prevent the final tragedy, but must stand by at two deathbeds as nurse, chief mourner, and sole survivor. From the outset it is clear that, as innkeeper in the "aul toun," she embodies one side of an evolving value conflict between rude old and fraudulent new. Her point of view is dramatized in her hatred of the gloss and pretense of the new spa. Her symbolic stance is defined in terms of her housekeeping; the symbolism of *St. Ronan's Well* is as replete with houses and housekeepers as that of *Bleak House*. Meg's tyrannies are grounded in "extreme and scrupulous nicety" (7). Her housekeeping is contrasted normatively with the absent-minded clutter of Cargill's manse, with the pathetic attempts of young Mowbray to "pick up" threadbare, disorderly Shaws-Castle for the picnickers, and with the superficial ornateness of the Well itself.

Political metaphors function logically to develop the same contrasts. They characterize Meg: "though hers was a severe and almost despotic government, it could not be termed a tyranny, since it was exercised, upon the whole, for the good of the subject" (7). Her rule is not romanticized; her bigoted lack of communication with the new is dangerous, and her protégé Tyrrel suffers from this as from the caprice of Touchwood. But politically the contrast favors Meg. The description of Well society opens with an epigraph of political satire:

There must be government in all society:
Bees have their queen, and stag-herds have their leader;
Rome had her consuls, Athens had her archons,
And we, sir, have our managing committee [27].

The Well "types" are presented in terms of political roles:

In watering-places, as in other congregated assemblies of the human species, various kinds of government have been dictated. . . . Sometimes the sole power has been vested in a master of ceremonies; but this, like other despotisms, has been of late unfashionable. . . . Committees of management . . . a more liberal mode of sway . . . the administration of the infant republic of St. Ronan's Well. This little senate . . . divided into two jarring and contending factions . . . all the animosity of political party [29–30].

Meg and Touchwood are at one extreme, benevolent despotism, with a petty republican factionalism at the other extreme. The novel presents no mean. Tyrrel finds no redemptive power on either side. Touchwood is as much the "petty politician" (401) as the Tory patron of Ravenswood in *The Bride*. He restates Meg's objections to the new "liberalism" of the Well, but his bigotry seems recklessly theoretical beside her concrete, personally felt judgments. While Touchwood can only spread ill news at last, she can only attend loyally on the dead and dying. Both end as symbols of political ineffectuality.

Meg Merrilies is a figure of political implications, too. Her ability to help Bertram-Brown derives from her matriarchal power as gypsy leader in the world outside the law. When Bertram-Brown enters the compact with Meg, he joins other Waverley heroes whose ordeals of identification and reinstatement also include temporary dependence on "natural" forces, forces outside the law, for which the protagonists then assume responsibility. Bertram-Brown's final action in recovering his name and place is to fulfill his obligation to Meg. To understand why, we must trace the origins of his disinheritance.

At the outset, the Bertrams are already in sharp decline. Godfrey Bertram, with his mild, incoherent nature, is the naive victim of economic exploiters such as Glossin, who (like his more worthy and dangerous counterpart, Ashton in *The Bride*) will add the finishing touches to the fall of the house. But first, Godfrey Bertram contributes the personal crime. As justice of the peace, he begins a program of legal reform, withdrawing his protection from two different, but allied, sets of outlaws: the gypsies and the smugglers. The narrator is explicit on Bertram's sins as reformer: "All this good had its rateable proportion of evil. Even an admitted nuisance of ancient standing should not be abated without some caution" (37). He has committed the crime of inhumanity, aggravated it by imprudence, and violated communal tradition: "We are not made of wood or stone, and the things which connect themselves with our hearts and habits cannot, like bark or lichen, be rent away without our missing them" (37). It is Meg, ranting among the gypsies' burning huts, who points the moral of his sins and prophesies the outcome: "Ride your ways, Godfrey Bertram! This day have ye quenched seven smoking hearths; see if the fire in your ain parlour burn the blyther for that. . . . Ride your ways, Ellangowan. Our bairns are hinging at our weary backs; look that your braw cradle at hame be the fairer spread up" (49–50). The smugglers receive comparable treatment and respond with comparable threats. But in the case of the gypsies, Bertram's ruthless legalism has violated a higher law, while in the case of Hatteraick he has simply been guilty of imprudence in correcting criminal indifference to the law.

When the boy disappears, both groups are suspected. But Meg has tried to protect the child from Hatteraick and has vowed to "set him in his father's seat, if every step was on a dead man" (402). She keeps her vow, and young Harry must reciprocate. He must follow Meg to the cave where Hatteraick lies hidden – where he lay hidden at the time of

271

the kidnapping – and prove his right to his father's neglected and abused authority by confronting and restraining
the evil that initially disinherited him. Meg is aware of this
ritualistic enactment of a moral climax, and it is apparent
that her creator shared her type of awareness and gave some
of his novels just such ritualistic integrities. One thinks
especially of the novel to come the year after *Mannering,
Old Mortality,* in which Morton's moral climax is also to
confront the author of his entanglement with lawlessness,
Balfour of Burley, as a devil in a cave.

But Bertram-Brown is not alone. Meg's ritualistic sense
allows one companion, Dandie Dinmont; the choice stresses
the sustained parallelism of herself and Dinmont as Bertram-Brown's most dedicated helpers. The parallelism contributes significantly to the shape of Harry Bertram's destiny.

We participate intensively in Bertram's experience, and
this makes him the protagonist Mannering fails to become.
But while Bertram's is the central experience, Mannering's
promises to be the significant moral development. There is
no sign that Bertram needs to develop morally. "Fate" has
involved him with two dangerously romantic personalities,
Mannering and his daughter, and, while he is determined to
win acceptance, he is consistently unbitter toward the father
and patient and understanding in his love for the daughter.
He knows nothing of his genteel lineage; hence, he is free of
the disagreeably gentlemanly postures and idioms of Lovel.
His early letter to an army friend reveals an energetic,
sensible, prudent young man capable of rising above his
anti-Mannering prejudice if given a chance. As he sets off
on his Scottish excursion to find Mannering and Lucy with
"firm step," with "erect and free carriage" (138), we suspect

that (a) he is the lost Harry Bertram, and (b) he is already fully deserving of good fortune.

We are not kept in suspense. The narrator makes clear that the narrative interest is to be elsewhere: namely, in the slow process of self-recognition Bertram undergoes. He meets Meg and Dandie; she stares, and he begins to sense the mystery of his identity. Following his initial adventures we lose touch with him for almost one fifth of the narrative (another flaw) and regain it when the accident with Hazelwood has caused him to flee, then return, and by accident come ashore at Ellangowan. The plight of the "harassed wanderer" (287), movingly summarized here, marks him as a Waverley protagonist; and a later passage relates him to others who likewise sense the mysterious control of their destinies by malevolent forces: "The strangeness of his destiny, and the mysteries which appeared to thicken around him, while he seemed alike to be persecuted and protected by secret enemies and friends, arising out of a class of people with whom he had no previous connection, for some time occupied his thoughts" (324). In short, he experiences the moment of paralyzing self-doubt which, in *Waverley, Redgauntlet, Peveril,* and *The Abbot,* for example, marks the hero's discovery of his fateful involvement with the terror of history. He expresses the same longing for stability and freedom which characterizes their yearning to escape their entanglements: "When will this uncertainty cease, and how soon shall I be permitted to look out for a tranquil home, where I may cultivate in quiet, and without dread and perplexity, those arts of peace from which my cares have been hitherto so forcibly diverted?" (345) The difference is that his plight lacks the historic and/or ideological dimension which characterizes their plights, and hence,

273

that his experience is without the inevitability and breadth of significance that mark theirs.

What significance it has comes in part from the contrast we have already noted between the prudent, sensible, energetic and optimistic Bertram, and the melancholy, capriciously romantic Mannerings. It comes, too, from the parallel importance to his excursion of Meg Merrilies and Dandie Dinmont.

Buchan sees Dinmont as one of "two centres of gravity in the book, two oases of peace in a disturbed country, which bring back the tale to normality, and rest and balance the reader's mind." He sees Dandie as "four-square, three dimensional, and vital."[12] But this does not explain the meaning and value of this oasis. The pastoral image of Charlieshope is a moving experience for Bertram, not because it is the delineation of the lost manners of storefarmers in the south of Scotland, but because it envisions a world of freedom and stability dominated by a natural aristocrat of devotion, generosity, tact, and (the trait Buchan singles out) "triumphant humanity."[13] In Dandie, the heir of Ellangowan encounters the book's most attractive social-political ideal; in Dandie, the disinherited son finds a natural father. Most important, in Dandie he finds a friend and protector through his own manifest worth and humanity; Dandie does not know his real name.

When Bertram goes to the rescue of Dandie, he goes simply as a human being; when Dandie reciprocates, he comes to the rescue of "Brown." The change of name to Bertram can have no effect on Dandie; thus Dandie's judgment of Harry serves as the norm by which Mannering's may be judged – Mannering, for whom Brown and Bertram *must* be different. Julia has, of course, loved Brown, and in this she resembles Dandie. When Dandie offers money, it is to Brown. When Meg offers money and protection, she is thinking only of the heir of the Bertrams. When the affectionate Dominie Sampson recognizes young Bertram, he sees only his long lost pupil. Bertram-Brown is the object of fidelity to many. But only Dinmont's serves as a genuine touchstone, for only his is grounded in natural humanity and individual obligation to the man who had saved him.

If the triumphant restoration of Ellangowan meant the triumph of Dandie Dinmont's "triumphant humanity," the book's ultimate thematic interest would be as consistent as its plot interest. But such is not the case. Instead, it seems to mean the fulfillment of the neofeudal dreams of Meg Merrilies and Guy Mannering, a feat accomplished too easily and uncritically. Thus the book's view of loss and gain in the crisis of Ellangowan is muddled at the last. It remains to ask what is the real issue of loss and gain in the crisis of St. Ronan's, or whether the failure of Meg Dods and Touchwood to accomplish their restoration has more definite meaning than the restoration accomplished by Meg Merrilies and her numerous allies.

Meg Dods, too, has been betrayed by an aristocracy which, in betraying her, has doomed itself and its traditional way of life. The Mowbrays, like the Bertrams, were already in a state of decay when the betrayal took place:

What I wonder at is the wretched chance that has attended us miserable lairds of St. Ronan's for more than a hundred years, that we have always been getting worse in the world, and never better. Never has there been such a backsliding generation, as the parson would say: half the country once belonged to my ancestors, and now the last furrows of it seem to be flying [106].

This is partly rationalizing in a young gambler who has recklessly thrown away his patrimony; his lawyer, his

275

"house's servant," sheds crocodile tears: "And now I am to see an end of it all, and just by the lad that I thought maist likely to set it up again better than ever" (109). The narrator initially concedes that the Mowbrays declined with their patron house of Douglas, but remained powerful in the seventeenth century, and then the narrator's concern shifts to the decline of St. Ronan's. The Bertrams "had made war, raised rebellions, been defeated, beheaded, and hanged, as became a family of importance, for many centuries" (7). The catastrophe of the Mowbrays is of more recent contrivance. It seems to have had its moral cause in the desertion by the Mowbrays of St. Ronan's "aul toun" fifty years before: "It became a common remark among the country folk that the decay of St. Ronan's began when Laird Lawrence and the crows flew off" (6). The deserted mansion has become Meg Dods's inn; and her complaint fastens the decline of the Mowbrays on their transferral of patronage and loyalty from stable, traditional values and manners of St. Ronan's – "They wad hae seen my father's roof-tree fa' down and smoor me before they wad hae gien a boddle a-piece to have propped it up; but they could a' link out their fifty pounds owerhead to bigg a hottle at the Well yonder" (21) – to the resort world of transiency, vulgarity, and chance, the world of the financial, social, and sexual gambler, the "not very select society of St. Ronan's Well" (59–60).

"Well" manners seem at once grotesque and unpleasantly plausible. "Well" society is founded not just in fraud, but in shallow corruption; hence the absurdity of judging the delineation in Austenite terms. The spa was founded to supply fraudulent medicinal powers for the curing of fraudulent ills in Lady Penelope Penfeather. Meg senses the dreadful travesty on restorative power which is basic to all forms of dishonesty at the Well when she refers to "the filthy puddle yonder, that they ca' the Waal" (147). The Well is a picture of disease pretending to health.[14] Its degeneracy is illustrated in Lady Pen's frivolous reference to her heroic past. "We were somewhat naughty in the forty-five, as you may have heard," she coyly tells the minister (234); such is a bitter "end of an auld sang" to contrast with the pathos of Redgauntlet or the tragicomedy of Waverley.

The society's guiding medical spirit is named Quackle-ben; its cultural leader Winterblossom, with a name suitable to his sterility, is neither "warm" nor "elevated," but "shrewd, selfish, and sensual" (33). Its chaplain, Simon Chatterly, reads prayers in the public room, is "a deviser of charades" (34) and is always available as a partner at whist. Its "Man of Peace," a Highland lieutenant on half-pay named MacTurk, one much concerned for the "credit of the place," finds "his chief delight in setting his friends by the ears, and then acting as umpire" (129). Its nobility is an English baronet, Sir Bingo Binks, who, having been tricked into marrying a cynical sensualist, is disowned by his family and forced to remain at the Well. The company is a social world adrift; its titles are fraudulent, its values sterile or brutalized, its chief concern sexual adventures, marital politics, and the gambling that accompanies both. The satiric tone of the whole delineation is best seen in the account of the voluptuous Lady Binks, whose "wild good-humour was entirely an assumed part of her character, which was passionate, ambitious, and thoughtful" (58). She caught Sir Bingo, to discover too late how revolted she would be by the folly and brutality of such a husband; thus she became "reserved, sullen, and haughty" (59), extravagant, and promiscuously available for extramarital adventures. The healthiest note in this health resort is in the frankly acquisitive courtship of the wealthy, unaffected grocer's widow, Mrs. Blower, by Dr. Quackleben.

Such is the substance of the "lamentable mirth" with which this "pitiful tragedy" is filled. Grierson agrees with Scott that the novel is justly described in such terms, but sees it as a poorly "harmonized whole." "The comic," he postulates, "must take colour from the tragic. . . . Meg Dods is admirable, and MacTurk, Mrs. Blower, and some others possibly, but the Smollett-like vein is not in harmony with the tragedy of poor Clara, for a tragic figure she is."[15] The meaning and force of the Mowbray tragedy rest on the achievement of imaginative unity in the book. Such unity is realized only if two conditions are met. First, the Mowbray tragedy must be assimilated to the satiric contrast between Meg's "aul toun" and the new Well. Second, both must assimilate the complicated legal fiction of Tyrrel's struggle for name and title with his villainous half brother Bulmer. Otherwise we have a book whose truth and power, unique in the novels, are blunted or dissipated by its disorganization.

As for the first, the comedy of the Well does derive its meaning from close and ambiguous relation to the plight of the Mowbrays, and their tragedy has its most pointed articulation in the connection. The Well is the place for the healing of lost fortunes and social displacements. Mowbray's is the blame for its creation; he hates his creation, yet is drawn to it first by a compulsive need to gamble, then by a reckless search for a cure for his decayed fortunes. Mowbray is thus a young, more culpable Wardour, turning for restoration to a tainted or fraudulent source. He obliges his sister, whom he loves, to mix in the Well society. His involvement, and the way it taints her, are well symbolized in the central episode of the mid-novel. Mowbray must entertain Well society at Shaws-Castle; the chief entertainment is a series of charades or romantic tableaux. Clara is obliged to participate, to become not just involved in the absurdly incongruous disguises, but even confused with the mean and petty women of the Well.

The confusion, however, is not just a matter of disguises. Clara's tragedy is grounded in character; she is insufficiently distinct from the Well women to remain untainted by their company. Hateful as it may seem to her admirers (e.g., Grierson), she is a more attractive form of Lady Binks; both are too wild, undisciplined. The difference is that in Lady Binks the "wild, hoydenish, half-mad humour, was only superinduced" (58). In Clara the humor is real: the lack of self-respect, the contempt for all forms, the fantastic dress and idiom. What began in an education on old romances became the dangerously whimsical, anarchic spirit of the girl and young woman, and is now the fatalistic conviction that life is a tragic farce. She cannot make herself out the victim of her brother's sordidness; her own flaws prevent her playing the tragic heroine: "I shall be no Lady Clementina, to be the wonder and pity of the spring of St. Ronan's; no Ophelia neither, though I will say with her, 'Good-night, ladies – good-night, sweet ladies!' And now, not 'my coach, my coach,' but 'my horse, my horse!' " (79) When she forgets it and essays the betrayed ingenue, her brother justly reminds her that the role doesn't suit her, his address providing the most searingly antifictional moment of the book.

He has been trying to persuade her to cure her wounded reputation and their sick fortunes by marrying Bulmer. She haughtily refuses to see Bulmer. Her brother reminds her that such postures scarcely fit: "You cannot, I suppose, even

279

in the workings of your romantic brain, imagine that the
days of Clarissa Harlowe and Harriet Byron are come back
again, when women were married by main force? . . . You
are no such prize, methinks, that the days of romance are to
come back for you" (251). Tyrrel says naively to Meg Dods,
"No doubt Miss Clara's conduct deserves all sort of freedom" (24). Her brother is more judicious when he suggests
she has had too much freedom for her own safety and
character (252). For her there *is* no society left but that of
the Well. She and her brother, pathetic last heirs, share the
burden of their catastrophe, share a hateful entanglement
with the tawdry world of Binkses and Penfeathers, share a
real affection, and even share pathetically degenerate
dreams of innocence, of liberation from the shallow evil they
have created: "There is enough left of the old acres to keep
us in the way you like best," he raves, "and that I will learn
to like. I will work in the garden, and work in the forest,
mark my own trees, and cut them myself." "Oh!" she
responds, "could we not begin such a life to-morrow?" (117)
It is no accident that Mowbray's final moral act is to kill
Bulmer and then destroy the spa, or that Clara wanders to
the heart of the "aul toun" to die under Meg's protection in
the Mowbray Old Place.

All of this skirts the still lively issue of just what Clara had
done, and what she would have done had Scott disallowed
the bowdlerizing of James Ballantyne. Lockhart may simply
have been mistaken, or he may have been seeking to save
Scott from his own indiscretion, when he claimed that the
original plan carried Bulmer's deception (substituting himself for the bridegroom) actually through the wedding
night.[16] At any rate, the cancelled sheet published in 1893
shows that Clara "fell" through no deception, but through
premarital sport with her lover Tyrrel. Scott's contemptuous

words to Ballantyne – "You would never have quarrelled with it . . . had the thing happened to a girl in gingham: – the silk petticoat can make little difference" – perhaps make more sense, as Ker argues, when read as referring to the cancelled sheet.[17] Whichever the case (and I shall argue that both may be correct) the basic issue is the question of Clara's motivation, and the causes of her mental instability. The question is tangled with the question of Tyrrel's motivation.

Gradually and skillfully Scott builds his case for Clara's psychological and moral instability. But its causes are unclear. The oddness and whimsicality mentioned by Lady Pen (62) are confirmed by the doctor's view that the "poor thing" is "unsettled," a little "touched" (76), through capricious education and a neglected youth. The narrator suggests an instability prior to her disgrace, whatever its nature (77). Meg attributes the problem rather to the heart than to the head (159); Clara's talks with Tyrrel and her brother indicate that her unsettled state is the aftermath of a breakdown *following* her entanglement with Tyrrel and Bulmer. As a matter of fact, we cannot isolate the question of cause in Clara's instability from the general thematic fact that she is far from alone in her madness. We must associate that madness with other statements. We have as evidence (1) Bulmer's remark in his letter to Jekyll that his house is governed by "an ignis fatuus influence": "it poured its wildfire through my father's veins, it has descended to me in full vigour" (281); (2) Jekyll's reply, "The *ignis fatuus* . . . seems to have ruled the fortunes of your whole house, there is so much eccentricity in all that you have told me" (285); and (3) Touchwood's statement that "everybody that has meddled in this St. Ronan's business is a little off the hooks – something of a *tête exaltée* – in plain words, a little crazy, or so" (325) – and he itemizes (326–27). The whole world of St. Ronan's Well is unstable; madness runs through its rootless society. This is a persistent theme, and one senses the inspiration in the references throughout to *Hamlet*: Clara's comparison of herself to Ophelia and her Ophelia-like behavior, Touchwood's allusion to Hamlet in the midst of his exposition of the theme (326), and the vague but powerful concern with coarse sexuality and incest throughout. In a "mad world," no naturalistically sufficient, isolated motivation can "explain" Clara's instability.

But to see what motivation is offered, we need not go to cancelled sheets. Clara repeatedly hints at what Ballantyne thought Scott had eliminated, that the rumors are true; that "they can scarcely say worse of me than I deserve"; that she "did indeed" roam the woods "a little too much in my father's time" (383, 252). To Tyrrel she reminisces, "You and I would, you know, become men and women while we were yet scarcely more than children. We have run, while yet in our nonage, through the passions and adventures of youth, and therefore we are now old before our day, and the winter of our life has come on ere its summer was well begun" (98). The cancelled sheet matters only because *Bulmer tells Jekyll* that the report of Clara's fall was merely *his* ruse to get the minister to perform the mock ceremony (274). The cancelled sheet indicates that *Bulmer* was ignorant of the truth. So Scott's last-minute attempts to prove the fall a false report don't work because we have been previously convinced by Clara of its actuality.[18]

Tyrrel confirms this. He says he wants to protect her from Bulmer because he "of all men who live" owes it to her, since "I first persuaded her to quit the path of duty" (313). This vague phrase could refer simply to his encouraging her reckless independence and thus exposing her to danger. But

Tyrrel's motivation provides a problem as complex as Clara's. Welsh supplies a dubious solution. For him, "the entire credibility of the action in *St. Ronan's Well* hinges" on a point of honor. Why, he asks, cannot Frank Tyrrel rescue Clara by marrying her? Regardless, he says, "of who, if anyone, has slept with Clara Mowbray, both the manuscript and the subsequent editions of *St. Ronan's Well* report one much more narrow cause of the hero's estrangement." He quotes Tyrrel's insistence that even if law could completely free Clara from her pretended marriage, an impassable obstacle would remain for him: "the nuptial benediction has been pronounced over her and the man whom I must for once call *brother*" (313). "Thus," interprets Welsh, "the sense of honor goes much further than either law or religion in respecting the ceremony of marriage."[19] But this is to grasp for the abstract and bypass the obvious. The sentence preceding Welsh's quotation reads, "Whatever [rights] I might have had, were cancelled by the act of treachery through which your friend endeavoured too successfully to supplant me." The phrasing here, "too successfully to supplant," the strong emphasis on the word brother, the other hints of a horror of incest, even in the wording of Hannah Irwin's cancelled confession, all suggest motivation for both Tyrrel and Clara, an explanation of the several Hamlet allusions, and an accounting for Lockhart's "mistake." Buchan had not seen the cancelled sheet, apparently, for he assumes the truth of Lockhart's report and uses it to motivate Tyrrel's vehemence: "A mere trick like a mock-marriage could not have wrought such havoc, and it needed, too, a deeper wrong to justify Tyrrel's feelings towards his half-brother."[20] The "deeper wrong" would be the consummation of the mock marriage. Add this to Clara's prior sin with Tyrrel. The despair of Tyrrel and the madness

283

of Clara are both more adequately explained when we assume Scott originally intended actual incest in the vein of Shakespeare's Gertrude.

There are enough vague hints to raise strong possibilities. And, to touch on the question raised by Ker, the numerous vague hints make the long, late disclosure by Hannah Irwin, bowdlerized or not, an excrescence. The novel is better off with its structure of implications. But the explicitness of Hannah Irwin's confession is part of a more general flaw. Whatever the lucidity and richness of thematic development, plot contrivance in the novel is impossibly intricate, hence it cries out for the kind of summary explicitness Hannah Irwin provides. The result is a serious loss of imaginative force: "Lord Etherington's intrigues, for example," says Buchan, "and the dependence of his inheritance on marriage with a Mowbray are invented rather than imagined,"[21] are too arbitrary, I suppose he means, ever to become organic. Tyrrel's struggle with Bulmer seems unconnected to what matters, to what has imaginative and moral life in the novel: the question of the survival of St. Ronan's and the Mowbrays. The disinherited heir's plight and quest seem to have little to do with the tragic love of Tyrrel and Clara.

The objection is to some extent insurmountable. But to see only disconnectedness is to overlook basic moral facts. The evil that Bulmer embodies has two origins: (1) the secret marriage of Tyrrel's father and mother – and this was to be reenacted by Tyrrel and Clara, otherwise Bulmer could not have interceded; (2) the will of Touchwood's father, Scrogie Mowbray, and his absurd attempt to achieve name and dynasty by disowning a son in favor of a ridiculous marriage. These criminal follies are the same as are present in St. Ronan's Well and the Mowbrays themselves.

They are the causes of both tragedies: the fall of the Mowbrays and the impossible love of Clara and Tyrrel; the mean, cold-blooded Bulmer is simply the instrument of such evils. So there is potential moral and imaginative unity. But the abstract, technical nature of Bulmer's lengthy and needlessly explicit explanations obscures that unity by keeping imaginative response at a minimum.

We should not, however, neglect the way the battle of Bulmer and Tyrrel is assimilated through their placement in the controlling "place" structure. Tyrrel, in his honesty, simplicity, quiet seriousness, is placed in and allied with the "aul toun." His arrival provides Meg with the occasion to expound on the recent changes in St. Ronan's; his disappearance brings her out as maternal protector; his return calls for the intercession of Touchwood. His introduction to Well society displays that contrasting world from an "aul toun" perspective; his virtues make him as out of place there as Clara's license and whimsy make her. Appropriately, it is in his room at Meg's Inn that Clara dies. Bulmer, on the other hand, although his fatal deception was played out before the spa's creation, belongs to the Well from his first appearance, not just in his sexual adventures with Lady Binks, but in his mean dishonesties, his petty tricks to rob the mails. He embodies the corruptions of the Well. Thus the contest between the half brothers individualizes the conflict between the old and new worlds of St. Ronan's; this, and the Well-like absurdity of the legal intricacy by which Bulmer operates, provide more imaginative unity than is apparent at first glance.

There is no doubt about it. The issues of the survival of Ellangowan and Mowbray are made live, and provide controlling thematic structures. *Guy Mannering* may seem to be the smoother narrative. But moral urgency and tragic irony, the controlling opposition of rude, despotic old with coarse, fraudulent new, and the revelation of the futility of facile remedies for the sickness of a corrupt, unstable aristocracy, all make *St. Ronan's Well* far more powerful and significant, and perhaps what Balzac thought it: one of Scott's masterpieces.[22]

3. *THE PIRATE* (1821) AND *THE SURGEON'S DAUGHTER* (1827)

The novel closest to the tragic *St. Ronan's Well,* as Gordon has recently noted, is *The Bride of Lammermoor;*[23] it is significant that the most "realistic" and contemporary should invite comparison with the most "Gothic." Where *St. Ronan's Well* falls short imaginatively, *The Bride,* written four years earlier, succeeds most remarkably. Is this an accident, or does the difference indicate the importance historicity had for Scott's organizing imagination? Before considering the question with reference to *The Bride,* we can analyze it further by considering two lesser novels, both later than *The Bride,* in which Scott also sought to escape historicity by substituting exotic locales whose remoteness is not primarily historic. In *The Pirate* and *The Surgeon's Daughter* we are still in the romance world of the lost heir's search for identity and stability. The search is associated with a threat to the established way of life on which he intrudes. A crisis of historic survival is associated with the intrusion of a dangerously romantic personality. The victim of both is a rejected daughter, saved from the lawless designs of the romantic heir, but withdrawn from life in nunlike isolation. The heroine's father, representative of the threatened values, is in some measure responsible for his daughter's misfortune: (1) he has been deluded by the dangerous heir's romantic personality and has adopted him; (2) in adopting the romantic heir he has rejected the heir he should have chosen: the stable, selfless foil to the romantic heir-hero. The father's false choice breaks the continuity of his house and leaves his daughter stoically strong, but barren. Such is the tragic note on which each ends.

Both novels are partly Scottish in setting. But *The Pirate* is set in Zetland, where Scottish settlers are alien proponents of new and outlandish manners. *The Surgeon's Daughter* moves from Scotland to India, as the romantic heir's exotic aspirations draw him to the East, where he recklessly becomes involved in Asian political intrigue.

We begin, then, with the fact that each portrays the disastrous consequences of a romantic personality's intrusion upon a traditional society: the patriarchal island culture of Norwegian Zetland; the quiet, hard-working world of the Scottish village doctor. The confrontation is akin to the confrontation of the historical novels: the unromantic "natural," i.e., disciplined, stable, communal, becomes entangled temporarily with the romance of historic forces or the destinies of historic personalities. Such is the common fate of the doomed heroines, Minna Troil and Menie Gray. But the confrontation is primarily nonhistoric; and Scott must therefore explain his romantic intruders in other terms, account for their evil not as historic fatality, but as individual aberration. Such terms prove only superficially meaningful. Such figures are "fatal"; they are of mysterious origin, extralegal; they consort with forbidden powers and are thus doomed or fey. But for the Enlightenment Scott only historic fatality is real; fatality of character, so complex and central an idea for his fictional heirs, George Eliot and Hardy, can for him be only moral delinquency. His romantic heir-heroes can be dynamic people, yet be judged with little moral subtlety.

For one thing, interest is blunted in each case by the presence of an unromantic foil which provides an overly schematic polarity. This does not, of course, mean that the foil is the "hero" or even the normative protagonist by which the romantic foil is judged villain.[24] Hartley is a dull, priggish Dobbin of a fellow apprentice to Richard Middlemas. He tries ineffectually to serve as friend and counselor to Middlemas, saves his life, then is forced to rescue Menie, whom he loves from afar, from the designs of Middlemas in India. Hartley then considerately dies, and Menie returns to her heroic spinsterhood in Scotland. The story is about the mysterious disinherited child left with Dr. Gray, about his growth and corruption, his infatuation with romantic ideas of a noble destiny put in his head by a foolish nurse, and his effect on the lives of the Grays and Hartley. *The Surgeon's Daughter* begins and ends with the same focus on Menie and Middlemas.

The Pirate is less simple. We see in it the danger Scott confronted, given the formal conception of a counterpointing of romantic protagonist and unromantic counterhero. *Waverley* might have fallen prey to some such static division of focus had Fergus been less skillfully integrated with other elements of Edward's experience. The structure of *Redgauntlet*, never achieving dialectical resolution of the counterpointing of Latimer and Fairford, failed. The danger is absent from the Puritan-Cavalier novels, where controlling polarities embody rival fanaticisms in the experience of the heroic moderate. It is absent from *Kenilworth* and *The Abbot*, kept in the background in *Durward* to the problem of fidelity to Louis, and transformed in *The Fair Maid's* counterpointing of Conachar and Smith. But in *The Pirate* the impulse was to domesticate the Schilleresque robber-hero. The outcome is an unresolved division of focus, and a final shift of tragic emphasis to the heroine.

The danger is apparent in *Ivanhoe*, where Scott becomes so engrossed in the romantic fatality of his first nihilist hero, Bois-Guilbert, and his doomed stranger Rebecca, that the romance of Ivanhoe's reinstatement loses its central place. *The Pirate* is no more and no less historical than *Ivanhoe*. Both suggest an uncertainty of perspective and a resultant lapse of form when Scott treats the phenomenon of romantic lawlessness independently of the ordeal of historical change. Scott as moralist, and concurrently Scott as narrative artist, is less engaging when history is not an essential force, or when the ironic imperatives of history are not brought constantly into interplay with conventional motifs to animate their otherwise abstract polarities. When historic conflict-in-change is the problem, then prejudice, fanatic loyalty and courage, romantic values, are of paradoxical worth – not, certainly, as *felix culpa,* but at least as *infelix pietas. Infelix pietas* in primarily domestic novels easily becomes mere foolish family pride. The tragic romantic personality can be significantly engaging in the novels only when his idealistic commitment is to values temporarily viable to the reader. To make them so, Scott needed the larger problem of ideological conflict in historical change.

While much attention is given to the alienation of Middlemas by the poison of false romantic notions, his commitment to remote Indian rebellions has no reality for the reader. The focus shifts to the sketchy, dull romance of Menie's rescue, and Middlemas dwindles from quasi-tragic hero into insignificant, uninteresting villain. There is little more to be said about the book.

The Pirate is otherwise. Here the problem of romantic

personality is set in a dynamic of authentically imagined cultural conflict. The specific manners whose survival is at stake are, Scott admitted, "necessarily in a great degree imaginary, though founded in some measure on slight hints, which, showing what was, seemed to give reasonable indication of what must once have been, the tone of the society in these sequestered but interesting islands" (x). The fictional possibilities remind us of *Ivanhoe*. The "tone of society" of early eighteenth-century Zetland was as remote and unparticularized for Scott as the manners of twelfth-century England. Yet such a life must have been, he infers, "close to nature," determined, that is, by natural environment and by the insular persistence of tradition, and it could therefore be imagined organically unlike reconstructed milieux, literary in derivation. Not that literary derivations are absent or necessarily inorganic. *The Pirate* is decked with pseudo-Nordic recitatives in the "sublime" manner, with the neopagan Norna to chant them. But in the imagined world of the novel, such relics are accorded doubtful reality. They belong to a Romanticism which the novel rejects as unreal and dangerous in favor of more natural, humane, enlightened, concrete, modes of thought and feeling.[25]

The possibilities for a familiar thematic complexity and unity may be glimpsed in the facts with which Scott began. The facts proved so congenial, the opportunity for thematic expansion so unlimited by the need for the authenticity of manners, that the book became one of Scott's most densely thematic novels.

The Pirate might better be called *The Stranger*. The story germ is the descent of the pirate Gow on the Orkneys in 1724–25, his mixing in the life and culture of the islands, the tragic love a young Orcadian lady "of some property" bears for him, and the heroic stratagems of a young islander who effects his capture.[26] The central plot fact is the tragic love; the facts of richest thematic potentiality are his strangeness to the islands and the threat to their culture posed by a fascinating, powerful stranger.

In order to broaden the social structure to define the threat, Scott says he was "induced to go a generation or two farther back to find materials from which I might trace the features of the old Norwegian udaller, the Scottish gentry having in general occupied the place of that primitive race, and their language and peculiarities of manner having entirely disappeared" (ix–x) – back, that is, from the Orkneys of Scott's first or secondhand knowledge. By so doing he could expand the conflict between the pirate and the islands to include related conflicts between island values and numerous strangers embodying various threats. Those most evident are between the hospitable, humane old Udaller Magnus Troil and (1) the stranger Mertoun, and (2) the stranger Yellowley.

Mertoun is a mysterious, withdrawn Englishman, objectionably abstemious, antisocial, and coldly unnatural as a father to the novel's counterhero Mordaunt Mertoun. Magnus is the opposite of his tenant Mertoun in every respect: unmysterious, excessively sociable, heroically extravagant in eating and drinking, and naturally affectionate as a father to two daughters. With predictable ritualism Mordaunt substitutes this natural father for his own unnatural one, becomes suitor to both daughters, and then is forced to work out the mystery of his identity and destiny in terms of his relation to both "fathers."

Yellowley's conflict with Magnus is cultural and economic. He is a mean, speculative agricultural reformer, perhaps the first ludicrous utilitarian in nineteenth-century fiction, from mainland Scotland, spokesman for progress, utility, and economic efficiency, who raves continuously about the "deplorable defects" of the island culture and vows that "all shall be reformed and amended" (115, 54). Mordaunt finds himself in the middle of the conflict and warns Yellowley about giving vent to such speculative passion in Magnus's presence: "Magnus Troil's boat is kittle to trim; he likes his own ways, and his country-ways, and you will as soon teach your sheltie to dive like a sealgh as bring Magnus to take a Scottish fashion in the place of a Norse one" (115–16). Yellowley persists, however, and finally rouses Magnus to this statement of one of the book's basic themes: "You are a fine fellow, Master Factor Yellowley! You come to us from a strange land, understanding neither our laws, nor our manners, nor our language, and you propose to become governor of the country, and that we should all be your slaves." "My pupils, worthy sir, my pupils!" Yellowley shouts back, "and that only for your own proper advantage" (149). Such is Yellowley's evil as a stranger: he is the Jacobin, the inhuman speculator who, in ignorance of the actual culture, seeks with pedantic ruthlessness to impose a new one.[27] When the chief stranger, the pirate, is expelled, Yellowley remains, but not until he has been acclimatized and humanized. The novel finds its chief spokesman in Magnus with his tirades against strangers. But what Magnus opposes is not change, but an irreverent rejection of what is truly valid in the past; what he hates is not the stranger, but the bad stranger who threatens Magnus's house and island with his ignorance, his abstract prejudice, his inhumanity.

Magnus undergoes a complex process of acceptance and rejection of the book's centrally opposed strangers, Mordaunt Mertoun and the pirate Cleveland. Initially he adopts Mertoun as son and heir; then he hears false reports that cause him to reject Mordaunt and adopt Cleveland in his place, thus taking a destructive principle into his own house and bringing partial destruction on his lineage. He discovers his error too late. His romantic elder daughter has already devoted herself eternally to her idealization of the pirate. He readopts Mordaunt, the good stranger, who becomes his heir, marries his younger daughter Brenda, and carries on the timeless values of Magnus's house in a mixed lineage of stranger and islander.

The two central strangers are mysteriously close and yet instinctively hostile from Cleveland's first appearance. It would be neatly useful to Welsh's Romantic–anti-Romantic scheme if the kinship embodied a contrast between active Cleveland and passive Mertoun, or "natural" Cleveland and "societal" Mertoun.[28] But Cleveland, the Romantic personality, is artificial and urbane; his virtues exist, as he concedes, only in the idealizing imagination of Minna Troil. It is Mordaunt who is the *natural* leader in boyish sports, and Mordaunt, too, who is captivated by the "dark romance" of local legend and superstition (15). Most important, it is Mordaunt who grows up with the islanders as master and lover of their own manners:

He could play upon the "gue," and upon the common violin, the melancholy and pathetic tunes peculiar to the country; and with great spirit and execution could relieve their monotony with the livelier airs of the North of Scotland. When a party set forth as maskers, or, as they are called in Scotland, "guizards," to visit some neighbouring laird, or rich udaller, it augured well of the expedition if Mordaunt Mertoun could be prevailed upon to undertake the office of "skudler," or leader of the band [17].

The passage delineates Mordaunt as instinctive master of cultural synthesis. Norna of the Fitful Head, the fanatic extremist with insular hatred of strangers, calls him the "youth of a foreign land, but of a friendly heart" (55). His "friendly heart" makes him tolerant, humane, with the fanatic Norna, with the eccentric Yellowleys, with the odd pathetic poet Halcro, even with his unaffectionate father.

The only exception to Mordaunt's tolerance is Cleveland. His motives for hating Cleveland are mixed, plausibly human, and yet significantly mysterious. It is he who saves Cleveland's life at the time of the shipwreck, and his humanity is thus responsible for Cleveland's coming to the island. When Cleveland replaces him in the Troil household and the island games, his boyish pride is hurt. His resentment of the worldly sophistication and charm of the new stranger is equally authentic or natural. But there is more than boyish pride in the hostility he feels, and he tries in vain to account for "a sort of repelling influence about the man" (91). Yet he has saved the man's life, is responsible for his presence; he has compounded the ordeal of loyalty to an unnatural, withdrawn father with responsibility for a powerful, lawless stranger. It is inevitable, given the logic of moral relationships by which the book is governed, that ultimately he should discover Cleveland to be his half brother and the true son of his father.[29]

The more sophisticated Cleveland accepts the paradoxical nature of their relationship. He awaits a chance to repay Mordaunt's gift of life and finally saves his preserver from drowning. (The islanders' reaction is significant: "Just let the twa strangers help ilk other, and stand by the upshot" [180].) He admits to Minna: "I cannot be friend to this young man; there is a natural dislike – an instinctive aversion – something like a principle of repulsion, in our mutual nature, which makes us odious to each other. Ask himself – he will tell you he has the same antipathy against me"

(235–36). The working of hostile principles in polar oppositions of personality types, given complex plot expression in a
tangle of family relations, tempts one to call the novel Scott's
Wuthering Heights. But the analogy does not yield the
meaning for Scott's book of the instinctive "principle of
repulsion in our mutual nature."

To interpret the hostility in terms of a supposedly pervasive "Waverley" opposition of Romantic lawlessness and
anti-Romantic discipline is to risk falsification. Not that
The Pirate lacks evidence for such a reading. Mordaunt's
final appearances are meek enough; and the novel seems to
impose a conventional moral judgment on Cleveland. For
Norna, Cleveland is "bold, haughty, and undaunted, unre-
strained by principle, and having only in its room a wild
sense of indomitable pride, which such men call honour"
(408). The narrator places Cleveland with those "who are
involved in evil rather by the concurrence of external
circumstances than by natural inclination." But these judgments pertain to Cleveland's piracy, a thing of the past. Our
concern in the book has been with his doomed attempt to
escape from that past, to create a new identity, find a new
life with Minna Troil in sequestered Zetland. He is wholly
sincere; he feels genuine love for Minna, which she, in her
romantic infatuation, cannot feel for him. The problem of
Mordaunt's present hostility is not solved by judgments of
Cleveland's past.

What Mordaunt senses is Cleveland's threat to the island
culture. In Cleveland's posture of superiority, in his attitudes toward the essential values of island life, he is a
destructive principle. Mordaunt, as the good stranger cher-
ishing the manners he has adopted, senses that Cleveland
the sceptic, the cosmopolite, the fatalist, is the bad stranger.

Such is the proposition disputed by the two sisters.

295

Brenda is disturbed by her sister's growing attachment to Cleveland. Norna tells the sisters of her own fatal passion for a mysterious stranger. She had been meant for Magnus; then came her "fatal stranger," "full of arts unknown to us, and graces which to the plain manners of your father were unknown" (207). "We loved in secret," she recalls, "we met in secret, till I gave the last proof of fatal and of guilty passion!" (207) In stealing out to run away with her lover, she shut her father's door, and the next morning he was dead of "suffocating vapour" (208). She is doubly guilty of two sins also connected, symbolically, in Minna's fateful love of Cleveland: reckless passion and parricide.

The sisters argue the story's applicability to the two present strangers. Minna warns Brenda against Mordaunt, "the nameless and birthless stranger," reminiscent of the stranger who "ruined Norna's peace for ever" (214–15). Brenda warns, in reply, "There are other strangers at Burgh-Westra besides this poor Mordaunt Mertoun" (215). The sensible, humane Brenda is spokesman for Magnus's view of the difference between the strangers. Norna's "fatal stranger" was a stranger "not only in birth, but in manners . . . in character, temper, birth, manners, and morals; some wandering adventurer, perhaps" (215). Mordaunt is not the stranger of the Cleveland-Yellowley-Mertoun Sr. type, the destructive, withdrawn intruder, but the sympathetic participant in their culture. In the face of such an argument, Minna characteristically shifts her grounds, reveals her infatuation, and identifies herself as the book's arch-Romantic, who, like Norna, is so fanatic in her dedication to an ideal image of her lineage, that she tragically deludes herself into finding that ideal embodied in one who can only be its destroyer.

Such is Minna's character, as schematically differentiated

from Brenda's as Mordaunt's is from that of his half brother. From this crucial midpoint the counterpointing of the sisters occupies a position of thematic centrality. "With determined consistency," says Welsh, "Scott invokes the contrast of his two heroines throughout *The Pirate.*" Welsh's own consistency in classifying them with other Waverley heroines is more determined still. It is all, we hear, a matter of complexion. The Romantic brunette, the "dark heroine does outlive the dark hero" – achieves resignation to life, but wears it out "in exile, or the cloister, or upon the sands of Zetland." She is more profound, sublime, natural, and passionate, more voluptuous; her hair is more abundant, less governable, symbolizing "her freedom from convention and restraint." (He is speaking of Die Vernon.) "The proper heroine of Scott," on the other hand, "is a blonde," sensible, prudent, less voluptuous, less hirsute, less "available," and in Brenda's case "at once less deeply emotional and more civilized," "molded by society," eminently suited to marry the "passive hero" (who in *The Pirate* is far less passive than the "dark hero"), happy, and less intellectual.[30]

There is enough general truth in this typology to provide Welsh with a plausible case, at the sacrifice, unfortunately, of essential differences between novel and novel, heroine and heroine. The fatal woman, whatever her coloring, is invariably more involved with Romantic values; the providential one serves to rectify or repudiate those values. But the heroines and the values vary significantly from novel to novel, as do the passive and nonpassive heroes. What implications prevail, for instance, in the extended contrast of Minna and Brenda? Brenda *is* the dutiful daughter until her father makes the wrong choice, and then it is Brenda, defiant of both father and general opinion, who remains true to Mordaunt the outcast and is proved right, while Minna dutifully chooses Cleveland. Minna is La Penserosa, Brenda L'Allegra. Minna is placid, pale, retiring, grave, *unworldly*. Brenda is buoyant, sociable, sensible, and *loyal*. (Minna quickly drops Cleveland to keep her threatened ideal intact.) As for voluptuousness, we are always more physically aware of Brenda. She persists in blushing "over every part of her beautiful skin which her dress permitted to be visible, including her slender neck and the upper region of a finely-formed bosom"; at one point her bodice is half unlaced (124, 214). Brenda's physical solidity is consistent with her views of what a lover should be. Her objections to Cleveland are several. "Can you think," she asks Minna, "of being yoked with a spirit so unsettled and stormy, whose life has hitherto been led in scenes of death and peril, and who, even while sitting by your side, cannot disguise his impatience again to engage in them?" Minna answers, "My lover must scorn the mockeries by which our degraded race strive for distinction. . . . My lover must be a sea-king" (217). Such sentiments are natural in one whose longing is the "aspiration of a soul bent on more important objects than those by which she was surrounded" (19), with a "high feeling for the solitary and melancholy grandeur of the scenes in which she was placed" (20). Brenda's inability to understand such a love would seem to relegate her to Welsh's "proper heroine" class and justify the more grandiloquent condescension of Norna of the Fitful Head, who says of Mordaunt's choice: "You cannot be so dull of heart, so poor of spirit, as to prefer the idle mirth and housewife simplicity of the younger sister to the deep feeling and high mind of the noble-spirited Minna?" (353) But Norna is scarcely a fitting judge, and to take hers as a judicious account of the Minna-Brenda contrast is to misread the book.

The chief difference – Halcro the poet renders it in his

repeated night versus day symbolism – is intellectual, and in this area Brenda is proved sound and Minna absurdly deluded. She has a "high mind" indeed; is customarily wrapped "in some vision of the imagination," has a "warmer fancy" (158, 212). Brenda, "in recompense for a less portion of imagination than her sister, was gifted with sound common sense" (283). Brenda, then, is incapable of doing what Minna does. She cannot find the reincarnation of the Viking hero, one above the law and fated to liberate her oppressed "race" (it isn't hers at all: she is the dark Celt, Brenda the Nordic blonde!) from the pettiness of ignoble strangers, in one who knows himself merely an "unfortunate buccanier" (237), who fears "that the descendant of an ancient sea-king will scarce acknowledge a fitting acquaintance in a modern rover" (237). To her racist-nationalist defiances of the "prejudices" that England and Scotland call laws, he warns, "Remember, it is yourself that throw me back upon a mode of life which the laws of Britain denounce as criminal, and which the violent passions of the daring men by whom it is pursued have rendered infamous" (240). The pirate seeks to flee from his lawless past to law and stability, only to be forced back into it by the reckless idealizing imagination of a girl who "has been bred in such remote simplicity, and utter ignorance of what is evil, that she compares our occupation with that of the old Norsemen." He admits, to his credit and to the comic refutation of Norna's judgments of himself and Minna, that he had to disenchant her, that he could not "so utterly play the part of a fallen spirit as to avail myself of her enthusiastic error" (335–36).

Minna may be more passionate, but her passion, like Flora MacIvor's, is wholly intellectual, and it renders her intellectually incompetent. She can love only an ideal.

299

Brenda's chief objection to the lover Minna sees in Cleveland is that he doesn't love her, and thus as an individual lover is inadequate (216). Brenda is not a conventionalist; she is a realist. Minna may be more attached to the sublime in nature; Brenda is more "natural." Minna responds only to the abstract, Brenda to the concretely human. As always in Scott, the normative contrast is between the ideal and the human commitment, the impersonal and the personal, the Jacobin and the anti-Jacobin.[31] Minna is deficient in humanity, and thus, ironically, she is susceptible to the kind of delusion which can only destroy the valuable reality for which she has tragically little respect. We have seen in evil strangers such as Mertoun and Yellowley that humanity is what they lack, humanity is the comprehensive value threatened by evil strangers – hospitality, forbearance, and the kind of concrete concern Brenda feels for her sister.

Other values are threatened, some necessarily. The book avoids Romantic primitivisms, and recognizes that the preservation of a traditional humanity may require the sacrifice of other traditional manners and beliefs.[32] Emphasized are the islanders' code concerning their right to whatever the sea brings them, which ironically makes them as piratical as "the pirate," and their doggedly held pagan superstitions. The task of working out a satisfactory attitude toward each of these belongs to the good stranger, Mordaunt Mertoun. Mordaunt's devotion to his adopted manners makes him hesitant to reject either custom; yet his humanity and enlightenment tell him he must. He is thus an intensely committed version of the Waverley protagonist-mediator, akin to Morton and Ravenswood.

Concerning the first, while the islanders profess to despise the commercial values introduced by strangers in the name of hospitality and generosity, they persist in the ruthlessly mercenary belief that it is disastrous to save a drowning man. If there are no survivors, a ship is lawful plunder. Mordaunt is urged not to save Cleveland; his adopted society opposes his action. For them, in the words of the fictitious Old Play's epigraph to Chapter 14, custom is law itself. Mordaunt refuses to identify custom with law; takes upon himself the burden of solitary appeal to a higher, humane code; and soon becomes aware that in so doing he has started the machinery of his fate working. The pattern is duplicated in *The Bride of Lammermoor* and *The Black Dwarf*. As it does for Morton and Waverley, this solitary act of humanity leads to temporary alienation, even entanglement with evil and resultant misrepresentation. In acting thus, however, he unknowingly allies himself with the island's future, to which his own lineage will belong, and justifies his own role as mediator, upon which the continuity of island culture depends. He has contributed to the obliteration of a custom which has made the islanders themselves pirates. Cleveland upon landing recognizes the custom is that "this is good doctrine, and more men than one may trim their sails to such a breeze" (90); his lieutenant sees no distinction between the "honesty" of the islander and the piracy of the pirate (385). Magnus recognizes retributive justice in the island custom and the islanders' vulnerability: "Till we learn to regard the rights of them that suffer by the winds and waves, we shall deserve to be oppressed and hagridden, as we have been and are, by the superior strength of the strangers who rule us" (186–87). We know from this that Mordaunt is his true heir, and it becomes not just ironic, but fitting, that he should temporarily reject Mordaunt when he hears the false report emanating from the "serpent," the destructive principle, Cleveland, that Mordaunt seeks a Troil wife only for her property value.

The second custom presents a more complex problem. Welsh quotes Coleridge's complaint, written in his copy of *The Pirate,* that Scott, in reporting preternatural superstitions, "is most anxious to let his readers know, that he himself is far too enlightened not to be assured of the folly and falsehood of all he yet relates as *truth,*" in such a way as to "save his own (Sir Walter's) character as an enlightened man."[33] This was not the case in *The Monastery* or in *The Betrothed,* and we have yet to consider his most careful dramatizing of the preternatural in *The Bride.* In the introduction to *The Pirate* Scott discusses the Radcliffian method – the ultimate naturalistic explanation of the preternatural – and finds in it "a degree of improbability almost equal to an absolute goblin narrative." This method having proved unsatisfactory, Scott is left with the choice of offering a "probability" which the reader finds anachronistic or a "probability" which the narrator admits he cannot accept. True, in *The Pirate* the narrator takes pains to detach himself from the time and place that could give credence to Norna's "pretensions to supernatural knowledge" (53). Norna's faith in her powers is presented as a form of pathetic madness associated with her neurotic withdrawal from life: she was "taken from humanity," she says, "to be something pre-eminently powerful, pre-eminently wretched!" (208–9). Her ceremonial acts of weather control recall the astronomer in *Rasselas,* and the epigraph to Chapter Ten proves the association deliberate. She is suffering from the diseased imagination from which Minna is ultimately saved. Nevertheless the book returns repeatedly to the question, what is the most viable and humane attitude toward Norna's kind of superstition?

The question does not imply that the superstition can be viewed with intellectual seriousness. It asks how, assuming disbelief, the custom of the superstition can be set aside without inhumane neglect of the feelings of those who harbor it and without losing the essential truth such a custom must contain. The evil strangers are cynically destructive; Mertoun Sr. and Cleveland mock Norna's superstition (223). Mordaunt is cautious and moderate, but neither timorous nor credulous. When Brenda errs on the side of scepticism, as her sister does on the side of credulity, Magnus reprimands her. However unsuperstitious himself, he defines destructive irreverence as a sin and notes the habit of "strangers in general" of finding "reasons for things which remained sufficiently obscure to those whose ancestors had dwelt there for ages" (223). He reveres superstition as a custom and defines his own essential conservatism: "I believe, Brenda . . . according to the belief of my forefathers. I pretend not to be a wiser man than they were in their time; and they all believed that, in cases of great worldly distress, Providence opened the eyes of the mind and afforded the sufferers a vision of futurity" (285).

The terms he uses echo his enlightened conservative kin in other Waverley Novels. A belief in supernatural power is a belief in Providence, and to this belief Norna does not aspire. Norna, like most fanatics in the novels, is self-doomed by her fatalism. She assures Mordaunt that "Fate has high views on" him (55). She believes herself withdrawn from humanity by fate through fatal love for a fatal stranger. "We drive on the stream of fate," she tells Mertoun Sr., "without oar or rudder" (275). And when he recognizes in her the Ulla Troil he had loved, he reveals his own desperate fatalism: "We fly from our fate in vain!" (276) She sees Cleveland as "of that temperament which the dark Influences desire as the tools of their agency" (408). Magnus, captured by pirates, has faith in Providence.

Norna remains a fatalist to the end, convinced in her ultimate delusion that fate has tricked her into condemning her own son, Cleveland; whereas he is providentially saved for one act of humanity, by which he lifts himself above his fatalism in the name of a providential and humane code.

The final awakening from fatalism is Minna's. Hers is the spirit that must grow out of delusion, and with characteristic ceremonial formality she chooses the Orcadian Stonehenge as the setting in which to "offer up to a better and a more merciful God . . . the vain ideas with which my youthful imagination has been seduced" (427). She commands Cleveland to redeem himself but vows never to see him again. Hers becomes a life of service, humanity, and yet monastic withdrawal. To this is devoted the pietistic closing paragraph, while the brief prior paragraph sets the happiness of Brenda and Mordaunt, who "laughed, sung, danced, daffed the world aside, and bid it pass" (448), on obviously a lower mimetic level. Considering Mordaunt's preparation as agent of conciliation and continuity, this is disappointing, but we are not surprised. The book in its last half has focused more and more sharply on Minna as tragic heroine, and the image of her saintly solitude is as logical a finale as is that of the dutiful spinster Menie Gray for *The Surgeon's Daughter*. The reason may be shamelessly didactic, the lesson the same one taught in the final depriving of Rebecca of conventional happiness: for such virtue, following salvation from such evil, there is no easy worldly reward. Or perhaps this is the moral realism of the suggestion that for Menie Gray, after such a "romance" ordeal, no simple adjustment to the "real" world is possible; for Minna, certainly, the shattering of delusion has equally irreversible effect.

The pious resolution seems unworthy of the novel's

complexity. What happens? No facile reference to the author's fatigue or disinterest or to the proverbial difficulty of "winding novels up" will do. Other suggestions will be forthcoming, but one seems obvious. If Cleveland and Minna were the tragic romantic pawns of a more authentically historic fatality like the MacIvors, Redgauntlets, Ashtons, Ravenswoods, or Mowbrays, their pathos would be more memorable, less dependent on arbitrary romance plotting or conditioned by a morality which places crippled romantic personalities beyond hope of social or political redemption. As we have seen, and shall see once more, the contest of the fateful and the providential becomes vivid and plausible in a Waverley Novel only when Fate assumes the guise of historic determinism and Providence works through a humane vision and will that merit and strive for historic survival.

4. THE BLACK DWARF (1816) AND THE BRIDE OF LAMMERMOOR (1819)

In St. Ronan's Well, The Surgeon's Daughter, and The Pirate, we have seen types of the tragic romantic heroine. In The Bride of Lammermoor (1819), though the motivating conflict is between two ostensibly well-meaning men, the ultimate antagonists are women, one tragically strong, the other tragically weak. Much could be made of the recurrence in the novels of the archetypes of deserted maiden and virago – both fatal, one passively so, the other arrogantly, both destructively. "If we resort to Jungian psychology," writes Clyde Ryals of early Tennyson, "we may equate the maidens with the poet's 'soul-image,' which is always represented, says Jung, in terms of the opposite sex.

305

Into the figure of the suffering maiden Tennyson projected that part of the self which had been frustrated in its desire for articulation and has been left isolated and deserted."[34] The Jungian loosed at the Author of Waverley might argue likewise. A dialectic emergent in conflict between fatalistic and providential males is dissipated in the final centrality of the deserted anima. More suitably archetypal even than Flora, Rebecca, Menie, or Minna is that pathetic anticipation of Tennyson's Elaine figures, Lucy Ashton, ironically the "bride."

Less Jungian terms may suffice. For Scott the stoic, the most strenuous projections of humane conciliation as a means to cultural survival sometimes fade in historical pessimism. For the political moralist, under some evil conditions cultural fragmentation and decay are so irreversible as to seem fated. Whatever the terms, the fiction remains impressive enough to challenge the Pritchett view of Scott the comedist and the Welsh view of the apologist of civil prudence. Few may agree that *The Bride* is the Waverley masterpiece; few can disagree that *The Bride* and *St. Ronan's Well* prove the "comic" classification based on *The Antiquary* kind of novel wholly misleading. No one can forget the tragic heroine, finally mad and violently dead in both.

Not that the *Lammermoor* hero is unimpressive. Ravenswood is the most complex and energetic of protagonists. In him is the most perfect internalizing of cultural conflict in all the novels. Yet his chief role is as a force externally realized; he is an instrument of fate in the destiny of others. Moreover, the collapse of the familiar son-in-law/father-in-law myth of reconciliation and continuity, repudiating the comic potentiality of other Waverley Novels, provides two impressive protagonists for this one.

Finally, the economy of the novel depends in part on its peculiar relation to the domestic novels of fallen houses. Its use of houses as central symbols recalls our discussions of *Woodstock* and *Kenilworth*, *Old Mortality* and *Peveril*, as well. But the house in *The Bride* is a Gothic ruin. Its threatened but animated persistence, its hint of imminent disintegration, its mystery of ancestral immanence, all function, in the Gothic mode, as symbolic ambience for the noble ruin of the master of the house. Its disequilibrium, to borrow Michael Sadleir's terms, is an outward sign of a fatal disequilibrium of spirit within.[35] To adapt Leslie Fiedler's, Gothic heroine and hero-villain alike, "only alternate versions of the same plight," are inseparably linked in an anxious fatality attendant on an ambiguous loyalty to the past that the ruin recalls and perpetuates as a threat to the present.[36]

For these and other reasons, it is useful to conclude with *The Bride of Lammermoor*. Its various and integrated excellences provide a suitable final test for any summary formulation of meaning and value in the novels. It is the triumph of the domestic novels. But it is made so by its superior articulation of a frightened, saddened sense of historic fatality, and by its economical use of historic milieu to validate conventional motif. Classification is difficult. Superficially it belongs with the Jacobite group. Its time setting places it shortly before *Rob Roy*, at the precise moment of Thackeray's *Esmond*. Its satiric delineation of early Jacobite intrigue is as devastating as anything in *Waverley* or *Redgauntlet*. Its quest for enlightened humanity, thwarted by rival fanaticisms, and its milieu of moral and political chaos place it with *Old Mortality* and *Peveril*. Its protagonist resembles the heroic moderates of those novels. In its aura of primitive violence and barbaric pride, it seems as remote as some of the romances of decadent chivalry. It belongs to all three groups insofar as history threatens private stability and contentment. Yet its chief impact is as a tragedy of domestic fidelities and conflicts. The ominous arbitrariness with which demonic history plays its fatal role has led to its being likened to a Border ballad; in its use of folk chorus and preternatural suggestion it warrants the analogy. But the way in which history and ideology are translated into irrational psychological forces is better suggested by reference to its "Gothic" quality. The Gothic classification tells most about *The Bride of Lammermoor*'s unique fusion of domestic novel and historical romance.[37]

A problem arises, however. We can say the same things about Scott's other Gothic effort, set at almost precisely the same historical moment, removed from public history to almost the same degree. *The Black Dwarf* (1816) is remembered only as the first Waverley failure. Why should the novel which most nearly resembles it succeed so magnificently? *The Black Dwarf* is potentially the same impressive Gothic fiction as *The Bride of Lammermoor;* it is spoiled by major flaws or lapses not found in *The Bride*.

At the center of both is the embattled heroine, daughter of a noble house whose ambitious entanglements in the political and ideological feuds of the times render its survival in doubt. Her destiny is largely controlled by her father, whose nature is split neurotically between his natural affection as a parent and his anxious, manipulative character as a politician. The heroine's suitor is scion of a neighboring rival house. He is an enlightened man who comes to believe that reconciliation – that is, marriage – is possible. He is shocked to find his enlightened optimism confronted by preternatural powers, whose reality and influence he must acknowledge. In *The Black Dwarf* the acknowledgment invokes an agency of Providence to save the heroine and her marriage from the political chaos that threatens both. In *The Bride* the acknowledgment is too tardy or impious. In both the pathos is focused on the heroine, the ethical dilemma on her father. In both, the hero is less a protagonist than an unwitting instrument of Fate.

Fatality has concerned us repeatedly in the "house" novels. It is in treating such irrational, even preternatural forces that Scott shows kinship with the Gothic novelist and with his antecedent political moralists Johnson and Burke in that shifting commitment to the Enlightenment all share.[38] Since it is primarily in the confrontation of such forces that the essential power of the "Gothic" is presumed to reside, we had best begin with them.

One of the tests of humane prudence the stranger must pass in *The Pirate* tries his attitude toward traditional beliefs in preternatural agents. In *The Dwarf* and *The Bride* both heroes fail the test; both, in their naive enlightenment, refuse to recognize their entanglement with mysterious forces: one refusal is a denial of Providence; the other is an infatuated defiance of Fate. The denial is remediable, for in *The Black Dwarf* Providence is implausibly embodied in the dwarf himself. In *The Bride* Fate has no such grotesque embodiment. But the beliefs of the fatalists are the more plausible for that. Norna's nearest kin here are two old women: blind Alice, a poor but educated woman for whom Fate, while terrifying, is a naturalistically explicable force; and Ailsie Gourlay, a grimly plausible Hardyesque folkwitch, for whom it is a destructive psychological power she can manipulate and thus sell. A sense of Fate is uniquely potent in *The Bride* because of their pragmatically grounded convictions and because fatality is embodied only in the divided personality of the hero himself and in the ironic shape of his tragedy.

In *The Black Dwarf*, Scott's decision to identify the dwarf of Border folk demonology with the monstrous, withdrawn secret benevolist Mauley, risked the loss of plausibility for any hint of supernaturalism. Nonetheless, until the dwarf's identity is known, he serves well enough as a symbol, and his symbolism is the broader and richer for his loss of supernatural status. The gain and the loss may be seen if we trace his evolution.

This first "Tale of My Landlord," like its successors, begins with a chapter of Gandercleugh gab. The talkers are visitors whose differences of opinion on the preternatural dwarf anticipate differences in the novel. The debaters are a sceptical farmer and an old servant. Of the tales of Elshie the dwarf, the farmer scoffs, "I dinna believe a word o't frae beginning to end." The servant is indignant. "Your father believed it unco stievely, though." "Ay, very true, Bauldie," retorts the farmer; "but that was in the time o' the black-faces; they believed a hantle queer things in thae days, that naebody heeds since the lang sheep cam in." That is, "cracking about Black Dwarfs and siccan clavers" are relegated to a past economic era "when the short sheep were in the fashion" (2–3). Conflicting attitudes toward such beings are framed in conflicting attitudes toward changed manners. The narrator seems neutral. But he concludes the chapter with a sly attack on the kind of "enlightenment" the farmer represents. When the farmer is drunk enough, he reveals that his "liberality of thinking" and his "freedom from ancient prejudices" are largely adornments of his new economic status. He retains "a lurking belief in the traditions of his forefathers" (4).

The attitudes of those through whose eyes we first see the

dwarf conflict in the same way. His reappearance on Muck-lestane-Moor is, to the inhabitants, a threat to the enlightenment of a peaceful, stable era. His fearful strangeness becomes an issue of symbolic importance. To the young Borderer Hobbie Elliott he is a figure of superstitious dread. To the returning heir of Earnscliff, "somewhat entertained with the gradual declension of superstition from one generation to another" (22) – in short, complacently enlightened – he is a challenge. Moreover, in his misanthropic alienation, the dwarf embodies a rejection of Earnscliff's code, "common humanity," that Enlightenment catchword which the dwarf scornfully rejects, and "Nature" (15). To Hobbie's grannie, the dwarf is a portent of returning violence and disorder: "weary fa' thae evil days! what can evil beings be coming for to distract a poor country, now it's peacefully settled, and living in love and law?" (19) She is, nevertheless, tied to the past. "The carline, she sits in the neuk yonder upbye, and cracks about the grand shooters and hunters lang syne" (9). For all her fear, she represents a fatal attraction to the forces of violence which the dwarf recalls.

The danger of such an attraction is brought home to both Earnscliff and Isabella Vere. Earnscliff returns as a slain father's heir to a region dominated by folk memory and by a folk morality which expects him to avenge his father's death on Isabella's family, the house of Ellieslaw. Earnscliff says "Fie! fie!" to the idea. For him, the accident was "a foolish brawl, occasioned by wine and politics" (10). Hobbie challenges his complacency. Ellieslaw "kens naething about thae newfangled notions o' peace and quietness; he's a' for the auld-warld doings o' lifting and laying on" (10). Thus the "country folk look for something atween ye" (10), and Earnscliff finds he has wandered into the romance world

311

traversed by Waverley, Morton, and Ravenswood. The peril they encounter is tellingly defined by Hobbie's mother: "God bless him! he's a real Earnscliff; he's his father's true son, a leal friend" (51). The peril is confronting one's heritage only to find one is one's father's son indeed. As Morton with Burley, Ravenswood with Caleb and old Alice, Roland with his grandmother, he is expected to inherit the past's prejudicial inhumanity. Such is the sonship expected of Earnscliff; such is the role upon which his hereditary identity depends. His response utilizes the catchword already mentioned: "I hope we shall have no war of so unnatural and unchristian a kind in our time." Hobbie throws his norm of nature back with a changed meaning: "It wad be but a wee bit neighbour war, and Heaven and earth would make allowances for it in this uncultivated place. It's just the nature o' the folk and the land" (11).

Isabella experiences the same shocked surprise as hereditary violences and fanatic loyalties break through the façade of Enlightenment optimism and humanity. She, like Earnscliff, has the somewhat glib common sense of Brenda, while her friend Lucy has "romantic" expectations more valid than Minna's self-delusions. Lucy lectures Isabella on her suitability for romantic intrigue with Earnscliff. "How can you talk so wildly, Lucy?" she replies. "Your plays and romances have positively turned your brain." "You laugh at my skill in romance," Lucy warns; "but, I assure you, should your history be written, like that of many a less distressed and less deserving heroine, the well-judging reader will set you down for the lady and the love of Earnscliff" – which the reader has already done, not anticipating that his judgment was to define a thematic issue. Lucy responds with the fatal half-truth of the superficially enlightened: "But these are not the days of romance but of sad reality, for there stands the castle of Ellieslaw" (36–37). "Reality" proves less simple, less distinguishable from "romance." There stands the castle, indeed; but the fact turns out to be ambiguous, as the outbreak of ideological intrigue threatens to turn the solid, unromantic castle into a scene of Gothic mystery and terror. The educative process reverses that of *Northanger Abbey*. Isabella is too much the antiheroine for her own safety. Her complacent assertion, incidentally, is repeated later by the prudent and devoted aide of the dwarf, Ratcliffe. When Ratcliffe says, "These are not the days of romance, when ladies are carried off merely for their beauty" (81), however, he is making a sound comment on the very unromantic realities of Jacobite intrigue which have caught up Isabella temporarily in the terrors of romance.

The crucial fact in *The Bride of Lammermoor* is that the Master of Ravenswood is in the same peril as Earnscliff, and recognizing this means disagreeing with most recent commentators on the novel. For Welsh, what matters is that Ravenswood be proved a passive hero. But Welsh slights important facts in the interests of his thesis; and the Nassau Senior statement he quotes as authoritative support oversimplifies Ravenswood's plight: "His misfortunes spring from the enmity of Bucklaw and Lady Ashton; both arising from causes out of his own controul, and as likely to have arisen if he had been the meekest of mankind."[39] Welsh acknowledges that Ravenswood is active in temperament, but this is not enough. From his first fierce vows through his final defiance of the Ashtons, he is a principal instrument of his own disaster through his infatuated denial of the fatality of his own nature. But we must first consider the issue between Daiches and Gordon concerning Ravenswood's obsolescence. They agree that Ravenswood embodies obsolete virtues, but Gordon claims Daiches "goes astray" in arguing

313

that Scott finds this remnant degenerate. "Edgar and Caleb," says Gordon, "have their eccentricities, but they are to be regarded, not ironically, but sympathetically, as embodiments of ancient virtues in a world that has abandoned those virtues." Thus, for Gordon, Edgar Ravenswood is the protagonist of a novel of "Tory pessimism," and not the "grim mockery" projected by a satirizing modernist.[40] Both Daiches and Gordon overlook what Edgar stands for, or tries to stand for.

Part of the oversight is an accident. The opening descriptions present the "forfeited nobleman" who "inherited the pride and turbulence" of his house and refer to "hot, fiery, and imprudent character" (15). It is not until his funeral that we realize these have all been references to the father. To the son, the Master, these qualities come only with his father's final curses, and he hears them "as if they had conveyed to him a legacy of vengeance" (19). At the funeral the son ostensibly dons the hereditary character for violence; he vows to accept the heritage and the role. Nothing could be closer to the returning Earnscliff's situation, or more remote from his enlightened, humane reaction to it. But in fact, having played his violent opening, Edgar spends the remainder of the novel trying to escape that role. Had he been merely his father's son, there would be no tragedy; for he would never have allowed himself the hope of reconciliation and thus could not have become the tool of Ashton's ill-fated conciliatory designs.

What the Master stands for is tragically at war with his hereditary identity. When old Alice warns Ashton concerning the Master, she insists that he is honorable, open, free, generous, noble, but warns that he is still a Ravenswood (37–38). Ashton is deaf to such warnings; but so is the

314

Master. His description marks him as of Gothic lineage, afflicted and alienated by "some secret sorrow, or the brooding spirit of some moody passion" (44). But he is no Gothic type. He denies his own fatality; he is free of superstitious belief in portents and other preternatural events. He believes his vows have no binding force. He charges old Alice with inhumanity, with blasphemy, with ferocious anachronism when she speaks to him of the fatality attendant on his projected marriage to an Ashton (176–77). In crucial scenes which contrast enlightened or naturalistic with primitive or supernaturalistic modes of vision, he is consistently the naturalist blind to the ominous. When, "to a superstitious eye," Lucy Ashton seems the reincarnation of the nymph of the fountain, doomed by consorting with a Ravenswood, Ravenswood sees only "a female exquisitely beautiful" (180). The scene ends with the ominous death of the raven at their feet, Lucy's dress covered with its blood which has been shed by her relative in defiance of the traditional role of the Ravenswoods as the ravens' protector. A folk observer or chorus is present to observe the portent, and to confirm the fatalistic symbolism of the novel's own descriptive mode. But the enlightened Ravenswood refuses to see.

The climax of Ravenswood's dogged clinging to enlightenment is his confrontation of the wraith of old Alice at the fountain. The narrator, while slightly apologetic, remains neutral, telling the tale "as we have received it" (217). Ravenswood persists in his naturalism, reflecting desperately on what seems a "breach" in the "laws of nature." His enlightened scepticism – "he despised most of the ordinary prejudices about witchcraft, omens, and vaticination, to which his age and country still gave such implicit credit" (223) – has been sorely tried. But he remains basically

315

enlightened, and thus blinded to his own fate. In his destiny, the warning given the young farmer in the introduction to *The Black Dwarf* is tragically fulfilled.

His enlightenment extends to moral and political values as well. His independence of the follies of ancestral pride is evident in his comic dealings with Caleb Balderstone. He dislikes the petty politics of the time from the point of view of the enlightened humanitarian, *not* that of chivalric anachronism. In the scene with Craigengelt and Bucklaw we see a cautious, restrained Ravenswood contrasted with another ruined scion, the reckless Bucklaw. Ravenswood, like Earnshaw, is expected to act by the code of the vendetta. He refuses. His fight with Bucklaw is forced on him; Bucklaw is turbulent, imprudent; Ravenswood cool and humane, conciliatory. When Bucklaw urges action, he advises prudence. When his powerful kinsman seeks to involve him with the Jacobites, Ravenswood makes his moderatism quite clear: "When I recollect the times of the first and second Charles, and of the last James, truly I see little reason that, as a man or a patriot, I should draw my sword for their descendants." He looks beyond petty factionalism to "the day when Justice shall be open to Whig and Tory, and when these nicknames shall only be used among coffee-house politicians, as 'slut' and 'jade' are among apple-women, as cant terms of idle spite and rancour" (83). No Morton or Everard is more energetically committed to moderatism; yet Edgar is supposedly the Gothic decadent among Waverley heroes.

The conversation with the Jacobites is crucial to our understanding of his tragedy. On behalf of enlightened justice he feels contempt for the "speculative politics" of the partisan or revolutionary. We recall Morton when Edgar's prudence and reasonability are mistaken by Bucklaw for coldness, for cowardly noncommitment. But Bucklaw speaks a tragic truth excluded from *Old Mortality* when he predicts the Master's own blood will overthrow his "present humour of moralizing on political truths" when his "blood is up." Ravenswood's answer is pathetically ominous: "Perhaps," he says, "you read me more rightly than I can myself" (84). He acknowledges to Lucy that his vows of revenge were a deadly sin (183). But we are reminded that "they had been heard and registered in the book of fate" (157). An heir of Ravenswood, contrary to his own enlightened humanity, he is forced to recognize his fated role as God's instrument against the Ashtons. The pathetic irony of his futile resistance is symbolized in his visit to Ravenswood Castle. As he enters he recalls his youth and his broken-hearted father, in sorrow, not in anger. But Ashton's younger son is terrified to see in him the reincarnation of his ancestor Malise, whose portrait "is up in the old Baron's hall that the maids launder the clothes in" (170), and who, in the violent past, had returned with twenty men to rid his castle of another usurper and leave his blood on the hearth. The Master cannot escape his bloody heritage, although his virtues and the values governing the book make it unambiguously desirable he should do so.

Any Waverley hero might find himself compelled to play such a role, to prove his loyalty to an unworthy heritage in order to liberate himself, to be his father's son in order to become himself. For some this means undergoing a ritual death or maiming: Morton must come "back from the dead"; Waverley must attend on Fergus's death and join Bradwardine in his cave; Bertram confronts his devil in a cave; Ivanhoe is persistently weak or ill; the young moderate in Montrose is wounded. From Ravenswood's death there is no issue; his loyalties lead nowhere, his enlightened values are lost. He vanishes, as if unreal, except as a pawn of his own doomed lineage; his death is not providential. But the destruction of the Ashtons is providential. The tragedy is not Edgar's, but theirs. The title focuses the Gothic bridal-funeral on the bride, and reminds us that the book's tragedy marks the rise and fall of the Ashtons. The active moral center of that tragedy is the deluded, weak father, Sir William Ashton, who, with a marvelous mixture of intentions, seeks to stabilize his house and make his daughter happy and in the process destroys both.

Once more *The Black Dwarf* prepares us. Its concern with fathers to the bride, natural and unnatural, is more pronounced than its concern with the enlightened young man threatened with fatal sonship. Richard Vere, Laird of Ellieslaw, is the chief local Jacobite. He is as ignoble as Richard Waverley; in his mean quixoticism, he anticipates Rashleigh Osbaldistone and Redgauntlet. But his role is primarily domestic; we watch in him, as in Ashton, a complex war between his nature as a father and his political anxieties. At the novel's climax, his rationalizings provide the psychological center. The moral complexity of his self-delusions, of his self-assurances that he really does love his daughter, is confirmed in his long letter from continental exile, in which he is congratulating himself on not standing in his daughter's way (he has been forced out of it) and for not resenting the treatment accorded him by her protector and his persecuted rival Mauley, the dwarf.

Ellieslaw is Isabella's real but unnatural father. Her "natural father" is the grotesquely unnatural Mauley. We have noted the conflicting uses of "natural" in the talk of Earnscliff and Hobbie; the same ambiguous word, we recall, provides a leitmotiv in the novel chronologically following, *Old Mortality.* The term's meanings focus on the dwarf, nature's monster. It is he who, in misanthropy and withdrawal from human involvement, claims to live the life of nature: "solitary, self-sufficing, and independent" (118). Isabella provides the opposing view. His may be the "nature" of the savage, she argues; "but it is not the law of nature in general" (118–19). Ironically she has hit upon his true nature, whose function is to bring providential aid to those who faithfully seek it. His "blackness" recalls his derivation from Goldsmith's secret benevolist. His agent Ratcliffe explains the difference between the "nature" he invokes and his truly natural, i.e., kindly, humane, actions: "No man's words and actions have been at such a wide difference, nor has any hypocritical wretch ever been more ingenious in assigning good motives for his vile actions than this unfortunate in reconciling to his abstract principles of misanthropy a conduct which flows from his natural generosity and kindness of feeling" (114).

Ratcliffe has the power to see the true nature of the man beneath the dwarf's unnatural appearance and his "unnatural" Naturalism. Others must acquire this vision before the dwarf's providential powers operate; we recall here the Enlightenment humanist's comparable interpretation of the magical potency of Saladin's talisman. *The Black Dwarf* enacts this ceremony in two parallel actions. Two houses are threatened; two heirs come for help. Hobbie Elliott's house is burned, his bride kidnapped. Hobbie's initial reaction is fear of the dwarf. To his grannie, the dwarf portends the return of old violence; and Hobbie inherits her reliance on the old law of revenge, the way of their fathers. "And what signifies deaving us wi' tales about our fathers," asks one of his friends, "if we're to sit and see our friends' houses burnt ower their heads, and no put out hand to revenge them? Our fathers did not do that, I trow?" (49) But he seeks the dwarf's aid; and when his betrothed is returned and his house reinstated, he sees the dwarf as agent of Providence (51, 67–68, 70).

In her plight Isabella repeats Hobbie's gesture of faith, overcoming her fears to surrender her will to Providence. Hobbie has called him a "queer-looking father" (75), and Isabella says, "I come to you, father," as if to a spiritual counselor in his cell (116). Her effect on the dwarf is akin to Lovel's on the antiquary: she activates a benevolence withdrawn from life. Mauley has been supposed dead; and appropriately, when he interrupts the forced marriage, he speaks from the tomb of Isabella's dead mother, his former love. Mauley is able to save Isabella only because he has previously won Hobbie's loyalty as a "son" and hence his support and that of his friends. The "natural" father is returned to life when those who need him see by enlightened faith through his unnatural aspect to his natural humanity. Thus, while the dwarf may be tossed off, in Buchan's terms, as "a piece of Gothick extravagance, Matt Lewis crossed with Byron," he provides an interesting study in Enlightenment Gothic, an Enlightened folklorist's translation of a figure of folk legend into a natural agent of Providence.[41]

The contrast of Mauley the man of nature with Ellieslaw the unnatural father who would sacrifice his daughter to his political anxieties, defines the book's significance as a Waverley Novel. The dwarf cannot, however, be made plausible. The book has other problems. Young Earnscliff and Isabella as lovers are of thematic interest; but while their union is symbolic of reconciliation and continuity, their characters and their alliance receive little attention as narrative reality. Having faced the threat of inheriting a traditional revenge role, Earnscliff loses his centrality to the dwarf. His efforts on behalf of Isabella are accidental; he rescues her by chance, and his attraction seems a coincidence. Moreover, in a novel which contains Scott's most effective satiric sketch of Jacobitism (see the Bunyanesque dialogues of anti-Union discontents [94–95]) Earnscliff lacks even a negative relation to ideological conflict. Isabella, too, after her initial display of naive scepticism, remains wholly external in her plight. Ultimately, setting aside the dwarf as richly significant but improbable, we are left with two interesting and plausible figures: the matter-of-fact, but devoted humanitarian Ratcliffe (a minor proto-Jarvie), and the morally complex and unstable father.

Sir William Ashton is political opposite to Ellieslaw, but this is incidental. He is a more complete portrayal of the same kind of weakness and unnaturalness. E. M. Forster describes his central position, then fails to recognize the formal achievement he has described and classifies Ashton's development as a "ragged end": "Scott presents the Lord High Keeper in this book with great emphasis and with endless suggestions that the defects of his character will lead to the tragedy, while as a matter of fact the tragedy would occur in almost the same form if he did not exist – the only necessary ingredients in it being Edgar, Lucy, Lady Ashton and Bucklaw."[42] The fact is that *every* element is a "necessary ingredient," including the precise historical moment, the timeless folk chorus, the notorious trickster and bore Caleb Balderstone. But the central agent is Sir William Ashton, who succeeds, where Ellieslaw fails, in destroying his daughter, ironically in a feeble attempt to marry her to the man she loves because he wants her to be happy and sees the only safety for his new "house" in the ancient name and honor of his persecuted enemies the Ravenswoods. Without his infatuated drive for reconciliation, the basic Waverley objective, there could have been no tragedy. Were it not for his character and the inherited character of his weak, timid daughter, the tragedy might have ended instead in triumph.

We see him first in the hall he has won from the Ravenswoods by legalistic and economic manipulation, hearing of the funeral and of the Master's vows of revenge. His problem is the book's occasion: what to do about such a threat. His initial response is his final one: politic resolution undermined by moral irresolution and fearfulness. As he learns from his daughter and old Alice of the ancient family, he expresses a dangerously facile hope for reconciliation. To old Alice he says she must *accept* change; she replies she will *endure* it (36), and for the first of numerous times we see the timorous opportunist cowed by a strength fanatically opposed to reconciliation. The process Forster describes commands the middle chapters: Ashton's intentions and machinations are the focus of the narrative; he alone is continuously internalized. Our initial impression is of cynical dishonesty, as he traps Ravenswood with the Author of Waverley's own arguments for humane tolerance and reconciliation. Ravenswood is gradually deceived; but so, we note with greater interest and are shown with stronger emphasis, is Ashton.

As Ashton anxiously seeks protection against imminent political change, the Union of 1707 which he fails utterly to understand, he persuades himself of his own generosity. Such is the ironic climax to a long analytic narration of Ashton's anxiety, perplexity, and rationalization which would bear rhetorical and psychological comparison with Stendhal's description of the baffled Count Mosca in *The Charterhouse*. By the time Ravenswood's captivation is complete, Ashton is overcome with the sentimental conviction that his daughter and Edgar are made for each other:

His eyes glistened as he looked upon a couple who were obviously becoming attached, and who seemed made for each other. . . . His daughter – his favourite child – his constant playmate – seemed formed to live happy in a union with such a commanding spirit as Ravenswood; and even the fine, delicate, fragile form of Lucy Ashton seemed to require the support of the Master's muscular strength and masculine character [157].

The narrator ominously adds: "Long after the catastrophe of their love, he used to warn his hearers against permitting their feelings to obtain an ascendency over their judgment, and affirm, that the greatest misfortune of his life was owing to a very temporary predominance of sensibility over self-interest" (157–58). But Ashton is never to perceive the delicate interweaving of sensibility and self-interest in the infatuation with which he engineers that misfortune.

For the time being, Ashton remains rhetorically central, anxiously reassuring himself how ideal the match is and how pleased his wife will be. The climax of his dominance comes when he brings his ancient enemy home, both of them supposing the enemy comes as heir-conciliator. Its termination is the return of his arrogant, overbearing wife; till now she has been absent from the narrative, her absence essential to the tragic complication, as her presence is to its denouement. From this point on (we are two-thirds of the way through the book) the father, having made the tragedy, recedes into the comic impotence of the henpecked husband, too weak to quell his haughty wife's resistance. As he loses both power and property after the Union and the coming of Queen Anne's Tory ministry to power, he is pathetic, mean, and in the words of Ravenswood's equally mean noble kinsman "a broken-down fanatic" (263). But he has been much more; and Lucy is truly his dearest, closest child.

Spiritual kinship is as real and symbolic a fact here as in *The Pirate,* indeed, as in *Wuthering Heights;* spiritual hostility is also quite real. Father and daughter are tragically close in spirit, as is evident from the early moment the anxious father hears her song:

> Look not thou on beauty's charming,
> Sit thou still when kings are arming,
> Taste not when the wine-cup glistens,
> Speak not when the people listens,
>
> Stop thine ear against the singer,
> From the red gold keep thy finger,
> Vacant heart, and hand, and eye,
> Easy live and quiet die [26].

The song certifies, before Lucy appears, that her character is her fate. As Donald Davie has observed, her desire to withdraw or remain neutral in life is the final condition of her doom.[43] She shares her father's timidity, and he loves her gentleness. She is the passive, will-less romantic dreamer, the anima figure, the Elaine whose erotic attraction to the powerful protective Ravenswood is a fatal curse to one of her nature. Erotic symbolism abounds in the episode that introduces the lovers. A wild bull threatens Lucy; her father, pathetically devoted, places himself meekly between her and the beast (40). Ravenswood saves them both; they both turn to his strength as a bulwark against the brutal forces of history. And the Elaine-like Lucy, while her father weaves policy, makes her own enchanted web of dreams of being saved by Ravenswood from the bull (48–49).

Throughout the following chapters she is present, susceptible, but passive. Like Ravenswood and her father, she is
blind to portent. But we are little concerned with her until
the love is reciprocal and recognized; and then two implications of her passive romantic character become clear: (1)
like her father, she is too weak to oppose her mother; (2) as
the barren child of a spiritually and culturally barren misal-
liance between Ashton and his haughtily aristocratic wife,
she is spiritually unfitted for a marriage of reconciliation
with Ravenswood. Like her lover, she is more than the
temporary pawn of history; she is spiritually disintegrated or
crippled by her heritage. And while Ashton persists in his
sentimentality, the lovers learn they are *not* "made for each
other." Lucy "perceived too plainly that her lover held in
scorn the manners and habits of a father to whom she had
long looked up as her best and most partial friend, whose
fondness had often consoled her for her mother's contemptuous harshness" (190). Ravenswood

saw in Lucy a soft and flexible character, which, in his eyes
at least, seemed too susceptible of being moulded to any
form by those with whom she lived. He felt that his own
temper required a partner of a more independent spirit.
. . . [Yet] he felt that the softness of a mind, amounting
almost to feebleness, rendered her even dearer to him
[190–91].

And so he blinds himself to his inclination to desert her and
remains as her protector and destroyer.

All the essential conditions for tragedy exist, then, in the
three central characters prior to the return of Lady Ashton
with her scheme to marry Lucy to Bucklaw. Her Whiggish
arrogance and the Marquis's Tory arrogance, to be sure,
provide the final impetus. Necessary, too, are the times.
Opposing, equally corrupt factions make futile all hopes of

325

reconciliation: Lady Ashton and the Marquis are haughty counterparts. Essential, too, but only as extensions of spiritual factors in the principals, are the divisive forces of the past, still ludicrously potent on both sides: Lady Ashton and Caleb Balderstone are ridiculous, dangerous counterparts in anachronism and deceit. But most essential are the ill-fated, ill-sorted natures and self-deceptions of the three optimistic principals. The tragedy originates in character, conditioned and corrupted by heritage, aggravated and crystallized by the times, which in turn suffer from the persistence of divisive fanaticisms of the past. All of this is known by the folk chorus, but they call it Fate. And such is the complex, bitterly ironic inevitability of the catastrophe that the reader experiences throughout – whatever "enlightenment" he supposes he shares with the narrator: a growing sense of fatality, at once historic, natural, and spiritual. No experienced form elsewhere in the novels can match this one for force and economy.

The full achievement is dependent in part on the rhetorical uniqueness of *The Bride* as a narrative, a uniqueness appropriate to the novel's Gothic character. In Chapter One, the fictitious narrator Peter Pattieson argues with Dick Tinto, a painter. Tinto complains that Pattieson's characters "*patter* too much," resulting in whole pages of "mere chat and dialogue," a confusion of narrative with drama.[44] Romance, he argues, is essentially descriptive; Pattieson should visualize his conceptions, using words not to inform, but to evoke. The whole picturesque premise is stated shortly:

You have accustomed yourself so much to these creeping twilight details of yours, that you are become incapable of receiving that instant and vivid flash of conviction which darts on the mind from seeing the happy and expressive combinations of a single scene, and which gathers from the position, attitude, and countenance of the moment, not only the history of the past lives of the personages represented, and the nature of the present business on which they are immediately engaged, but lifts even the veil of futurity, and affords a shrewd guess at their future fortunes [9–10, 13].

Ian Jack, while recognizing the dramatic stress on dialogue as Scott's chief innovation, has suggested that the picturesque might be used "as the central concept in a study of Waverley Romances."[45] Evidences of a taste for "striking contrast" are found in many of the novels. But as recent theorists of the Gothic have shown, it was in Gothic fiction that picturesque theory found its most congenial literary expression, sharing as it does with Gothic apologetic a strongly perspectivist and affective aesthetic.[46] Logically, it is Scott's single Gothic triumph that consistently applies Dick Tinto's precepts, substituting for the characteristic dramatic unit of scene-dialogue the pictorial unit of the picture-tableau. The novel is as informed by portentous visualized moments as *Henry Esmond:* the funeral; the image of the Ashtons with Ravenswood in the crumbling tower, seeking shelter amid ominous ruin; the prophetic emblem of Edgar and Lucy at the Well; the entrance of Ravenswood into his ancestral hall, now the home of the usurper. In such images, memory and omen contribute symbolically to present reality, and the interplay between setting and character, between material milieu and spiritual principle, is so dynamic as to create a single ambience of symbolic intensity.

The consequences suggest much about *The Bride's* singularity among the novels. For one thing, the narrative mode of Gothic-picturesque, stressing emotive ambience and symbol,[47] facilitates significant and powerful unity of mood, thus strengthening the reader-observer's sense of motive force or fatality. For another, the descriptive mode, as opposed to the dramatic, encourages – as in characteristically Gothic novels, whether Radcliffian or Godwinian – emphasis on interior or psychological narration. We have noted the unusual degree of explicit internalizing in Ashton, and to a lesser extent in Lucy and Edgar. This in turn makes for sustained manipulation of point of view, a technical control rarely exercised, because rarely invited, in the succession of dramatic scenes of the other novels. Thus, while Ravenswood is internalized sufficiently to show us his tragic inward struggle between fatal hereditary role and enlightened self, his most memorable function in the book is as an ambivalent force or symbol in the timid, anxious machinations of Ashton and Lucy. The descriptive mode allows him to fulfill such a function. In most of the portentous tableaux, he appears through the vision and feeling of Ashton or Lucy as a powerfully ambiguous figure, at once Malise the destroyer and Edgar the benevolent protector. He can hover in reality between legendary or fatal force, the incarnation of his lineage, and the conscious individuality of character. Even his final disappearance can serve a primarily symbolic function. We know of its natural causes; but we see it through the vision of Caleb and of an Ashton, and for both, as for us, its dreadful arbitrariness and finality are all we really know.

Also contingent on the descriptive mode is the unique guise of historicity anticipated in *The Black Dwarf*, but defined with full effect only in *The Bride*. The novel is precisely historical, yet its imaginative grounding in Gothic vision and folk or primitive fatalism makes it seem more remote from historical reality than almost any other of the novels. The narrator dissociates his work from the tale of horror by claiming that his is an "OWER TRUE TALE" (305).

Its historic truth is perhaps more particularized than that of any other Waverley Novel, as may be seen from the need for unusually precise dating. Gordon agrees with Daiches that the book portrays conflict between feudalism and modernism shortly *after* the Union of 1707.[48] But their dating must be wrong: Scots Parliament and Privy Council are still in existence, otherwise Ashton's position would be different. Lady Ashton still has a powerful friend in the Duchess of Marlborough. The possibility of Edgar's appeal to the House of Lords is still impending, and Ashton does not realize what that means. The book's "moment" is as precise as the Stendhalian moment celebrated by Auerbach. We are at the opening of the eighteenth century amid the corruption and instability of Scottish rule just before the Union, and in the aftermath of Ashton's most powerful, acquisitive period in the 90s, following the defeat of James's forces and the disaster of Darien. The unique moment is essential to the tragedy.

But the precision coexists, paradoxically, with the remoteness of historic milieu. History as public panorama or epoch is coincidental; history as particular condition, as amoral force, is not only present, but uniquely domesticated, even internalized. Thus, historicity is rendered psychological or affective, not generic or mimetic as in more characteristic usages; and for this, too, the Gothic mode is primarily responsible.

The imaginative remoteness of historical time is sustained in part by the importance of the folk chorus, for whom history scarcely exists, except in the primitive sense of mythic reenactment. But equally influential is the operation in the book of two independent chronologies, reminiscent of *Othello*. The domestic tragedy is initiated and complicated so rapidly that no time lapse makes itself felt until it is too late for reflection. Ravenswood saves Ashton and Lucy the day following the funeral; that night he meets Bucklaw and Craigengelt. After three or four days comes the hunt, the Ashtons spend one night, and the next morning Ashton tells Edgar of Craigengelt's reports to the Privy Council and Ashton's own efforts on Ravenswood's behalf. It is as if outside history were moving with un-natural rapidity to precipitate domestic tragedy. Lady Ash-ton was in Edinburgh, has now moved to London, will shortly be in Northumberland, where she is arranging Lucy's marriage to Bucklaw, whose rich aunt, living a moment ago, now, it appears, is dead, leaving Bucklaw a wealthy heir. From old Ravenswood's funeral to Edgar's betrothal is no more than six days. While history con-tributes precisely to the domestic tragedy, it remains a reality remote from the domestic, local, primitive world of the tragedy.

Finally, the Gothic descriptive mode helps translate the most typical Waverley character in the novel into something rich and strange without changing his complex value as an element in the narrative. The ludicrous and devoted, infu-riating and pathetic Caleb Balderstone provides a crucial test for the formal and tonal integrity of *The Bride*. Rela-tively remote from the tragicomic, "mixed" world of public history, the domestic novels all seem to invite easier classification into "tragedy" or "comedy." The two "trage-dies," mixing the severely ironic with the loftily pathetic, raise more complex problems of formal integrity than do any others of the novels. Ian Jack sees a "fatal lack of homoge-neity" in *St. Ronan's Well;* this I have tried to disprove in answering Grierson's similar complaint. It is more surpris-ing, in view of his awareness of Shakespearian antecedents, to hear Jack criticize Caleb and *The Bride:* "By using Caleb

Balderstone not only as a choric character but also as comic relief Scott destroys the unity of the book: although Balderstone is one of his finest comic creations his presence prevents everything in the tale from being in key."[49] He presents no such problem for Daiches and Gordon, only by virtue of their oversimplification of his role and of the book's "key." The problem is real. The solution is to recognize in Caleb's "comic relief" considerable and relevant tragic and ironic seriousness of implication.

Daiches sees Caleb as an ironic figure; he is the enlightened modernist's mockery of anachronistic feudal virtues.[50] This is true. His pretences of huge dinners destroyed by soot, his saving the family's "honor" by breaking its crockery, his attempts to concentrate "all the lightnings of aristocracy in his eye" and overwhelm the villagers with arguments "from antique custom and hereditary respect" (117 – 18) – all provide the desolation of the Ravenswoods with a comic center. His climactic stroke of folly is to avoid entertaining the Marquis by seeming to set fire to the tower. Nowhere is the tragic futility of Ravenswood's enlightened optimism more strikingly symbolized, and this in a comic gesture of vain folly. The only fidelity left Ravenswood is that of this ancient retainer, in whom fidelity has become a bore, a nuisance; and now the servant, whose fidelity to the house makes him a fool, sacrifices all to a fraudulent honor, even the house itself. Daiches is right.

But Gordon, describing his "novel of Tory pessimism," finds Caleb, like Edgar, profoundly sympathetic.[51] He is. Because Edgar is admirable in his enlightenment, his humanity, and his courage, his faithful retainer also receives our sympathy. Our sympathy lends approbation to Caleb's numerous statements on behalf of "the gude auld times, when authority had its right," his lamentations for "that due and fitting connexion betwixt superior and vassal, whilk is in some danger of falling into desuetude, owing to the general license and misrule of these present unhappy times" (132). His fidelity is indefatigable; the "house" is his only life. He is the sole survivor, who pines away in a year. He is the pathetic demon of his Gothic tower, and his death following his Master's is the final cessation of animistic life in the house.

Both views are correct: Caleb is ludicrous, ironic; Caleb is pathetic, sympathetic, an element in the tragedy. Moreover, to see the rhetorical complexity of Caleb as a flaw in the novel's form is to misunderstand both Caleb and the novel, to ignore the activities which take up so much of Caleb's and the reader's time. Caleb is not just the pathetic demon of a house; he is the absurd embodiment of the house's tragic degeneracy. In behalf of the family "honor," he is consistently the deceiver, destroyer, and thief. If he represents the "gude auld times" under the Ravenswoods, one is not surprised to find no remnant, among the villagers he exploits and robs, of loyalty to the ancient lairds. In Caleb's mouth, sentiments of archaic fidelity are the tools of the confidence man, however benevolent his ends. Caleb exploits the first rumors of the marriage to win favors. While Ashton is using the new language of "humanity" to trap Edgar, Caleb, equally cynical, is using the old one of fidelity to exploit the villagers. It is by duplicity and fraud that Caleb has supported the house for years, and even his fire is a trick. To Edgar, then, he must be a ludicrous reminder of the unreality of family "honor," and his loyalty is an extremely ambiguous, though inescapable, blessing. In his deceit he resembles not his Master, but Ashton; in his fanatic and destructive pride he resembles Lady Ashton; in his reckless opportunism he is associated with the political cynicism of the Tory Marquis – all this, of course, on a low comic level, under the heading of "comic relief." All in all, he symbolizes the degeneracy Edgar can never redeem and never escape. Thus, as "comic relief," he embodies the essence of the tragedy.

Like other victims of history – Fergus and Brian and Cleveland, Conachar and Redgauntlet and the inhabitants of St. Ronan's Well, and many ambiguous figures in later Scottish fiction[52] – he belongs to that Border roughly located by Northrop Frye where tragedy and irony meet or overlap. Ravenswood lacks the foresight to deal with him; Ravenswood lacks the romantic wisdom to recognize his own fatality, and the practical wisdom to avoid a mediatorial role he cannot possibly play in the interests of a conciliation for which there is no natural ground. As is shown by other mediatorial hopefuls and would-be agents of Providence, either role, played without piety or with an optimism too superficially enlightened, can lead to disaster – that is, to the ultimate triumph of historic fatality. The price of such blasphemous imprudence is, in the words of a recent reviewer of Chekhov, to become one of "the feckless and the defeated, who were bound to go down the drain of history."[53] The double tragedy of *The Bride* leaves no one to endure, no survivor; in terms appropriate to the "new Gothic" of the Brontës, the two principles, unreconciled and irreconcilable, are self-destructive, marking the degeneration and death of both old and new. For some Earnshaws and some Lintons, reconciliation, hence, survival, is impossible. Following self-conquest, marriage is possible for the passionate but spiritually timid Jane Eyre and the passionate but spiritually decadent Edward Rochester. *The Bride* permits no self-conquest, hence no transcendence of historic fatality.

333

The claim that a seemingly irrefutable historic fatalism may have engendered the most nearly perfect of the novels saves us from the Pritchett view of Scott as the comedist of the "normal." But it should not lead us to the worse mistake of a "tragic" label. Rather, it should help us to recognize that the serious thematic concern, the problem of individual humanity in cultural crisis, of all the novels has both tragic and comic possibilities, even where the tragic ones prevail or persist into an otherwise comic restabilization. Moreover, *The Bride's* subtle and complex economy in the use of history as frame and condition of a domestic tragedy should, if earlier discriminations have not, save us from a facile defining of Waverley historism. Cultural continuity is as much at stake in the "house" novels as in *Durward* or *Woodstock;* while their milieux are domestic, their "givens" are as historic as those of the historically various Renaissance novels. Finally, *The Bride's* effective dependence on the Gothic mode of symbolic-picturesque should point to the general absurdity of the romance-novel discrimination, by calling climactic attention to the meaningful juxtaposing throughout the novels of "romance" and "reality," of fictive experience in the archetypal or projective genre, with fictive imitation in the novelistic or analytic genre. Characters and settings and events of different kinds of reality mingle in most of the novels; in the successful ones they are significantly coordinated or counterpointed.

Such sophistications as these would seem to forestall any generalization whatsoever about the Author of Waverley. It will be enough if a fairly exhaustive "reading" of over two dozen thick novels helps to dispel or at least to redefine certain orthodoxies. In the matter of form, it is my conclusion that the Author of Waverley could most certainly construct, and that in the better novels thematic richness and coherence are inseparable from formal success. In the best novels the success is augmented by the coordination of an effectively romantic protagonist, a dynamic central experience, a vivid logical pertinence of other character groupings, and even related patterns of symbolic imagery. In the matter of historic vs. nonhistoric subject, I conclude that history is often essential as a limiting cultural condition, often essential as a major threat to the natural stabilities of human character and society, always essential as the occasion for a crisis of cultural continuity and an ordeal of personal identity. The four areas I have distinguished provided various interpretations and complications of the same basic crisis and ordeal, various occasions for the same quest for a conservative, yet enlightened humanity that, guided by Providence, could survive the nightmare of history. But such conclusions leave two persistent charges in the mouths of two of the Author of Waverley's first admirers and disparagers: Carlyle and Hazlitt. Both were prejudiced against him; both admired him extremely; yet both posed ultimate questions for Waverley criticism.

The Carlyle charge that he believed in nothing, had no "message," has I hope been refuted. The charge that he lacked religious passion and insight need not be. The ordeals in the best novels are dramatized with power and plausibility. They are ordeals of conscience: but conscience, for the Author of Waverley, is a political or cultural concept, grounded in an imperative to preserve and honor a *natural* humanity. He is not a religious novelist, but a political one. Can we, then, on the basis of the novels, classify him as a political moralist?

The trick may be as difficult as Orwell found it to be with Dickens.[54] He is "Conservative." He believes in cultural piety and continuity; he also deplores and mocks decadent or

335

reckless aristocracies, breathes conviction into the libertarianism of the defiant outlaw, and satirizes Romantic visions of the "child of nature" even as he finds essential truth in the sagacity of the "primitive." No easy consistency here. His association with Burke was more definitive before Old Burkeans and New Conservatives began to disagree on Burke's own ambiguous Utilitarianism and his equally ambiguous Rationalism.[55] Occasionally one sights a Stoic Naturalism in the novels; occasionally a Gothic supernaturalism. But rarely. So if Burke contains both, then the Author of Waverley must find some more enlightened Conservative antecedent: Montesquieu, perhaps, whose ambiguous historical relativism is a striking anticipation;[56] or Johnson, whom Scott worshipped, and whose ambiguous Conservatism in the *Journey to the Western Islands* he knew well.

Scott never went through the early Radicalism which lingers to rouse our suspicions of the later Toryism of his literary fellow Conservatives. But recent interpreters make it illuminating to place the Author of Waverley in their company. Todd reminds us that the antibourgeois Wordsworth remained something of a Jacobin and confessed himself a Chartist.[57] Carnall reminds us that the ex-Pantisocrat Southey was to earn a place among the ancestor-heroes of British socialism and would have sympathized with Engels' denunciations of a brutalized industrial "society."[58] Colmer recalls the "sacred principle" of the proto-Keynsian Coleridge and in so doing defines the major political themes of the Waverley Novels: "that a person can never become a thing, nor be treated as such without wrong"; that church and state are instruments of cultural continuity and fulfillment; that property is not a legal "given," but a sacred trust.[59] It is surprising, too, that Carlyle, the Conservative Sansculottist of the Old Clothes Market, could not recognize some of his own political ambiguity in the Author of Waverley. But then, only recent analysts have recognized it in the others.

The Hazlitt charge is perhaps more insistent. Only the past is of concern to the Author of Waverley; his interest encompasses only what is settled, done. Having lost control of the present, he looks for order to the past. To this view there are many rejoinders, and on their efficacy depends the plausibility of my entire book. For one, we recall Ortega's observation that *every* novelist limits his reader's horizons, makes of him a temporal provincial.[60] The Waverley provinces are in time and place, neither singly. For another, there is the Daiches view that Scott's vision of history is not statically escapist, but ambiguously modernist; or the Peckham view that Scott found in various pasts "orientative analogies" to the present. Finally, there is Lukacs's recent postulation, which may be hopefully applied to one of his idols, Scott:

There is an intimate connection between a writer's ability to create lasting human types (the real criterion of literary achievement) and his allegiance to an ideology which allows of a belief in social development. Any attempt to substitute a static immobilism for the dynamic movement of history must reduce the significance, the universality, of the typology in question.[61]

The novels themselves allow us to save the truth from the dogma in all these generalizations. Whatever their responses to it, the novels recognize "the dynamic movement of history." They dramatize crises of continuity, always by their nature forward-looking; they enact ordeals of identity which look back only for liberation from or transcendence of the past. Theme is never focused on what is *done,* but on what is still alive, still redeemable, still unresolved. Every past scene is the present. The times in such pasts are always out of control; the question is always how to live with, how morally to survive such times, such presents, and how to stabilize the present by redeeming the past. In such critical presents, the good man – the man of natural humanity and personal fidelity – cannot escape his historicity by naïveté or weakness or noncommitment. But by a willed commitment to the "romance of his situation," and by an active faith in the providential power of natural humanity, he may transcend the terrors of history and survive to participate in a new stability. If the Author of Waverley's study in the politics of survival is not still timely, it is hard to imagine one that is.

NOTES

NOTES TO THE INTRODUCTION

¹ J. P. Eckermann, *Conversations with Goethe*, trans. J. Oxenford, ed. J. K. Moorhead (London, 1930), Oct. 9, 1828.

² Hazlitt, *The Spirit of the Age, Collected Works*, ed. Waller and Glover (London, 1902), IV, 241–42, 245–47. Hazlitt would be astonished to hear from Georg Lukacs that "what in Morgan, Marx and Engels was worked out and proved with theoretical and historical clarity, lives, moves and has its being poetically in the best historical novels of Scott" (*The Historical Novel*, trans. H. and S. Mitchell [London, 1962], p. 56). On Balzac cf. James P. Hillhouse, *The Waverley Novels and Their Critics* (Minneapolis, 1936), pp. 258–59; for Carlyle, the *Critical and Miscellaneous Essays* (London, 1899), V, 75–77; for Bagehot, the *Literary Studies* (London, 1911), II, 153–55, 158–60.

³ Cf. Richard Stang, *The Theory of the Novel in England: 1850–1870* (New York, 1959); for Eliot on Scott, see *The George Eliot Letters*, ed. Gordon S. Haight (New Haven, 1954–55), III, 15–16; V, 144, 170, 175; VII, 65. Booth, *Anthony Trollope* (Bloomington, Ind., 1958), p. 139.

⁴ Mackenzie writes: "The real battle in my youth was over Scott, and the brutal truth that by the last decade of the nineteenth century we had outlived Scott must be coldly set down" (*Literature in My Time* [London, 1933], p. 22). Leslie Stephen, in an essay written before the turn of the century, has not noticed Mackenzie's "brutal truth" and records the sustained sales; but he poses the question: "Will our posterity understand at least why he was once a luminary of the first magnitude, or wonder at their ancestors' hallucination about a mere will-o'-the-wisp" (*Hours in a Library* [New York, 1907], I, 186–87)? Pritchett, *The Living Novel* (London, 1949), p. 43. Craig, *Scottish Literature and the Scottish People: 1680–1830* (London, 1961), p. 215. J. H. Raleigh has obviously exaggerated in claiming that the novels proved "negligible to posterity." See his "What Scott Meant to the Victorians," *Victorian Studies*, VII (1963–64), 7–34.

NOTES: THE INTRODUCTION

[5] "Scott, it is quite obvious, never dreamed of 'composition' in fiction, in the way James uses it, as analogous to composition in painting" (*The Heyday of Sir Walter Scott* [London, 1961], p. 63). In fact, as Ian Jack has noted, the painting analogy was consistently important to Scott; but it is best not to assume access to Scott's dreams and judge his composition by performance.

[6] Craig, *Scottish Literature*, pp. 145, 155–57, 186–87. Van Ghent, *The English Novel* (New York, 1961), pp. 113–24, sets forth "the implications of incoherence in the work of art." I should admire the "aesthetic rigorism" (to borrow Vivas's term) of both these critics and trust it more had they proved themselves capable of rendering the particulars of a Waverley Novel less prejudicially.

[7] Davie, *Heyday of Scott*, pp. 16–19, cites Cruttwell's attempt to prove Scott "no romantic; . . . an Augustan," and disputes it. (See Cruttwell in *From Blake to Byron*, ed. Boris Ford [Harmondsworth, Middlesex, 1962], pp. 110–11.) My objection is to the debates over mere terminology and to the narrow, obsolete definitions of Romanticism they imply. Northrop Frye's "Towards Defining an Age of Sensibility" suggests the historical absurdity of such either/or's. His suggestion in *Anatomy of Criticism* (Princeton, 1957), p. 306, that Scott belongs to "a mysterious Northumbrian renaissance" misrepresents Scott and perpetuates the old war. I shall suggest that the English "Gothic" tradition best contains the ambivalences that have occasioned the Romantic–anti-Romantic battle in Scott's case.

[8] Sir William Gell records a conversation in which Scott, discussing a dissertation *contra* "Ossian MacPherson," imagines he has received the threatening letter and responds with an unconscious echo of Johnson's reply (*Reminiscences of Sir Walter Scott's Residence in Italy, 1832*, ed. J. C. Corson [London, 1957], p. 5).

[9] On publication of his *Life*, Lockhart received a letter from the father of "Tom Brown" Hughes, praising Scott as a "powerful barrier against the maudlin Byronianism of the French school, and the vagaries of Burke's 'sophisters, economists, and calculators' " (National Library of Scotland MS. 934 No. 114). Scott was enjoying a posthumous revenge for his rival poet's triumph when the Victorian Sage commanded, "Close thy Byron."

[10] Davie, *Heyday of Scott*, pp. 17–19.

[11] "When the crash of the French Revolution came in Scott's youth, Burke denounced its *a priori* abstract reasonings in the name of prescription." (One might prefer "Nature.") "A traditional order and belief were essential, as he urged, to the well-being of every human society. What Scott did afterwards was precisely to show by concrete instances, most vividly depicted, the value and interest of a natural body of traditions" (Stephen, *Hours*, I, 222). "Scott was really the first imaginative observer who saw distinctly how the national type of character is the product of past history, and embodies all the great social forces by which it has slowly shaped itself" (p. 224).

[12] Lukacs, *The Historical Novel*, pp. 20, 26–27, etc. Scott was as anti-Jacobin, Burkean, and antiquarian as Gibbon; neither thereby gave up his faith in Enlightenment.

[13] *Beyond the Tragic Vision* (New York, 1962), p. 191.

[14] Whatever he thought of Scott as a novelist, Lockhart came to deplore Scott's influence on historiography. As the *Quarterly Review* prepared to assault Macaulay's *History*, he wrote Croker: "Scott has been the great inspirer & misleader of all our recent history writers French & English." In 1850 he praised a historian for "abstaining from the trickeries at all events of the historical romance claptrap style" (Nat. Lib. Scot. MS. 1829 No. 175, MS. 1826 No. 155a).

[15] Praz, *The Hero in Eclipse in Victorian Fiction* (London, 1956), p. 56.

[16] Welsh, *The Hero of the Waverley Novels*, pp. 55–56, quotes Coleridge from *Miscellaneous Criticism*, pp. 341–42. Cf. Lukacs, *The Historical Novel*, p. 41: Scott's "profound grasp of the historical factor in human life"; Daiches, "Scott's Achievement as a Novelist," *Literary Essays* (Edinburgh, 1956), pp. 91–92. For Welsh and Davie, Scott seems more fully committed to the side of "prudent civility" and progress; they deny the balance Daiches identifies. I disagree with Daiches not in denying the balance, but in redefining the terms of the tension and in finding the ambivalence equally present in depictions of different kinds of historical transition.

[17] Pritchett, *The Living Novel*, p. 44.

[18] To begin with Nigel and Arthur Phillipson is to concede some difficulty (*The Hero of the Waverley Novels*, pp. 30–38). The handling of "possible exceptions" – Durward, Ravenswood, Smith – is also prejudicial.

[19] Peter L. Thorslev, *The Byronic Hero* (Minneapolis, 1962), p. 23.

[20] "The notion of fiction as an expressive or projective activity" may, as Welsh argues (*The Hero of the Waverley Novels*, p. 5), mark the novel aspect of Romantic fiction. But his demonstration obscures the extent to which Romantic novelists worked in complete consistency with mid-eighteenth-century notions of the mimetic and pragmatic functions of the novel. They differed primarily on the meaning, the connoted degree of particularity and inwardness, of the word "manners"; but the novelist remained prime delineator of manners. If Maria Edgeworth opened a new era with *Castle Rackrent* (1800), she did so in the guise of novelist as descriptive sociologist. Lockhart expressed representative contemporary views of fiction when he congratulated Washington Irving on having before him "the present state of manners in the United States of America," and said, "Could a Smollett, a Fielding, or a Le Sage have seen America as she is, he would at once have abandoned every other field, and blessed himself on having obtained access to the true *terra fortunata* of the novelist" (*Blackwood's*, VII [1820], 368–69). As E. A. Baker notes, "Any variety, any curious aspect, of human existence cried out for its novelist, whose business

was to give a veracious report" (*History of the English Novel*, VII, 63–64). The follower of William Godwin saw himself, to be sure, more as psychologist. But all such scientific rationales stressed fiction's analytic-descriptive function even to a degree unanticipated in the prior century. The influential "Gothic" tradition, meanwhile, had reintroduced its affective or projective function. But the "Gothic" remained in the analytic mode, and as a result created the internal conflict inherited by several Romantic novelists. Leslie Fiedler describes it best: "In many writers . . . projective and analytic modes are mingled often confusedly; for such authors are the heirs of a confusion at the heart of the gothic about its own method and meaning. Precisely because the early practitioners of the tale of terror were only half aware of the symbolic nature of the genre, they did not know what kind of credence to ask for their protagonists – presenting them sometimes as fully motivated characters in the analytic sense, and at others, as mere projections of unconscious guilt or fear" (*Love and Death in the American Novel* [New York, 1960], p. 124).

[21] *Anatomy of Criticism*, p. 44.

[22] *The Byronic Hero*, p. 141.

[23] *The Journal of Sir Walter Scott*, ed. J. G. Tait (Edinburgh, 1950), entry for June 22, 1826.

[24] *The Historical Novel*, pp. 58–59.

[25] Karl Kroeber, *Romantic Narrative Art* (Madison, Wisc., 1960), pp. 186, 187, 191.

[26] Welsh, *The Hero of the Waverley Novels*, p. 86 and note. The argument is futile not just because Scott was an unphilosophical novelist, but because it assumes the exclusive alternatives of a single Rationalist antihistorism and a single Romantic historism, neither of which, as Cassirer and Dilthey and Lukacs have argued, ever existed. It assumes that a genuine historism demanded a Stendhalian sense of the present, whereas almost every Romantic and early Victorian British novelist set his "presents" back in time, including George Eliot.

[27] *The Historical Novel*, pp. 40–41.

[28] It is unnecessary to document the persistence here. But let me acknowledge and applaud Donald Davie's position: "According to Mr. David Daiches, this holding of the balance between phases of history is the true theme of all Scott's good novels, the true 'plot' to which what Mr. Daiches calls 'the external plot' is irrelevant. That this is the true theme I would agree. But I do not think that the question of Scott's plots can be dismissed quite so easily. For if the apparent plot bears no relation to the true theme, this is surely a major flaw in the writing" (*Heyday of Scott*, p. 41). Cf. Daiches, "Scott's *Redgauntlet*," in *From Jane Austen to Joseph Conrad*, ed. Rathburn and Steinmann (Minneapolis, 1958), p. 58.

[29] *Hero in Eclipse*, p. 60.   [30] *Romantic Narrative Art*, p. 191.

[31] *European Literature in the Nineteenth Century* (London, 1925), p. 67.

[32] *Sir Walter Scott* (London, 1958), pp. 5–6.

NOTES TO SECTION ONE

[1] *The Letters of Sir Walter Scott,* ed. H. J. C. Grierson, 12 vols. (London, 1932–37), III, 478–79. Scott characteristically makes a joke of his serious concern with hero-making and temporarily sees Waverley from Flora's point of view. He is a "bad hand at depicting a heroe properly so calld and have an unfortunate propensity for the dubious characters of Borderers Buccaneers highland robbers and all others of a Robin Hood description." Note what follows: "I do not know why it should be so I am myself like Hamlet indifferent honest." The analogy is suggestive: Scott finds the thrusting of heroic sonship on an imaginative, enlightened young man a dreadful, intriguing spectacle. Scott's moral imagination often seems dominated by Shakespearian recollections. For Thackeray's statement see Anthony Trollope, *Thackeray* (New York, 1880), p. 121.

[2] Gordon Ray, *Thackeray: The Age of Wisdom* (New York, 1955), pp. 180–88.

[3] Lockhart dates the fragment April 26, 1808. *Waverley*'s first seven chapters were done in 1805; Scott returned to it in the months following the memoir, for Ballantyne announced it for publication in 1809–10. Thus the experiment in self-characterization in the memoir may well have aided in effecting the rhetorical control of the novel. If *Waverley* had begun with prolonged analysis of Romantic self and education, the memoir, in a sense, preempted that function and liberated Waverley from his comic origins.

[4] J. G. Lockhart, [*Memoirs of*] *The Life of Sir Walter Scott,* 10 vols. (Edinburgh, 1902), I, 32. Subsequent references are to "Lockhart." This edition reprints the text of the standard second edition of 1839, with the alterations and additions of the 1848 abridgment in footnotes.

[5] Praz, *Hero in Eclipse,* pp. 189–90.

[6] Intro. to *Waverley* (1829), in Dryburgh edition, I, xxvii–xxx; Lockhart, I, 155–56, 200–2. Ordinarily references to the novels are given parenthetically in my text to pages in the appropriate volumes of the Dryburgh edition.

[7] Preface to *A Personal Record* (New York, 1912), p. 14.

[8] *The Historical Novel,* p. 31.

[9] *Thackeray: The Age of Wisdom,* p. 177.

[10] British *Notes and Queries,* June 17, 1944, pp. 288–89.

[11] "The Unity of *Henry Esmond,*" *Nineteenth Century Fiction,* XV (1960–61), 346.

[12] Translated by Thomas Carlyle (New York, 1962), p. 246.

[13] "The Unity of *Henry Esmond,*" p. 346.

[14] *Ibid.,* p. 350. Thackeray's own "reading" appears to exclude the *bildungsroman* conception. His preference for George Brimley's review

345

of the novel appears to be based on Brimley's assertion of Lady Castle-wood's sustained importance; the book "is throughout a record of his attachment to one woman" (Ray, *Thackeray*, p. 188).

[15] *Waverley*, p. 371; subsequent references are in the text. The phrasing, closely examined, suggests extraordinary distance between protagonist and self, as between narrator and protagonist. The justification for his right to the pronouncement is, the context makes clear, in self-mastery; the self-mastery has come from sorrowful reflection on the individual tragedies wrought by "civil conflict."

[16] Tillyard, *The Epic Strain in the English Novel* (Fair Lawn, N.J., 1958), pp. 67–69, makes much of Flora's irony without indicating how the reader is saved from its influence. S. Stewart Gordon, *"Waverley* and the 'Unified Design,'" *ELH*, XVIII (1951), 116.

[17] *The Hero of the Waverley Novels*, pp. 71–76.

[18] *Anatomy of Criticism*, pp. 101, 196.

[19] *Thackeray the Novelist* (Cambridge, 1954), p. 9.

[20] *Ibid.*, pp. 80–81, 85.

[21] J. Y. T. Greig, *Thackeray: A Reconsideration* (London, 1950), pp. 159–60.

[22] *Ibid.*, p. 160.   [23] *The Historical Novel*, p. 40.

[24] *Thackeray*, p. 132.   [25] *Romantic Narrative Art*, p. 169.

[26] "Society" in the novels is neither static nor monolithic; "authority" is unstable, ambiguous, and may itself undergo transformation before proving worthy of the protagonist's faith. Self-mastery is crucial. The final societal stability may well be a new one, engineered in part by the protagonist's conciliatory power.

[27] Gordon, *"Waverley* and the 'Unified Design,'"* p. 112. Welsh, *The Hero of the Waverley Novels*, pp. 148, 208.

[28] Daiches, "Scott's Achievement," p. 94.

[29] Cf. "I am *in loco parentis* to you, and bound to see you scathless" (p. 63); "whom he had so much right to regard as his own son" (p. 262); "he gave way to the feelings of nature, threw his arms around Waverley's neck, and sobbed out – 'My son, my son! if I had been to search the world, I would have made my choice here'" (p. 415).

[30] *"Waverley* and the 'Unified Design,'"* pp. 115–16.

[31] *The Hero of the Waverley Novels*, p. 151.

[32] *"Waverley* and the 'Unified Design,'"* p. 116.

[33] *The Hero of the Waverley Novels*, pp. 147–48.

[34] Bradwardine, left behind in Chap. 16 (p. 97), reappears immediately *after* Fergus has presented Waverley to Charles Edward in Chap. 41 (p. 261), an absence of 165 pages in a narrative of 450. Cf. the temporary withdrawal of the paternal Geddes in *Redgauntlet* and of Heriot in *The Fortunes of Nigel*, discussed below.

[35] *Heyday of Scott*, p. 30.

[36] *"Waverley* and the 'Unified Design,'"* pp. 120–21, 117–18 n. (far too crucial for a note!).

[37] *Romantic Narrative Art*, p. 186.

[38] The question is posed by Davie (*Heyday of Scott*, p. 56). I agree that *Rob Roy* "comes badly out of the comparison." I regret disagreeing with Tillyard (*The Epic Strain in the English Novel*, pp. 98–110), for whom *Rob Roy* is "superbly plotted."

[39] *English Literature: 1815–1832*, pp. 207–10.

[40] Cf. Daiches, "Scott's Achievement," pp. 110–13. Four novels had intervened: two "domestic" studies, *Mannering* and *The Antiquary;* the "Gothic" *The Black Dwarf*, which uses Jacobitism; *Old Mortality*, which opens the way to a newer, profounder subject matter. Grierson (*Sir Walter Scott, Bart.*, p. 158) notes that *Rob Roy* is less of an historical novel than its immediate predecessor.

[41] *The Hero of the Waverley Novels*, p. 183.

[42] This is a clue to the essential importance of the presence of cultural crisis or historic fatality in the novels. Cf. the discussion in Section IV of *The Pirate* and *The Surgeon's Daughter*.

[43] *Heyday of Scott*, pp. 56–57.

[44] *The Hero of the Waverley Novels*, p. 183.

[45] *The Epic Strain in the English Novel*, pp. 99–102.

[46] Davie's change of mind is significant: "Osbaldistone (or rather not he, but the party he at this point represents – pre-eminently his father) stands by the principle of *credit*" (*Heyday of Scott*, p. 57).

[47] *Ibid.*, p. 59.

[48] See the discussion of "Tentative Fiction," pp. 189–98, in *The Hero of the Waverley Novels*. This is at once one of the most obscure and revealing parts of the book. Welsh seems merely to be *describing* romance, yet the "description" becomes a judgment of the inferiority of romance as a genre, adopted from W. P. Ker, which in turn becomes a condemnation of Scott for "tentativeness."

[49] I can agree with the descriptions of the novel-romance structural shift, then, if we accept Northrop Frye's distinction and its purely descriptive terminology. The "excursion" serves the function of such a shift in most of the novels, and the shift *may* be wholly defensible. The interplay of "novel" and "romance" realities is a structural principle and should be judged in each case by its workings.

[50] "Scott's Achievement," pp. 110–13; *Heyday of Scott*, pp. 60–61. Davie certainly avoids Daiches' oversimplification, p. 111.

[51] Daiches, "Scott's Achievement," p. 110.

[52] *Ibid.*, pp. 112–13. Given such terms, Davie is right to observe that in *Rob Roy* "the old gets less than justice" (*Heyday of Scott*, p. 60). Forced to apply such terms, we can conclude the same of many of the novels. But here, as often elsewhere, there is no such simple contrast.

[53] *Heyday of Scott*, p. 60.

[54] See the Introduction to Edgar Johnson's edition (Riverside) of *Rob Roy*.

[55] *Heyday of Scott*, p. 63. The evidence in *The Waverley Novels and Their Critics* suggests that critics from the beginning were undisturbed by such formalist concerns, though Scott himself, in the Preface (1822)

to *The Fortunes of Nigel,* had recognized the danger to form resulting from "cutting loose" with such characters as Dalgetty or Jarvie.

[56] I am thinking of Pritchett's description of Dickens's "solitaries" (*The Living Novel,* p. 78). I do NOT mean to agree with the view that such solitaries are of no thematic relevance. But the notion of "Dickensian exuberance" usually excludes the assumptions of thematic relevance.

[57] *The Hero of the Waverley Novels,* p. 199.

[58] This is the single novel in which Scott used the technique (*Redgauntlet* represents, in part, an uncontrolled experimental return to it). There is little evidence in the novels of the effects or values one associates with the technique: the kinds of irony, the potency of evaluative memory, the retrospective nostalgia of Thackeray or Dickens. An exception will be found in *The Antiquary,* with its many retrospective narrators.

[59] The opening chapter distinguishes significantly between Frank-narrator and Frank-hero. The old man speaks of his early follies from a later era of conciliation. But he shortly disappears, to return at the end to record his wife's death and his mourning.

[60] *The Hero of the Waverley Novels,* pp. 180–83.

[61] *Heyday of Scott,* pp. 58–59, 64.   [62] *Ibid.,* pp. 58–59.

[63] *Ibid.,* p. 63.   [64] *Ibid.*

[65] *The Waverley Novels and Their Critics,* p. 55. Daiches, "Scott's Achievement," p. 92. Buchan, *Sir Walter Scott,* p. 264.

[66] Cf. Lockhart, I, 128–29, 179, 200, 206–10.

[67] "Scott's *Redgauntlet,*" in *From Jane Austen to Joseph Conrad,* p. 46.

[68] During the year prior to beginning work on this study (1960–61), I had occasion to teach *The Heart of Midlothian* to an advanced class in Romantic literature at The Ohio State University. In the course of our discussions, a graduate student in his first year, Robert MacConnell, suggested to us all the extraordinary importance of mutually incomprehensible idioms in the novel. He noted that people throughout the middle of the novel simply could find no common language. I asked him to write an analysis of the novel in these terms in the hope that we might collaborate on a further investigation of the motif in the novels. Within a month he was tragically dead in an air crash, leaving a rough draft in my hands. I shall refer to it in its proper place. But it seems appropriate to declare here that parts of this book are in memory of one of the most delightful, promising, eagerly interested students I shall ever have.

[69] *The Scottish Tradition in Literature* (Edinburgh, 1958), p. 223.

[70] "Scott's *Redgauntlet,*" p. 47.   [71] *Ibid.,* p. 57.

[72] *The Hero of the Waverley Novels,* p. 68.

[73] "Scott's *Redgauntlet,*" p. 58. Cf. above, Introduction, n. 28.

[74] Cf. the discussion of tragic heroines in *The Pirate, The Surgeon's Daughter, St. Ronan's Well,* and of course *The Bride of Lammermoor,* in Section IV.

[75] *Heyday of Scott,* p. 45.

NOTES TO SECTION TWO

[1] Craig, *Scottish Literature,* pp. 196–97.

[2] *Ibid.,* pp. 175–78; 188–97. Craig is right to recognize a significant distinction here. But I suspect the distinction is between generations. The Author of Waverley was of Enlightenment Edinburgh; Lockhart and Hogg were not only not Edinburgh, they were clearly post-Enlightenment. Craig is wrong on one relevant point: *"Adam Blair* . . . is perfectly contemporary, not felt to be distanced in time – indeed, it represents the conventional moral feelings of the age" (174–75). It is set a half-century before: see the closing sentence. And its scandalized reception and pastoral idealizing of puritanical compassion suggest that it seemed anything but "conventional morality."

[3] Lockhart, X, 192–93. Within two or three months of the *Life's* completion, Lockhart, reading a life of Wilberforce, wrote to Croker: "After my long labours on Scott's energetic and tumultuous existence – all excitement of one sort or other – I could not but feel very strongly the beautiful composing and sustaining effect of religion in Wilberforce, and wishing from my heart that Sir Walter had had more of that element mixed in him." This does not, however, prove Lockhart made up the deathbed plea or, as is now asserted on the most precarious reasoning, had it made up for him by Mrs. Scott of Harden. Her surviving letter urges Lockhart "to mention any of the few sentences he uttered when his mind was clear, of a religious tendency . . . for there are wicked minded people who will take a *pleasure* in saying that he was not a religious man" (Nat. Lib. Scot. MS. 935 No. 58). The letter does not prove Lockhart false; the story, if true, does not prove Scott "religious."

[4] Carlyle, *Crit. and Misc. Essays,* V, 75–77. Bagehot, *Literary Studies,* II, 153–55, 158–60. Both had been anticipated, of course, by Hazlitt in *The Spirit of the Age* (1825).

[5] *Memorials of His Time* (Edinburgh, 1910), p. 197.

[6] *Scottish Literature,* pp. 144, 186–87, and *passim.*

[7] Tillyard, *The Epic Strain in the English Novel,* p. 65.

[8] *Letters,* IV, 293.   [9] *Ibid.*

[10] See *Scottish Literature,* pp. 185–88, for the view that Scott's impoverishment of imagination derived from his inability to conceive of a rational Presbyterian. *Woodstock* and *Peveril* provide refutations, and certainly, as Craig implies, *The Heart of Midlothian* does, too.

[11] In the Prefatory Letter to *Peveril,* Dryasdust complains that, "Your Puritan is faintly traced in comparison to your Cameronian." The Author of Waverley answers, "I still consider hypocrisy and enthusiasm as fit food for ridicule and satire, yet I am sensible of the difficulty of holding fanaticism up to laughter or abhorrence, without using colouring

349

which may give offence to the sincerely worthy and religious. Many things are lawful which we are taught are not convenient; and there are many tones of feeling which are too respectable to be insulted, though we do not altogether sympathize with them."

[12] *Scottish Literature*, p. 147.

[13] *The Hero of the Waverley Novels*, pp. 235; 238–41.

[14] *Ibid.*, p. 240.   [15] *Ibid.*, p. 256.

[16] *Ibid.*, p. 236.   [17] *Ibid.*, p. 231.

[18] *Scottish Literature*, p. 147.

[19] *Sir Walter Scott, Bart.*, p. 156. Grierson's concluding lamentation that Scott's heroes remained uncommitted is rightly challenged by Daiches. It comes to this: Scott's unconscious dualism shows itself in the novels "in the contradiction between his romantic sympathies and his sober judgment. He does not surrender himself to the full romance of his story as Dumas does" (p. 307). How do we know whether a novelist has "taken sides"? Should a novelist "surrender" himself? Could Scott possibly "take sides" and still "side" with the hope of reconciliation and a transcendence of historic conflict? As Lukacs argues, taking sides is *not* the representative activity of the epochal representative anyway; the majority are always uncommitted or unconsciously antiextremist. Scott's protagonist-mediator inherits the necessity of "taking sides" and attempts to overcome it, saving himself and healing his society by doing so.

[20] *The Hero of the Waverley Novels*, p. 231.

[21] *Scottish Literature*, p. 153.

[22] *The Hero of the Waverley Novels*, p. 233.

[23] The terms are those of Adolphus, quoted by Grierson, p. 157.

[24] *The Hero of the Waverley Novels*, p. 236.

[25] Cf. Buchan, *Sir Walter Scott* (London, 1932), p. 163.

[26] *The Hero of the Waverley Novels*, pp. 255–56.

[27] *Ibid.*   [28] *Sir Walter Scott*, p. 301.

[29] *Ibid.*, p. 302.   [30] *Ibid.*, p. 300.   [31] *Ibid.*

[32] "I am pressed to get on with *Woodstock*, and must try. . . . I must take my old way, and write myself into good-humour with my task" (*Journal*, p. 62); "We dined of course at home, and before and after dinner I finish about twenty printed pages of *Woodstock*, but to what effect others must judge. A painful scene after dinner, and another after supper, endeavouring to convince these poor dear creatures that they must not look for miracles" (p. 72); cf. also pp. 84, 100, 113, 152–53.

[33] Scott rejects in the *Journal* (Feb. 3, 1826) James Ballantyne's criticisms of his "imitations of Mrs. Radcliffe." "I have taken a wide difference – my object is not to excite fear of supernatural things in my reader, but to show the effect of such fear upon the agents in the story – one a man of sense and firmness – one a man unhinged by remorse – one a stupid uninquiring clown – one a learned and worthy but superstitious divine."

[34] *The Great Tradition* (London, 1950), pp. 5–6, n. 2.

[35] *Sir Walter Scott, Bart.*, pp. 208–9.

[36] *Sir Walter Scott,* pp. 253–55.

[37] *Ibid.,* p. 253.   [38] Lockhart, VII, 108.

[39] *The Hero of the Waverley Novels,* p. 119, stresses that in *Peveril* "hostility to the hero" is largely directed against his property. The threat to the "property" as such is a minor element in the struggle for power of the villains of the piece.

[40] The usually generous Goethe found Scott's alteration and "improvement" of Mignon unacceptable. Cf. Eckermann, *Conversations with Goethe,* Wed., Jan. 31, 1827. The mixture of Mignon and Ondine provides Lermontov with a character in *A Hero of Our Time.* See the translation by the Nabokovs (Garden City, N.Y., 1958), pp. 73–74.

[41] *Sir Walter Scott,* p. 192: "The book . . . lives by virtue of a single character, the immortal Rittmaster." Cf. Daiches, "Scott's Achievement," p. 114. On the early complaint that there was "too much, perhaps, of Dalgetty – or, rather, he engrosses too great a proportion of the work – for, in himself, we think he is uniformly entertaining," see Francis Jeffrey, *Contributions to the Edinburgh Review,* 3 vols. (London, 1846), III, 77.

[42] *The Historical Novel,* p. 40.   [43] *Contributions,* III, 77.

[44] Craig, in *Essays in Criticism,* VIII (1958), 217. Welsh, *The Hero of the Waverley Novels,* p. 127.

[45] See, especially, the "Heart of Midlothian" chapter of Dorothy Van Ghent, *The English Novel: Form and Function.*

[46] P. F. Fisher, "Providence, Fate, and the Historical Imagination in Scott's *The Heart of Midlothian,*" NCF, X (1955–56), 99–114 – an extremely suggestive essay whose influence may well be detected in my discussions of other novels.

[47] Introduction to *The Heart of Midlothian,* Rinehart edition (New York, 1948), p. vii.

[48] *Heyday of Scott,* Chap. II. While noting European analogues, one should consider Lukacs's general likening of the Scott novel to Goethe's narrative poem *Hermann und Dorothea* (*The Historical Novel,* pp. 51–52). This is more suggestive than the comparison with Pushkin. The heroic peasant girl is central in both; but Jeanie lacks Dorothea's epic sense of her own historic plight.

[49] References in the text are to the following: Welsh, *The Hero of the Waverley Novels;* Robin Mayhead, "*The Heart of Midlothian:* Scott as Artist," *Essays in Criticism,* VI (1956), 266–77, leading to rejoinders by Joan H. Pittock, also in *EIC,* VII (1957), 477–79, and David Craig, "*The Heart of Midlothian:* Its Religious Basis," *EIC,* VIII (1958), 217–25; also Van Ghent, *The English Novel.*

[50] *The English Novel,* p. 115; the prejudgment is built into the very phrasing of this page.

[51] *Ibid.,* pp. 117, 121.   [52] *Heyday of Scott,* p. 16.

[53] *Scottish Literature,* p. 172.

[54] *The Hero of the Waverley Novels,* p. 130.

[55] "Providence, Fate, and the Historical Imagination," p. 112.

[56] *Scottish Literature,* p. 169.   [57] *The English Novel,* p. 122.
[58] *The Living Novel,* p. 52.   [59] Rinehart ed., Intro., p. ix.
[60] *The English Novel,* p. 119.   [61] *Scottish Literature,* p. 168.
[62] My student, the late Robert MacConnell, first called my attention to this matter of language, to "the frequent inability of the central characters in *The Heart of Midlothian* to communicate with one another." He notes, in his memorandum, that "Jeanie is unable to communicate in any satisfactory way with Effie's seducer in the midnight encounter because his words are those of another language, as it were," and that Robertson shares another idiom with the magistrate who visits Davie. I feel a sense of personal loss at not having had his counsel during the writing of this book.
[63] Kroeber, *Romantic Narrative Art,* p. 191.
[64] "Scott as Artist," p. 277.
[65] Van Ghent, *The English Novel,* p. 116.
[66] *The Hero of the Waverley Novels,* pp. 129, 134.
[67] *Ibid.,* p. 140. Welsh (pp. 136 ff.) misrepresents the function of society in the novel. The realists of the novels are genuinely in touch with personal relations; the romantics are *lacking in* the "sense of solid and individual objects and persons" Welsh attributes to them. When Welsh seeks to demonstrate that the "reality" celebrated in the novel is an abstraction or a normative projection of social and economic relations, I must challenge him to produce a fictive or novelistic world that is *not.*
[68] Fisher, "Providence, Fate, and the Historical Imagination," p. 110.
[69] "Scott as Artist," pp. 270–71.   [70] *Heyday of Scott,* p. 14.
[71] "Providence, Fate, and the Historical Imagination," p. 107.
[72] *Ibid.,* p. 112.   [73] *Ibid.,* p. 104.

NOTES TO SECTION THREE

[1] *English Literature: 1815–1832,* pp. 207–10.
[2] But for this oversimplification, J. E. Duncan is refreshingly original and sound in "The Anti-Romantic in *Ivanhoe*," NCF, IX (1955), 293–300.
[3] *Miscellaneous Prose Works* (Edinburgh, 1834), VI, 11, 99, 19. Is the following a "Romantic" view of the Crusades: "The real history of the Crusades, founded on the spirit of Chivalry, and on the restless and intolerant zeal which was blended by the churchmen with this military establishment, are an authentic and fatal proof of the same facts [consequences of "the outrageous nature of the zeal which was supposed to actuate a Christian knight"]. The hare-brained and adventurous character of these enterprises," and so on? (*Ibid.,* p. 16).
[4] He records this himself in the later Introduction. Cf. Lockhart, VI, 160–61.
[5] *The Hero of the Waverley Novels,* pp. 78–80. The novel itself offers, so far as I can see, no indication that Rebecca's love for Ivanhoe

must be thwarted because it is "passionate" or "ill-assorted," or because she is a "dark heroine."

[6] "Providence, Fate, and the Historical Imagination," p. 106 n.

[7] *Ibid.,* p. 112: "The worship of Fate turns out to be the vice of the romantic, whose historical *Weltgeist* takes over from Providence by means of that blur of movement called progress." The villain is a fatalist, afflicted with the peculiarly Romantic *weltschmerz,* as redefined in Thorslev, *The Byronic Hero,* pp. 87–89. That is, his fatalism results from a paralysis of moral will caused by a neurotic excess of idealism turned to nihilism. Scott's providentialism implies a theodicy which takes the Byronic Hero as evil principle.

[8] In a fragment of letter to Ballantyne concerning the death of Proudfute in *The Fair Maid of Perth,* "I cannot afford to be merciful to Master Proudfute, although I am heartily glad there is any one of the personages sufficiently interesting to make you care whether he lives or dies. But it would cost my cancelling half a volume, and rather than do so, I would, like the valiant Baron of Clackmannan, kill the whole characters, the author, and the printer. Besides, *entre nous,* the resurrection of Athelstane was a botch. It struck me when I was reading Ivanhoe over the other day" (Lockhart, IX, 186). The fragment is of extreme interest, illustrating how persistently discouraging Scott found his printer's abundant criticisms; illustrating that at this point, at least (early Spring, 1828), Scott was rereading earlier novels as he wrote a new one; illustrating, too, that his initially rapid composition was often followed by extensive cancellation and revision of the sheets sent back by Ballantyne. Yet I can find no sign of the letter in Grierson's edition. I infer it must be among those "details about proofs dispatched" which Grierson and his assistants saw fit to exclude from their extract of the letter of Feb. 7, 1828.

[9] The effect is closely akin to the effect of the pathetic cabal scene at the end of *Redgauntlet.* The fact that heroic Saxonism is as much an "unreal anachronism" as late Jacobitism is satirically confirmed by ludicrous survival, where heroic death has been expected.

[10] The careful and suspenseful buildup of erotic anticipation in *The Betrothed* resembles the same buildup in Lockhart's *Adam Blair* (1822). *The Betrothed* is the novel Lockhart the mystifier would have written had he undertaken to imitate the author of *Ivanhoe.* Lockhart's account (VII, 353–54) of the near destruction and last-minute rescue of the novel is mysterious, especially since there is no sign in the *Letters* of such criticism from Ballantyne, or, indeed, that *The Betrothed* was ever written; no references in letters about *The Talisman* to this other work to be sneaked into the same publication. When was the novel written? Why has Lockhart printed no extracts illustrative of Ballantyne's disparagement and the author's despair? Is it significant that the "Archdeacon Williams" whose conversation about Wales supplied the idea was in fact *Lockhart's* close Oxford friend?

[11] Scott left no introduction for *Count Robert;* Lockhart, who had saved the disorganized novel for publication by extensive cutting and revision

(see the page proofs in the National Library of Scotland), supplied one
in his stead, referring the reader to Gibbon and Mills' *History of the
Crusades*.

[12] Introduction to *Quentin Durward*.

[13] In the essay "Why the Heroes of Romance Are Insipid," quoted by
Welsh, *The Hero of the Waverley Novels*, p. 64.

[14] *Ibid.*, pp. 63, 66.

[15] Hillhouse, *The Waverley Novels and Their Critics*, pp. 51–53:
Nassau Senior refused to see any new departure; Hillhouse says Senior
"rates *The Talisman* high, on the somewhat strained theory that as Scott
recedes into the more and more remote past his imagination supplies with
increased power the lack of actual historical material" – not a strained
theory at all. Cf. p. 121: Galt preferred *Ivanhoe* to more careful pictures
of manners. Lockhart thought *Ivanhoe* Scott's masterpiece of *art*. All
stress the departure from historicity.

[16] Cited by Welsh, p. 86 n., from the *Journal of Aesthetics and Art
Criticism*, VIII (1949–50), 111–12.

[17] There is, of course, no denying Burke's "organic conservatism." In
Father Canavan's words, Burke in his later years "elaborated a theory in
which human nature was seen as realizing itself through the artificial and
conventional order of civil society. In other words, instead of opposing
nature to history, Burke saw history as the expression and actualization
of nature" (*The Political Reason of Edmund Burke* [Durham, 1960],
p. 86). But this does not make him an historicist. On pp. 181–88 Father
Canavan deals with the ways in which Burke's statements may mis-
takenly provoke "the charge that his conception of providence was a
prelude to nineteenth-century historicism." Perhaps the most effective
proof that Burke's "historicism" was no Hegelian brand is in his devotion to the historic finality of the Glorious Revolution of 1688 and the
Constitution it ordained. And of course, if we accept the Christian Stoic
Burke of Peter Stanlis, historicism recedes even further. Burke proves,
then, that Scott, too, could be an "organic conservative" in his view of
history and yet no "historicist" in the nineteenth-century sense. In
Mimesis, the actual stress in not on the *difference* between Scott's atmospheric historism and atmospheric realism, but on their close connectedness. *Mimesis* (Anchor Book, Garden City, N.Y., 1957), p. 417:
"Michelet and Balzac are borne on the same stream." On p. 420, Auerbach notes that in attempting the history of manners, Balzac "feels encouraged by the example of Walter Scott's novels; so here we are completely within the world of romantic Historism." Consider Auerbach's
own illustration of Balzacian historism, from *La Vieille Fille*: "Les
époques déteignent sur les hommes qui les traversent. Ces deux person-
nages prouvaient la vérité de cet axiome par l'Opposition des teintes
historiques empreintés dans leurs physionomies, dans leurs discours, dans
leurs idées et leurs coutumes" (*Mimesis*, p. 421). Scott went further,
even in the Dedicatory Epistle to *Ivanhoe*. And we have Auerbach's word
that Balzac "far outdoes" Stendhal "in organically connecting man and

history" (p. 424). Welsh suggests that the development Auerbach describes came much later to England. The actual contrast Auerbach makes is on p. 434: the development of modern realism began much earlier in England, he says, and moved more gradually. Cf. Lukacs on Stendhal, *The Historical Novel*, p. 81. The passage by Victor Brombert – "This eminently 'modern' quality of Stendhal's writings owes much to this awareness of an historical *fatum*. . . . Yet there is here no mystique of History – quite the contrary. As Erich Auerbach reminds us, Stendhal is immune to romantic Historism," etc. – on pp. 2–3 of *Stendhal: A Collection of Critical Essays* (Englewood Cliffs, N.J., 1962) may be applied without change to Scott.

[18] *Heyday of Scott*, pp. 24–26.

[19] *The Philosophy of the Enlightenment* (Boston, 1955), p. 198; cf. Dilthey, *Pattern and Meaning in History*, ed. H. P. Rickman (New York, 1962), pp. 143–44.

[20] *The Historical Novel*, p. 61.   [21] *Ibid.*, p. 187.

[22] *Sir Walter Scott, Bart.*, p. 181.

[23] *The Historical Novel*, p. 187. Sainte-Beuve denied the "artistic significance" of such wholly nonhuman authenticity, and cited Scott in contrast.

[24] Cf. the description of Pompeiian houses in Chap. 3. Bulwer boasted he had rejected Scott the "property-man's" historical picturesque in the interests of accuracy and philosophical seriousness. But Curtis Dahl points out that "Bulwer's frequent perversion of history in order to make it analogous to Victorian conditions is more important than his intended accuracy" ("History on the Hustings," in *From Jane Austen to Joseph Conrad*, p. 61).

[25] *The Historical Novel*, p. 189.   [26] *Ibid.*, p. 188.

[27] *Last Days of Pompeii* (London, 1906), p. 65.

[28] *Waverley*, p. 3; *Ivanhoe*, p. xxiv.

[29] *The Historical Novel*, pp. 47–48.

[30] *The Hero of the Waverley Novels*, p. 86.

[31] Cf. the praise of Fielding in the Introductory Epistle to the first edition of *The Fortunes of Nigel*.

[32] *The Historical Novel*, p. 79.

[33] *Chronique du Règne de Charles IX* (Paris, 1890), p. i.

[34] *The Historical Novel*, p. 80.

[35] Cf. also, *Woodstock, The Pirate, The Bride of Lammermoor,* and *The Black Dwarf*, where Scott, as he himself recognized in defending *Woodstock*, evaded or minimized the problem of how to reanimate the historical fact of superstition by focusing on the psychological and cultural issues of such superstition and its role.

[36] *The Historical Novel*, pp. 40, 44.

[37] Grierson (*Sir Walter Scott, Bart.*, p. 199) anticipates this observation and thus, by implication, the revision I hypothesize.

[38] *Mimesis*, pp. 402–3.

[39] To recognize this and define its failure seems ample refutation of Hesketh Pearson's cute dismissal: "There is nothing to be said for it, so nothing need be said, since it is a waste of words to criticize a waste of words" (*Sir Walter Scott* [London, 1954], p. 158).

[40] *The Historical Novel*, p. 48.

[41] This is what Grierson, e.g., fails to note in calling the novel a masterpiece "*of its kind,* that is the romantic reconstruction of the history of a time the life of which lies beyond our ken" (*Sir Walter Scott, Bart.*, p. 201). The description is truer of *Nigel*. For Buchan, the novel is "Scott's masterpiece in sheer craftsmanship as distinct from inspiration," whatever that means, and he praises the intricate, tightly knit narrative structure (*Sir Walter Scott*, pp. 231–32). I would apply to *Kenilworth* Edwin Muir's phrase for *Nigel*: "Scott's most baroque work" (*Essays on Literature and Society* [London, 1949], p. 77).

[42] *The Hero of the Waverley Novels*, p. 32.

[43] *Ibid.*, pp. 34–35, 214–16.

[44] A close examination shows that Grierson is wrong in saying that *this* hero is "the peep-hole, the magic lantern," for our contemplation of the picture of London (*Sir Walter Scott, Bart.*, p. 203).

[45] *The Hero of the Waverley Novels*, pp. 48–49. This seems to me sheer perversity. Grierson is like Welsh: he defines "Scott's way" obtusely or irrelevantly. Thus, Grierson (p. 200) sees in Roland only another Edward Waverley, and laments: "Surely George Douglas should have been the hero and the story a tragedy throughout. But that was not Scott's way," and so on. Does anyone seriously suggest that Jane Fairfax should have been the heroine of *Emma*? Why not recognize "Scott's way" was meaningfully to *include* the ideological tragedies of George Douglas, of Fergus, of Brian, of Conachar within tragicomic plots of historic survival?

[46] It is significant, I believe, that the two books recall the period of Scott's first major literary effort, the translation of Goethe's *Goetz*. One can argue that the first imaginative shaping of the Author of Waverley's sense of historic change came from the fifteenth-century world of *Durward* and *The Fair Maid*, Froissart and Malory.

[47] P. Hume Brown, *History of Scotland* (Cambridge, 1902), I, 197; R. L. Mackie, *A Short History of Scotland* (Oxford, 1952), p. 152; Appendix III in W. C. Mackenzie, *The Highlands and Isles of Scotland* (Edinburgh, 1937). The discussion of *The Fair Maid* is taken largely from my article, "*The Fair Maid,* Manzoni's *Betrothed,* and the Grounds of Waverley Criticism," in *Nineteenth-Century Fiction,* XVIII (1963), 103–118, reprinted by permission of the Regents of the University of California.

[48] On pp. 42–43, Welsh (*The Hero of the Waverley Novels*) makes too much of the fact that, while Quentin "nearly finishes" the villain, "the rules of passive heroism" prevent his completing it. This does not save Quentin from the taint of violence; it simply gives him more to do at the climax. He sacrifices his right to the completion of the deed – hence, to Isabel – in order to perform an act of humanity. Quentin has

been brought up in a code of revenge. It is a growing humanity, not a conventional propriety, that eliminates violence from his life. Henry Wynd or Smith is more violent. But Ivanhoe *has been* violent before the romance of his humanization begins. And Henry, too, whatever his class, must have his strength softened, humanized.

⁴⁹ The scenes of the storming of La Ferette and the mob execution of Archibald de Hagenbach in *Anne of Geierstein* also suggest the anti-Jacobin historian of Revolutionary France which Scott had, by this time, become.

⁵⁰ *Woodstock* was underway before the Crash and completed before Lady Scott died. *Anne* (1829) was too huge in conception for the energy left to carry it out. Then came only *Count Robert* and *Castle Dangerous* (both 1831).

⁵¹ *Conversations,* Oct. 3, 1828.

⁵² Lockhart makes much, properly, of Scott's "secret motive" of expiating his sin of inhumanity at the death of his younger brother Daniel, guilty of criminal cowardice. Lockhart is reminded, and Scott concurs, of Johnson bareheaded on the market place of Uttoxeter. In Connachar there is apparent an extraordinary degree of personal scrutiny. See the *Journal,* entry for Dec. 5, 1827; and Lockhart, IX, 196–99.

⁵³ *The Hero of the Waverley Novels,* p. 45.

⁵⁴ Pritchett, *The Living Novel,* p. 45.

⁵⁵ *Heyday of Scott,* p. 63.

⁵⁶ *Sir Walter Scott,* p. 318.

⁵⁷ *Conversations,* Oct. 3, 1828.

⁵⁸ The startling scene which Buchan cites as illustrative of a "new technique" of "ironic subtlety" involves the dead Proudfute and the living Dwining. The apothecary, having been largely responsible for Proudfute's murder, is called into the house of mourning to save the murdered man's child, near death with croup. He succeeds, rejects the offered reward of the murdered man's beads, and hurries away, strangely elated that he has saved the child (Buchan, *Sir Walter Scott,* p. 318).

⁵⁹ *The Pirate,* pp. 372–73.

⁶⁰ *European Literature in the 19th Century,* p. 166.

⁶¹ *The English Novel,* p. 121.

⁶² Colquhoun, *Manzoni and His Times,* pp. 165–66.

⁶³ What judgment this implies of *Anne of Geierstein* (1829) and *Count Robert of Paris* (1831) has been accounted for earlier. The final Waverley Novel, *Castle Dangerous* (1831), has received no mention, and no extended analysis seems called for. The novel is difficult to classify. Its title suggests the symbolic focus of a threatened house; the Castle Douglas does prove to be a complex embodiment of dangers: social, psychological, and spiritual. The commandant's honor is at stake; the dangerousness of the castle's position jeopardizes social bonds, as two noble knights gradually allow anxiety and distrust to ruin their friendship and raise a barrier of pride and silence between them. This theme is mixed with others, also familiar. The book often verges on the militant pacifism of *The Fair Maid,* and the absurd inhumanity of

357

chivalric violence is underlined in the same way. The book's violent climax occurs in an historic confrontation at a church on Palm Sunday, allowing for much bitter reflection on how proud men desecrate days of peace with violence. The chivalric spirit does serve, ultimately, as a reconciling power, even bringing temporary peace between the two great enemies, de Walton and the Douglas. The "dangerousness" of the Castle to all is, of course, due to the foolish vow of the heroine that she would marry the man who could hold the Castle for a year and a day in her favor. Her journey *incognito* is additional folly and puts the Castle in double jeopardy. The excursion and the education in unromantic reality are hers, then. The crisis is hers, when, lost in the wilderness, she must accept the guidance of the Knight of the Sepulchre – and does so, knowing that she risks herself and her knight, but trusting completely in Providence: "beset and hard pressed as I am, to ask me to form a resolution for myself is like calling on a wretch, in the act of falling from a precipice [recall young Arthur in *Anne*], to form a calm judgment by what twig he may best gain the chance of breaking his fall. His answer must necessarily be, that he will cling to that which he can easiest lay hold of, and trust the rest to Providence" (p. 313). In so doing she survives her own folly and earns the role of peacemaker between de Walton and the Douglas. She is, then, the only female Waverley protagonist in the Waverley mode. Like *Count Robert, Castle Dangerous* begins with an anecdote in Scott's *Essay on Chivalry;* it, too, envisions a repudiation and at the same time a redemption of chivalric idealism. Consider this key passage: "The blood darted rapidly through the lady's veins at the thought of being thus unceremoniously presented to the knight in whose favour she had confessed a rash preference more agreeable to the manners of those times, when exaggerated sentiments often inspired actions of extravagant generosity, than in our days, when everything is accounted absurd which does not turn upon a motive connected with the immediate selfish interests of the actor himself" (p. 324). The most moving element of the disorganized, often ill-written narrative, is part of its composition: the journey to the Castle with Lockhart (who later "saved" the novel, as he did *Count Robert*, by substantial cutting and revision of page proofs) in the summer of 1831, for close observation of the locale to be described. See Lockhart, X, 72–76. A final note on *The Fair Maid:* having formed and tested my own judgment, I now discover this intriguing, but undocumented report in W. P. Ker, *Collected Essays*, ed. C. Whibley, 2 vols. (London, 1925), I, 197: "Some judges think [*The Fair Maid*] the best of his historical novels."

NOTES TO SECTION FOUR

[1] *The Living Novel*, p. 44.

[2] *Ibid.*, pp. 49–50. Ian Jack, in *English Literature: 1815–1832*, p. 192, notes: "From the brilliant opening scene onwards it becomes evi-

dent that the dominant spirit of the book, unlike that of its predecessors, is the spirit of comedy."

[3] Lockhart, V, 129–30. Such different recent critics as Daiches ("Scott's Achievement," pp. 90–91) and Tillyard (*The Epic Strain*, pp. 64–65) are committed to what the latter calls "the modern orthodoxy" that the novels that matter are the first seven and *Redgauntlet* – the "Scotch novels." Pearson (*Walter Scott*, pp. 129–30) is willing to acknowledge that Scott had to recall his plot and "change the entire atmosphere of the story" halfway through. And Buchan (*Sir Walter Scott*, pp. 149–50) gives the devil's advocate his turn to admit that the plot is elaborate and unimportant, the construction careless, and the writing often pompous. Grierson (*Sir Walter Scott, Bart.*, p. 130) goes along with Lockhart in stressing its closeness to Scott's experience.

[4] *Aspects of the Novel* (New York, 1954), pp. 53–62.

[5] *Ibid.*, p. 62.   [6] *Ibid.*, pp. 48–51.   [7] *Ibid.*, p. 55.

[8] Reading through and correcting it, Scott notes (*Journal*, July 28, 1826), "The fashionable portraits are not the true thing. I am too much out of the way to see and remark the ridiculous in society." R. H. Hutton's is the typical Victorian criticism: "He was beyond his proper field. . . . Miss Austen would have made Lady Penelope Penfeather a hundred times as amusing" (*Sir Walter Scott*, English Men of Letters [New York, 1901], p. 104). Hutton was prejudiced against the "domestic novel." Buchan (pp. 260–64) shows that it is possible to be fair to the book; still, for him it is the "romancer" turned "realist," and since we have rejected the terms, we cannot accept his idea of the book's uniqueness. Pearson suggests, "*St. Ronan's Well* gives us a rough idea of what might have happened if Jane Austen had written *Wuthering Heights*" (*Walter Scott*, p. 192). The suggestion of Charlotte writing *Mansfield Park* might make more sense; but the reader of Susan Ferrier, Galt, and Lockhart will have less trouble "placing" the novel in a Scottish context. There is no Austen at all in the novel. E. A. Baker noted that "the social comedy in *St. Ronan's Well* was less akin to the Edgeworth and Austen strain than to Scott's own delineation of nondescript humours in *The Antiquary* or *The Heart of Midlothian*, with more than a dash of satirical pungency very like Smollett's" (*History of the English Novel*, VI, 194). What if Godwin had written *Humphrey Clinker*?

[9] Lockhart, V, 130, suggests Scott must have seen "the founder of the Abbotsford Museum, in the inimitable portraiture of the Laird of Monkbarns." Grierson (p. 130) says, "Oldbuck is Scott himself."

[10] Tillyard is quite fair in his strictures on the rhetorical artifice (*The Epic Strain in the English Novel*, pp. 65–67).

[11] Cf. the importance of Ratcliffe, discussed earlier, as Jeanie Deans' protector – providential, though outside the law.

[12] *Sir Walter Scott*, p. 141.

[13] Welsh, *The Hero of the Waverley Novels*, p. 229, notes the "healthy and thriving occupation" of Dinmont as norm, though I must disagree

on its operation. Jack sees only the "manners" interest in Dinmont: "The hero's interruption of his journey to see Julia Mannering is not very credible; and while Scott is more careful than he would have been in *Waverley* to give Dandie Dinmont some part in the plot, the true reason for his introduction remains too evident" (*English Literature: 1815–1832*, p. 190).

[14] Cf. the complex ironic meaning of the titular place of *The Heart of Midlothian;* Scott's use of place as structural symbol is as always activated by his "Gothic" sense of place, Gothic in the Ruskinian and Dickensian sense of the word.

[15] *Sir Walter Scott, Bart.*, pp. 216–17. [16] Lockhart, VII, 191.

[17] The words are quoted by Lockhart, *ibid.* The canceled sheet was published by J. M. Collyer, in *Athenaeum*, February 4, 1893. Ker's argument is in *Collected Essays of W. P. Ker*, ed. C. Whibley, 2 vols. (London, 1925), II, 204–6. Welsh reports (p. 211 n.) that the manuscript, which is in the Morgan Library in New York and which I have not seen, confirms Collyer's evidence.

[18] Lockhart, VII, 191, recognizes that the cancellation of "about twenty-four pages" was only enough "to obliterate, to a certain extent, the dreaded scandal [though he defined it differently] – and in a similar degree, as he always persisted, to perplex and weaken the course of his narrative, and the dark effect of its catastrophe." Such appears to be Scott's meaning in the *Journal*, July 28, 1826: "The story is terribly contorted and unnatural, and the catastrophe is melancholy, which should always be avoided."

[19] *The Hero of the Waverley Novels*, p. 211.
[20] *Sir Walter Scott*, p. 262. [21] *Ibid.*, p. 261.
[22] W. P. Ker (*Collected Essays*, II, 202–4) analyzes Balzac's "high estimate of *Les Eaux de Saint-Ronan*," as "partly due to Scott's anticipation of his own methods and favourite subjects. The St. Ronan's Hotel was just the right place for Balzac. . . . The Maison Vauquer shows what he could have made of it."

[23] Robert C. Gordon, "*The Bride of Lammermoor*: A Novel of Tory Pessimism," *NCF*, XII (1957–58), 122–23.

[24] Welsh, *The Hero of the Waverley Novels*, p. 40, may be obliged by his thesis to call Hartley the "hero" of the book, just as Menteith must be the "proper hero" of *Montrose* (p. 43). Both are subordinate characters, however they may resemble Waverley protagonists.

[25] Here is another bit of evidence to suggest that the objectionably conventional or artificial in a Waverley Novel may, if read properly in context, serve a legitimate rhetorical function. Cf. the theatrical Staunton and Madge in *The Heart of Midlothian*.

[26] The story had come via the mode of the ballad collector, not from books. An "old sibyl" named Bessie Millie, who "sold winds" to mariners at Stromness, had told Scott of Gow from her own memory during Scott's "Lighthouse Tour" in 1814: see *The Pirate*, pp. ix, 454; and Scott's tour diary in Lockhart, IV, 239.

[27] Cf. Burke on the Jacobin legislators in *Reflections on the Revolution in France.*

[28] *The Hero of the Waverley Novels*, pp. 65, 76. Note, however, Welsh's observation of Cleveland's ambiguity, on p. 63: "If it were possible for a character in the Waverley Novels to escape entirely from his past, Cleveland would survive as a close relative of the passive hero." But it is not the burghers of Kirkwall who prevent the escape; it is Minna Troil's imagination.

[29] One thinks, throughout this unusually parabolic novel, not just of the Brontës, but of secret kinship as it articulates the theme of connectedness in, say, *Great Expectations* and *Bleak House.*

[30] On Minna and Brenda, cf. *The Hero of the Waverley Novels*, pp. 74–78; on the heroines in general, pp. 70–82 *passim.*

[31] An illuminating gloss on the application to the idea of fidelity of Scott's Romantic anti-abstractionism appears in Henry Aiken's recent remarks on Gabriel Marcel: "From Marcel's existentialist perspective, any morality of principle which demands that I act not only in accordance with but for the sake of an idea, is anathema. Fidelity to a principle, in his view, amounts not just to a sacrifice, but to a betrayal, of a 'thou,' i.e., an individual person who is truly an incarnate being" (*New York Review of Books*, Aug. 20, 1964, p. 11). Scott would accept such a distinction, even as he too excoriates the "fanaticism of the ideal."

[32] Nowhere is it more vividly clear that Scott was the reflective conservative, not the unselective reactionary, than in this distinction between values that must be conserved and values that must be sacrificed in the interest of conserving the others. Here is not the least of reasons why the Waverley Novels seem timely in the 1960's.

[33] *The Hero of the Waverley Novels*, p. 23.

[34] *Theme and Symbol in Tennyson's Poems to 1850* (Philadelphia, 1964), p. 61.

[35] In *The Northanger Novels: A Footnote to Jane Austen*, English Association Pamphlet No. 68 (Oxford, 1927), pp. 6–8.

[36] *Love and Death in the American Novel* (New York, 1960), pp. 111–12.

[37] There is nothing new in classifying the novel as "Gothic." R. C. Gordon, in "*The Bride of Lammermoor*: A Novel of Tory Pessimism," *NCF*, XII (1957–58), 111 n., gives ample documentation. What is new is the recent seriousness of theoretic attempts at redefining and reassessing the "Gothic." In his new selection, *The Castle of Otranto, The Mysteries of Udolpho, Northanger Abbey* (Rinehart ed., New York, 1963), Andrew Wright holds that "it is not too much to say that an understanding of the literature of the last two hundred years requires a knowledge of the nature of Gothic" (p. viii).

[38] Cf. Jeffrey Hart's suggestive phrase for Dr. Johnson – "his complicated commitment to the Enlightenment" – in "Johnson's *A Journey to the Western Islands*: History as Art," *EIC*, X (1960), 57.

[39] *The Hero of the Waverley Novels*, p. 44.

[40] *"The Bride of Lammermoor:* A Novel of Tory Pessimism," pp. 111–12; Daiches, "Scott's Achievement," *Literary Essays,* pp. 113–14.

[41] Buchan, *Sir Walter Scott,* p. 159.

[42] *Aspects of the Novel,* pp. 55–56.

[43] *Heyday of Scott,* p. 160.

[44] For Balzac, the special genre of Scott was "drama in dialogue." In 1840 Eugene Sue is reproached by Balzac for clumsiness in dialogue, which, though the lowest of literary forms, has been raised to new heights by Scott (Philippe Bertault, *Balzac and the Human Comedy,* English version by Richard Monges [New York, 1963], pp. 173–75).

[45] *English Literature: 1815–1832,* p. 207.

[46] Wylie Sypher, for instance, discusses the "Gothic" in a chapter significantly entitled "Psychological Picturesque," in *Rococo to Cubism in Art and Literature* (New York, 1960), pp. 107–9.

[47] *Ibid.,* pp. 91–92; Walter Allen, *The English Novel,* p. 93.

[48] *"The Bride of Lammermoor:* A Novel of Tory Pessimism," p. 111. The Scottish Parliament met for the last time March 25, 1707. The Privy Council was abolished the following year.

[49] *English Literature: 1815–1832,* p. 205.

[50] "Scott's Achievement," pp. 113–14.

[51] *"The Bride of Lammermoor:* A Novel of Tory Pessimism," pp. 112, 117–18.

[52] I think especially of the tragic-ironic hero as powerfully drawn in George Douglas Brown's *The House with the Green Shutters* (1900) and J. MacDougall Hay's *Gillespie* (1914). See my essay in *Studies in Scottish Literature,* Vol. II, No. 1. The tragic irony one associates with Scotland's traditional ballads persists in the tonal complexity of its prose fiction. It might be argued that by virtue of such complexity, *The Bride of Lammermoor* might be considered the most Scottish of the novels. If it is also the best, then we have a rejoinder to Mr. Craig.

[53] *New York Times,* Sun., July 5, 1964, Section 2, p. 1.

[54] "Charles Dickens," in *Critical Essays* (London, 1954).

[55] See Peter Stanlis, *Edmund Burke and the Natural Law* (Ann Arbor, 1958), and Francis P. Canavan, S.J., *The Political Reason of Edmund Burke* (Durham, 1960).

[56] It would be inappropriate to document the influence of Montesquieu on late eighteenth-century British social and political thought here. But let me cite Isaiah Berlin's suggestive paper in *Proc. Brit. Acad.,* XLI (1955), 267–96, which defends Montesquieu's historism the way Lukacs defends Scott's – i.e., against the views of his nineteenth-century successors. Montesquieu is an Aristotelian empiricist: "There is a kind of continuous dialectic in all Montesquieu's writings between absolute values which seem to correspond to the permanent interests of men as such, and those which depend upon time and place in a concrete situation" (p. 293). Montesquieu has "a dry sense of historical reality, as concrete as Burke's and free from his violent prejudices and romantic distortions" (p. 296).

[57] F. M. Todd, *Politics and the Poet* (London, 1957), *passim,* but especially pp. 14, 213.

[58] G. Carnall, *Southey and His Age* (Oxford, 1960), p. 193.

[59] J. Colmer, *Coleridge Critic of Society* (Oxford, 1959), especially p. 170.

[60] "Notes on the Novel," in *The Dehumanization of Art and Other Writings* (Garden City, N.Y., 1956), p. 83.

[61] *Realism in Our Time* (New York, 1964), p. 57.

INDEX

INDEX

SCOTT'S NOVELS
The Plotting of
Historic Survival

was composed, printed
and bound by
Kingsport Press, Inc.,
Kingsport, Tennessee.
The types are Fairfield
and Deepdene, and the
paper is Warren's Olde Style.
Design is by Edward Foss.